Text by Judith Ferguson
and Celia Norman

Photography by Peter Barry

Designed by Philip Clucas MSIAD

Produced by Ted Smart, Gerald
Hughes and David Gibbon

THE COMPLETE
MICROWAVE
COOKBOOK

JUDITH FERGUSON

COLOUR LIBRARY BOOKS

CONTENTS

I may be known for my Irish accent and a spot of broadcasting, but I've never been renowned for my culinary skills, a fact which I am sure my family will be more than happy to confirm! For years I've tried the old excuse of time or the lack of it, so for me the microwave has been the most wonderful invention – fast, clean and versatile – not just a kitchen luxury but an absolute necessity. There are times when I think my family would be on bread and cheese if it weren't for the speed and convenience of microwave cooking. Unpredictable schedules and last minute hitches could mean no calories at all, but I have them so well trained these days that they're all mad on the micro.

My love affair with the microwave begins at 7.30am. Breakfast... bacon is wonderful done in the microwave – no pans and no dirty, greasy grills, and the same goes for scrambled eggs – no sticky pots to scrape. And as for the little things in life, well, ever since I discovered I could soften frozen butter in a few seconds in the micro I was hooked!

Chasing my tail, as I usually do, I find that a lot of my entertaining is done at fairly short notice, perhaps when friends drop in unexpectedly at the weekend. I love it, but I used to panic at the sight of the first car drawing up at the front door, and then I would be seen sneaking out of the back to the nearest shop to try to find something tasty to eat! Nowadays, with a well stocked freezer and my trusty microwave, suddenly I'm the calmest hostess in the district.

Vegetables are ideal when they're cooked in the microwave. I like them still to look green and crunchy on the plate, and the microwave method is perfect for that – no more of the mushy peas and limp cabbage that used to adorn my table.

Fish cooks beautifully in minutes, a steak or chops can come from freezer to table in a very short time, not to mention being able to thaw a roast when, once again, I've been so disorganised that I've forgotten to take it out of the freezer before going to work.

Of course, many people are under the impression that microwave ovens are just for de-frosting or re-heating, but I have found them invaluable for a whole range of cooking applications – a fact very much reflected in the huge number and variety of recipes in this book. I remember, in the seventies, having one of the first microwaves to arrive in Northern Ireland on trial for a few months. At that time there were no cookery books in Britain to tell you how to really use it, which tended to result in a certain amount of confusion. However, things are much more straightforward these days and, although in recent years there have been many publications on microwave cooking, I think you will agree that this is the most comprehensive to date. It contains hundreds of recipes for quick meals, pre-prepared meals, lunches for unexpected guests, dinner parties and outdoor eating.

Judith Ferguson has done a magnificent job in compiling, editing and putting together a wealth of different recipes covering the many aspects of microwave cookery today.

Each and every one of them, by the way, has been tested and prepared in her own kitchen – all so wonderful that I did suggest gently that our family move in for a while, but then, as Judith pointed out, once the cookery book was finished I'd be able to do it all myself. Just think, from here on my friends and family will be under the illusion that I'm a wonderful cook – they'll be staggered by the culinary delights I'll be setting in front of them and, as an extra bonus, no slaving over a hot stove – just my microwave.

So whether you are experimenting with your first microwave, or are already a well seasoned microwave cook looking for new ideas, this book is for you. I hope you enjoy it and wish you many hours of successful and rewarding cooking.

Microwave
SOUPS AND APPETIZERS

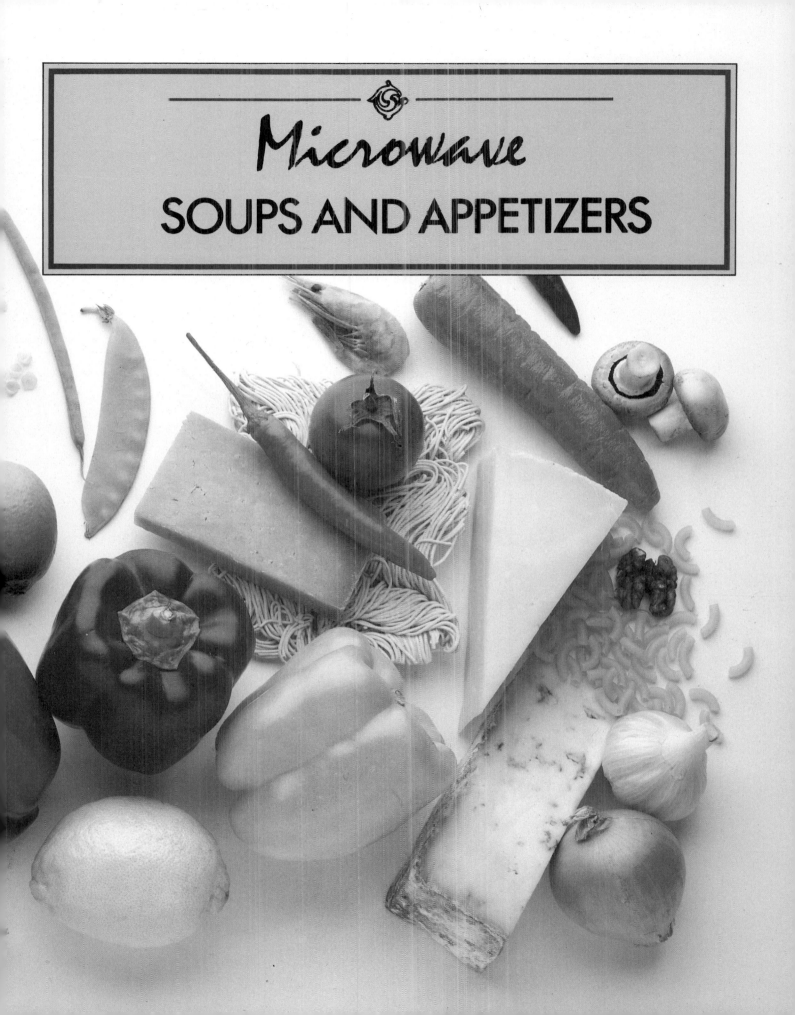

Microwave
SOUPS AND APPETIZERS

Soups and starters or appetizers are the beginnings of a great meal. To make a memorable start, carefully consider how the soup or starter will co-ordinate with the rest of the meal. Consider color, texture and variety of ingredients.

Are soup and starters reserved only for the beginning of a meal? Absolutely not. They can be meals in themselves: soups, accompanied by salads and good bread, make wonderful cold weather lunches and dinners, while starters can double as light meals anytime. Microwave cooking makes light work of a light meal.

Soups can easily be made in small quantities in a microwave oven. Depending on your oven and your own preference, you may want to add 1½ times the flour quantity when adapting soup recipes for microwave cooking. Liquids do not evaporate as fast in microwave cooking as they do in conventional cooking and so more thickening may be required. The soup recipes in this book have been designed to include standing time, but always allow 1 to 2 minutes when adapting any soup recipe for your microwave oven.

Sauce recipes may need more flour, too, depending on your oven. These recipes were tested in a 700 watt maximum oven, but ovens with a lower maximum wattage may require a recipe with more flour.

Soufflés wait for no one, and those made in a microwave oven are no exception. I've included one, though, because they cook in a matter of minutes and are great fun to watch. Beware of over-cooking, though.

Pâtés are one food the microwave oven cooks excellently, and in a fraction of the time taken in a conventional oven. A custard cup of water in the oven with the pâté or terrine keeps the mixture moist.

A microwave oven can be a great boon when giving a dinner party. Preparations can be made ahead of time and then your first course can be reheated in a matter of minutes while you relax with your guests. Better still, soups and starters can be cooked and reheated in their serving dishes, providing they are safe for the microwave oven. Think of the advantage that will give when the time comes to washing the dishes!

Microwave
SOUPS AND APPETIZERS

CREAM AND PURÉE SOUPS

Crab Bisque

PREPARATION TIME: 15 minutes

MICROWAVE COOKING TIME:
17 minutes

SERVES: 4 people

SOUP
450g/1lb crabmeat, fresh or frozen
45g/1½ oz/3 tbsps butter or margarine
45g/1½ oz/3 tbsps flour/plain flour
1 shallot finely chopped
570ml/1 pint/2 cups milk
140ml/¼ pint/½ cup cream
280ml/½ pint/1 cup fish or chicken stock
1 bay leaf
Salt
Pepper
Tabasco
30ml/2 tbsps dry sherry

CROÛTONS
30g/1oz/2 tbsps butter or margarine
2 slices bread, crusts removed
Salt
Pepper
Paprika

Put butter and shallot into a casserole. Cover and cook for 3 minutes on HIGH, stirring occasionally. Stir in the flour and cook for 2 minutes on HIGH. Stir in the milk, stock, seasonings, bay leaf and a few drops of tabasco and cover and cook on HIGH for 5 minutes, stirring frequently. Blend in the crabmeat and sherry. Cook on MEDIUM for 3-4 minutes. To prepare croûtons, place butter in a small bowl and cook on LOW for 15-20 seconds or until softened. Cut each slice of bread into 12-16 squares, depending on the size and thickness of the slices. Toss the cubes of bread in the melted butter with salt and pepper. Spread the bread out on a flat plate. Sprinkle the bread with paprika and cook on HIGH for 1½-2 minutes or until the croûtons are firm but not crisp. Stir and turn the croûtons several times during

This page: **Crab Bisque (top) and Cream of Chicken Soup (bottom).** Facing page: **Cream of Cucumber Soup (top) and Leek and Potato Soup (bottom).**

cooking. Let them stand for 5 minutes before serving. Re-heat the soup on HIGH for 1 minute. Stir in the cream just before serving, top with the croûtons and dust with more paprika.

Leek and Potato Soup

PREPARATION TIME: 10 minutes

MICROWAVE COOKING TIME: 20 minutes

SERVES: 4 people

3 leeks, washed and sliced thinly
550g/1½lbs/3½ cups potatoes, diced
45g/1½ oz/3 tbsps butter or margarine
570ml/1 pint/2 cups milk
430ml/¾ pint/1½ cups chicken or
vegetable stock
1 bay leaf
1.25ml/¼ tsp thyme
Salt
Pepper

GARNISH
1 bunch chives, chopped
120ml/¼ pint/½ cup sour cream

Put leeks, potatoes and butter into a large bowl. Cover with plastic wrap and pierce several times. Cook on HIGH for 10 minutes. Add milk, stock, thyme, bay leaf and seasoning, and cook for 7 minutes on HIGH. Leave standing, covered, for 1 minute. Uncover and allow to cool slightly. Remove bay leaf, pour soup into a food processor, and purée until smooth. Check seasoning and heat through for 3 minutes on HIGH. Serve with a spoonful of sour cream and chopped chives for each individual portion.

Cream of Chicken Soup

PREPARATION TIME: 15 minutes

MICROWAVE COOKING TIME: 31 minutes

SERVES: 4 people

450g/1lb chicken breasts
430ml/¾ pint/1½ cups water
570ml/1 pint/2 cups milk

1 chicken bouillon cube
30g/1oz/2 tbsps butter
30g/1oz/2 tbsps flour/plain flour
60ml/2 fl oz/¼ cup heavy/double cream
1 bay leaf
1 sprig thyme
1.25ml/¼ tsp sage, fresh or dried
Salt
Pepper

GARNISH
1 bunch chives, chopped

Put the chicken into a large bowl with the water. Cover with plastic wrap, pierce several times, and cook for 15 minutes on HIGH. Remove chicken from bowl and leave to cool. Strain the liquid from the chicken and set it aside. Put butter and flour into the bowl and cook for 1 minute on HIGH. Gradually stir in the liquid from the chicken and the milk. Add bay leaf, thyme and seasoning, and cook for 4 minutes on HIGH, stirring occasionally. Remove skin and bone from chicken, and cut into small pieces. Crumble the stock cube and add to the bowl along with the chicken and sage. Cook, uncovered, for 10 minutes on HIGH. Add cream and cook for 1 minute on HIGH. Serve garnished with chopped chives.

Lentil Soup with Smoked Sausage

PREPARATION TIME: 10 minutes

MICROWAVE COOKING TIME: 60-70 minutes

SERVES: 4 people

225g/½lb smoked sausage
255g/9oz/1½ cups brown lentils, washed
1 medium onion, chopped
1 bay leaf
1.25ml/¼ tsp thyme
15ml/1 tbsp Worcester sauce
Powdered cloves
1 litre/1¾ pints/4 cups chicken or
vegetable stock

GARNISH
45g/1½ oz/⅓ cup Parmesan cheese,
grated

Put onion into a large bowl. Cover with plastic wrap and pierce in several places. Cook for 8 minutes on HIGH, or until onion is softened. Add lentils, herbs, Worcester sauce, pinch of powdered cloves and the stock. Re-cover bowl and cook on HIGH for about 20 minutes, stirring well. Reduce setting to MEDIUM and cook for about 20 minutes, stirring well. Remove skin from smoked sausage if desired. Add sausage to the bowl, and continue to cook for another 20-30 minutes, or until lentils are soft. Remove the bay leaf and the sausage. Purée the soup if desired. Slice the sausage into thin rounds and add to the soup. Stir soup well and adjust seasoning. Serve garnished with Parmesan cheese.

Creamy Spinach Soup

PREPARATION TIME: 15 minutes

MICROWAVE COOKING TIME: 16 minutes

SERVES: 4 people

900g/2lbs fresh spinach, washed and
stems removed
30g/1oz/2 tbsps butter or margarine
30g/1oz/2 tbsps flour/plain flour
1 shallot, finely chopped
430ml/¾ pint/1½ cups milk
430ml/¾ pint/1½ cups chicken or
vegetable stock
140ml/¼ pint/½ cup cream
1.25ml/¼ tsp marjoram
Squeeze of lemon juice
Grated nutmeg
Salt
Pepper

GARNISH
1 hard-boiled egg, chopped

Put washed spinach into a roasting bag and tie loosely. Stand the bag upright in the oven and cook for 2 minutes on HIGH, or until spinach

Facing page: Creamy Spinach Soup (top) and Lentil Soup with Smoked Sausage (bottom).

has wilted. (It can also be cooked in a bowl covered with pierced plastic wrap.) Put shallot and butter into a large bowl, cover and cook for 5 minutes on HIGH. Add flour, and cook for 2 minutes on HIGH. Stir in the milk and stock, and add marjoram, bay leaf and grated nutmeg. Cook for 2 minutes on HIGH, stirring occasionally. Add spinach, salt, pepper and lemon juice, and cook for 3 minutes on HIGH. Pour soup into a food processor and purée until smooth. Add cream, and adjust seasoning. Heat through for 2 minutes on HIGH. Serve garnished with egg.

Bouillabaisse

PREPARATION TIME: 15 minutes

MICROWAVE COOKING TIME: 10 minutes

SERVES: 4 people

450g/1lb assorted fish (eg monkfish, red snapper, cod, white fish, rock salmon)
225g/½lb assorted cooked shellfish (shrimp, lobster, crab)
2 leeks, cleaned and thinly sliced
1 small bulb Florentine fennel, sliced
30ml/2 tbsps olive oil
4 tomatoes, skinned, seeded and roughly chopped
15ml/1 tbsp tomato paste
850ml/1½ pints/3 cups water
150ml/6 fl oz/⅔ cup white wine
1 clove garlic, crushed
1 strip orange rind
2.5ml/½ tsp saffron
1 bay leaf
5ml/1 tsp lemon juice
15ml/1 tbsp chopped parsley
Salt
Pepper

GARNISH
4 slices French bread, toasted
60ml/2 fl oz/¼ cup prepared mayonnaise, mixed with 1 clove garlic, crushed, and a pinch of Cayenne pepper

Cut fish into 5cm (2″) pieces. Remove shells from shellfish and cut crab and lobster into small pieces. Put leeks, fennel, garlic and olive oil

into a large casserole. Cover and cook for 3 minutes on HIGH. Add orange rind, saffron, bay leaf, lemon juice, water and wine. Stir in the tomato paste and seasoning, and mix well. Add fish and tomatoes and cook for 5 minutes, covered, on HIGH. Add shellfish and parsley, and cook for 2 minutes on HIGH. Mix the mayonnaise, garlic and Cayenne pepper and spread on the pieces of toasted French bread. Place bread in the bottom of the serving dish and spoon over the soup.

Cream of Celery Soup

PREPARATION TIME: 10 minutes

MICROWAVE COOKING TIME: 32 minutes

SERVES: 4 people

1 large head/4 cups chopped celery, leaves reserved
1 shallot, finely chopped
30g/1oz/2 tbsps butter
30g/1oz/2 tbsps flour
280ml/½ pint/1 cup chicken or vegetable stock
430ml/¾ pint/1½ cups milk
140ml/¼ pint/½ cup heavy/double cream
15ml/1 tbsp celery seeds (optional)
1 bay leaf
1 sprig thyme
Salt
Pepper

This page: Bouillabaisse.
Facing page: Cheddar Cheese Soup (top) and Cream of Celery Soup (bottom).

Put butter into a large casserole and heat for 1 minute on HIGH. Add celery and shallot, then cover and cook for 10 minutes on HIGH, stirring frequently, or until celery and shallot are soft. Stir in the flour and cook for 1 minute on HIGH. Add stock, milk, bay leaf, thyme and seasoning. Cover and cook for 18 minutes on HIGH, stirring frequently. Allow the soup to cool slightly. Remove bay leaf and thyme, and pour soup into a food processor. Purée until smooth, and return the soup to the bowl. Add celery seeds and re-heat for 2 minutes on HIGH. Just before serving, stir in the cream, and garnish with reserved celery leaves.

Cheddar Cheese Soup

PREPARATION TIME: 10 minutes

MICROWAVE COOKING TIME: 22 minutes

SERVES: 4 people

225g/8oz/2 cups mature Cheddar cheese and Red Leicester/Colby cheese, grated and mixed
1 carrot, peeled and diced
2 sticks celery, diced
45g/1½ oz/3 tbsps butter
30g/1oz/¼ cup flour/plain flour
570ml/1 pint/2 cups milk
430ml/¾ pint/1½ cups chicken or vegetable stock
1 bay leaf
1.25ml/¼ tsp thyme

GARNISH
Chopped parsley

Put butter, celery and carrot into a bowl. Cover with plastic wrap and pierce several times. Cook for 5 minutes on HIGH. Stir in the flour, and add the stock gradually, mixing well. Add thyme and bay leaf, and cook for 10 minutes on HIGH, uncovered. Add milk and cook for 5 minutes on HIGH. Put cheese into a bowl and stir in 140ml/¼ pint/½ cup of the liquid from the soup. Return cheese mixture to soup and cook, uncovered, for 2 minutes on HIGH. Serve with a garnish of chopped parsley.

Cream of Cucumber Soup

PREPARATION TIME: 10 minutes

MICROWAVE COOKING TIME: 22 minutes

SERVES: 4 people

1 large cucumber
1 shallot, finely chopped
30g/1oz/2 tbsps butter
30g/1oz/2 tbsps flour/plain flour
280ml/½ pint/1 cup chicken or vegetable stock
570ml/1 pint/2 cups milk
140ml/¼ pint/½ cup light/single cream
15ml/1 tbsp chopped parsley
1 small clove garlic, crushed
1 bunch dill, finely chopped
Grated nutmeg
Salt
Pepper

Put butter, shallot and garlic into a large bowl. Cover with plastic wrap and pierce several times. Cook for 3 minutes on HIGH. Add flour and blend thoroughly. Wash cucumber, reserve 4 slices for garnish, and grate the rest. Add it to the bowl and cook for 5 minutes on HIGH, until cucumber is slightly softened. Stir in the stock, parsley, nutmeg, chopped dill and seasoning. Re-cover bowl and cook for 7 minutes on HIGH. Stir in the milk and cream and pour into a food processor. Purée until smooth and return to the bowl. Heat through for 3 minutes on HIGH and serve garnished with the cucumber slices. Serve hot or cold.

Clam Chowder

PREPARATION TIME: 15 minutes

MICROWAVE COOKING TIME: 16 minutes

SERVES: 4 people

1 litre/1 quart clams
280ml/½ pint/1 cup water, mixed with 5ml/1 tsp lemon juice
1 shallot, roughly chopped
4 strips green streaky bacon (rindless and boneless)
340g/12oz/2 cups diced potatoes
1 onion, finely sliced

1 litre/1¾ pints/3¼ cups milk
30g/1oz/2 tbsps butter
30g/1oz/2 tbsps flour/plain flour
Light/single cream as necessary
1 bay leaf
1.25ml/¼ tsp thyme
30ml/2 tbsps chopped parsley
Salt and pepper

GARNISH
Paprika

Scrub clams well and discard any that are open or broken. Put into a large bowl with the water, shallot and bay leaf. Cover with pierced plastic wrap and cook for 2 minutes on HIGH. Drain through a fine strainer and reserve. Remove clams from shells and set aside. Put butter, sliced onion and diced bacon into the rinsed-out bowl, cover, and cook on HIGH for 3 minutes. Stir in flour and cook a further 2 minutes on HIGH, stirring frequently. Add potatoes, milk, reserved clam liquid, thyme and seasoning. Cook for 10 minutes on HIGH, stirring occasionally. Add parsley and clams and, if soup is very thick, some cream to thin it down. Cook for 1 minute on HIGH. Serve sprinkled lightly with paprika.

Vichyssoise

PREPARATION TIME: 10-12 minutes

MICROWAVE COOKING TIME: 25 minutes

SERVES: 4 people

45g/1½ oz/3 tbsps butter or margarine
3 leeks
2-3 medium potatoes, peeled and sliced
850ml/1½ pints/3 cups chicken or vegetable stock
90ml/3 tbsps/⅓ cup sour cream
140ml/¼ pint/½ cup milk
Salt and pepper

Facing page: Clam Chowder (top) and Vichyssoise (bottom).

1 sprig fresh rosemary
Salt
Pepper

GARNISH
Parsley leaves

Put leeks, potatoes, carrots and butter into a large bowl. Cover with plastic wrap, and pierce several times. Cook for 10 minutes on HIGH. Add milk, stock, bay leaf, sprig of rosemary and seasoning. Re-cover and cook for 7 minutes on HIGH. Leave standing, covered, for 1 minute. Put parsley leaves and 15ml/1 tbsp water into a small dish. Cover with plastic wrap and pierce several times. Cook on HIGH for 1 minute. Uncover the soup and allow it to cool slightly. Remove bay leaf and rosemary, pour soup into a food processor, and purée until smooth. Check seasoning and heat through for 3 minutes on HIGH. Serve with a garnish of parsley leaves.

Pumpkin Soup

PREPARATION TIME: 20 minutes	
MICROWAVE COOKING TIME: 25 minutes	
SERVES: 4-6 people	

1 whole pumpkin, weighing about 1kg/ 2lbs
2 medium potatoes, peeled and sliced
2 small onions, finely chopped
30g/1oz/2 tbsps butter
850ml/1½ pints/3 cups chicken stock
280ml/½ pint/1 cup milk
140ml/¼ pint/½ cup heavy/double cream
2.5ml/½ tsp tarragon
2.5ml/½ tsp chopped parsley
Nutmeg
Salt
Pepper

GARNISH
1 small bunch chives

Trim the white part of the leeks, slice thinly and wash well. Shred the green part finely, wash well and set aside. Put butter into a large bowl and cook, uncovered, for about 1½ minutes on HIGH. Add potatoes and white part of leeks to the butter. Cover with plastic wrap and pierce several times. Cook for 5 minutes on HIGH, stirring frequently. Add half the stock, re-cover and cook on HIGH for about 14 minutes or until the vegetables are very soft. Cool slightly, pour into a food processor, and purée until smooth. Add remaining stock and milk, and adjust the seasoning. Put reserved green part of the leeks into a small bowl with 2-3 tbsps of water. Cover the bowl with plastic wrap and pierce several times. Cook for about 2 minutes on HIGH. Re-heat soup on HIGH for 3 minutes.

Add more milk if the soup is too thick. To serve, top with the soured cream and the thinly shredded green part of leeks. Serve hot or cold.

French Country Soup

PREPARATION TIME: 10 minutes	
MICROWAVE COOKING TIME: 21 minutes	
SERVES: 4 people	

3 leeks, washed and sliced thinly
180g/6oz/1 cup chopped carrots
350g/12oz/2 cups diced potatoes
570ml/1 pint/2 cups milk
570ml/1 pint/2 cups chicken or vegetable stock
45g/1½ oz/3 tbsps butter or margarine
1 bay leaf

This page: Pumpkin Soup.
Facing page: French Country Soup.

Cut top off pumpkin and scoop out pulp and discard seeds. Push as much of the pulp as possible through a sieve. Using a small, sharp knife or tablespoon, remove pumpkin flesh from inside shell, leaving a 1cm (½") lining of flesh. Put flesh, pulp, potatoes and onions into a large bowl with the butter. Cover with plastic wrap and pierce several times. Cook on HIGH for 10 minutes. Add stock, milk, thyme, parsley, nutmeg, and salt and pepper. Re-cover the bowl and cook on HIGH for 10 minutes. Pour the soup into a food processor and purée until smooth. Add double cream and mix in well. Wash pumpkin shell and top, and dry well. Return soup to the bowl and re-heat for 5 minutes on HIGH. Pour soup into cleaned pumpkin shell to serve, and garnish with chopped chives.

Watercress and Potato Soup

PREPARATION TIME: 10 minutes

MICROWAVE COOKING TIME: 22 minutes

SERVES: 4 people

1 bunch (about 2 cups) watercress
675g/1½lbs/3 cups diced potatoes
430ml/¾ pint/1½ cups chicken or
    vegetable stock
430ml/¾ pint/1½ cups light/single
    cream, or milk
1 shallot, finely chopped
45g/1½ oz/3 tbsps butter or margarine
Nutmeg
Lemon juice
Salt and pepper

Put the butter, shallot and potatoes into a large bowl. Cover with plastic wrap and pierce several times. Cook for about 2 minutes on HIGH. Add stock, salt and pepper, and pinch of nutmeg. Re-cover the bowl and cook on HIGH for about 10 minutes or until the vegetables are soft. Chop the watercress leaves, reserving 4 sprigs for garnish. Add the chopped leaves to the other ingredients in the bowl, re-cover and cook for another

2 minutes on HIGH. Put into a food processor and purée until smooth. Return to the bowl. Stir in the cream and cook for 3-4 minutes on LOW until heated through. Do not allow the soup to boil. Stir in the lemon juice to taste, and adjust the seasoning. Serve the soup garnished with sprigs of watercress. Serve hot or cold.

Bean and Bacon Soup

PREPARATION TIME: 10 minutes

MICROWAVE COOKING TIME: 1 hour 35 minutes and 10 minutes standing time

SERVES: 4 people

225g/½lb navy/haricot beans, picked
    over and washed
225g/½lb smoked streaky bacon
1 large onion, finely chopped
1 stalk celery, finely chopped
1 bay leaf
1.25ml/¼ tsp thyme
Pinch of sage
½ clove garlic, crushed
15ml/1 tbsp chopped parsley
Salt
Pepper

This page: Watercress and Potato Soup.
Facing page: Bean and Bacon Soup (top) and Cream of Onion Soup (bottom).

Put beans into a large casserole and add 1150ml/2 pints/4 cups water. Cover and cook for 10 minutes on HIGH, or until boiling. Allow to boil for 2 minutes, then set aside, covered, for 1 hour. Heat a browning dish for 5 minutes on HIGH and brown the bacon for 2 minutes. Crumble and set aside, reserving the fat. Put onion, celery, garlic and bacon fat into a large casserole and cook on HIGH for 2 minutes. Drain beans, and add to the casserole along with the thyme, sage and bay leaf. Pour on 1150ml/2 pints/4 cups of fresh water, cover, and cook for 45-55 minutes on HIGH. Then stir in the bacon, reserving 4 tbsps for garnish. Re-cover dish and cook a further 25-35 minutes on HIGH, or until beans are soft but not breaking apart. Add water as necessary during cooking. Allow to stand, covered, for 10 minutes. Remove the bay leaf and serve garnished with the reserved bacon.

Mulligatawny Soup

PREPARATION TIME: 12 minutes

MICROWAVE COOKING TIME: 36-38 minutes

SERVES: 4 people

180g/6oz/1 cup onions, thinly sliced
2 apples, peeled and grated
60g/2oz/4 tbsps butter
60g/2oz/4 tbsps flour/plain flour
1 tbsp tomato paste
10ml/2 tsps curry powder
15ml/1 tbsp mango chutney
60g/2oz/⅓ cup quick-cooking rice
1150ml/2 pints/4 cups beef or chicken stock
1 small bunch fresh coriander leaves
1 bay leaf
1 clove garlic, crushed
Salt
Pepper

GARNISH
90ml/3 fl oz/⅓ cup plain yogurt

Reserve 4 sprigs of coriander for garnish and chop 1 tbsp of the remainder. Put butter, onion and garlic into a large casserole. Cover and cook for 5 minutes on HIGH. Blend in the flour and curry powder, then cover and cook for 2 minutes on HIGH. Add tomato paste, stock and 1 tbsp coriander, and cook for 5 minutes on HIGH until boiling. Add apple, chutney, rice and seasoning, and cook for 10 minutes on MEDIUM, or until rice is tender. Cook an additional 2 minutes on HIGH if necessary. Serve topped with yogurt and reserved coriander leaves.

Cream of Mushroom Soup

PREPARATION TIME: 10 minutes

MICROWAVE COOKING TIME: 17 minutes

SERVES: 4 people

340g/¾lb mushrooms
1 shallot, finely chopped
570ml/1 pint/2 cups chicken or vegetable stock
430ml/¾ pint/1½ cups milk
30g/1oz/2 tbsps butter or margarine
45g/1½ oz/3 tbsps flour/plain flour
1.25ml/¼ tsp thyme
30ml/2 tbsps dry sherry
90ml/3 fl oz/⅓ cup heavy/double cream
Salt
Pepper

Reserve 4 mushrooms to use as garnish, and chop the rest finely. Put them with the butter and shallot into a large glass bowl. Cover with plastic wrap and pierce several times. Cook for 4 minutes on HIGH or until mushrooms are soft. Stir occasionally. Add flour and stir well. Gradually add the stock, re-cover, and cook for 5 minutes on HIGH. Stir the mixture several times while cooking. Add milk, thyme and sherry, and cook on HIGH for 6 minutes, or until boiling. Stir several times during cooking. Allow the soup to stand for 1-2 minutes, covered. Slice remaining mushrooms thinly. Put them in a small bowl with 1 tbsp of water and a squeeze of lemon juice. Cover bowl with plastic wrap and pierce several times, and cook for 1 minute on HIGH. Add cream to the soup and cook for 2 minutes on HIGH. Serve the soup garnished with the slices of mushroom.

Cream of Broccoli Soup

PREPARATION TIME: 10 minutes

MICROWAVE COOKING TIME: 20 minutes

SERVES: 4 people

450g/1lb broccoli spears, fresh or frozen
30g/1oz/2 tbsps butter
30g/1oz/2 tbsps flour/plain flour
430ml/¾ pint/1½ cups chicken or vegetable stock
570ml/1 pint/2 cups milk
1 bay leaf
1.25ml/¼ tsp thyme
15ml/1 tbsp chopped parsley
140mil/¼ pint/½ cup heavy/double cream
Salt
Pepper

Chop broccoli roughly, reserving 4-8 small flowerets for garnish. Put chopped broccoli into a loosely tied roasting bag with 2 tbsps water. Cook on HIGH for 5 minutes. (The broccoli may also be cooked in a bowl covered with pierced plastic wrap.) Put butter into a large bowl and cook for 1 minute on HIGH. Stir in the flour, and add the milk, stock, thyme, parsley, bay leaf and seasoning. Cook for 7 minutes on HIGH, stirring several times. Add broccoli and cook a further 3 minutes on HIGH. Pour the soup into a food processor and purée until smooth. Put reserved flowerets of broccoli into a small bowl with 1 tbsp of water. Cover with pierced plastic wrap and cook for 2 minutes on HIGH. Set aside. Add cream and re-heat the soup for 2 minutes on HIGH. Serve with a garnish of broccoli florets.

Facing page: Cream of Mushroom Soup (top) and Mulligatawny Soup (bottom).

140ml/¼ pint/½ cup cream
650ml/1½ pints/3 cups beef stock
60ml/4 tbsps/¼ cup white wine
1 bunch dill
1 bay leaf
Salt
Pepper

GARNISH
140ml/¼ pint/½ cup sour cream

Reserve 4 sprigs of dill for garnish and chop the rest. Put the dill, carrot, onion, potatoes, cabbage, garlic, bay leaf, seasoning, and half the stock into a large casserole. Cover and cook on HIGH for 15 minutes or until vegetables soften. Add the remaining stock, beets, wine and tomato paste, and cover and cook on HIGH for 10 minutes. Stir occasionally. Remove bay leaf. Pour soup into a food processor and purée until smooth. Add cream and blend thoroughly. Return soup to bowl and re-heat for 2 minutes on HIGH. Serve topped with sour cream and sprigs of dill.

Stilton Cheese and Walnut Soup

PREPARATION TIME: 10 minutes

MICROWAVE COOKING TIME: 18 minutes

SERVES: 4 people

225g/8oz/2 cups Stilton cheese, crumbled (half Cheddar and half blue cheese may be substituted)
1 large onion, finely chopped
45g/1½ oz/3 tbsps butter
30g/1oz/2 tbsps flour/plain flour
430ml/¾ pint/1½ cups chicken stock
430ml/¾ pint/1½ cups milk
60ml/4 tbsps/¼ cup cream
90g/3oz/½ cup walnuts, finely chopped
1 bay leaf
1 sprig thyme
Salt and pepper

Cream of Onion Soup

PREPARATION TIME: 10 minutes

MICROWAVE COOKING TIME: 18 minutes

SERVES: 4 people

675g/1½lbs onions, finely chopped
30g/1oz/2 tbsps butter
30g/1oz/2 tbsps flour
570ml/1 pint/2 cups beef or chicken stock
430ml/¾ pint/1½ cups milk
15ml/1 tbsp Madeira
140ml/¼ pint/½ cup cream

GARNISH
4 green onions, sliced

Put the butter into a large bowl and cook for 1 minute on HIGH. Add onions, and cook for 5 minutes on HIGH, stirring occasionally until light brown. Stir in the flour, stock, bay leaf, and salt and pepper. Cook for 10 minutes on HIGH. Pour the soup into a food processor and purée until smooth. Pour milk into a small bowl and heat for 2 minutes on HIGH. Pour the soup back into a bowl, add the milk, and stir well. Re-heat on HIGH for 2 minutes and add the Madeira. Stir in the cream before serving and garnish with the sliced green onions.

Creamy Borscht

PREPARATION TIME: 15 minutes

MICROWAVE COOKING TIME: 27 minutes

SERVES: 4 people

3 beetroots, grated
255g/9oz/1½ cups cabbage, shredded
1 medium carrot, thinly sliced
2 medium potatoes, peeled and thinly sliced
1 medium onion, finely chopped
1 small clove garlic, crushed
1 teaspoon tomato paste

This page: Creamy Borscht. Facing page: Cream of Broccoli Soup (top) and Stilton Cheese and Walnut Soup (bottom).

Jerusalem Artichoke and Almond Soup

PREPARATION TIME: 15 minutes

MICROWAVE COOKING TIME:
33-38 minutes

**CONVENTIONAL
OVEN TEMPERATURE:**
180°C, 350°F, Gas Mark 4

SERVES: 4 people

1kg/2½lbs Jerusalem artichoke
2 shallots, finely chopped
30g/1oz/¼ cup blanched almonds
30g/1oz/2 tbsps butter or margarine
280ml/½ pint/1 cup chicken stock
430ml/¾ pint/1½ cups milk
140ml/¼ pint/½ cup heavy/double
  cream
60ml/2 fl oz/¼ cup white wine
1 bay leaf
Grated nutmeg
Lemon juice
Salt
Pepper

GARNISH
30g/1oz/¼ cup sliced almonds, browned

Peel artichokes and keep in a bowl of cold water and lemon juice. Thinly slice them and put them into a bowl with shallots, butter and almonds. Cover with plastic wrap and pierce several times, and cook for 4 minutes on HIGH. Pour in the stock and wine, add the bay leaf, grated nutmeg and seasoning, and cook, uncovered, for 10 minutes on HIGH. Remove bay leaf, add cream and milk, and pour into a food processor. Purée until smooth and adjust seasoning. Meanwhile, brown almonds for garnish in a conventional oven for 15 minutes or in a microwave-convection oven on Combination for 7 minutes, stirring often. Re-heat soup for 2 minutes on HIGH, and serve garnished with the browned almonds and more grated nutmeg.

Put onion and butter into a large bowl. Cover with plastic wrap and pierce several times. Cook for 6 minutes on HIGH. Stir in flour, add the stock gradually and mix well. Add bay leaf, thyme, salt and pepper, and cook, uncovered, for 10 minutes on HIGH. Remove the herbs. Crumble the cheese into a bowl and add 140ml/¼ pint/½ cup of the soup to the cheese. Stir in well. Return cheese mixture to the rest of the soup and add cream. Cook 1 minute, uncovered, on HIGH. Add the walnuts to the bowl, reserving about 2 tbsps for garnish. Cook on HIGH for 1 minute. Serve garnished with the reserved walnuts.

This page: Jerusalem Artichoke and Almond Soup (top) and Cream of Carrot and Orange Soup (bottom). Facing page: Spiced Tomato Soup (top) and Green Pea Soup (bottom).

Green Pea Soup

PREPARATION TIME: 10 minutes

MICROWAVE COOKING TIME: 12 minutes

SERVES: 4 people

450g/1lb frozen peas
30g/1oz/2 tbsps butter
30g/1oz/2 tbsps flour
280ml/½ pint/1 cup chicken or vegetable
 stock
430ml/¾ pint/1½ cups milk
140ml/¼ pint/½ cup light/single cream
1 shallot, finely chopped
1 small bunch fresh mint
1.25ml/¼ tsp marjoram
15ml/1 tbsp chopped parsley
Salt
Pepper

Put butter and shallot into a large bowl and cover with pierced plastic wrap. Cook for 5 minutes on HIGH, then add the peas to the bowl, reserving 90g/3oz/½ cup. Add the stock, milk, marjoram, parsley and seasoning. Cook for 5 minutes on HIGH. Pour into a food processor and purée until smooth. Chop the mint, reserving 4-8 leaves for garnish, if desired. Return soup to the bowl, and add chopped mint, cream and reserved peas. Re-heat soup for 2 minutes on HIGH. Garnish with the mint leaves.

Cream of Lettuce Soup

PREPARATION TIME: 10 minutes

MICROWAVE COOKING TIME: 18 minutes

SERVES: 4 people

2-3 potatoes, peeled and diced
1 onion, finely chopped
1 head romaine/cos lettuce
280ml/½ pint/1 cup chicken stock
570ml/1 pint/2 cups milk
30g/1oz/2 tbsps butter or margarine
140ml/¼ pint/½ cup cream
Ground nutmeg
1.25ml/¼ tsp thyme
15ml/1 tsp chopped parsley
Salt
Pepper

Put potatoes and onion into a large bowl with the butter and stock. Cover with plastic wrap and pierce several times. Cook on HIGH for 10 minutes. Wash lettuce well and shred leaves finely, reserving a small amount for garnish. Add to the bowl with the seasoning, thyme and ground nutmeg, and cook for 1 minute on HIGH. Add the milk and pour the soup into a food processor, and purée until smooth. Add the cream. Return to the bowl and re-heat for 7 minutes on HIGH. Serve soup garnished with reserved shredded lettuce. Serve hot or cold.

Spiced Tomato Soup

PREPARATION TIME: 10 minutes

MICROWAVE COOKING TIME: 22 minutes

SERVES: 4 people

800g/28oz can tomatoes
2 onions, finely chopped
570ml/1 pint/2 cups beef stock
15ml/1 tbsp cornflour/cornstarch
1 tbsp tomato paste
60ml/2 fl oz/¼ cup port or brandy
5ml/1 tsp thyme
½ stick cinnamon
2 whole cloves
3 black peppercorns
3 allspice berries
1 bay leaf
Salt
Sugar

GARNISH
2 tomatoes
60ml/4 tbsps heavy/double cream

Put tomatoes and their juice, stock, onion, herbs, spices and salt into a large bowl. Cook, uncovered, for 20 minutes on HIGH. Add a pinch of sugar if necessary, to bring out the tomato flavor. Sieve tomatoes, extracting as much pulp as possible. Blend cornstarch and port and stir into the soup. Put tomatoes for garnish into a bowl of water and cook on HIGH for 1 minute. Drain and put into cold water. Peel, remove seeds, cut into thin shreds and set aside. Return soup to oven and cook, uncovered, for 2 minutes on HIGH, stirring often. Adjust seasoning, and serve soup garnished with a swirl of double cream and the shreds of tomato.

Cream of Carrot and Orange Soup

PREPARATION TIME: 10 minutes

MICROWAVE COOKING TIME: 18 minutes

SERVES: 4 people

450g/1lb/3 cups grated carrots
1 shallot, finely chopped
30g/1oz/2 tbsps butter or margarine
280ml/½ pint/1 cup chicken or vegetable
 stock
570ml/1 pint/2 cups milk
100ml/6 tbsps/⅓ cup heavy/double
 cream
Juice and rind of 1 orange
1 bay leaf
1 sprig of thyme
1 small bunch chives, chopped
Salt
Pepper

Pare the rind from the orange and squeeze the juice. Put butter into a large bowl and heat for 1 minute on HIGH. Add onion and cook for 5 minutes on HIGH. Add carrots, stock, bay leaf, thyme, and salt and pepper. Cover with pierced plastic wrap and cook for 10 minutes on HIGH. Add milk, orange juice and orange rind and cook for 1 minute on HIGH. Remove bay leaf, thyme, and orange rind, and pour into a food processor. Purée until smooth. Return soup to bowl, and heat through for 2 minutes on HIGH. Stir in the chives and the cream before serving. Serve hot or cold.

Facing page: Cream of Lettuce Soup.

Microwave
SOUPS AND APPETIZERS

VEGETABLE AND PASTA SOUPS

Chicken Vegetable Soup

PREPARATION TIME: 15 minutes

MICROWAVE COOKING TIME:
23 minutes

SERVES: 4 people

450g/1lb chicken parts
1150ml/2 pints/4 cups water
1 chicken bouillon cube
1 small turnip, diced
1 onion, finely chopped
3 sticks celery, sliced
2 medium carrots, diced
60g/2oz/¼ cup frozen peas
60g/2oz/¼ cup fresh or frozen sliced
   green beans
60g/2oz/½ cup mushrooms, quartered
1.25ml/¼ tsp thyme
1 bay leaf
15ml/1 tbsp chopped parsley

Put the chicken parts and the water
into a large casserole with the thyme,
bay leaf and seasoning. Cover and
cook on HIGH for 15 minutes.
Remove chicken and leave to cool.
Remove the skin and bones and cut
the chicken into small pieces. Set
aside. Strain stock. Return stock to
casserole and skim any fat from the
surface. Taste and, if necessary, add
the stock cube. Add the carrot,
onion, celery and turnip; cover and
cook for 10 minutes on HIGH. At
this stage, if using fresh beans, cut
into even sized lengths and add to
the stock with the mushrooms.
Cover and cook for 4 minutes on
HIGH. Add frozen peas and parsley
and cook a further 1 minute on
HIGH. (If using frozen beans, add
with the peas.) Add chicken. Adjust
seasoning, and heat through for
3 minutes on HIGH. Serve.

Greek Lemon Soup

PREPARATION TIME: 8 minutes

MICROWAVE COOKING TIME:
17 minutes

SERVES: 4 people

3 lemons
1 onion, finely chopped
45g/1½ oz/3 tbsps butter or margarine
30g/1oz/2 tbsps flour/plain flour
90g/3oz/1 cup quick-cooking rice
1 litre/1¾ pints/4 cups chicken stock
1.25ml/¼ tsp powdered oregano
Nutmeg
Salt
Pepper

Put butter and onion into a bowl.
Cover with plastic wrap and pierce
several times. Cook on HIGH for
about 3 minutes. Add flour to bowl
and cook on HIGH for an additional
1½-2 minutes. Gradually stir in the
stock. Grate rind and squeeze juice
from 2 lemons, and add to the bowl
with the bay leaf, pinch of nutmeg,
oregano, salt and pepper. Cook on
HIGH for 5 minutes. Add rice,
re-cover the bowl, and cook for
5 minutes on HIGH, stirring
frequently. Additional cooking time
may be needed if the rice is not
tender. Leave to stand, covered,
about 2 minutes. Slice remaining
lemon thinly and garnish each
serving of soup with a slice of lemon.

Minestrone

PREPARATION TIME: 15 minutes

MICROWAVE COOKING TIME:
26 minutes

SERVES: 4 people

2 small leeks, washed and cut into thin
   strips
30ml/2 tbsps oil
225g/8oz/1½ cups canned tomatoes
1 green pepper, sliced
215g/7oz can canellini, or haricot, beans
1 carrot, cut into 2.5cm (1") strips
2 sticks celery, cut into 2.5cm (1") strips
1 zucchini/courgette, cut into 2.5cm (1")
   strips
1 clove garlic, crushed
120g/¼lb ham, cut into thin strips
1150ml/2 pints/4 cups stock (preferably
   ham)
30g/1oz/⅓ cup macaroni
1 bay leaf
2.5ml/½ tsp basil
2.5ml/½ tsp oregano
2.5ml/½ tsp fennel seed
Salt and pepper
Sugar

GARNISH
90g/3oz/½ cup Parmesan cheese, grated

Put oil, leeks, carrot, celery, garlic and
herbs in a large casserole. Cover and
cook 6 minutes on HIGH. Add
macaroni, tomatoes and their juice,
stock, ham, drained beans, salt,
pepper and a pinch of sugar, and
cook, covered, on HIGH for
6 minutes. Add zucchini/courgette,
green pepper and parsley, and cook
5 minutes on HIGH, or until pasta is
tender. Serve with grated Parmesan
cheese.

Facing page: Minestrone.

Cream of Asparagus Soup

PREPARATION TIME: 10 minutes

MICROWAVE COOKING TIME: 32 minutes

SERVES: 4 people

450g/1lb asparagus, fresh or frozen
45g/1½ oz/3 tbsps butter or margarine
45g/1½ oz/3 tbsps flour/plain flour
1 shallot, finely chopped
850ml/1½ pints/3 cups chicken stock
140ml/¼ pint/½ cup cream
1 bay leaf
1.25ml/¼ tsp thyme
Salt
Pepper
Nutmeg

Place butter and shallot into a large casserole. Cover and cook on HIGH for 6 minutes. Stir in the flour and cook a further 1 minute on HIGH. Stir in the stock and cook for 15 minutes on HIGH, until boiling. Chop asparagus roughly and, if using fresh, reserve 4 tips for garnish. Add asparagus, bay leaf, seasoning, and a pinch of grated nutmeg, and cook for 10 minutes on MEDIUM. Remove the bay leaf, and pour the soup into a food processor and purée until smooth. Put reserved asparagus tips into a small bowl with 1 tbsp of water. Cover with plastic wrap and pierce several times. Cook for 1 minute on HIGH and set aside. Add the cream to the soup, cover, and re-heat for 2-3 minutes. Serve garnished with the reserved asparagus tips and more grated nutmeg.

French Onion Soup

PREPARATION TIME: 10 minutes

MICROWAVE COOKING TIME: 27 minutes

SERVES: 4 people

675g/1½lbs onions, thinly sliced
60g/2oz/4 tbsps butter or margarine
30g/1oz/2 tbsps flour/plain flour
140ml/¼ pint/½ cup dry cider or white wine
30ml/2 tbsps Calvados or brandy

1150ml/2 pints/4 cups beef stock
1.25ml/¼ tbsp thyme
1 bay leaf
4 slices French bread, toasted and buttered
60g/2oz/½ cup Gruyère or Swiss cheese
Salt
Pepper

Place onions, butter, salt and pepper into a large bowl and cook on HIGH for 8 minutes. Stir occasionally. Stir in the flour, add the stock, cider, Calvados, thyme and bay leaf. Cover bowl with plastic wrap and pierce several times. Cook on HIGH for 10 minutes. Uncover and stir occasionally. Reduce the setting to LOW and cook a further 8 minutes.

Leave the bowl to stand covered for 1-2 minutes. Put slices of toast on a plate, and sprinkle over the grated cheese thickly. Cook on LOW until cheese starts to melt, and then grill/broil conventionally until lightly browned. Spoon the soup into individual micro-proof bowls. Top each with the cheese toast and heat through for 1 minute on HIGH. Serve immediately.

This page: Chicken Vegetable Soup. Facing page: Cream of Asparagus Soup (top) and French Onion Soup (bottom).

the soup and cook, stirring several times, for 5 minutes on HIGH. Drain noodles and add them to the bowl with the sesame seed oil. Heat soup through for 2 minutes on HIGH. Serve garnished with more chopped spring onion if desired.

Potato Soup

PREPARATION TIME: 10 minutes

MICROWAVE COOKING TIME: 21 minutes

SERVES: 4 people

675g/1½lbs/4 cups diced potatoes
45g/1½oz/3 tbsps butter or margarine
1 onion, thinly sliced
280ml/½ pint/1 cup water
850ml/1½ pints/3 cups milk
1 bay leaf
1 sprig of thyme
Salt
Pepper
Nutmeg

GARNISH
60g/2oz/½ cup Red Leicester/Colby cheese, grated

Put potatoes, onions and butter into a large bowl. Cover with plastic wrap and pierce several times. Cook for 10 minutes on HIGH. Add milk, water, thyme, bay leaf, seasoning and grated nutmeg, and cook for 7 minutes on HIGH. Leave standing, covered, for 1 minute. Uncover and allow to cool slightly. Remove bay leaf and thyme, pour soup into a food processor, and purée until smooth. Check seasoning and consistency. If too thick, add more milk. Cover and heat through for 3 minutes on HIGH. Serve garnished with the grated cheese.

Chinese Chicken and Mushroom Soup

PREPARATION TIME: 8 minutes

MICROWAVE COOKING TIME: 36 minutes

SERVES: 4 people

6 dried Chinese mushrooms
2 chicken breasts
280ml/½ pint/1 cup water
1 small can water chestnuts, sliced
1 small can bamboo shoots, sliced
1 bunch spring/green onions, sliced diagonally
120g/¼lb fine Chinese egg noodles
120g/¼lb pea pods/mangetout
15ml/1 tbsp (light) soy sauce
30ml/2 tbsps dry sherry
5ml/1 tsp sesame seed oil
15ml/1 tbsp cornstarch/cornflour
850ml/1½ pints/3 cups chicken stock
Salt and pepper

Put mushrooms into a small bowl and cover with cold water. Cover bowl with plastic wrap and pierce several times. Heat on HIGH for 2 minutes and leave to stand. Put chicken breasts into a bowl with 280ml/½ pint/1 cup water. Cover with pierced plastic wrap and cook for 15 minutes on HIGH. Put noodles into a bowl with 1150ml/2 pints water. Cover with pierced plastic wrap and cook for 3 minutes on HIGH. Leave standing, covered, for 5 minutes. Drain and slice mushrooms, and put into a large bowl with the stock. Cover with pierced plastic wrap and cook for 1 minute on HIGH. Skin, bone and shred chicken and add to bowl with spring onions, pea pods/mangetout, water chestnuts and bamboo shoots and cook for 1 minute on HIGH. Mix cornflour/cornstarch, soy sauce and sherry with a tbsp of the hot liquid. Pour into the bowl with the rest of

This page: Potato Soup (top) and Greek Lemon Soup (bottom).
Facing page: Chinese Chicken and Mushroom Soup.

Chili Corn Chowder

PREPARATION TIME: 15 minutes

MICROWAVE COOKING TIME:
24 minutes

SERVES: 4 people

45g/1½ oz/3 tbsps butter or margarine
1 shallot, finely chopped
4 strips/rashers smoked streaky bacon
    (rindless and boneless)
45g/1½ oz/3 tbsps flour/plain flour
570ml/1 pint/2 cups chicken stock
430ml/¾ pint/1½ cups milk
2 medium potatoes, peeled and cut into
    1cm (½") dice
1 red pepper, diced
1 green chili pepper, finely chopped
280g/10oz/1½ cups corn/sweetcorn,
    frozen
140g/¼ pint/½ cup light/single cream
15ml/1 tbsp chopped parsley
1.25ml/¼ tsp ground cumin
1 bay leaf

GARNISH
4 green onions

Put butter into a bowl and cook for 1 minute on HIGH. Dice bacon and add it with the shallot to the butter. Cover with pierced plastic wrap and cook for 5 minutes on HIGH until onions are softened. Stir in the flour and cumin, and cook for 1 minute on HIGH. Gradually stir in the stock and milk, and add potatoes and bay leaf. Cook for 6 minutes on HIGH or until boiling. Add red pepper and as much of the chili pepper as desired. Cook for 10 minutes or until potatoes soften. Remove bay leaf, add corn, cream, parsley and seasoning, and cook for 3 minutes on HIGH. Serve garnished with chopped green onion.

Italian Onion Soup

PREPARATION TIME: 10 minutes

MICROWAVE COOKING TIME:
16-23 minutes and 1-2 minutes
standing time

SERVES: 4 people

675g/1½lbs onions, thinly sliced
450g/16oz can plum tomatoes

45g/1½ oz/3 tbsps butter or margarine
30g/1oz/2 tbsps flour/plain flour
140ml/¼ pint/½ cup red wine
430ml/¾ pint/1½ cups beef stock
1.25ml/¼ tsp basil
1.25ml/¼ tsp oregano
1 bay leaf
Salt
Pepper
Tomato paste
4 slices French bread, toasted and
    buttered
60g/2oz/2 tbsps Parmesan cheese, grated
60g/2oz/2 tbsps Cheddar cheese, grated

Place onions, butter, salt and pepper into a large bowl and cook on HIGH for 6 minutes. Stir occasionally. Stir in flour, add the stock, tomatoes, red wine, basil, oregano and bay leaf. Cover the bowl with plastic wrap and pierce several times. Cook on HIGH for 8 minutes. Uncover and stir occasionally. Reduce setting to LOW and cook for a further 4 minutes. Leave the bowl to stand covered for 1-2 minutes. Adjust seasoning and add tomato paste, if necessary, for color and flavor. Mix the cheeses together, put the slices of toast on a plate, and sprinkle over the grated cheese. Cook on LOW until cheese starts to melt, and then grill/broil conventionally until lightly browned. Use the Combination setting on convection microwave oven for 7 minutes. Spoon the soup into individual micro-proof bowls. Top each with the cheese toast and heat through for 1 minute on HIGH.

This page: Chili Corn Chowder.
Facing page: Curried Cauliflower
Soup (top) and Italian Onion Soup
(bottom).

Curried Cauliflower Soup

PREPARATION TIME: 10 minutes

MICROWAVE COOKING TIME:
15 minutes

SERVES: 4 people

4 cups cauliflowerets, or 1 small
  cauliflower cut into flowerets
2 shallots finely chopped
30g/1oz/2 tbsps butter or margarine
30g/1oz/2 tbsps flour/plain flour
10ml/2 tsps curry powder
430ml/¾ pint/1½ cups chicken or
  vegetable stock
570ml/1 pint/2 cups milk
Salt
Pepper

GARNISH
60g/2oz/⅓ cup sliced almonds, browned

Put cauliflowerets into a roasting bag
with the shallot and bay leaf. Tie bag
loosely and cook for 8 minutes on
HIGH. (Cauliflower may also be
cooked in a bowl covered with
pierced plastic wrap.) Put butter into
a large bowl and cook for 1 minute
on HIGH until melted. Stir in the
curry powder and flour, and cook for
1 minute on HIGH. Add milk and
cook for 3 minutes on HIGH, stirring
occasionally. Pour the soup into a
food processor, add the cauliflower,
and purée until smooth. Return the
soup to the oven to heat through for
2 minutes on HIGH. Serve garnished
with the browned sliced almonds.

Vegetable Soup

PREPARATION TIME: 10 minutes

MICROWAVE COOKING TIME:
21 minutes

SERVES: 4 people

1 large carrot, peeled and diced
1 large turnip, peeled and diced
2 leeks, washed and sliced thinly
2 potatoes, peeled and diced
60g/2oz/¼ cup frozen peas
60g/2oz/¼ cup frozen corn/sweetcorn
90g/3oz/½ cup fresh or frozen sliced
  green beans
120g/¼lb okra (optional)

450g/16oz can plum tomatoes
570ml/1 pint/2 cups chicken or
  vegetable stock
60g/2oz/⅓ cup soup pasta
1 bay leaf
1.25ml/¼ tsp marjoram or savory
15ml/1 tbsp chopped parsley
Pepper

Put butter into a large bowl and cook
for 45 seconds on HIGH until it
melts. Add carrots, turnips, leeks and
potatoes and mix together. Cover
with plastic wrap and pierce several
times. Cook on HIGH for 10 minutes
or until vegetables begin to soften.
Stir occasionally. Add stock,
tomatoes, bay leaf, marjoram, pasta,

salt and pepper. Cover and cook for
7 minutes on HIGH. Slice beans (if
fresh), trim okra, and slice into
rounds, and add to bowl. Re-cover
bowl and cook for 2 minutes on
HIGH. Add corn, peas and parsley.
Cook for 1 minute on HIGH or until
pasta is tender. Sprinkle with more
chopped parsley, if desired, before
serving.

**This page: Vegetable Soup.
Facing page: Jellied Vegetable
Terrine with Tomato Dressing.**

TARTS, TERRINES AND PÂTÉS

Jellied Vegetable Terrine with Tomato Dressing

PREPARATION TIME: 15 minutes

MICROWAVE COOKING TIME: 11 minutes

SERVES: 4 people

TERRINE
1 tbsp gelatine
1 chicken bouillon cube
570ml/1 pint/2 cups boiling water (less 2 tbsps)
30ml/2 tbsps dry sherry
225g/8oz green beans, ends trimmed
1 large carrot, peeled
1-2 Jerusalem artichokes, peeled
120g/4oz mushrooms, cleaned
120g/4oz/½ cup frozen peas

DRESSING
400g/14oz can tomato sauce
1 tsp tomato paste
Juice and grate rind of half a lemon
1.25ml/¼ tsp chives, snipped
1.25ml/¼ tsp parsley, chopped
1.25ml/¼ tsp thyme, chopped
1.25ml/¼ tsp basil, chopped
45-60ml/3-4 tbsps olive oil
30ml/2 tbsps red wine vinegar
¼ tsp Dijon mustard
1 bay leaf
Sugar
Salt
Pepper

GARNISH
1 bunch watercress

Heat water in a glass measuring jug/cup for 3-4 minutes on HIGH until boiling. Add sherry and stir in the gelatine and bouillon cube. Leave to cool at room temperature, then put into a bowl of cold water. The aspic must be cold but liquid. If it sets too quickly in the cup, melt again for 1-2 minutes on HIGH. Then chill again in the cold water, and repeat the process again when necessary. Leave green beans whole and cook for 8 minutes on HIGH with 2 tbsps water in a small, shallow dish covered with pierced plastic wrap. Cut carrots lengthways into 0.5cm (¼") sticks and cook for 10 minutes in the same way as the beans. Cut artichokes into

Chicken and Asparagus Terrine with Lemon Mousseline Sauce

PREPARATION TIME: 15 minutes

MICROWAVE COOKING TIME: 33 minutes

SERVES: 4-6 people

TERRINE
450g/1lb chicken breasts
430ml/¾ pint/1½ cups cream
340g/12oz low-fat cheese
30ml/2 tbsps white wine
140ml/¼ pint/½ cup water
3 eggs
450g/1lb asparagus spears, fresh or frozen
Salt
Pepper
Nutmeg
1 bay leaf

SAUCE
60g/2oz/½ cup butter
3 egg yolks
Rind and juice of 1 lemon
60ml/4 tbsps/¼ cup whipping cream
1 bay leaf
1 blade mace
Salt
Pepper

Cut tips off asparagus spears, trim stalk ends, and cook on HIGH for 6 minutes with 2 tbsps water in a shallow dish covered with pierced plastic wrap. Leave to cool. Put chicken breasts into a bowl with the white wine, water and bay leaf. Cover with pierced plastic wrap and cook for 15 minutes on HIGH. Cool and remove skin and bones. Put chicken, cheese, seasoning, nutmeg and 2 eggs into a food processor, and purée until smooth. In a clean bowl, purée the asparagus spears with 1 egg, salt and pepper. Put half the chicken mixture into a loaf pan and smooth evenly. Cover with half the asparagus mixture and layer on the reserved asparagus tips. Cover with remaining

This page: Chicken and Asparagus Terrine with Lemon Mousseline Sauce.
Facing page: Tomato Tarts Niçoise (top) and Cheese and Mushroom Tarts (bottom).

thin rounds and cook for 8 minutes. Remove stalks from mushrooms and slice caps thinly. Cook them for 3 minutes on HIGH, then the frozen peas for 1 minute on HIGH. Dampen a 450g/1lb loaf pan with water and pour in a 0.5cm (¼") layer of cool aspic. Chill until set. Arrange a layer of peas on top and pour over a thin layer of aspic to set the peas in place. Chill until set, then add more aspic to just cover the peas. Chill again until set. Repeat the process with a layer of artichokes, green beans, carrots and mushrooms. Fill the pan to the top with aspic and chill for

1-2 hours until firm. Meanwhile, put tomato sauce, paste, garlic, bay leaf, seasoning and sugar into a bowl. Cover with pierced plastic wrap and cook for 10 minutes on HIGH, stirring frequently. Allow sauce to cool completely. Whisk oil, vinegar and mustard together until thick. Whisk in the tomato sauce, add chopped herbs, and adjust seasoning. Unmould the terrine and cut into 1cm (½") slices. Serve with tomato dressing and small bouquets of watercress or parsley.

asparagus mixture, then the remaining chicken mixture. Cover the dish with plastic wrap and cook for 10 minutes on HIGH. Cover and weight down the top, leaving to stand for 5 minutes. Serve hot with the lemon mousseline sauce.

To make sauce: Put the butter into a glass measuring jug/cup or a small, deep bowl and cook for 1 minute on HIGH to melt. Put lemon juice, bay leaf and mace into another bowl and heat for 1 minute on HIGH. Beat egg yolks, lemon rind and seasoning, and strain on the juice. Pour egg yolk mixture into the butter and stir well. Have a bowl of ice water ready. Put the sauce mixture into the oven and cook for 15 seconds on HIGH. Remove and stir, repeating the process until sauce has thickened – approximately 2 minutes. Put the jug immediately into the ice water to stop the cooking. Whip cream, fold into the sauce and serve at once with the terrine.

Country Pâté

PREPARATION TIME: 10 minutes

MICROWAVE COOKING TIME: 15 minutes

SERVES: 6-8 people

225g/½ lb minced/ground pork
225g/½ lb minced/ground veal
120g/¼ lb ham, minced
120g/¼ lb pigs'/pork liver
90g/3oz minced pork fat
1 clove garlic, crushed
60ml/4 tbsps brandy
Ground allspice
Thyme
1 bay leaf
2 tsps green peppercorns in brine, rinsed
8 slices (streaky) bacon, bones and rind removed
Salt
Pepper

Line a 1lb glass loaf dish with the bacon. Remove skin and ducts from liver, mince in a food processor, and mix with the minced/ground meats, garlic, herbs, spices, brandy, peppercorns and seasoning. Press meat mixture into the dish on top of

bacon. Place bay leaf on top. Fold edges of bacon over the top and cover with plastic wrap. Put a ramekin dish of water into the oven with the pâté, and cook on MEDIUM for 6 minutes. Leave to stand for 5 minutes and cook for a further 10 minutes on MEDIUM. Cover with foil, press down and weight. Leave to chill 2-4 hours. Remove the bay leaf, and cut mixture into thin slices (about 18) to serve.

Asparagus with Orange Hollandaise

PREPARATION TIME: 10 minutes

MICROWAVE COOKING TIME: 11 minutes

SERVES: 4 people

900g/2lbs asparagus spears
60g/2oz/½ cup butter
3 egg yolks
Juice of half a lemon
Grated rind and juice of ½ an orange
1 small bay leaf
1 blade mace
Salt
Pepper

Trim any thick ends from the asparagus spears and rinse them well. Put into a shallow casserole with 45-60g/3-4 tbsps water. Cover and cook for 7 minutes until just tender. Leave covered while preparing sauce. Put the butter in a glass measuring cup or jug, or small, deep bowl and cook for 1 minute on HIGH to melt. Put orange juice, lemon juice, bay leaf and mace into another bowl and heat for 1 minute on HIGH. Beat egg yolks, orange rind and seasoning together, and strain on the juice. Pour egg yolk mixture into the butter and stir well to mix. Have a bowl of ice water on hand. Put the sauce mixture into the oven and cook for 15 seconds on HIGH. Remove and stir well, and repeat the process until sauce is thickened. It should take about 2 minutes. Put the jug immediately into the ice water to prevent sauce from cooking further. Serve at once with the asparagus.

Cheese and Mushroom Tarts

PREPARATION TIME: 10 minutes

MICROWAVE COOKING TIME: 11 minutes

SERVES: 4 people

60g/2oz/1½ cups wholewheat biscuits/ crackers
60g/2oz/½ cup butter or margarine
60g/2oz/½ cup Cheddar cheese, grated
225g/½lb mushrooms, roughly chopped
60ml/4 tbsps chopped chives
15g/½ oz/1 tbsp flour
15g/½ oz/1 tbsp butter
90ml/5 tbsps/⅓ cup chicken or vegetable stock
1 egg, beaten
30ml/2 tbsps light/single cream
60g/2oz/½ cup Red Leicester/Colby cheese, grated
Cayenne pepper
Salt
Pepper

Crush the crackers/biscuits into a food processor and grate in the cheese. Melt 45g/1½ oz/⅓ cup of the butter on HIGH for 1 minute and pour into the crumbs and cheese. Process to mix. Press the mixture firmly into 8 individual tart pans or a muffin pan. Cook for 2 minutes on HIGH, and cool. Melt the remaining butter on HIGH. Mix in flour, chives, seasoning and stock, and cook for 2 minutes on HIGH, or until sauce has thickened. Fill the tart shells with the mushrooms. Beat egg, cream, Cayenne pepper and seasonings together until frothy. fold in the Red Leicester/Colby cheese. Pour on top of the mushroom filling and cook for 2 minutes on HIGH until the cheese custard sets. Tops may be browned under a grill/broiler if desired, or cooked for 5 minutes on the Combination setting in a microwave convection oven. Serve immediately.

Facing page: Country Pâté (top) and Asparagus with Orange Hollandaise (bottom).

1lb glass loaf dish with the ham slices. Press mixture firmly onto the ham. Cover with plastic wrap and cook for 6 minutes on MEDIUM. Leave to stand for 5 minutes, then cook for a further 7 minutes on MEDIUM. Cover with foil and weight down the top. Leave to chill for 4-5 hours, and serve with tarragon sauce.

To make sauce: Have ready a bowl of ice water. Beat egg and sugar in a small glass bowl until creamy. Add vinegar and cook on HIGH for 30 seconds. Remove and stir. Repeat the process until sauce thickens (approximately 2 minutes). Put immediately into ice water to stop the cooking, and leave to go cold, stirring occasionally. Whip the cream and fold into the sauce with the chopped tarragon.

Tomato Tarts Niçoise

PREPARATION TIME: 20 minutes

MICROWAVE COOKING TIME:
10 minutes

SERVES: 4 people

PASTRY
150g/5oz/1 cup flour/plain flour
20g/¾ oz/1½ tbsps butter or margarine
20g/¾ oz/1½ tbsps baking powder
90ml/5 tbsps/⅓ cup milk
Pinch salt
*15ml/1 tbsp chopped parsley, basil and
   thyme, mixed*

FILLING
1 onion, finely slicd
*225g/½lb tomatoes, skinned and thickly
   sliced*
15ml/1 tbsp olive oil
16 black olives, stoned
1 tbsp capers
8 anchovies
1.25ml/¼ tsp oregano or basil
60g/2oz/½ cup Gruyère cheese, grated

To make pastry: Sift flour with salt and cut in the butter until mixture resembles fine breadcrumbs. Add herbs and milk, and mix to a soft dough. It may not be necessary to add all the milk. Turn out and knead lightly Divide dough into 4 pieces

Terrine of Duck and Cherries with Tarragon Sauce

PREPARATION TIME: 15 minutes

MICROWAVE COOKING TIME:
15 minutes

SERVES: 6-8 people

TERRINE
1 2kg/5lb duck, skinned and boned
6 slices boiled ham
145g/5oz/⅓ cup ground/minced pork
145g/5oz/⅓ cup ground/minced veal
½ clove garlic, crushed
*225g/8oz can black/morello cherries,
   drained and pitted*

60ml/4 tbsps white wine
Allspice
10ml/2 tsps tarragon, chopped
15ml/1 tbsp kirsch
Salt
Pepper

SAUCE
1 egg
45ml/3 tbsps tarragon vinegar
1.25ml/¼ tsp chopped fresh tarragon
45g/1½ oz/2 tbsps sugar
140ml/¼ pint/½ cup whipping cream

To prepare terrine: Mince duck meat in a food processor and mix with pork and veal. Add garlic, kirsch, wine, tarragon, allspice and seasoning. Fold in the cherries. Line a 450g/

Facing page: Terrine of Duck and Cherries with Tarragon Sauce. This page: Ham and Mushroom Pâté (left) and Stuffed Tomatoes Provençal (right).

and roll each out to line a muffin pan or 8 tart pans.
To make filling and assemble tarts: Bring 570ml/1 pint/2 cups water to the boil for 3 minutes on HIGH. Put in the tomatoes for 5 seconds, remove and plunge them into cold water. Peel, drain and slice them. Put olive oil in a bowl, add onion, and cook for 3 minutes on HIGH or until softened. Season, mix with half the cheese. Put into the bottom of each pastry shell. Layer tomatoes,

seasoning and sprinkling the herbs between each layer. Decorate with anchovies, capers and olives, and sprinkle with remaining cheese. Bake for 4 minutes on HIGH, turning pans once. Brown under a grill/broiler if desired. Do not overbake or pastry will become hard.

Ham and Mushroom Pâté

PREPARATION TIME: 10 minutes
MICROWAVE COOKING TIME: 20 minutes
SERVES: 6-8 people

450g/1lb cooked ham, minced
120g/4oz/1 cup fresh white breadcrumbs
3 eggs
45g/1½ oz/3 tbsps butter
120g/4oz mushrooms, finely chopped
1 shallot, finely chopped
1 clove garlic, crushed
30ml/2 tbsps dry sherry
1.25ml/¼ tsp thyme
1.25ml/¼ tsp parsley
Nutmeg
Salt and pepper

Melt the butter in a small bowl and add the shallot. Cover with pierced plastic wrap and cook for 2 minutes on HIGH. Add the thyme, parsley and mushrooms, and cook for a further 4 minutes, uncovered, on HIGH. Add the seasoning and 30g/1oz/¼ cup of the breadcrumbs. Leave to cool. Add 1 beaten egg only if necessary to bind together. Mix ham, remaining breadcrumbs, garlic, sherry, nutmeg and seasonings. Beat in up to 2 of the eggs, 1 at a time, until mixture holds together. Put half the ham mixture into a 450g/1lb glass loaf dish and pack down firmly. Make a channel down the centre and mound the mushroom mixture into it. Cover with remaining ham mixture, packing it carefully around the mushroom mixture to cover it completely. Cover dish with plastic wrap and put into the microwave oven with a ramekin dish of water. Cook for 10 minutes on MEDIUM, leave to stand for 2 minutes, then cook for another 2 minutes on MEDIUM until firm. Cover with foil and weight the top of the dish. Chill for 4-5 hours and cut into slices to serve with toast or French bread.

Stuffed Tomatoes Provençal

PREPARATION TIME: 10 minutes
MICROWAVE COOKING TIME: 6 minutes
SERVES: 4 people

4 large ripe tomatoes
225g/8oz mushrooms, finely chopped
1 shallot, finely chopped
30g/1oz/2 tbsps butter or margarine
*45g/1½ oz/1 cup fresh white
    breadcrumbs*
15ml/1 tbsp white wine
1 clove garlic, crushed
1 tsp Dijon mustard
5ml/1 tsp chopped parsley
5ml/1 tsp chopped basil
1.25ml/¼ tsp thyme

GARNISH
Parsley sprigs

Cut the rounded ends of the tomatoes off to form caps, and remove the green cores from the bottoms. Scoop out the pulp and seeds, and strain the juice. Put the butter into a small bowl with the garlic and shallot and cook for 2 minutes on HIGH. Stir in the mushrooms and wine and cook for 2 minutes on HIGH. Add breadcrumbs, herbs, seasoning, mustard

and tomato pulp, and mix well. Stuff the tomatoes and put into a shallow dish. Place the tops on at a slight angle and cook, uncovered, for 2 minutes on HIGH. Garnish with the parsley sprigs.

Langoustine Parisienne

PREPARATION TIME: 10 minutes
MICROWAVE COOKING TIME: 14 minutes
SERVES: 4 people

*450g/1lb scampi/langoustines, shelled
    and uncooked (Gulf shrimp may be
    substituted)*
225g/8oz mushrooms
75g/2½ oz/⅔ cup butter or margarine
45g/1½ oz/3 tbsps flour/plain flour
1 shallot, finely chopped
430ml/¾ pint/1½ cups milk
15ml/1 tbsp chopped parsley
30ml/2 tbsps dry sherry
60g/2oz/⅓ cup dry breadcrumbs
Lemon juice
Paprika
Salt
Pepper

Cut mushroom stalks level with the caps and cut mushrooms into quarters. Put 45g/1½ oz/3 tbsps of the butter into a large bowl, then add shallot and cook for 1 minute on HIGH. Stir in the mushrooms and cook, uncovered, for 6 minutes on HIGH. Add flour and seasoning, and stir in the milk and sherry. Cook for 3 minutes on HIGH, stirring frequently. Add parsley, and set aside. Put scampi into a small bowl with 2 tbsps water, cover with pierced plastic wrap and cook for 2 minutes on HIGH. Cut each scampi into 2 or 3 pieces if large, then stir them into the mushroom sauce. Heat a browning tray and melt the remaining butter. Stir in the breadcrumbs and cook until golden brown and crisp. Put the shellfish-mushroom mixture into 4 ramekins or shells and scatter over the crumbs. Sprinkle over the paprika and heat for 2 minutes on HIGH. If using a microwave convection oven, melt the butter for 1 minute on HIGH microwave

setting, mix in the crumbs, fill the ramekins with the shellfish-mushroom mixture and scatter the crumbs over. Sprinkle with paprika and cook for 3 minutes on the Combination setting to brown.

Chicken Liver Pâté

PREPARATION TIME: 8 minutes
MICROWAVE COOKING TIME: 9 minutes
SERVES: 4 people

450g/1lb/chicken livers
1 shallot, finely chopped
1 clove garlic, crushed
1 large sprig rosemary
5ml/1 tsp parsley
15ml/1 tbsp Madeira
15ml/1 tbsp cream
45g/1½ oz/⅓ cup butter
Nutmeg
Salt
Pepper

GARNISH
Juniper berries
Small sprigs of rosemary

Pick over the livers, removing any discolored parts. Put livers, shallot, garlic, 1 sprig rosemary, half the butter, seasonings and a pinch of nutmeg into a bowl. Cover with pierced plastic wrap and cook for 6 minutes on HIGH, stirring once. Remove rosemary and put the mixture into a food processor with the Madeira, cream and parsley, and purée until smooth. Divide between 4 ramekin dishes. Put remaining butter in a bowl and cook for 3 minutes on HIGH until boiling. Leave to stand and skim off salt rising to surface. Spoon the butter oil over each pâté to seal. Chill until firm, decorate with small sprigs of rosemary and juniper berries, and serve with hot toast or French bread.

Facing page: Chicken Liver Pâté (top) and Langoustine Parisienne (bottom).

Microwave
SOUPS AND APPETIZERS

MEAT AND SEAFOOD APPETIZERS

Sparkling Shrimp

PREPARATION TIME: 5 minutes

MICROWAVE COOKING TIME: 2½ minutes

SERVES: 4 people

675g/1½lbs peeled shrimp or prawns
15ml/1 tbsp peppercorns packed in brine, rinsed
140ml/¼ pint/½ cup dry sparkling white wine
140ml/¼ pint/½ cup heavy/double cream
Juice and grated rind of half an orange
Salt
Pepper

GARNISH
12 thin orange slices

Put orange rind and juice, pepper-corns, seasoning and wine into a bowl. Heat for 30 seconds on HIGH. Stir in the prawns and heat for 1 minute on HIGH. Lightly whip the cream, fold in, and heat for a further 1 minute on HIGH. Adjust seasoning before putting into serving dishes. Garnish with the orange slices.

Moûles Marinière à la Moutarde

PREPARATION TIME: 5 minutes

MICROWAVE COOKING TIME: 9 minutes

SERVES: 4 people

1 litre/2 pints mussels
20g/¾ oz/1½ tbsps butter or margarine
2 shallots, finely chopped
1 clove garlic, crushed
4 tbsps Dijon mustard

280ml/½ pint/1 cup white wine
140ml/¼ pint/½ cup heavy/double cream
15g/½ oz/1 tbsp flour/plain flour
15ml/1 tbsp parsley, chopped
15ml/1 tbsp dill, chopped
Salt
Pepper

This page: Moûles Marinière à la Moutarde.
Facing page: Sparkling Shrimp.

Scrub mussels well and discard any that are open or broken. Put butter into a large bowl and cook for

1 minute on HIGH. Add shallot, garlic, wine and seasoning. Cover with pierced plastic wrap and cook for 2 minutes on HIGH. Add mussels, and cover and cook for 3 minutes or until the shells are open. Stir half-way through the cooking time. Remove mussels from the bowl, put into a serving dish and keep them warm. Strain the liquid from them and set it aside. Put flour into a clean bowl and gradually pour on the mussel liquid, stirring well to mix. Cook, uncovered, for 2 minutes on HIGH or until thick, stirring occasionally. Stir in the mustard, cream and chopped herbs and heat through for 1 minute on HIGH. Pour over the mussels and serve with French bread.

Pork Satay with Peanut Sauce

PREPARATION TIME: 10 minutes and 1 hour to marinate pork

MICROWAVE COOKING TIME: 13 minutes

SERVES: 4 people

675g/1½lbs pork fillet/tenderloin, cut into 2.5cm (1") cubes
1 large red pepper, cut into 2.5cm (1") slices
30ml/2 tbsps oil
Lime juice
1 clove garlic, crushed
1 small green chili pepper, finely chopped
60g/2oz/½ cup crunchy peanut butter
140ml/¼ pint/½ cup chicken or vegetable stock
5ml/1 tsp ground cumin
5ml/1 tsp ground coriander
1 shallot, finely chopped
Salt
Pepper

GARNISH
1 bunch fresh coriander leaves (optional)
Lemon wedges

Mix lime juice, salt and pepper together and mix in the pork. Leave in a cool place for 1 hour. Heat 1 tbsp oil in a small bowl and add shallot. Cook for 2 minutes on HIGH, add chili pepper and cook for 1 minute

more on HIGH. Stir in stock, peanut butter, spices and seasoning. Cook for 1 minute on HIGH. Set aside. Thread meat and red pepper onto 12 small, wooden skewers. Heat a browning tray for 5 minutes on HIGH. Add oil and brown the satay for 3 minutes on HIGH, turning frequently. Transfer onto a roasting rack, and cook for 6 minutes on MEDIUM. Arrange sprigs of coriander leaves on serving plates and put the satay on top. Spoon over some of the peanut sauce and serve the rest separately.

Spicy Chicken Kebabs with Avocado Sauce

PREPARATION TIME: 10 minutes

MICROWAVE COOKING TIME: 6 minutes

SERVES: 4 people

CHICKEN AND MARINADE
3 chicken breasts, skinned and boned
30ml/2 tbsps vegetable oil
1 clove garlic, crushed

**This page: Pork Satay with Peanut Sauce (top) and Spicy Chicken Kebabs with Avocado Sauce (bottom).
Facing page: Stuffed Zucchini/Courgettes.**

15ml/1 tbsp curry powder
1.25ml/¼ tsp Cayenne pepper
15ml/1 tbsp chopped coriander leaves
Juice and grated rind of 1 lime
Salt
Pepper

SAUCE
1 large avocado, peeled and stone removed
140ml/¼ pint/½ cup plain yogurt
15ml/1 tbsp vegetable oil
2.5ml/½ tsp finely chopped onion
5ml/1 tsp mango chutney
Lime juice

Cut chicken into strips 2.5cm (1") wide. Combine ingredients for the marinade and mix in the chicken to coat each piece. Leave to marinate for 1 hour. Thread the meat onto wooden skewers and put onto a roasting rack. Cook for 5 minutes on

HIGH. Turn kebabs while cooking. Leave to stand, covered in plastic wrap, for 1 minute. Put oil and onion for the sauce into a small bowl. Cook for 1 minute on HIGH, and stir in chutney. Put avocado flesh into a food processor with seasoning, yogurt and lime juice. Add onion and chutney, and process until smooth. Serve with the chicken kebabs.

Stuffed Zucchini/ Courgettes

PREPARATION TIME: 10 minutes

MICROWAVE COOKING TIME: 18 minutes

SERVES: 4 people

4 small, even-sized zucchini/courgettes
120g/¼lb crabmeat, fresh or frozen
1 shallot, finely chopped
140ml/¼ pint/½ cup cream cheese
60g/2oz/½ cup mushrooms, chopped
¼ tsp tomato paste
45g/1½oz/¼ cup grated Parmesan cheese
60g/2oz/4 tbsps dry breadcrumbs
30ml/2 tbsps milk
15ml/1 tbsp chopped parsley
60g/2oz/4 tbsps butter, melted
Tabasco
Salt and pepper

Top and tail the zucchini/courgettes and put into a large dish with 1 cup of water. Cover with pierced plastic wrap and cook for 4-5 minutes on HIGH. Rinse in cold water until completely cooled. Cut in half lengthways, and carefully scoop out the flesh with a teaspoon, leaving a thin lining of flesh inside the skin. Leave to drain. Chop flesh roughly and set aside. Melt 30g/1oz/2 tbsps of butter in a bowl for 1 minute on HIGH. Add the shallot and mushrooms, and cook, covered, for 2 minutes on HIGH. Add zucchini/ courgette flesh, cover and cook for 1 minute on HIGH. Beat the cream cheese, tomato paste and milk together. Add crabmeat, parsley, seasoning, and a few drops of tabasco. Stir into the zucchini/ courgette mixture and pile the filling into each zucchini/courgette shell.

Mix breadcrumbs and Parmesan cheese together, and top each filled zucchini/courgette. Melt the remaining butter and sprinkle over the zucchini/courgettes. Heat through, uncovered, for 5 minutes on HIGH and brown under a grill/broiler or on the Combination setting of a microwave convection oven for 10 minutes. Serve immediately.

Potted Smoked Fish

PREPARATION TIME: 15 minutes

MICROWAVE COOKING TIME: 8 minutes

SERVES: 4 people

2 smoked white, or kippered, fish fillets
15g/½ oz/1 tbsp butter or margarine
15g/½ oz/1 tbsp flour/plain flour
90ml/5 tbsps/⅓ cup cream cheese
90ml/5 tbsps/⅓ cup milk
6-8 pimento-stuffed olives, sliced
2 tsps Dijon mustard
Salt and pepper

GARNISH
60g/2oz/½ cup butter for clarifying
Pimento-stuffed olives
Black peppercorns

Skin the fish fillets and break up into small pieces. Melt butter for 1 minute on HIGH. Stir in the flour and cook for 2 minutes on HIGH. Blend in the cheese, milk, half the olives, mustard and seasoning. Add fish and mix until well blended. Put into 4 ramekin dishes and smooth the top. Cover each with plastic wrap and cook for 1 minute on HIGH to set the mixture. Put butter into a medium bowl and heat for 3-4 minutes on HIGH, or until boiling. Leave to stand for 10-15 minutes. Skim the salt off the top and spoon the butter oil carefully over each pot of fish. Fill nearly to the top, and leave until almost set. Then place the remaining olives and peppercorns on top of the butter. Chill and when set, cover the decoration with another thin layer of clarified butter and refrigerate again until set. Serve with hot toast.

Artichokes with Mustard Butter

PREPARATION TIME: 8 minutes

MICROWAVE COOKING TIME: 21 minutes

SERVES: 4 people

4 globe artichokes
15ml/1 tbsp lemon juice
Pinch salt
570ml/1 pint/2 cups water
15ml/1 tbsp oil
1 bay leaf
1 slice onion

SAUCE
60g/2oz/½ cup butter
3 tbsps Dijon mustard
Salt and pepper
Squeeze of lemon juice

Break stems from the base of each artichoke and twist to remove any stringy fibres. Trim the base of each so the artichokes sit level. Trim tips of artichoke leaves using kitchen scissors. Wash artichokes under cold running water. Put lemon juice, salt, water, oil, bay leaf and onion slice into a large bowl and cook 3-4 minutes on HIGH, or until the water boils. Put artichokes upright in the bowl, cover with plastic wrap and pierce several times. Cook for 15 minutes on HIGH, or until lower leaves can be pulled away easily. Leave to stand covered while preparing the sauce. Put butter, seasoning and lemon juice into a glass measuring cup or jug and cook for 2 minutes on HIGH, or until butter has melted. Beat in the mustard until sauce holds together. Put artichokes onto special artichoke serving plates, or onto small serving plates each on top of a larger plate, to give room for the discarded leaves. Serve the sauce separately, or remove the "choke" and serve the sauce in the centre of the artichoke.

Facing page: Potted Smoked Fish (top) and Artichokes with Mustard Butter (bottom).

Microwave

SOUPS AND APPETIZERS

CHEESE AND EGG APPETIZERS

Eggs Florentine

PREPARATION TIME: 15 minutes

MICROWAVE COOKING TIME:
18 minutes

SERVES: 4 people

1kg/2¼lbs fresh spinach, washed and
*   stems removed*
30g/1oz/2 tbsps butter or margarine
4 eggs
2 tomatoes, skinned and seeded
Nutmeg
Salt
Pepper

MORNAY SAUCE
45g/1½ oz/3 tbsps butter or margarine
45g/1½ oz/3 tbsps flour/plain flour
430ml/¾ pint/1½ cups milk
45g/1½ oz/⅓ cup Cheddar cheese, grated
Dry mustard
Cayenne pepper
Salt
Pepper

To prepare spinach and tomatoes:
Put spinach into a roasting bag and
tie loosely. Stand upright and cook
for 5 minutes on HIGH. (Spinach
may also be cooked in a bowl
covered with pierced plastic wrap.)
Drain spinach well, and chop roughly.
Boil 570ml/1 pint/2 cups of water in
a large bowl on HIGH and put in the
tomatoes for 5 seconds. Put the
tomatoes immediately into cold
water. Peel, squeeze out the seeds and
juice, and chop roughly.
To poach the eggs: Pour water into
each of 4 ramekin dishes/custard
cups to a depth of 2.5cm (1"). Put the
dishes in a circle and heat on HIGH
until the water boils. Break 1 egg into
each cup and pierce the yoke with a
sharp knife. Cook on DEFROST or

LOW for 3 minutes, or until whites
have set. Turn the dishes at 1 minute
intervals.
To prepare Mornay sauce: Melt
butter in a medium bowl for 1 minute
on HIGH. Stir in the flour, mustard
and a pinch of Cayenne pepper, and
add the milk gradually. Cook for 4-5
minutes on HIGH, stirring frequently.
Add the cheese, reserving some for
the top. Add seasoning and stir until
blended. Melt 30g/1oz/2 tbsps of
butter for 1 minute on HIGH. Stir in
the spinach, seasoning and grated
nutmeg to taste. Heat for 1 minute on
HIGH, then add tomatoes. Put some
of the spinach mixture into each
individual serving dish and top with
a poached egg. Coat each with
Mornay sauce and sprinkle on grated
cheese. Brown under a grill/broiler,
or on the Combination setting in a
microwave convection oven for
2 minutes.

Baked Eggs with Mushrooms and Mustard Cream

PREPARATION TIME: 10 minutes

MICROWAVE COOKING TIME:
9 minutes

SERVES: 4 people

225g/8oz mushrooms, finely chopped
4 eggs
140ml/¼ pint/½ cup cream, whipped
30g/1oz/ chopped chives
5ml/1 tsp sherry
10ml/2 tsps Dijon mustard
Paprika
Salt
Pepper

Melt butter in a small bowl for
1 minute on HIGH. Add mushrooms
and cook for 4 minutes on HIGH.
Add chives, sherry and seasoning and
divide into 4 ramekin dishes. Make a
slight well in the center of each
portion and break an egg into it.
Pierce the yoke with a small, sharp
knife. Fold the mustard, cream and
seasonings together and spoon over
the eggs. Sprinkle with paprika and
cook for 4 minutes on HIGH. Leave
to stand for 1 minute before serving.

Cheese Custards

PREPARATION TIME: 10 minutes

MICROWAVE COOKING TIME:
30 minutes

SERVES: 4 people

30g/1oz/¼ cup butter or margarine
30g/1oz/¼ cup flour/plain flour
2.5ml/½ tsp mustard powder
280ml/½ pint/1 cup light/single cream
140ml/¼ pint/½ cup heavy/double
*   cream*
340g/12oz/¾ cup Cheddar cheese,
*   grated*
4 eggs, separated
1.25ml/¼ tsp cream of tartar
Cayenne pepper
Salt
Pepper
Paprika

Melt the butter for 1 minute on
HIGH. Add the flour, mustard,
Cayenne pepper and seasoning to the

Facing page: Eggs Florentine (top)
and Cheese Custards (bottom).

bowl and stir in the cream gradually. Cook for 6 minutes on HIGH, stirring frequently until thickened. Add 225g/8oz/½ cup of the cheese and stir to melt. Beat in the egg yolks and whip egg whites with the cream of tartar until stiff but not dry. Fold whites into cheese mixture and pour into 8 ramekin dishes/small custard cups. Arrange in a larger dish filled with hot water. Cook for 3 minutes on HIGH. Turn the cups and cook for 1½ minutes more on HIGH. If the mixture appears set and begins to pull away from the sides of the cups/dishes, turn the custards out. If not, cook for 30 seconds longer on HIGH. Put the custards into individual baking dishes, allowing 2 per person. Pour over the heavy/double cream and sprinkle on the remaining cheese and paprika. Bake for 2 minutes on HIGH and serve immediately.

Sour Cream and Caviar Cheesecake

PREPARATION TIME: 10 minutes

MICROWAVE COOKING TIME: 15 minutes

SERVES: 4 people

225g/8oz/1 cup Cheddar cheese
    crackers/biscuits
30g/1oz/¼ cup butter
30g/1oz/2 tbsps Parmesan cheese
225g/8oz package/carton cream cheese
120g/4oz/1 cup Gruyère cheese, grated
60ml/2 fl oz/¼ cup milk
2 eggs
140ml/¼ pint/½ cup sour cream
1 bunch/⅓ cup chives, chopped
1 jar red salmon caviar
1 jar black lumpfish caviar

Crush the crackers/biscuits in a food processor and melt the butter for 1 minute on HIGH. Add half the Parmesan cheese and all the butter to the crumbs in the processor and work until well mixed. Mix cream cheese, Gruyère and remaining Parmesan together. Beat in eggs and sour cream, reserving 30ml/2 tbsps for the top, and stir in the chives. Add seasoning. Line the base of a 15cm (6″) microwave cake pan with

wax/greaseproof paper and pour in the cheesecake mixture. Bake for 5 minutes on HIGH until lightly set. Sprinkle on the crumbs and press down gently. Bake for another 10 minutes on MEDIUM. Leave to cool at room temperature, then chill for 1 hour. Invert onto a serving dish, spread with remaining sour cream and decorate the top with caviar. Cut into wedges to serve.

Eggplant/Aubergine Caviar

PREPARATION TIME: 30 minutes

MICROWAVE COOKING TIME: 13 minutes

SERVES: 4 people

This page: Sour Cream and Caviar Cheesecake.
Facing page: Baked Eggs with Mushrooms and Mustard Cream (top) and Eggplant/Aubergine Caviar (bottom).

1 large or 2 small eggplants/aubergines
1 clove garlic, crushed
60ml/4 tbsps olive oil
Juice of half a lemon
10ml/2 tsps chopped fresh coriander
15ml/1 tbsp chopped parsley
5ml/1 tsp cumin seeds
1 cap pimento, finely chopped
Cayenne pepper
Salt
Pepper
Pitta bread

Dice the aubergine/eggplant, then spread out on paper towels, sprinkle

with salt and leave for 30 minutes to draw out any bitterness. Rinse and dry well. Put into a large bowl with 4 tbsps water, cover with pierced plastic wrap and cook for 10 minutes on HIGH, stirring 2-3 times. Drain and leave to cool. Put cumin seeds on a plate and roast, uncovered, for 3 minutes on HIGH, stirring occasionally. Put the aubergine/ eggplant into a food processor with the garlic, and blend until smooth, adding olive oil slowly through the feed tube. Add lemon juice, seasoning, Cayenne pepper and cumin seeds, and process once. Add herbs and pimento and process again once. Adjust seasoning and chill. Wrap pitta bread in paper towels and warm for 30 seconds on HIGH. Cut into triangles and serve·with the aubergine/eggplant caviar.

Pasta Shells Stuffed with Garlic Cheese

PREPARATION TIME: 10 minutes

MICROWAVE COOKING TIME: 20 minutes

SERVES: 4 people

8 large pasta shells (conchiglie) or small shells
2 pkts garlic and herb soft cheese
4 tomatoes, skinned and seeded
45g/1½ oz/3 tbsps butter or margarine
45g/1½ oz/3 tbsps flour/plain flour
570ml/1 pint/2 cups milk
60g/2oz/½ cup Gruyère cheese, grated
15ml/1 tbsp chopped parsley
Nutmeg
Salt and pepper

Heat 1150ml/2 pints/4 cups water on HIGH for 5 minutes, until boiling. Put in the tomatoes for 5 seconds, then remove them and put immedi ately into cold water. Peel, seed and shred them thinly, then set aside. Put the pasta into the water with 1 tbsp oil and cook for 9 minutes, or until just tender. Leave to stand for 5 minutes. Drain and dry. Beat cheese to soften. Put into a pastry/piping bag fitted with a wide, plain tube. Fill each shell with the garlic cheese and put into 4 baking dishes. Melt butter in a small bowl for 1 minute on HIGH and stir in the flour. Stir in the milk and seasoning, and blend well. Heat for 2-3 minutes on HIGH, stirring frequently. Add half of the cheese, stirring to melt. Stir in the tomato strips and coat over the pasta shells in the baking dishes. Sprinkle on the remaining cheese. Heat for 2 minutes on HIGH.

This page: Pasta Shells Stuffed with Garlic Cheese.
Facing page: Stuffed Vine Leaves Bordelaise.

VEGETABLE APPETIZERS

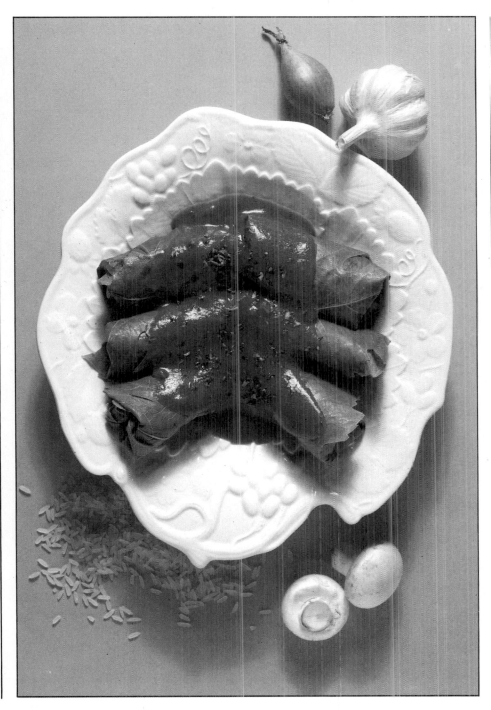

Stuffed Vine Leaves Bordelaise

PREPARATION TIME: 15 minutes

MICROWAVE COOKING TIME:
53 minutes and 5 minutes standing time

SERVES: 4 people

12 packaged vine leaves
30g/1oz/¼ cup butter
1 shallot, finely chopped
175g/6oz/1 cup mushrooms, finely chopped
90g/3oz/½ cup rice
4 strips green streaky bacon (rind and bones removed)
30g/1oz/2 tbsps dried blackcurrants
15ml/1 tbsp parsley
Salt and pepper

SAUCE
1 shallot, finely chopped
15g/½ oz/1½ tbsps flour/plain flour
15g/½ oz/1½ tbsps butter or margarine
180ml/7 fl oz/¾ cup red wine
180ml/7 fl oz/¾ cup beef stock
1 clove garlic, crushed
1 tsp tomato paste

To make stuffed vine leaves: Put 850ml/1½ pints/3 cups water and the rice into a large, deep bowl. Cover with pierced plastic wrap and cook for 14 minutes on HIGH. Add the blackcurrants and leave to stand for 5 minutes. Drain and cool. Put the butter and shallot for the filling into a bowl, cover and cook for 1 minute on HIGH. Add mushrooms and cook for 6 minutes on HIGH, stirring occasionally. Heat a browning dish for 3-4 minutes on HIGH and cook the bacon for 1 minute each side until crisp. Crumble the bacon and add to the mushrooms with the

rice, parsley and seasoning. Mix well and put a mound of filling on each leaf. Roll up, tucking in the sides to enclose the filling completely.
To make the sauce: Heat a browning dish for 3-4 minutes on HIGH. Melt the butter and add shallot and flour. Cook until golden brown, or about 4 minutes on HIGH. Put into a bowl and stir in the stock, wine, garlic, tomato paste and seasoning. Cook, covered with pierced plastic wrap, for 4 minutes on HIGH. Put vine leaves into a casserole, seamed side down, and pour over the sauce. Cover and cook for 5 minutes on HIGH. Serve immediately.

Celeriac Moutarde

PREPARATION TIME: 10 minutes

MICROWAVE COOKING TIME: 15 minutes

SERVES: 4 people

1 large root celeriac, peeled
30ml/2 tbsps white wine

MUSTARD CREAM SAUCE
45g/1½ oz/3 tbsps butter
45g/1½ oz/3 tbsps flour/plain flour
570ml/1 pint/2 cups milk
60ml/4 tbsps Dijon mustard
15ml/1 tbsp celery seed
Salt and pepper
60ml/4 tbsps dry breadcrumbs
30g/1oz/2 tbsps butter or margarine

Cut celeriac into 5mm (¼") slices, then into sticks about 2cm (1") long. Put into a bowl with the wine, and toss to mix. Cover with pierced plastic wrap and cook for 4 minutes on HIGH. Melt butter in a small deep bowl for 1 minute on HIGH. Add flour and cook for 1 minute more on HIGH. Stir in milk, mustard, celery seed and strained cooking liquid from the celeriac. Season and cook for 3 minutes on HIGH, stirring occasionally, until sauce has thickened. Put celeriac into 4 baking/gratin dishes and coat with the sauce. Heat a browning tray for 3-4 minutes on HIGH. Put in 30g/1oz/2 tbsps butter and dry bread-

crumbs, and cook until golden brown. Sprinkle the breadcrumbs on top of the celeriac and heat through for 2 minutes on HIGH. If using a microwave convection oven, melt the butter for 1 minute, then stir in the breadcrumbs. Sprinkle on top of the celeriac and cook on the Combination setting for 5 minutes. Serve immediately.

Vinaigrette de Jardin

PREPARATION TIME: 15 minutes

MICROWAVE COOKING TIME: 7 minutes

SERVES: 4 people

SALAD AND DRESSING
120g/4oz pea pods/mangetout
2 zucchini/courgettes, sliced in rounds
4 spring/green onions, sliced
120g/4oz broccoli flowerets
1 small head cauliflower, cut into flowerets
2 carrots, sliced in rounds
4 tomatoes, seeded and sliced into strips
1 banana pepper, sliced into strips
100ml/6 tbsps olive oil
30ml/2 tbsps white wine vinegar
15ml/1 tbsp Dijon mustard
15ml/1 tbsp herbs (eg chives, chervil, parsley, basil), chopped
Salt and pepper

GARLIC BREAD
1 small loaf French bread
45g/1½ oz/⅓ cup butter
1 clove garlic, crushed
2 tbsps poppy seeds

Cook each of the vegetables on HIGH in 2 tbsps water, in a shallow, covered dish: pea pods/mangetout, 2 minutes; zucchini/courgettes, 3 minutes; broccoli, 3 minutes; cauliflower, 5 minutes; carrots, 5 minutes. When cooked, rinse immediately in cold water to stop the cooking. Drain and leave to dry. Boil 570ml/1 pint/2 cups water for 3-4 minutes on HIGH and put tomatoes in for 5 seconds. Then put them immediately into cold water, peel and quarter them, remove the seeds, and cut them into thin shreds. Cut pepper into thin slices and add,

with the tomato, to the drained vegetables. Mix oil, vinegar, Dijon mustard, herbs and seasoning, and pour over the mixed vegetables. Toss lightly and leave to marinate. Serve with the garlic bread.
To make garlic bread: Cut the loaf into thick slices without cutting through the base. Mix the butter, garlic and poppy seed, and spread between each slice. Wrap loosely in paper towels and heat for 1½ minutes on HIGH or until butter has melted. Serve with the vegetable salad.

Cheese and Herb Soufflés

PREPARATION TIME: 8 minutes

MICROWAVE COOKING TIME: 8-10 minutes

SERVES: 4 people

180g/6oz/1 cup Red Leicester/Colby and Parmesan cheese, grated and mixed
30g/1oz/¼ cup butter or margarine
45g/1½ oz/¼ cup flour/plain flour
430ml/¾ pint/1½ cups milk
6 eggs, separated
5ml/1 tsp cream of tartar
1.25ml/¼ tsp parsley, chopped
1.25ml/¼ tsp chives, chopped
1.25ml/¼ tsp thyme, chopped
1.25ml/¼ tsp sage, chopped
Dry mustard
Paprika
Salt
Pepper

Put the butter in a bowl and heat for 1 minute on HIGH. Stir in the flour, Cayenne pepper and mustard, and blend in the milk. Cook for 4 minutes on HIGH, stirring frequently until thickened. Add cheese, herbs and seasoning. Beat egg yolks into the cheese mixture one at a time. Whisk egg whites until stiff but not dry with the cream of tartar, and fold in carefully. Divide the mixture

Facing page: Cheese and Herb Soufflés (top) and Celeriac Moutarde (bottom).

lining inside the shell. Sprinkle the scooped-out flesh and shell with lemon juice. Heat a browning tray for 3 minutes on HIGH, brown bacon for 1 minute each side, crumble it and set aside. Brown shallot, pepper and mushrooms lightly for 1 minute in the bacon fat and combine with avocado flesh. Melt 15g/½ oz/1 tbsp butter for 1 minute on HIGH. Stir in flour and milk. Heat for 2 minutes until thickened, stirring frequently. Add all ingredients save cheese and breadcrumbs. Stir in seasoning and a few drops of tabasco. Pile into the shells. Sprinkle on the cheese and breadcrumbs. Melt remaining butter for 1 minute. Sprinkle over the avocado and cook for 3 minutes in a microwave-convection oven on Combination setting, or brown under a grill/broiler. Serve immediately.

Stuffed Mushrooms

PREPARATION TIME: 8 minutes

MICROWAVE COOKING TIME: 6-8 minutes

SERVES: 4 people

12-16 large mushrooms
120g/4oz ham, finely chopped
60g/2oz/½ cup fresh white breadcrumbs
75g/2½ oz/⅓ cup finely chopped walnuts
1 egg, beaten
1 bunch snipped chives
15ml/1 tbsp chopped parsley
15ml/1 tbsp Dijon mustard
Dry breadcrumbs
45g/1½ oz/3 tbsps butter, melted
Salt
Pepper

Clean the mushrooms, trimming stalks, and chop them finely. Mix with the ham, breadcrumbs, walnuts, herbs, mustard and seasoning. Beat in the egg gradually to bind. Pile on top of the mushrooms, then put on a plate and cook for 5 minutes on

between 4 small soufflé dishes. Cook on MEDIUM for 4-6 minutes. The COMBINATION setting of a microwave convection oven may be used for 6 minutes. Sprinkle with paprika and serve immediately.

Stuffed Avocados

PREPARATION TIME: 10 minutes

MICROWAVE COOKING TIME: 10 minutes

SERVES: 4 people

2 large avocados
4 slices smoked streaky bacon
60g/2oz/1 cup peeled prawns or cooked shrimp, shelled
1 shallot, finely chopped
60g/2oz/½ cup mushrooms, roughly chopped
1 green pepper, roughly chopped
20g/¾ oz/1½ tbsps butter or margarine
30g/1oz/2 tbsps flour/plain flour
140ml/¼ pint/½ cup milk
2 tomatoes, skinned, seeded and chopped
60g/2oz/⅓ cup Parmesan cheese
4 tbsps dry breadcrumbs
15ml/1 tbsp parsley
5ml/1 tsp marjoram
Tabasco
Salt and pepper
Lemon juice

Halve avocados and remove stones. Scoop out flesh, leaving 5mm (¼″)

This page: Vinaigrette de Jardin. Facing page: Stuffed Avocados (top) and Stuffed Mushrooms (bottom).

HIGH. Sprinkle over the dry crumbs and melted butter. Cook for a further 1 minute on HIGH. Brown under a grill/broiler, or cook for 2 minutes in a microwave-convection oven on the Combination setting.

Spinach Gnocchi in Ricotta Sauce

PREPARATION TIME: 10 minutes

MICROWAVE COOKING TIME: 8 minutes

SERVES: 4 people

GNOCCHI
450g/1lb fresh spinach, washed and stems removed
120g/4oz/1 cup Gruyère cheese, grated
4 slices white bread, crusts removed·
2 tbsps finely chopped walnuts
1 tbsp finely chopped shallot
1 clove garlic, crushed
1 egg, beaten
Nutmeg
Salt
Pepper

RICOTTA SAUCE
225g/8oz Ricotta cheese
45g/1½ oz/3 tbsps grated Parmesan cheese
2.5g/½ tsp basil, fresh or dried
1.25g/¼ tsp chopped parsley
190ml/⅓ pint/⅔ cup cream or milk
Salt
Pepper
Paprika

To prepare gnocchi: Put spinach into a roasting bag and tie loosely. Stand upright and cook for 3 minutes on HIGH. (Spinach may also be cooked in a bowl covered with pierced plastic wrap.) Drain the spinach well, and chop finely. Make crumbs from the bread slices using a food processor or liquidiser. Add to the spinach along with the Gruyère, walnuts, nutmeg, seasoning and egg. Beat well and shape into 5cm (2″) balls or ovals. Put gnocchi onto a plate, cover loosely with plastic wrap, and cook for 2 minutes on HIGH. Set aside and keep warm.
To make sauce: Mix Ricotta cheese with the other ingredients except the

paprika and heat for 1 minute on HIGH.
Divide the gnocchi between 4 gratin dishes and coat with the sauce. Sprinkle with paprika and heat for 2 minutes on HIGH. Serve at once.

Salade Alsacienne

PREPARATION TIME: 10 minutes

MICROWAVE COOKING TIME: 13-15 minutes

SERVES: 4 people

340g/¾lb new potatoes, scrubbed but not peeled (or regular/old potatoes, peeled)
Half head (white) cabbage, shredded
30ml/2 tbsps white wine
225g/8oz smoked sausage or kielbasa
10ml/2 tsps caraway seeds
60g/2oz/½ cup blue cheese, crumbled
140ml/¼ pint/½ cup sour cream
15ml/1 tbsp white wine vinegar
45ml/3 tbsps vegetable oil
1.25ml/¼ tsp French mustard
Salt
Pepper

GARNISH
4 green onions, chopped

Prick potato skins with a fork, if using new potatoes. Put potatoes into a casserole dish with 2 tbsps water, cover, and cook for 10-12 minutes on HIGH until tender. Drain and cut into large pieces. Mix vinegar, oil, mustard and seasoning together and pour over the potatoes. Stir and leave to stand. Prick sausage skin and cook, covered, for 1 minute on

HIGH. Slice thinly and add to the potatoes. Put cabbage into a casserole dish with the wine, caraway seeds and seasoning. Cover and cook for 2 minutes on HIGH. Add to the potatoes and sausages. Add blue cheese and sour cream, and mix carefully, so that the potatoes do not break up. Garnish with chopped green onions.

Fondue Pots

PREPARATION TIME: 10 minutes

MICROWAVE COOKING TIME:
10-13 minutes

SERVES: 4 people

FONDUE
225g/8oz/2 cups Gruyère cheese, grated

Facing page: Spinach Gnocchi in Ricotta Sauce.
This page: Salade Alsacienne (left) and Fondue Pots (right).

225g/8oz/2 cups Swiss cheese, grated
430ml/¾ pint/1½ cups dry white wine
20ml/1½ tbsps cornstarch/cornflour
20ml/1½ tbsps kirsch
1 clove garlic, crushed
Dry mustard
Nutmeg
Salt and Pepper

BREADSTICKS
12 slices white bread, crusts removed
115g/4oz/1 stick butter
60g/4 tbsps herbs (eg thyme, parsley, sage) chopped

To make breadsticks: Roll out each slice of bread to flatten. Mix herbs and half the butter together and spread over the bread. Roll up from each end to the middle and cut in half to form 2 breadsticks. Melt remaining butter for 1 minute on HIGH and brush over breadsticks. Put bread onto a plate and cook for 5 minutes in a microwave convection oven on the Combination setting until pale brown. Keep warm. (Breadsticks may also be baked in a conventional oven for 20 minutes at 200°C, 400°F, Gas Mark 6.)
To make fondue: Put garlic, wine, mustard, nutmeg and seasoning into a bowl and cook for 5 minutes on HIGH. Mix cornflour, kirsch and cheese, and blend well into the wine. Cook for 5-8 minutes on MEDIUM, stirring frequently until thick and

creamy. Heat individual ramekin dishes and pour fondue mixture into each. Serve immediately with the warm breadsticks or raw vegetables.

Garlic Mushrooms

PREPARATION TIME: 5 minutes

MICROWAVE COOKING TIME: 6 minutes

SERVES: 4 people

675g/1½lbs mushrooms, cleaned and
    quartered
2 cloves garlic, crushed
30g/1oz/¼ cup butter
45ml/3 tbsps white wine
8 slices French bread, 1.5cm (½") thick
1.25ml/¼ tsp fresh thyme, chopped
1.25ml/¼ tsp fresh sage, chopped
1.25ml/¼ tsp parsley, chopped
Salt
Pepper

GARNISH
30ml/2 tbsps chopped chives

Heat butter for 1 minute on HIGH or until melted in a large bowl. Add garlic and cook for 2 minutes on HIGH. Mix in the herbs, wine, seasoning and mushrooms. Pour into a shallow casserole, and cook, uncovered, for 3 minutes on HIGH. Heat the bread for 1 minute on HIGH. Garnish with snipped chives and serve on French bread.

Leek and Ham Tarts Bernaise

PREPARATION TIME: 10 minutes

MICROWAVE COOKING TIME: 19½ minutes

SERVES: 4 people

TART SHELLS AND FILLING
8-12 slices wholewheat bread, crusts
    removed
1-2 leeks, washed and sliced
30g/1oz/¼ cup butter or margarine
115g/4oz ham, chopped
45g/1½ oz/2½ tbsps flour
45ml/3 tbsps white wine
30ml/2 tbsps milk or chicken stock

BERNAISE SAUCE
60g/2oz/½ cup butter
3 egg yolks
15ml/1 tbsp white wine or tarragon
    vinegar

This page: Leek and Ham Tarts
Bernaise (top) and Garlic
Mushrooms (bottom).
Facing page: Pumpkin Creams with
Dill Sauce.

1 bay leaf
1 blade mace
5ml/1 tsp chopped tarragon
5ml/1 tsp chopped parsley
Salt
Pepper
Lemon juice

To prepare shells and filling: Roll out the slices of bread to flatten slightly. Cut out large rounds with a pastry cutter. Melt half the butter for 1 minute on HIGH and brush over both sides of the bread rounds. Mould into custard cups/ramekin dishes or a muffin pan and cook for 3 minutes on HIGH until crisp. Melt the remaining butter in a bowl for 1 minute on HIGH and add the leek slices. Cover with pierced plastic wrap and cook for 8 minutes on HIGH, stirring occasionally. Add ham and flour, and cook for 1 minute on HIGH. Stir in the wine, milk or stock, and seasoning. Cook, uncovered, for 2 minutes or until sauce thickens. Set aside.

To make Bernaise sauce: Have a bowl of ice water ready. Melt the butter in a deep bowl on HIGH for 1 minute. Put vinegar, bay leaf and mace in a small dish and heat through for 30 seconds on HIGH. Beat egg yolks and seasoning together and strain on the vinegar. Pour into the bowl with the butter and stir well. Cook for 15 seconds on HIGH, remove bowl and stir sauce. Repeat until sauce has thickened – which takes about 2 minutes. Put jug/bowl immediately into ice water to stop the cooking. Remove the prepared shells from the custard cups/ramekin dishes and put onto a plate. Fill with the ham and leek mixture and coat each with a spoonful of the Bernaise sauce. Broil/grill until lightly browned. Serve immediately.

Pumpkin Creams with Dill Sauce

PREPARATION TIME: 15 minutes

MICROWAVE COOKING TIME: 27 minutes

SERVES: 4 people

450g/1lb/2½ cups mashed pumpkin
1 shallot, finely chopped
60g/2oz/½ cup Ricotta cheese
90g/3oz/½ cup Parmesan cheese, grated
2 eggs
60ml/2 fl oz/¼ cup sour cream
140ml/¼ pint/½ cup heavy/double cream
15ml/1 tbsp parsley
2 bunches dill
Crushed garlic (optional)
Nutmeg
Salt
Pepper

GARNISH
Whole sprigs of dill

Put the mashed pumpkin into a food processor and add eggs, shallot, cheeses, parsley, nutmeg and seasoning. Process until well blended. Divide between 4 ramekin dishes and cook for 6 minutes on HIGH until set. Leave to stand for 5 minutes before turning out. Heat the cream for 2 minutes on HIGH in a small bowl with the crushed garlic, if desired. Chop the dill finely, reserving 4 whole sprigs. Stir the chopped dill into the hot cream with the sour cream. Turn out the pumpkin creams and serve immediately with the dill sauce. Garnish with whole sprigs of dill.

Microwave
FISH AND SEAFOOD

Microwave
FISH AND SEAFOOD

A microwave oven is a fish kettle par excellence. In fact, many people prefer microwaved fish and shellfish to that cooked by conventional methods. Microwave cooking retains the natural moisture of food, something that is important in well-prepared fish. Fish and shellfish both require quick cooking, so the microwave oven really comes into its own.

Poaching is the fish cooking method that the microwave oven performs best. Use a shallow dish or a cooking bag and add white wine or water and lemon juice with peppercorns, onion slices and aromatic herbs, spices and vegetables. In a microwave oven all the flavor cooks into the fish, and low evaporation means plenty of liquid to make a good sauce.

A whole fish, such as a salmon or sea bass, can easily be poached providing the fish is not too large to allow it to turn freely. It is best to choose a fish no heavier than 1kg/2.2lbs in weight. Use a large cooking bag, securely tied, or a large, shallow dish covered with plastic wrap/cling film. Wrap the head and tail with foil to keep them from over-cooking and falling off. Cook 7-10 minutes on HIGH, or slightly longer on MEDIUM. The fish will continue to cook as it stands, so

keep it covered while preparing sauces to accompany the fish. If you are not sure whether the fish is cooked, check close to the bone in an inconspicuous place. The flesh should be firm and opaque.

Even frying is possible, after a fashion, in a microwave oven. Dredge fish fillets or small whole fish with seasoned flour and preheat a browning dish. Fry in butter briefly on both sides to get a light brown, slightly crisp coating; a surprising result from a microwave oven.

Shellfish need careful cooking in a microwave oven or they toughen. Cook them no longer than 3 minutes on the highest setting or add them to a hot sauce at the last minute.

In the classification of fish there are four main categories: Flat fish, such as sole; Round fish, such as trout; Shellfish and Smoked fish, more popular in England and Europe than in the United States. Flat fish and round fish can be subdivided into oily fish, such as trout or salmon, and whitefish, such as sole or cod. But whatever fish you choose, your microwave oven will help you cook it to perfection.

FISH SOUPS

Spicy Clam Chowder

PREPARATION TIME: 15 minutes

MICROWAVE COOKING TIME: 12 minutes

SERVES: 4 people

30g/1oz/2 tbsps butter or margarine
1 green pepper, diced
1 onion, finely sliced
340g/12oz/1½ cups potatoes, diced
450g/1lb can plum tomatoes
450g/1lb can clams, liquid reserved
1 small chili pepper, finely chopped
Pinch cinnamon
Pinch nutmeg
Salt and pepper

Melt the butter in a large bowl for 30 seconds on HIGH. Add the green pepper, onion, potatoes and the liquid from the clams. Cover the bowl loosely and cook for 10 minutes on HIGH or until the potatoes are tender. Add the plum tomatoes, clams, chili pepper, cinnamon, nutmeg, and salt and pepper. Cook, uncovered, for 2 minutes more on HIGH. Serve immediately.

Mariners' Chowder

PREPARATION TIME: 15 minutes

MICROWAVE COOKING TIME: 12 minutes

SERVES: 4 people

225g/8oz whitefish
225g/8oz/½ pint clams
225g/8oz/½ pint mussels
225g/8oz raw shrimp/prawns, peeled
45g/1½ oz/3 tbsps butter
45g/1½ oz/3 tbsps flour/plain flour
1 onion, finely chopped

850ml/1½ pints/4 cups milk
60ml/2 fl oz/¼ cup white wine
140ml/¼ pint/½ cup cream
1 bay leaf
30g/1oz/2 tbsps chopped parsley
Salt and pepper

This page: Mariners' Chowder (top) and Spicy Clam Chowder (bottom). Facing page: Cheese and Clam Chowder (top) and Curried Prawn Soup (bottom).

Scrub the clams and mussels well. Discard any with broken or open shells. Put into a bowl with 30ml/ 2 tbsps water and cover loosely. Cook for 4 minutes on HIGH until the shells open. Discard any shellfish that do not open, remove the others from their opened shells, and set them aside. Combine the fish, shrimp and wine in a casserole and cook for 4 minutes, covered, on HIGH. Melt the butter for 30 seconds on HIGH in a large bowl. Add the onion and cook for 2 minutes on HIGH. Add the flour, milk, wine from the fish, salt and pepper. Cook for 5 minutes on HIGH, stirring frequently. Add the fish, shellfish, cream and parsley. Heat through for 1 minute on HIGH. Remove the bay leaf and serve.

Cheese and Clam Chowder

PREPARATION TIME: 15 minutes

MICROWAVE COOKING TIME: 13 minutes

SERVES: 4 people

2 450g/1lb cans clams, liquid reserved
340g/12oz/2 cups diced potatoes
1 onion, finely chopped
2 sticks celery, chopped
1 green pepper, chopped
1 litre/1¾ pints/3¼ cups milk
30g/1oz/2 tbsps butter or margarine
30g/1oz/2 tbsps flour/plain flour
2.5ml/½ tsp dry mustard
Light/single cream as necessary
1 bay leaf
1.25ml/¼ tsp thyme
Dash Worcestershire sauce
30ml/2 tbsps chopped parsley
120g/4oz/1 cup grated Colby/Red
    Leicester cheese
Salt and pepper

Put the butter, onion, celery and pepper into a large bowl. Cover loosely and cook on HIGH for 2 minutes. Stir in the flour, mustard, milk and clam liquid. Blend well and add potatoes, thyme, salt and pepper. Put in the bay leaf, and cook on HIGH for 10 minutes, stirring occasionally. Remove the bay leaf and add the clams, cheese and

Worcestershire sauce. Heat for 2 minutes on MEDIUM to melt the cheese. Add light cream to thin the soup if it is too thick. Add the parsley to the soup and serve immediately.

Curried Prawn Soup

PREPARATION TIME: 10 minutes

MICROWAVE COOKING TIME: 8 minutes

SERVES: 4 people

45g/1½ oz/3 tbsps butter or margarine
45g/1½ oz/3 tbsps flour/plain flour
30g/1oz/2 tbsps curry powder
1 shallot, finely chopped
5ml/1 tsp mango chutney
15ml/1 tbsp lime juice
850ml/1½ pints/3 cups milk
280ml/½ pint/1 cup fish or chicken stock
225g/8oz cooked shrimp/prawns
Salt and pepper

GARNISH
Fresh coriander leaves or parsley
Plain yogurt

Melt the butter for 30 seconds on HIGH in a large bowl. Add the curry powder and the shallot and cook for 1 minute on HIGH. Stir in the flour, milk, stock, chutney, lime juice, salt and pepper. Cook for 5-6 minutes on HIGH until thickened. Add the shrimp and cook for 30 seconds on HIGH. Serve garnished with coriander and yogurt.

Lobster Bisque

PREPARATION TIME: 15 minutes

MICROWAVE COOKING TIME: 9 minutes

SERVES: 4 people

1 large lobster tail, uncooked
60g/2oz/4 tbsps butter or margarine
60g/2oz/4 tbsps flour/plain flour
1 shallot, finely chopped
570ml/1 pint/2 cups milk
280ml/½ pint/1 cup cream
280ml/½ pint/1 cup fish or chicken stock
1 bay leaf
Celery salt

Pepper
Cayenne pepper
60ml/2 fl oz/4 tbsps dry sherry

Remove the lobster tail meat from the shell. Break the shell into small pieces. Melt the butter in a small bowl for 30 seconds on HIGH. Put in the shell pieces and the shallot and cook for 1 minute on HIGH or until the shell turns red. Strain the butter into a large, clean bowl. Cut the lobster meat into small pieces and add to the butter. Cook for 1-2 minutes on HIGH. Remove the meat and set it aside. Stir the flour, celery salt and Cayenne pepper into the butter. Add the bay leaf, milk and stock. Cook for 5-6 minutes on HIGH to thicken. Add the sherry and the lobster meat and heat through for 1 minute on HIGH. Remove the bay leaf and swirl the cream through the soup. Serve immediately.

Smoked Salmon Cream Soup

PREPARATION TIME: 15 minutes

MICROWAVE COOKING TIME: 7-8 minutes

SERVES: 4 people

225g/8oz whitefish, cut into 2.5cm (1")
    chunks
225g/8oz smoked salmon, cut into 2.5cm
    (1") pieces
45g/1½ oz/3 tbsps butter or margarine
30g/1oz/2 tbsps flour/plain flour
140ml/¼ pint/½ cup white wine
850ml/1½ pints/3 cups milk
140ml/¼ pint/½ cup light/single cream
Pepper

GARNISH
Sour cream
Chopped chives

Cook the whitefish and wine for 2 minutes on HIGH. Melt the butter for 30 seconds on HIGH. Stir in the

Facing page: Smoked Salmon Cream Soup (top) and Lobster Bisque (bottom).

flour and milk, the whitefish and its cooking liquid. Cook for 5-6 minutes, stirring frequently, until thick. Add pepper, smoked salmon and cream. Work in a food processor until smooth. Re-heat for 1 minute on HIGH and add salt to taste. Garnish each serving with a spoonful of sour cream and a sprinkling of chopped chives.

Creamy Crab Soup

PREPARATION TIME: 15 minutes

MICROWAVE COOKING TIME: 9 minutes

SERVES: 4 people

450g/1lb crabmeat, fresh or frozen
60g/2oz/4 tbsps butter or margarine
60g/2oz/4 tbsps flour/plain flour
1 shallot, finely chopped
850ml/1½ pints/3 cups milk
140ml/¼ pint/½ cup cream
140ml/¼ pint/½ cup stock
30ml/2 tbsps white wine
Cayenne pepper
Salt and pepper

GARNISH
Chopped chives

Put the butter and shallot into a casserole. Cover and cook for 3 minutes on HIGH, stirring occasionally. Stir in the flour, milk, stock, Cayenne pepper, salt and pepper. Cook for 5 minutes on HIGH, stirring frequently until thickened. Add the crabmeat, cream and wine, and cook for a further 1 minute on HIGH. Serve garnished with chopped chives.

Shrimp and Chinese Mushroom Soup

PREPARATION TIME: 15 minutes

MICROWAVE COOKING TIME: 9 minutes

SERVES: 4 people

120g/4oz fine Chinese egg noodles
8 dried Chinese mushrooms
120g/4oz/¾ cup shrimp/prawns, cooked and peeled
1 small can water chestnuts, sliced

1 small can bamboo shoots, sliced
Bunch green/spring onions, sliced diagonally
120g/¼ lb peapods, mangetout, trimmed
15ml/1 tbsp light soy sauce
30ml/2 tbsps dry sherry
5ml/1 tsp sesame seed oil
15g/1 tbsp cornstarch/cornflour
1150ml/2 pints/4 cups chicken or fish stock
Salt and pepper

Put the mushrooms into a small bowl with enough water to cover. Cook on HIGH for 2 minutes and leave to stand. Mix the cornflour with 30ml/ 2 tbsps stock, and set aside. Combine the remaining stock, peapods and noodles. Cook for 2 minutes on HIGH. Add the cornstarch mixture and all the remaining ingredients, and cook for a further 5 minutes on HIGH. Serve immediately.

Oyster and Watercress Soup

PREPARATION TIME: 15 minutes

MICROWAVE COOKING TIME: 13 minutes

SERVES: 4 people

450g/1lb can oysters
Bunch watercress
675g/1½ lbs/3 cups diced potatoes

430ml/¾ pint/1½ cups liquid reserved from oysters
430ml/¾ pint/1½ cups light/single cream
280ml/½ pint/1 cup milk
1 shallot, finely chopped
45g/1½ oz/3 tbsps butter or margarine
Nutmeg
Lemon juice
Salt and pepper

Drain the oysters and add water to the liquid, if necessary, to measure 430ml/¾ pint/1½ cups. Melt the butter in a large bowl for 30 seconds on HIGH. Add the potatoes, shallot, stock, nutmeg, salt and pepper. Cover loosely and cook on HIGH for 10 minutes, or until the potatoes are tender. Add the milk and half the oysters. Chop the watercress, reserving 4 sprigs for garnish, and add to the bowl. Cook, uncovered, for 2 minutes on HIGH. Put into a food processor and purée until smooth. Return to the bowl and add the remaining oysters, cream and lemon juice. Heat through for 1 minute on HIGH. Serve garnished with the reserved watercress.

This page: Shrimp and Chinese Mushroom Soup. Facing page: Creamy Crab Soup (top) and Oyster and Watercress Soup (bottom).

APPETIZERS AND FIRST COURSES

Florentine Shrimp Tarts

PREPARATION TIME: 20 minutes

MICROWAVE COOKING TIME: 9-10 minutes

SERVES: 4 people

4 slices wholewheat bread
60g/2oz/¼ cup butter, melted
675g/1½ lbs fresh spinach, washed (or
    340g/¾ lb frozen spinach, thawed)
30ml/2 tbsps heavy/double cream
Nutmeg, grated
8 large, unpeeled shrimp/prawns, cooked

SAUCE
120g/4oz/½ cup butter
3 egg yolks
15ml/1 tbsp white wine vinegar
Cayenne pepper
Salt and pepper

GARNISH
Fresh chives or chervil

Cut the crusts off the bread and roll out each slice very thinly. Cut out a 10cm (4") round from each slice and brush both sides with melted butter. Mould into 4 individual pie or flan pans, preferably false-bottomed. Cook on HIGH for 2-3 minutes until crisp. Cook the fresh spinach in a large bowl, loosely covered, for 2 minutes on HIGH with 30ml/ 2 tbsps water. Drain the spinach well, squeezing out all the moisture whether using fresh or frozen spinach. Heat 15g/½ oz/1 tbsp of the remaining butter in a large bowl for 1 minute on HIGH. Toss in the spinach, salt, pepper and nutmeg. Stir in the cream and set aside. Peel the shrimp carefully and set aside. Prepare the sauce by melting the butter in a small, deep bowl for 1 minute on HIGH. Mix the egg yolks, salt, pepper, Cayenne pepper and vinegar together, and pour into the hot butter, beating constantly. Have a bowl of ice water ready. Cook the sauce for 30 seconds on HIGH, then beat well. Repeat until the sauce thickens, which takes about 2 minutes. Put the sauce bowl immediately into ice water to stop the cooking. Remove and set aside. Put the spinach into the bread shells and top with the shrimp. Heat through for 30 seconds on HIGH. Pour over the sauce and heat for 20 seconds on MEDIUM. Serve garnished with chives or chervil.

This page: Florentine Shrimp Tarts. Facing page: Shrimp Kebabs Vera Cruz.

Shrimp Kebabs Vera Cruz

PREPARATION TIME: 15 minutes

MICROWAVE COOKING TIME:
4 minutes

SERVES: 4 people

2 dozen large shrimp, peeled and
    uncooked
120g/4oz chorizo or pepperoni, cut into
    5mm (¼") slices.
1 large green pepper
30ml/2 tbsps olive oil
1 ripe avocado
2 tomatoes, peeled, seeded and finely
    chopped
1 clove garlic, crushed
Cayenne pepper
Lemon juice
Salt and pepper

Alternate the shrimp, sausage and
green pepper on wooden skewers.
Brush with oil. Peel and mash the
avocado with the garlic, lemon juice,
Cayenne pepper, and salt and pepper.
Stir in the tomatoes. Cook the
kebabs on a roasting rack for
3 minutes on HIGH, and heat the
sauce for 30 seconds on HIGH.
Serve immediately.

Layered Seafood Terrine

PREPARATION TIME: 20 minutes

MICROWAVE COOKING TIME:
12 minutes, plus 5 minutes standing
time

SERVES: 4 people

340g/12oz whitefish, skinned and cut
    into chunks
90g/3oz crabmeat
90g/3oz lobster
60g/2oz/¼ cup cream cheese
2 eggs
60g/2oz/1 cup fresh white breadcrumbs
30ml/1oz/2 tbsps heavy/double cream
30ml/1oz/2 tbsps white wine
Chopped parsley
Cayenne pepper
Salt and pepper

BERNAISE SAUCE
3 egg yolks
120g/4oz/½ cup butter
15ml/1 tbsp chopped mixed herbs

15ml/1 tbsp white wine vinegar
Salt and pepper

Combine the eggs, whitefish, cheese,
cream, crumbs, wine, salt and pepper
in a food processor and work until
smooth. Divide the mixture into
thirds. Mix the crab and parsley into
one third, the lobster and Cayenne
pepper into another third, and leave
the remaining third plain. Line a
450g/1lb glass loaf pan/dish with
wax/greaseproof paper, and layer in
the crabmeat, whitefish and lobster
mixtures. Cover well with plastic
wrap and cook for 10 minutes on
MEDIUM. Put a small dish of water
into the oven with the terrine to
keep it moist. Allow to stand for
5 minutes while preparing the sauce.
Beat the egg yolks, vinegar, herbs and
salt and pepper together. Melt the
butter for 1 minute on HIGH in a
small, deep bowl. Beat the egg yolks
into the butter. Have a bowl of ice
water ready. Cook the sauce
ingredients for 15 seconds on HIGH
and then stir well. Repeat the process
until the sauce thickens, which takes
about 2 minutes. Put the sauce
immediately into the bowl of ice
water to stop the cooking. Slice the
terrine and serve with the Bernaise
Sauce.

Crab-Stuffed Pea Pods

PREPARATION TIME: 20 minutes

MICROWAVE COOKING TIME:
2 minutes

SERVES: 4 people

450g/1lb pea pods/mangetout

FILLING
120g/4 oz/½ cup crabmeat
1 package/carton garlic-and-herb soft
    cheese
30ml/2 tbsps white wine
15ml/1 tbsp milk or light/single cream

Mix the filling ingredients together,
breaking up the crabmeat well. Wash
the pea pods/mangetout and
carefully split down one side of each
to form pockets. Blanch for 1 minute
on HIGH with 60ml/4 tbsps water in
a loosely-covered bowl. Rinse under

cold water and dry well. Carefully
open each pocket. Put the filling into
a pastry bag fitted with a 15mm (½")
plain tube and pipe the filling into
the pea pods/mangetout. Arrange on
individual dishes and heat for
30 seconds on HIGH. Serve with
lemon slices or wedges.

Herbed Fish Pâté with Lemon-Orange Hollandaise Sauce

PREPARATION TIME: 20 minutes

MICROWAVE COOKING TIME:
12 minutes, plus 5 minutes standing
time

SERVES: 4 people

450g/1lb whitefish (sole, flounder or cod)
120g/4oz Parma ham, thinly sliced
60ml/4 tbsps chopped mixed herbs
60g/2oz/1 cup fresh white breadcrumbs
2 eggs
60g/2oz/¼ cup low-fat soft cheese, or
    Ricotta cheese
30ml/2 tbsps heavy/double cream
Salt and pepper

HOLLANDAISE SAUCE
3 egg yolks
120g/4oz/½ cup butter
15ml/1 tbsp lemon juice
15ml/1 tbsp orange juice and rind
Salt and pepper

Line a 450g/1lb glass loaf pan/dish
with the slices of Parma ham. Skin
and cut the fish into chunks.
Combine all the remaining pâté
ingredients in a food processor and
work until smooth. Spoon onto the
ham and smooth out. Fold the ends
of the ham over the pâté mixture.
Cover well with plastic wrap and
cook on MEDIUM for 10 minutes, or
until just firm. Put a small dish of
water into the microwave oven with
the pâté to keep it moist. Leave to
stand for 5 minutes before turning
out and slicing for serving. To

**Facing page: Layered Seafood
Terrine (top) and Herbed Fish
Pâté with Lemon-Orange
Hollandaise Sauce.**

90g/3oz/½ cup crabmeat
2.5ml/½ tsp grated horseradish
15ml/1 tbsp snipped chives or chopped
    green spring onion
15ml/1 tbsp sesame seeds
15ml/1 tbsp poppy seeds
30ml/2 tbsps butter, melted
Salt and pepper

Scrub, but do not peel, the potatoes,
Pierce them several times with a fork.
Mix the cheese, crab, horseradish,
chives and salt and pepper together.
Cook the potatoes with enough
water to barely cover for 4 minutes
on HIGH. When cooked, slice 1.5cm
(½″) off the top of each potato and
reserve. Spoon 5ml/1 tsp of the crab
filling into the bottom portion of the
potatoes. Top with the lids and put
the filled potatoes onto a plate. Pour
some of the melted butter over each
potato and sprinkle on a mixture of
the sesame and poppy seeds. Heat for
30 seconds on HIGH.

Scallops with Red and Gold Sauces

PREPARATION TIME: 15 minutes

MICROWAVE COOKING TIME:
12 minutes

SERVES: 4 people

900g/2 lb fresh scallops
225g/½ lb fresh bean sprouts
1 large, ripe avocado
60ml/2oz/4 tbsps lime juice
2 sweet red peppers
2 yellow peppers
15ml/1 tbsp grated ginger
280ml/½ pint/1 cup water
30ml/2 tbsps desiccated coconut
15ml/1 tbsp ground almonds
Pinch Cayenne pepper
Salt and pepper

Put scallops in a casserole with
60ml/4 tbsps water and 8ml/1½ tsps
lime juice. Cover loosely and cook

prepare the sauce, melt the butter in
a small glass bowl for 1 minute on
HIGH. Beat the egg yolks with the
salt, pepper, lemon juice, orange juice
and rind. Mix the egg yolks with the
butter, stirring constantly. Have a
bowl of ice water ready. Cook the
sauce for 15 seconds on HIGH. Stir
well, and repeat the process until the
sauce thickens, which takes about
2 minutes. Put the sauce immediately
into the bowl of ice water to stop the
cooking. Serve with the pâté.

Crab-Stuffed New Potatoes

PREPARATION TIME: 15 minutes

MICROWAVE COOKING TIME:
5 minutes

SERVES: 4 people with
3 potatoes each

12 small new potatoes, uniform in size
90g/3oz/½ cup cream or low-fat soft
    cheese

**This page: Scallops with Red and
Gold Sauces. Facing page: Crab-
Stuffed Pea Pods (top) and Crab-
Stuffed New Potatoes (bottom).**

on HIGH for 1 minute. Turn the scallops over after 30 seconds. Slice the scallops in half through the middle if they are large. Slice the red and yellow peppers, and put them into separate bowls with half the remaining lime juice and water in each. Cover with pierced plastic wrap and cook each for 5 minutes on HIGH, or until the peppers are very soft. Put the yellow peppers and liquid into a food processor with the ginger and salt and pepper, and work to a smooth purée. Strain if necessary. Work the red peppers in the same way but with the almonds, coconut, Cayenne pepper, and salt and pepper. Peel and slice the avocado thinly. Divide the red sauce evenly on 4 salad plates, covering one side, and put the equivalent gold sauce on the other side of each plate. Arrange the scallops, bean sprouts and avocado slices on top of the sauce to serve.

Oysters Florentine

PREPARATION TIME: 15 minutes

MICROWAVE COOKING TIME:
5 minutes

SERVES: 4 people

2 dozen oysters on the half shell
450g/1lb spinach, washed, or 225g/½ lb
*   frozen spinach, thawed*
60ml/2 fl oz/¼ cup heavy/double cream
Nutmeg
Salt and pepper

SAUCE
3 egg yolks
120g/4oz/½ cup butter
1 shallot, finely chopped
30ml/2 tbsps lemon juice mixed with
*   Tabasco*

GARNISH
Lemon slices

Cook the spinach with 15ml/1 tbsp water for 1 minute on HIGH in a large bowl loosely covered. Drain well and season with salt and pepper. Add the nutmeg and cream. Put a spoonful of spinach on top of each oyster. Melt the butter on HIGH for 1 minute with the shallot. Mix the

egg yolks with lemon juice and Tabasco, and pour into the hot butter, beating constantly. Have a bowl of ice water ready. Cook for 30 seconds on HIGH and stir. Repeat the process until the sauce thickens (about 2 minutes). Put the sauce bowl immediately into ice water to stop the cooking. Remove and set aside. Top each oyster with a spoon-ful of the sauce and heat through for 30 seconds on MEDIUM. Garnish with lemon slices.

NOTE: Oysters can be opened easily in microwave ovens. Clean the shells well, and leave to soak in clean water

for 2 hours. Cook for 45 seconds on HIGH, insert a knife near the hinge and pry open.

Crab-Stuffed Avocados

PREPARATION TIME: 15 minutes

MICROWAVE COOKING TIME:
3 minutes

SERVES: 4 people

This page: **Crab-Stuffed Artichoke (top) and Crab-Stuffed Avocados (bottom). Facing page: Oysters Florentine.**

2 ripe avocados, cut in half and stones
    removed
225g/½ lb crabmeat
1 green pepper, diced
2 sticks celery, diced
2 green/spring onions, chopped
280ml/½ pint/1 cup prepared
    mayonnaise
30ml/2 tbsps heavy/double cream
15ml/1 tbsp chili sauce
Lemon juice
Salt and pepper
Paprika

Scoop out some of the avocado and chop the flesh roughly. Sprinkle the shell and the chopped flesh with lemon juice. Put the pepper, celery and onion into a small bowl with 30ml/2 tbsps water. Cover loosely and cook for 2 minutes on HIGH to soften. Drain away the water and mix in the crab, mayonnaise, cream, chili sauce and salt and pepper. Carefully fold in the reserved avocado flesh. Pile into the avocado shells and sprinkle with paprika. Cook for 1 minute on HIGH, with the narrow end of the avocados pointing to the middle of the dish. Serve immediately.

Stuffed Artichokes

PREPARATION TIME: 20 minutes

MICROWAVE COOKING TIME:
17-19 minutes

SERVES: 4 people

4 globe artichokes
1 bay leaf
1 slice lemon

FILLING
225g/8oz/1 cup crabmeat, flaked
45g/1½ oz/3 tbsps butter
45g/1½ oz/3 tbsps flour/plain flour
30ml/1oz/2 tbsps Dijon mustard
30ml/2 tbsps snipped chives
280ml/½ pint/1 cup milk
140ml/¼ pint/½ cup white wine
Salt and pepper

Trim the points of the artichoke leaves and cut the stems so that the artichokes will sit upright. Put them into a large, deep bowl with enough water to barely cover. Add the bay

leaf and lemon slice. Cook for 15 minutes on HIGH. Drain upside-down. Melt the butter in a small, deep bowl for 30 seconds on HIGH. Stir in the flour, milk, wine, salt and pepper. Cook for 2-3 minutes on HIGH. Stir every 30 seconds. Add the mustard and chives. Add the crabmeat and keep warm. Remove the center leaves of the artichoke and carefully lift away the thistle-like choke with a teaspoon. Pour in the crabmeat filling and serve hot.

Lobster Julienne

PREPARATION TIME: 20 minutes

MICROWAVE COOKING TIME:
9-10 minutes

SERVES: 4 people

1 large lobster tail, uncooked
30g/1oz/2 tbsps butter or margarine
2 carrots, cut in thin, 5cm (2") strips
1 leek, cut in thin, 5cm (2") strips
2 zucchini/courgettes, cut into 5cm (2")
    strips
2 sticks celery, cut in 5cm (2") strips
8 mushrooms, thinly sliced
140ml/¼ pint/½ cup white wine
10ml/2 tsps cornstarch/cornflour
15ml/1 tbsp lemon juice
140ml/¼ pint/½ cup whole milk yogurt
10ml/2 tsps crushed tarragon
Salt and pepper

GARNISH
Chopped parsley

Melt half the butter for 30 seconds on HIGH in a small casserole. Add the carrot and celery and 15ml/1 tbsp white wine. Cover and cook for 1 minute on HIGH. Add the zucchini/courgette, leek and mushrooms. Cover the casserole and cook for 2 minutes on HIGH and set aside. Heat a browning dish for 3 minutes on HIGH. Remove the lobster tail meat from the shell and cut into 1.5cm (½") slices. Drop the remaining butter into the browning dish and add the lobster meat. Cook for 1 minute on HIGH. Remove the lobster and mix with the vegetables. Mix the cornstarch with the lemon juice, remaining wine, tarragon, salt

and pepper. Cook for 1-2 minutes on HIGH until thickened. Stir in the yogurt and heat through for 30 seconds on HIGH. Toss the lobster and vegetables with the sauce and serve immediately, garnished with chopped parsley.

Chinese Shrimp/Prawn Parcels

PREPARATION TIME: 20 minutes

MICROWAVE COOKING TIME:
6-7 minutes

SERVES: 4 people

1 head Chinese cabbage/Chinese leaves

FILLING
90g/3oz/½ cup cashew nuts
4 green/spring onions, chopped
225g/8oz cooked shrimp/prawns
120g/4 oz/½ cup chopped water
    chestnuts
450g/1lb/2 cups bean sprouts
8 dried Chinese mushrooms, soaked
1 red pepper, chopped
15g/½ oz/1 tbsp cornstarch/cornflour
30ml/1oz/2 tbsps white wine

**SWEET AND SOUR MUSTARD
SAUCE**
30ml/2 tbsps honey
30ml/2 tbsps white wine vinegar
60ml/4 tbsps Dijon mustard
15g/½ oz/1 tbsp cornstarch/cornflour
140ml/¼ pint/½ cup white wine
140ml/¼ pint/½ cup water
30ml/2 tbsps soy sauce

Separate 8 of the largest and best-looking leaves of the Chinese cabbage. Trim down their spines to make them easier to roll up. Put them into a large bowl with 30ml/2 tbsps water. Cover the bowl loosely and cook the leaves for 30 seconds on HIGH to soften slightly. Slice the mushrooms and roughly chop the cashews, then mix with the remaining

**Facing page: Lobster Julienne
(top) and South Seas Tidbits
(bottom).**

1 papaya, peeled and cut into 2.5cm (1")
    chunks
225g/8oz raw shrimp, peeled
225g/8oz scallops

SAUCE
30g/1oz/2 tbsps brown sugar
15g/½ oz/1 tbsp cornstarch/cornflour
15ml/½ oz/1 tbsp soy sauce
15ml/½ oz/1 tbsp cider vinegar
Large pinch ground ginger
30g/1oz/2 tbsps desiccated coconut
2 green/spring onions, chopped

Mix all the sauce ingredients, except
the coconut, together with 180ml/
6 fl oz/¾ cup reserved pineapple
juice. Cook for 2-3 minutes on
HIGH, stirring until thickened. Add
the shrimp and scallops and cook for
a further 2 minutes on HIGH. Add
the pineapple, papaya and coconut
and cook for a further 30 seconds on
HIGH. Serve as an appetizer.

Steamed Crabmeat Wontons

PREPARATION TIME: 20 minutes

MICROWAVE COOKING TIME:
5 minutes for wontons; 2-3 minutes
per sauce

SERVES: 4 people

30 fresh wonton skins

FILLING
340g/12oz cooked crabmeat, fresh or
    frozen
2 green/spring onions, chopped
6 water chestnuts, chopped
15ml/1 tbsp grated fresh ginger root
15ml/1 tbsp sherry or white wine
15ml/1 tbsp sesame seed oil
1 egg
Salt and pepper

SWEET AND SOUR SAUCE
180ml/6 fl oz/¾ cup orange juice
30ml/2 tbsps soy sauce
25ml/1½ tbsps brown sugar
25ml/1½ tbsps cider vinegar
10ml/2 tsps cornstarch/cornflour
25ml/1½ tbsps ketchup

HOT MUSTARD SAUCE
60ml/4 tbsps dry mustard
8ml/1½ tsps cornstarch/cornflour

filling ingredients. Put 2 leaves
together, slightly overlapping, and
divide the filling equally among all
the leaves. Tuck the sides of the
leaves around the filling and roll up.
Repeat with the remaining leaves and
filling. Put folded edge down in a
large casserole with 30ml/2 tbsps
water. Cover loosely and cook for
3 minutes on HIGH. Set aside while
preparing the sauce. Mix all the sauce
ingredients together and cook for
2-3 minutes on HIGH. Stir every
30 seconds until the sauce thickens.
Set aside

**Above: Chinese Shrimp/Prawn
Parcels (top) and Steamed
Crabmeat Wontons (bottom).**

South Seas Tidbits

PREPARATION TIME: 15 minutes

MICROWAVE COOKING TIME:
5-6 minutes

SERVES: 4 people

450g/1lb can pineapple chunks, juice
    reserved

60ml/4 tbsps white wine vinegar
140ml/¼ pint/½ cup water
60ml/2 fl oz/¼ cup honey
Salt

Mix all the filling ingredients
together. Just before filling each skin,
brush both sides with water. Put a
rounded tsp of the filling in the
center of each skin and pinch the
edges together, leaving some of the
filling showing. Lightly grease a plate
or microwave baking sheet and place
the wontons on it. Pour 30ml/1oz/
2 tbsps water over the wontons.
Cover them loosely with plastic wrap
and cook for 1 minute on HIGH.
Lower the setting to LOW and cook
for 4 further minutes. Cook in two
batches. Brush the wontons several
times with water while cooking.
Serve with one or both of the sauces.
For the sweet and sour sauce, mix the
sauce ingredients and cook in a small,
deep bowl, uncovered, for
2-3 minutes on HIGH. Stir every
30 seconds until the sauce has
thickened. For the hot mustard
sauce, mix the mustard and corn-
starch/cornflour together. Beat in the
water, vinegar and honey gradually
until the sauce is smooth. Add salt
and cook, uncovered, in a small, deep
bowl for 2-3 minutes on HIGH. Stir
every 30 seconds until thickened.

Coriander Mussels

PREPARATION TIME: 15 minutes

MICROWAVE COOKING TIME:
4-6 minutes

SERVES: 4 people

900g/2lbs/1 quart mussels
2 shallots, finely chopped
280ml/½ pint/1 cup white wine
15ml/½ oz/1 tbsp coriander seeds,
   crushed
15g/½ oz/1 tbsp butter
15g/½ oz/1 tbsp flour/plain flour
140ml/¼ pint/½ cup cream
15ml/½ oz/1 tbsp chopped coriander
15ml/½ oz/1 tbsp chopped parsley
Salt and pepper

Scrub the mussels well and discard
any with broken or open shells. Put
the mussels into a large bowl with

the shallots, wine and coriander
seeds. Cook for 1-2 minutes on
HIGH, stirring every 30 seconds,
until shells open. Discard any
mussels that do not open. Strain the
cooking liquid. Melt the butter in a
small, deep bowl for 30 seconds on
HIGH. Stir in the flour, cream,
strained liquid, and salt and pepper.
Cook for 2-3 minutes on HIGH until
thickened, stirring every 30 seconds.
Add the chopped coriander and
parsley. Divide the mussels into
individual bowls and pour over the
sauce to serve.

Above: Coriander Mussels.

Brandied Shrimp

PREPARATION TIME: 10 minutes

MICROWAVE COOKING TIME:
4 minutes

SERVES: 4 people

1kg/2¼ lbs uncooked shrimp, peeled
175g/6oz/1½ cups dry breadcrumbs
60ml/2 fl oz/4 tbsps brandy

120g/4oz/½ cup butter
2 shallots, chopped
60ml/4 tbsps chopped parsley
Paprika
Salt and pepper

GARNISH
4 lemon wedges

Mix the shallot, salt, pepper, parsley
and shrimp together and divide
between 4 small baking dishes. Pour
brandy over each dish and cook for
30 seconds on HIGH. Heat a
browning dish for 5 minutes on
HIGH. Drop in the butter and cook
for a further 30 seconds on HIGH.
Stir in the breadcrumbs and cook for
1-2 minutes to brown. Spoon the
breadcrumbs over the shrimp and
sprinkle on the paprika. Cook for
1 minute on HIGH or until the
shrimp are cooked. Serve with lemon
wedges.

Marinated Herring with Tomatoes

PREPARATION TIME: 20 minutes

MICROWAVE COOKING TIME:
5-7 minutes

SERVES: 4 people

8 herring fillets

MARINADE
2 onions, finely chopped
200ml/6 fl oz/¾ cup red wine vinegar
60ml/2 fl oz/¼ cup water
60g/2oz/¼ cup sugar
6 black peppercorns
2 whole allspice berries

SAUCE
4 tomatoes, peeled, seeded and cut into
  thin strips
30ml/2 tbsps tomato purée/paste
30ml/2 tbsps snipped chives
90ml/3 fl oz/⅓ cup vegetable oil
60ml/2 fl oz/¼ cup reserved marinade
Salt and pepper

Combine the marinade ingredients
and cook, uncovered, for 5-7 minutes
on HIGH until rapidly boiling. Allow
to cool slightly, and pour over the
fish fillets. Leave the fish to cool

completely in the marinade. Mix the
oil and strained reserved marinade
together with the tomato purée,
chives, salt and pepper. Pour over the
herring and top with the tomato
strips to serve.

Smoky Cheese and Shrimp Dip

PREPARATION TIME: 15 minutes

MICROWAVE COOKING TIME:
5 minutes

SERVES: 4 people

180g/6oz/1½ cups shredded Cheddar
cheese

**This page: Smoky Cheese and
Shrimp Dip. Facing page:
Brandied Shrimp (top) and
Marinated Herring with Tomatoes
(bottom).**

120g/4oz/1 cup shredded smoked or
  smoky cheese
15g/½ oz/1 tbsp butter
1 shallot finely chopped
120g/4oz/½ cup shrimp, chopped
180ml/6 fl oz/¾ cup light/single cream
15g/½ oz flour/plain flour
Salt and pepper
Raw vegetables

Melt the butter in a small, deep bowl
for 30 seconds on HIGH. Add the
shallot and cook for 1 minute on

HIGH to soften. Toss the cheese and flour together and add to the bowl with the shallot. Stir in the cream, salt and pepper. Cook for 4 minutes on MEDIUM or until the cheese has melted. Stir the mixture twice while cooking. Serve hot with vegetable crudités for dipping.

Herring in Mustard Dill Sauce

PREPARATION TIME: 20 minutes

MICROWAVE COOKING TIME: 7-9 minutes

SERVES: 4 people

4 herring fillets, cut in chunks

MARINADE
2 onions, finely chopped
200ml/6 fl oz/¾ cup white wine vinegar
60ml/2 fl oz/¼ cup water
60g/2oz/¼ cup sugar
4 sprigs fresh dill
15ml/1 tbsp dried dill
6 black peppercorns
2 whole allspice berries

SAUCE
15g/½ oz/1 tbsp flour/plain flour
30ml/1oz/2 tbsps mustard
15ml/1 tbsp chopped dill
60ml/2 fl oz/¼ cup sour cream

Combine the marinade ingredients and cook, uncovered, for 5-7 minutes until rapidly boiling. Allow to cool slightly, and pour over the fish. Leave the fish to cool in the marinade. Strain the marinade and beat gradually into the flour. Add the mustard and cook for 2 minutes on HIGH, stirring every 30 seconds until thickened. Mix with the chopped dill, and chill. Mix in the sour cream and herring. Serve as an appetizer/starter, or on a bed of lettuce as a first course.

Oysters Romanoff

PREPARATION TIME: 10 minutes

MICROWAVE COOKING TIME: 1 minute

SERVES: 4 people

2 dozen oysters on the half shell
20ml/1½ tbsps snipped chives
280ml/½ pint/1 cup sour cream
1 jar red lumpfish or salmon caviar
Lemon juice
Salt and pepper

Put a drop of lemon juice on each oyster. Mix the chives and cream together with salt and pepper. Put a spoonful of the mixture on top of each oyster. Heat through for 1 minute on HIGH on a large plate. Heat in 2 batches if necessary. Put a spoonful of the caviar on each oyster before serving. Serve with lemon wedges and watercress.

This page: Pickled Mussels (top) and Herring in Mustard Dill Sauce (bottom). Facing page: Oysters Romanoff.

Pickled Mussels

PREPARATION TIME: 15 minutes

MICROWAVE COOKING TIME: 6 minutes

SERVES: 4 people

900g/2lbs/1 quart mussels
140ml/¼ pint/½ cup white wine
140ml/¼ pint/½ cup white wine vinegar

30g/1oz/2 tbsps sugar
15ml/½ oz/1 tbsp mustard seed
1 cinnamon stick
4 whole allspice berries
4 black peppercorns
4 whole cloves
2 shallots, finely chopped
Salt and pepper

Scrub the mussels well and discard any with broken or open shells. Put the mussels into a large bowl with 30ml/2 tbsps water. Cook on HIGH for 45-50 seconds, until the shells open, stirring twice. Discard any mussels that do not open. Combine the remaining ingredients, and cook for 5 minutes on HIGH or until boiling. Allow to cool slightly. Remove the mussels from their shells and combine with the pickling mixture. Leave to cool and then refrigerate. Keep no longer than 2 days.

Salmon Terrine

PREPARATION TIME: 15 minutes

MICROWAVE COOKING TIME: 10 minutes

SERVES: 4 people

450g/1lb salmon
2 eggs
60g/2oz/1 cup fresh white breadcrumbs
60g/2oz/¼ cup cream cheese
30ml/2 tbsps heavy/double cream
Salt and pepper

DRESSING
1 cucumber, grated
280ml/½ pint/1 cup sour cream
140ml/¼ pint/½ cup prepared
   mayonnaise
30ml/2 tbsps chopped dill
Salt and pepper

GARNISH
Red lumpfish caviar

Skin the salmon and cut into chunks. Combine with the remaining terrine ingredients in a food processor and work until smooth. Line the bottom of a 450g/1lb glass loaf pan/dish with waxed/greaseproof paper. Fill with the salmon mixture and smooth out.

Cover well with plastic wrap and cook for 10 minutes on MEDIUM, with a small dish of water to keep it moist. Allow to cool and then chill well. Turn out and cut into slices. Mix all the dressing ingredients together and serve with the terrine. Garnish with the lumpfish caviar.

Smoked Oyster Pâté

PREPARATION TIME: 15 minutes

MICROWAVE COOKING TIME:
10 minutes, plus 5 minutes standing time

SERVES: 4 people

1 can smoked oysters
450g/1lb whitefish
60g/2oz/1 cup fresh white breadcrumbs
Butter
2 eggs
60g/2oz/¼ cup cream cheese
30ml/2 tbsps cream
15ml/½ oz/1 tbsp chopped parsley
10ml/2 tsps Worcestershire sauce
15ml/1 tbsp lemon juice
Salt and pepper

Roughly chop the smoked oysters. Combine the remaining ingredients in a food processor and work until smooth. Fold in the oysters. Line the bottom of a 450g/1lb glass loaf pan/dish with waxed/greaseproof paper. Spoon in the pâté mixture and smooth out. Cover well with plastic wrap and cook for 10 minutes on MEDIUM. Put a small dish of water into the oven with the pâté to keep it moist. Leave to stand for 5 minutes, then chill before serving. Serve with buttered toast.

Paprika Shrimp

PREPARATION TIME: 15 minutes

MICROWAVE COOKING TIME:
10 minutes

SERVES: 4 people

900g/2lbs raw shrimp/prawns, peeled
60g/2oz/¼ cup butter or margarine
15ml/1 tbsp paprika
2 chopped shallots
1 red pepper, thinly sliced

30ml/2 tbsps chopped parsley
430ml/¾ pint/1½ cups sour cream
15ml/1 tbsp lemon juice
Salt and pepper

TOPPING
60g/2oz/¼ cup butter or margarine
120g/4oz/½ cup breadcrumbs

Heat a browning dish for 5 minutes on HIGH. Melt the butter for the topping and stir in the breadcrumbs. Cook on HIGH for 2 minutes, stirring every 30 seconds. Set aside. Melt the remaining butter in a large casserole for 30 seconds on HIGH. Add the paprika, shallot and sliced pepper. Cook for 2 minutes on HIGH, stirring frequently. Add the shrimp, lemon juice, salt and pepper, and continue cooking for 2 minutes more on HIGH. Stir in the sour cream. Put into individual serving dishes and sprinkle over the browned crumbs. Cook for 30 seconds on MEDIUM to heat through, and serve with hot rolls or French bread.

Calamares España

PREPARATION TIME: 20 minutes

MICROWAVE COOKING TIME:
8 minutes

SERVES: 4 people

2 medium-sized squid
30ml/2 tbsps olive oil
30g/1oz/2 tbsps flour/plain flour
1 clove garlic, finely chopped
450g/1lb/2 cups canned plum tomatoes
1 chili pepper, finely chopped
Grated rind and juice of 1 orange
140ml/¼ pint/½ cup white wine
15ml/1 tbsp tomato purée/paste
5ml/1 tsp oregano
5ml/1 tsp basil
1 bay leaf
Salt and pepper

GARNISH
Fresh coriander leaves

Facing page: Smoked Oyster Pâté (top) and Salmon Terrine (bottom).

This page: Garlic Shrimp/Prawns and Mushrooms. Facing page: Paprika Shrimp (top) and Calamares España (bottom).

Separate heads of the squid from the tails. Remove the ink-sac and reserve for the sauce if desired. Remove the quill and discard. Cut the tentacles above the eyes, and reserve. Discard the eyes and head. Peel the purplish membrane off the tail portion of the squid. Split the tail in half, length-wise, and wash it well. Cut the tail into pieces about 5cm (2") wide. Score each section in a lattice pattern at 5mm (¼") intervals. Separate the tentacles. Put the squid, bay leaf and onion into a casserole with hot water. Cover loosely and cook for 1 minute on HIGH. Heat the olive oil for 30 seconds on HIGH in a medium-sized bowl. Add the garlic and onion, and cook for a further 1 minute on HIGH. Stir in the flour. Mix the cooking liquid from the squid with the tomatoes and the other sauce ingredients. If using the ink, break the ink-sac into the sauce ingredients. Cook the sauce, uncovered, for 5 minutes on HIGH. Mix with the squid and serve garnished with fresh coriander leaves.

Garlic Shrimp/Prawns and Mushrooms

| **PREPARATION TIME:** 10 minutes |
| **MICROWAVE COOKING TIME:** 3-4 minutes |
| **SERVES:** 4 people |

4-8 (depending on size) oyster or wild mushrooms
120g/4oz/½ cup butter
675g/1½ lbs raw shrimp/prawns, peeled
1 large clove garlic, chopped
30ml/2 tbsps chopped parsley
Salt and pepper
Lemon juice

Leave the mushrooms whole, but remove the stalks. Melt the butter in a shallow casserole for 30 seconds on HIGH. Add the mushrooms, garlic, salt, pepper and lemon juice. Cook for 2 minutes on HIGH. Remove and set aside. Add the shrimp to the casserole and cook on HIGH for 1 minute, stirring several times. Cook for 30 seconds more on HIGH, if required, to cook the shrimp thoroughly. Mix in the parsley and add more seasoning if necessary. Arrange the mushrooms in individual dishes and spoon over the shrimp and any remaining butter in the dish. Serve with French bread.

Microwave

FISH AND SEAFOOD

LIGHT DISHES

Codfish Pie

PREPARATION TIME: 15 minutes

MICROWAVE COOKING TIME:
11-12 minutes

SERVES: 4 people

4 cod fillets
30ml/2 tbsps lemon juice
30ml/2 tbsps water
1 bay leaf

SAUCE
45g/1½ oz/3 tbsps butter
1 shallot, finely chopped
45g/1½ oz/3 tbsps flour/plain flour
430ml/¾ pint/1½ cups milk
30ml/2 tbsps chopped parsley
Salt and pepper

TOPPING
2 large potatoes, peeled and very thinly
    sliced
60g/2oz/¼ cup grated Colby/Red
    Leicester cheese
Paprika

Put the fillets in a casserole with the
water, lemon juice and bay leaf.
Cover loosely and cook for 2
minutes on HIGH. Melt the butter in
a deep bowl for 30 seconds on
HIGH. Add the shallot and cook for
a further 1 minute on HIGH. Stir in
the flour, milk, liquid from the fish,
salt, pepper and parsley. Cook for
2-3 minutes on HIGH or until thick,
stirring frequently. Pour over the cod.
Slice the potatoes on a mandolin or
with the fine blade of a food

**This page: Codfish Pie (top) and
Tuna, Pea and Fennel Casserole
(bottom). Facing page: Sea Lion.**

processor. Layer on top of the cod and season with salt and pepper. Cover the dish tightly and cook for 3 minutes on HIGH. Sprinkle on the cheese and paprika and cook, uncovered, for a further 2 minutes on MEDIUM to melt the cheese. Serve immediately.

Crab Lasagne

PREPARATION TIME: 15 minutes

MICROWAVE COOKING TIME: 10 minutes

SERVES: 4 people

8 quick-cooking green lasagne noodles
4 tomatoes, peeled and sliced
225g crabmeat, flaked
340g/12oz Ricotta cheese
60g/2oz/¼ cup grated Parmesan cheese
140ml/¼ pint/½ cup milk
1 small clove garlic, minced
Pinch marjoram
Pinch nutmeg
Pinch dry mustard
Salt and pepper

TOPPING
60g/2oz/¼ cup seasoned dry
   breadcrumbs
15g/½ oz/1 tbsp butter
Paprika

Boil 1 litre/1¾ pints/3½ cups water on HIGH with a pinch of salt. Put in the lasagne and leave for 1 minute. Remove the noodles and rinse under hot water. Dry on paper towels. Mix the remaining ingredients, except the tomatoes, together. If the mixture is very thick, add more milk. Layer up the noodles, tomatoes and crabmeat filling, ending with filling. Melt the butter on HIGH for 30 seconds and stir in the breadcrumbs. Scatter over the top of the lasagne and sprinkle on some paprika. Cook for 3 minutes on HIGH and serve immediately.

Sea Lion

PREPARATION TIME: 20 minutes

MICROWAVE COOKING TIME: 5 minutes

SERVES: 4 people

CRABMEAT BALLS
450g/1lb crabmeat, flaked
45ml/1½ fl oz/3 tbsps sherry
15ml/½ fl oz/1 tbsp soy sauce
4 water chestnuts, finely chopped
2 green/spring onions, finely chopped
30ml/2 tbsps cornstarch/cornflour
1 egg white, lightly beaten
Pinch ginger
Salt and pepper

ACCOMPANIMENT
1 head Chinese cabbage/leaves, shredded
15ml/1 tbsp cornstarch/cornflour
30ml/2 tbsps soy sauce
5ml/1 tsp sugar
140ml/¼ pint/½ cup chicken stock

GARNISH
Sesame seeds

Mix all the ingredients for the crabmeat balls together and shape into 5cm (2") balls. Place them in a large casserole with 30ml/1 fl oz/ 2 tbsps water. Cover loosely and cook for 2 minutes on MEDIUM. Remove from the casserole and keep warm. Combine the ingredients for the accompaniment and cook in the casserole for 2 minutes on HIGH, or until the cornstarch/cornflour thickens. Put the crabmeat balls on top of the cabbage and heat through for 1 minute on HIGH. Sprinkle over the sesame seeds to serve.

Monkfish Provençale

PREPARATION TIME: 20 minutes

MICROWAVE COOKING TIME: 19 minutes

SERVES: 4 people

675g/1½ lbs monkfish tails
1 aubergine/eggplant, cut in 1.5cm (½")
   chunks
2 zucchini/courgettes, cut in 1.5cm (½")
   chunks
1 large red pepper, cut in thin strips
90g/3oz/¾ cup sliced mushrooms
1 large onion, thinly sliced
30ml/1oz/2 tbsps olive oil
1 clove garlic, crushed
140ml/4oz/½ cup white wine
200g/7oz can plum tomatoes
30ml/1oz/2 tbsps tomato purée/paste

Pinch dried thyme
1 bay leaf
Salt and pepper
120g/4oz/½ cup grated cheese

Cut the eggplant/aubergine in half lengthways and lightly score the surface. Sprinkle with salt and leave to stand for 30 minutes. Wash and pat dry before cutting in cubes. Heat the olive oil in a browning dish for 3 minutes on HIGH. Add the vegetables and garlic. Cook for 2 minutes on HIGH. Add the canned tomatoes, tomato paste, thyme, bay leaf, half the wine, salt and pepper. Pour the contents into a casserole dish, cover, and cook for 10 minutes on HIGH. Stir 3 or 4 times during cooking. Cook the fish separately in the remaining wine for 2 minutes on HIGH. Transfer the fish to a baking dish and cover with the Provençale vegetables. Sprinkle on the cheese and cook for 2 minutes on MEDIUM to melt.

Tuna, Pea and Fennel Casserole

PREPARATION TIME: 15 minutes

MICROWAVE COOKING TIME: 10 minutes, plus 10 minutes standing time

SERVES: 4 people

225g/8oz green and whole-wheat
   noodles
120g/4oz/1 cup frozen peas
1 small bulb Florentine fennel chopped
225g/8oz can tuna, drained
45g/1½ oz/3 tbsps butter or margarine
45g/1½ oz/3 tbsps flour/plain flour
60ml/2oz/¼ cup white wine
360ml/⅔ pint/1¼ cups milk
Pinch oregano
1 small clove garlic, minced
Salt and pepper

TOPPING
Paprika
Parmesan cheese

Facing page: Monkfish Provençale (top) and Crab Lasagne (bottom).

Put the noodles in a large bowl with 1 litre/1¾ pints/3½ cups water. Cook for 6 minutes on HIGH and then leave to stand for 10 minutes. Drain, rinse under hot water, then leave to dry. Put the fennel into a casserole with 30ml/1 fl oz/2 tbsps water. Cover and cook for 1 minute on HIGH. Drain and combine with the noodles, tuna and peas. Melt the butter for 30 seconds on HIGH with the garlic. Stir in the flour, wine, milk, oregano, salt and pepper. Pour over the noodles and mix well. Sprinkle on grated Parmesan cheese and paprika. Heat for 2 minutes on HIGH before serving.

Shrimp/Prawn Curry

PREPARATION TIME: 10 minutes

MICROWAVE COOKING TIME:
5-7 minutes

SERVES: 4 people

45g/1½ oz/3 tbsps butter or margarine
45g/1½ oz/3 tbsps flour/plain flour
1 small onion, finely chopped
15g/½ oz/1 tbsp curry powder
430ml/¾ pint/1½ cups milk
60ml/2oz/¼ cup plain yogurt
1 cap pimento, chopped
225g/8oz shrimp/prawns, cooked and
* peeled*

This page: Seafood Stir-fry. Facing page: Shrimp/Prawn Curry (top) and Pasta alla Vongole (bottom).

*Desiccated coconut or chopped green/
  spring onion*

Melt the butter for 30 seconds on HIGH. Add the onion and cook for 30 seconds on HIGH to soften. Stir in the curry powder and cook for 1 minute on HIGH. Add the flour, salt, pepper and milk. Cook for 3-4 minutes, stirring often until thickened. Add the yogurt, pimento and shrimp. Heat for 30 seconds on

HIGH and serve on a bed of rice. Sprinkle on the coconut or onion.

Seafood Stir-fry

PREPARATION TIME: 20 minutes

MICROWAVE COOKING TIME: 16 minutes

SERVES: 4 people

120g/4oz thin Chinese egg noodles
30ml/1 fl oz/2 tbsps vegetable oil
2 large or 4 small scallops
90g/3oz/½ cup crabmeat, flaked
90g/3oz/½ cup shrimp/prawns, cooked
  and peeled
4 water chestnuts, sliced
4 ears baby corn
60g/2oz peapods/mangetout
1 small red pepper, sliced
225g/8oz bean sprouts
140ml/¼ pint/½ cup chicken or fish stock
30ml/1 fl oz/2 tbsps soy sauce
15ml/1 tbsp cornstarch/cornflour
15ml/1 tbsp sherry
Dash sesame seed oil
Salt and pepper

Boil 1 litre/1¾ pints/3½ cups water with a pinch of salt for 5 minutes on HIGH. Put in the noodles and leave them to stand for 6 minutes. Drain and rinse under hot water and leave to dry. Heat the oil for 5 minutes on HIGH in a browning dish. Cook the scallops for 3 minutes on HIGH, turning several times. Add the pepper, peapods/mangetout and baby corn. Cook for 1 minute on HIGH. Add the bean sprouts and noodles. Mix the remaining ingredients together and add to the dish with the shrimp and crab. Toss the ingredients together and heat for 2 minutes on HIGH or until the sauce thickens. Serve immediately.

Pasta alla Vongole

PREPARATION TIME: 15 minutes

MICROWAVE COOKING TIME: 9 minutes, plus 10 minutes standing time

SERVES: 4 people

180g/6oz/2 cups red, green and plain
  pasta shells (or other shapes)

3 tomatoes, peeled, seeded and sliced in
  strips
45g/1½ oz/3 tbsps butter or margarine
½ clove garlic, crushed
2 shallots, finely chopped
45g/1½ oz/3 tbsps flour/plain flour
140ml/¼ pint/½ cup white wine
280ml/½ pint/1 cup milk, or light/single
  cream
30ml/1 tbsp chopped parsley
Pinch oregano or basil
340g/12oz/1½ cups small clams, shelled
Salt and pepper
Grated Parmesan cheese

Put the pasta into 1 litre/1¾ pints/ 3½ cups hot water with a pinch of salt. Cook for 6 minutes on HIGH. Leave to stand for 10 minutes, then drain and rinse in hot water. Melt the butter in a small, deep bowl for 30 seconds on HIGH. Add the garlic and shallot and cook for 30 seconds on HIGH to soften. Stir in the flour, wine and milk or cream, and add the herbs, salt and pepper. Cook for 2-3 minutes on HIGH, stirring every 30 seconds. Cut the tomatoes into thin strips and add to the hot sauce with the clams. Heat through for a further 30 seconds on HIGH. Toss the sauce and pasta together and serve with grated Parmesan cheese if desired.

MAIN DISHES

Turbot with Almonds and Emerald Sauce

PREPARATION TIME: 20 minutes

MICROWAVE COOKING TIME: 11 minutes

SERVES: 4 people

4 turbot fillets
1 slice onion
1 bay leaf
2 black peppercorns
140ml/¼ pint/½ cup water

SAUCE
450g/1lb fresh spinach, well washed
15ml/1 tbsp fresh chives, chopped
15ml/1 tbsp white wine vinegar
Nutmeg
Cayenne pepper
15g/1 tbsp butter
140ml/¼ pint/½ cup cream

GARNISH
90g/3oz/½ cup sliced/flaked almonds

Heat a browning dish for 5 minutes on HIGH and toast the almonds for 1-2 minutes on HIGH, stirring frequently until browned. Put the fish into a casserole with the slice of onion, bay leaf, peppercorn, lemon juice and water. Cover loosely and cook on HIGH for 2 minutes. Set aside. Put the spinach, nutmeg, Cayenne pepper and butter into a large bowl with 15ml/1 tbsp water. Cover loosely and cook on HIGH for 2 minutes. Purée in a food

This page: Salmon and Broccoli Fricassee. Facing page: Turbot with Almonds and Emerald Sauce.

processor. Add the cream, chives and some of the fish cooking liquid if the sauce is too thick. Sprinkle the toasted almonds on the fish and serve with the emerald sauce.

Garlic-Braised Tuna Steaks

PREPARATION TIME: 20 minutes

MICROWAVE COOKING TIME: 11-12 minutes

SERVES: 4 people

4 tuna steaks, cut 2.5cm (1") thick
1 clove garlic, peeled and cut in thin
    slivers
225g/8oz button or pickling onions,
    peeled
15g/½ oz/1 tbsp butter
140ml/¼ pint/½ cup red wine
140ml/¼ pint/½ cup water
1 bay leaf

SAUCE
Cooking liquid from the fish
15g/½ oz/1 tbsp butter or margarine
15g/½ oz/1 tbsp flour/plain flour
15ml/1 tbsp tomato paste or purée
2.5ml/½ tsp thyme
15ml/1 tbsp chopped parsley
Squeeze lemon juice
Salt and pepper

GARNISH
450g/1lb fresh spinach, washed and
    thinly shredded
15g/½ oz/1 tbsp butter

Make small slits in the tuna steaks with a knife and insert a sliver of garlic into each slit. Heat a browning dish for 3 minutes on HIGH. Drop in 15g/½ oz/1 tbsp butter and the peeled onions. Heat for 1-2 minutes on HIGH, stirring occasionally, until the onions begin to brown. Pour in the water and wine. Transfer the contents of the browning dish to a large casserole. Add the bay leaf and fish to the casserole, cover loosely and cook for 5 minutes on HIGH. Remove the fish and onions from the casserole and keep them warm. Melt 15g/½ oz/1 tbsp butter in a small, deep bowl for 30 seconds on HIGH. Stir in the flour and cook for 1-2 minutes on HIGH or until the flour

is lightly browned. Pour in the cooking liquid from the fish, and add the tomato purée and thyme. Cook for 2-3 minutes on HIGH, stirring occasionally until thickened. Add the parsley, lemon juice, salt and pepper, and set aside with the fish. Melt the remaining butter in a small casserole on HIGH for 30 seconds. Put in the spinach, cover loosely and cook for 1-2 minutes on HIGH. Spread the spinach onto a serving plate and combine the fish and sauce to re-heat for 30 seconds on HIGH. Arrange the fish and onions on top of the bed of spinach and pour over the sauce to serve.

Salmon and Broccoli Fricassee

PREPARATION TIME: 20 minutes

MICROWAVE COOKING TIME: 10-12 minutes

SERVES: 4 people

900g/2lbs salmon fillets or tail pieces
60g/2oz/½ cup sliced/flaked almonds,
    toasted
450g/1lb broccoli
140ml/¼ pint/½ cup white wine
180g/6oz/1 cup sliced mushrooms
15g/½ oz/1 tbsp butter
15g/½ oz/1 tbsp flour/plain flour
120g/4oz/1 cup chow mein noodles
5ml/1 tsp chopped dill
5ml/1 tsp chopped parsley
200ml/6 fl oz/¾ cup cream
Salt and pepper

Put the fillets into a casserole with enough water to barely cover. Cover the dish loosely and cook for 2 minutes on HIGH. Reserve the cooking liquid, flake the fish and set aside. Put the broccoli into a bowl with 30ml/2 tbsps water. Cover loosely and cook for 4 minutes on HIGH. Drain and arrange the broccoli in a casserole with the flaked salmon. Melt the butter in a small bowl for 30 seconds on HIGH. Stir in the flour, cream, fish liquid and sliced mushrooms. Cook for 2-3 minutes on HIGH. Season with salt and pepper. Add dill and parsley and pour over the fish and broccoli.

Sprinkle over the almonds and noodles. Heat through for 2 minutes on HIGH before serving.

Halibut à la Normande

PREPARATION TIME: 15 minutes

MICROWAVE COOKING TIME: 5-7 minutes

SERVES: 4 people

4 halibut fillets or steaks
140ml/¼ pint/½ cup white wine, dry
    cider or unsweetened apple juice
60ml/4 tbsps/¼ cup water
15g/½ oz/1 tbsp flour/plain flour
30g/1oz/2 tbsps butter or margarine
1 shallot finely chopped
2 medium-sized apples/dessert apples
60ml/2oz/¼ cup light/single cream
1 bay leaf
Salt and pepper
Lemon juice

GARNISH
Chopped parsley

Put the halibut into a casserole with the wine, cider or juice, water and bay leaf. Cover loosely and cook for 2 minutes on HIGH. Set aside and keep warm. In a small bowl melt half the butter. Add the shallot and cook, uncovered, for 1 minute on HIGH, stirring once. Peel and chop one of the apples. Add the shallot, cover the bowl loosely and cook for 2 minutes on HIGH, or until the apple is soft. Stir in the flour, add the cooking liquid from the fish and heat for 2 minutes on HIGH. Stir the sauce twice until thickened. Add the cream and heat for 30 seconds on HIGH. Season with salt, pepper and lemon juice to taste. Heat a browning dish for 5 minutes on HIGH and drop in the remaining butter. Core and slice the second apple, but do not peel it. Brown the slices for 1-2 minutes on HIGH in the butter. Coat the fish with the sauce and garnish with the parsley. Serve surrounded with the apple slices.

Facing page: Garlic-Braised Tuna Steaks

Monkfish Medallions Piperade

PREPARATION TIME: 15 minutes

MICROWAVE COOKING TIME:
7 minutes, plus 1 minute standing time

SERVES: 4 people

900g/2lbs monkfish tails
140ml/¼ pint/½ cup white wine
430ml/¾ pint/1½ cups tomato sauce
1 shallot, finely chopped
1 red pepper, sliced
1 green pepper, sliced
1 yellow pepper, sliced
1 clove garlic, finely minced
2.5ml/½ tsp thyme
1 bay leaf
Salt and pepper

GARNISH
Chopped parsley

Cut the monkfish tails into round slices 15mm (½″) thick. Put into a casserole with the wine and bay leaf. Cover loosely and cook for 2 minutes on HIGH. Set aside. Combine the shallot, garlic and thyme in a small, deep bowl. Pour on the fish cooking liquid and cook, uncovered, for 3 minutes on HIGH to reduce by half. Add the tomato sauce, peppers, salt and pepper. Cover loosely and cook for 2 minutes on HIGH. Leave to stand for 1 minute and pour over the fish to serve.

Salmon in Chive Sauce

PREPARATION TIME: 15 minutes

MICROWAVE COOKING TIME:
5 minutes

SERVES: 4 people

1 side of salmon (about 675-900g/
*   1½-2lbs)*
30g/1oz/2 tbsps butter or margarine
280ml/½ pint/1 cup sour cream
120ml/¼ pint/½ cup light/single cream
5ml/1 tsp cornstarch/cornflour
45g/1½ oz/3 tbsps snipped chives
5ml/1 tsp coarsely ground black pepper
Salt

Slice the salmon horizontally into very thin slices. Heat a browning dish for 3 minutes on HIGH. Drop in the butter and heat for 30 seconds on HIGH. Lay in the salmon slices and cook for 30 seconds each side. Cook the fish in several batches. Remove the fish from the dish. Cover and keep warm. Mix the cream, sour cream, and cornstarch together. Pour into the dish and cook for 30 seconds on HIGH. Stir well and repeat the process until the cornstarch has cooked and thickened

This page: Monkfish Medallions Piperade. Facing page: Halibut à la Normande (top) and Salmon in Chive Sauce (bottom).

the sauce. The sauce should not bubble too rapidly, but the cornstarch will help prevent the sour cream from curdling. Stir in the chives, pepper and salt, and pour over the salmon slices. Serve with fine green noodles.

Sole in Lettuce Leaf Parcels

PREPARATION TIME: 20 minutes

MICROWAVE COOKING TIME:
5 minutes

SERVES: 4 people

4 double fillets of sole or flounder
8 large leaves of romaine/cos lettuce
225g/8oz small shrimp/prawns
1 finely chopped shallot
90g/3oz/½ cup chopped mushrooms
60ml/2 tbsps chopped parsley

4 large caps canned pimento
1 cap pimento, chopped
140ml/¼ pint/½ cup white wine
140ml/¼ pint/½ cup heavy/double cream
120g/4oz/1 cup low-fat soft cheese
Salt and pepper

Combine the shrimp/prawns, mushrooms, half the parsley, salt and pepper, and stuff the pimento caps with the mixture. Roll the fish fillets around the pimento and set aside. Put the lettuce leaves into a large casserole with 30ml/2 tbsps water.

This page: **Sole in Lettuce Leaf Parcels.** Facing page: **Mackerel and Mustard (top) and Trout with Hazelnuts (bottom).**

Cover tightly and cook for 30 seconds on HIGH to soften. Roll the leaves carefully around the stuffed fillets. Put seam-side down into a casserole with the wine and shallot. Cover loosely and cook for 3 minutes on HIGH. Remove the parcels and keep them warm. Cook

the wine for a further 2-3 minutes on HIGH to reduce. Stir in the cream and bring to the boil for 2 minutes on HIGH. Add the cheese, salt, pepper, the remaining parsley and chopped pimento. Serve the sauce with the sole parcels.

Trout with Hazelnuts

PREPARATION TIME: 15 minutes

MICROWAVE COOKING TIME: 12-13 minutes

SERVES: 4 people

4 small rainbow trout, cleaned
60g/2oz/4 tbsps butter
120g/4oz/¾ cup crushed hazelnuts
4 green/spring onions, shredded
Juice of 1 lemon
Salt and pepper

Heat a browning dish for 5 minutes on HIGH. Put in the hazelnuts and cook for 2-3 minutes on HIGH, stirring often until browned. Set aside. Melt half the butter in the browning dish. Add the trout and cook for 5 minutes per side. If the butter has browned too much, wipe out the dish. Melt the remaining butter and allow to brown lightly. Add the nuts, lemon juice and green onion, and season with salt and pepper. Pour over the fish to serve.

Hangchow Fish

PREPARATION TIME: 15 minutes

MICROWAVE COOKING TIME: 19 minutes

SERVES: 4 people

1 sea or freshwater bass, 900-1kg/
    2-2¼ lbs in weight, cleaned
140ml/¼ pint/½ cup white wine
140ml/¼ pint/½ cup water
1 small ginger root, sliced
60g/2oz/¼ cup sugar
90ml/3 fl oz/⅓ cup rice vinegar
30ml/1 fl oz/2 tbsps soy sauce
15g/½ oz/1 tbsp cornstarch/cornflour
1 clove garlic, minced
1 carrot, thinly sliced in rounds
4 water chestnuts, thinly sliced

4 green/spring onions, diagonally sliced
Salt and pepper

Combine the wine, water and a few slices of ginger in a large casserole. Cut 2 or 3 slashes on each side of the fish to help it cook faster, and put it into the casserole. Cover and cook for 25 minutes on MEDIUM. Set the fish aside and keep it warm. Combine the cornstarch, sugar, vinegar, soy sauce, salt, pepper and 140ml/ ¼ pint/½ cup of the fish cooking liquid. Add the garlic and cook on HIGH for 2 minutes, stirring frequently. Add the water chestnuts, carrots and remaining slices of ginger. Cook the sauce for a further 1-2 minutes on HIGH. Add the green/ spring onions and pour over the fish to serve.

Mackerel and Mustard

PREPARATION TIME: 15 minutes

MICROWAVE COOKING TIME: 14-16 minutes

SERVES: 4 people

4 small mackerel, cleaned
280ml/½ pint/1 cup white wine
5ml/1 tsp whole mustard seed
3 whole peppercorns
1 bay leaf
1 slice onion

SAUCE
25g/¾ oz/1½ tbsps flour/plain flour
25g/¾ oz/1½ tbsps butter
30ml/1oz/2 tbsps Dijon or spicy brown
    mustard
30ml/1oz/2 tbsps chopped herbs
    (eg chives, parsley, thyme, dill)
140ml/¼ pint/½ cup milk
Salt and pepper

Put the mackerel into one or two casseroles (do not crowd the fish) and cook in two batches if necessary. Pour over the white wine and add the mustard seed, peppercorns, bay leaf and onion. Cover loosely and cook for 12 minutes on HIGH. Set aside and keep warm. Melt the butter in a small, deep bowl for 30 seconds on HIGH. Stir in the flour, milk and strained liquid from the fish. Cook, uncovered, for 2-3 minutes on

HIGH, stirring often until thickened. Add salt, pepper, mustard and herbs. Peel the skin from one side of the mackerel and coat each one with some of the sauce to serve. Serve the remaining sauce separately.

Crab-Stuffed Trout

PREPARATION TIME: 15 minutes

MICROWAVE COOKING TIME: 14 minutes

SERVES: 4 people

4 rainbow trout
60g/2oz/4 tbsps butter
Juice of 1 lemon

STUFFING
225g/8oz flaked crabmeat
3 green/spring onions, chopped
2 sticks celery, finely chopped
1 small green pepper, finely chopped
60g/2oz/¼ cup black olives, sliced
Fresh breadcrumbs from 4 slices of white
    bread, crusts removed
30ml/2 tbsps chopped parsley
30ml/2 tbsps sherry
Salt and pepper

GARNISH
Lemon slices
Chopped chives

Buy the trout fresh or frozen with the bones removed. Mix the stuffing ingredients together and fill the trout. Put the trout into a large casserole and cook, covered, in two batches if necessary. Cook 4 trout together for 12 minutes on HIGH, or 2 trout for 6 minutes on HIGH. Melt the butter for 2 minutes on HIGH and add the lemon juice and pour over the trout before serving. Garnish with lemon slices and chives.

Facing page: Hangchow Fish.

Sole and Asparagus Rolls

PREPARATION TIME: 15 minutes

MICROWAVE COOKING TIME: 7 minutes

SERVES: 4 people

8 fillets of sole
16 asparagus spears
140ml/¼ pint/½ cup water
15ml/1 tbsp lemon juice

SAUCE
3 egg yolks
30ml/2 tbsps lemon juice
120g/4oz/½ cup butter
Cayenne pepper
Salt

This page: Sole and Asparagus Rolls. Facing page: Crab-Stuffed Trout.

Cook the asparagus with 30ml/ 2 tbsps water for 2 minutes on HIGH in a covered casserole. Rinse under cold water and drain dry. Divide the asparagus evenly between all the sole fillets and roll the fish around them. Tuck the ends of the fillets under the asparagus evenly between all the sole fillets and roll the fish around them. Tuck the ends of the fillets under the asparagus and

place in a casserole. Pour over the water and 15ml/1 tbsp lemon juice. Cover the dish loosely and cook for 2-3 minutes on HIGH. Set aside and keep warm. Melt the butter in a small, deep bowl for 1 minute on HIGH. Beat the egg yolks, lemon juice, salt and Cayenne pepper together. Have a bowl of iced water ready. Pour the yolk mixture into the butter and beat well. Cook for 30 seconds on HIGH and beat well. Repeat the process until the sauce thickens – about 2 minutes. Put the sauce bowl into the iced water to stop the cooking. Pour over the hot fish and asparagus rolls to serve. Sprinkle on paprika if desired.

Sole with Limes and Chili Peppers

PREPARATION TIME: 15 minutes

MICROWAVE COOKING TIME: 6 minutes

SERVES: 4 people

900g/2lbs sole fillets
2 limes
1 green chili pepper, very thinly sliced
1 small bunch chives
30g/1oz/2 tbsps butter
Salt and pepper

Melt the butter in a large casserole for 1 minute on HIGH. Put in the fish and cook for 30 seconds each side on HIGH. Remove from the casserole and keep warm. Grate the peel off one of the limes, pare off the white pith and cut the lime into very thin rounds. Squeeze the remaining lime for its juice. Pour the lime juice into the casserole with the butter. Add the chili pepper slices and cook for 30 seconds on HIGH. Add the lime slices, rind and snipped chives. Season and pour over the fish fillets to serve.

Salmon with Tomato Chive Hollandaise

PREPARATION TIME: 15 minutes

MICROWAVE COOKING TIME: 4 minutes

SERVES: 4 people

4 salmon fillets or tail portions
2 tomatoes, peeled, seeded and chopped
30ml/2 tbsps snipped chives
3 egg yolks
120g/4oz/½ cup butter
5ml/1 tsp red wine vinegar
Salt and pepper

Poach the fish fillets in enough water to come half way up the side of the fillets. Cover loosely and cook for 2 minutes on HIGH. Keep warm. Beat the yolks with salt, pepper and chives. Add the vinegar and set aside. Melt the butter for 1 minute on HIGH in a small, deep bowl. Beat the yolks into the butter. Have a bowl of iced water ready. Put the sauce ingredients into the oven and cook for 20 seconds on HIGH. Stir and cook for 20 seconds more. Repeat until the sauce thickens – about 2 minutes. Put the bowl into the iced water to stop the cooking process. Add the tomatoes to the sauce and serve with the salmon fillets.

Sole Bonne Femme

PREPARATION TIME: 20 minutes

MICROWAVE COOKING TIME: 8-11 minutes

SERVES: 4 people

900g/2lbs sole fillets
225g/8oz whole mushrooms, stalks removed
120g/4oz button or pickling onions, peeled
140ml/¼ pint/½ cup white wine
1 bay leaf

WHITE SAUCE
30g/1oz/2 tbsps butter or margarine
30g/1oz/2 tbsps flour/plain flour
140ml/¼ pint/½ cup milk
Salt and pepper

BUTTER SAUCE
2 egg yolks
60g/2oz/¼ cup butter
7ml/½ tbsp white wine vinegar
Salt and pepper

For the butter sauce, melt 60g/2oz/¼ cup butter in a small, deep bowl for 30 seconds on HIGH. Mix the egg yolks, vinegar, salt and pepper together and beat into the butter. Have a bowl of iced water ready. Cook the sauce for 15 seconds on HIGH and beat well. Repeat until the sauce has thickened – about 1 minute. Put immediately into a bowl of iced water to stop the cooking. Set the sauce aside. Tuck the ends of each sole fillet under and place the fish into a large casserole. Add the mushrooms, onions, wine and bay leaf. Cover loosely and cook for 5-6 minutes on HIGH. Arrange the fish, mushrooms and onions in a clean casserole or serving dish and keep warm. In a small bowl melt the remaining butter on HIGH for 30 seconds. Stir in the flour, milk, cooking liquid from the fish, salt and pepper. Cook for 2-3 minutes on HIGH, stirring frequently until thickened. Beat in the butter sauce and pour over the fish to serve.

Cod with Bacon

PREPARATION TIME: 15 minutes

MICROWAVE COOKING TIME: 12 minutes

SERVES: 4 people

4 fillets of cod
60ml/2oz/¼ cup white wine
8 strips bacon/streaky bacon, rind and bones removed
1 green pepper, diced
2 green/spring onions, chopped
15g/½ oz/1 tbsp flour/plain flour
140ml/¼ pint/½ cup milk
1 bay leaf
Salt and pepper

Put the cod, wine and bay leaf into a large casserole. Cover loosely and cook on HIGH for 3 minutes. Set aside. Heat a browning dish for 3 minutes on HIGH. Chop the bacon

Facing page: Sole Bonne Femme (top) and Salmon with Tomato Chive Hollandaise (bottom).

roughly, put it into the browning dish and cook for 2-3 minutes on HIGH. Stir frequently until the bacon has browned. Add the pepper and onion and cook for 30 seconds on HIGH. Stir in the flour, milk, salt, pepper and liquid from the fish. Cook for 2-3 minutes on HIGH, stirring frequently until the sauce has thickened. Pour over the fish and re-heat for 30 seconds on HIGH. Serve with parsley new potatoes.

Sole with Oranges

PREPARATION TIME: 15 minutes

MICROWAVE COOKING TIME: 5 minutes

SERVES: 4 people

900g/2lbs sole fillets
200ml/6 fl oz/¾ cup orange juice
15ml/1 tbsp lemon juice
10g/2 tsps butter
10g/2 tsps flour
200ml/6 fl oz/¾ cup heavy/double
  cream
15ml/1 tbsp chopped basil
Salt and pepper

GARNISH
2 oranges, peeled and cut in segments
Fresh basil leaves, if available

Tuck in the ends of the sole fillets. Put into a casserole with the orange and lemon juice. Cover loosely and cook on HIGH for 2 minutes. Set aside. Melt the butter in a small, deep bowl for 30 seconds on HIGH. Add the flour and fish cooking liquid. Stir in the cream, basil, salt and pepper, and cook, uncovered, for 2 minutes on HIGH. Stir frequently until the sauce thickens. Pour over the fish and serve with the orange segments and basil leaves.

Cod with Crumb Topping

PREPARATION TIME: 10 minutes

MICROWAVE COOKING TIME: 5-7 minutes

SERVES: 4 people

4 cod fillets
Lemon juice
140ml/¼ pint/½ cup water

TOPPING
60g/2oz/4 tbsps butter or margarine
180g/6oz/1½ cups seasoned breadcrumbs
30ml/2 tbsp paprika
60g/2oz/¼ cup grated Parmesan cheese
30ml/1oz/2 tbsps sesame seeds
Salt and pepper

GARNISH
Lemon wedges

Heat a browning dish for 3 minutes on HIGH. Melt the butter in the dish and add the breadcrumbs. Stir well and heat for 1 minute on HIGH to lightly brown. Add the remaining

This page: Cod with Crumb Topping (top) and Cod with Bacon (bottom). Facing page: Sole with Limes and Chili Peppers (top) and Sole with Oranges (bottom).

ingredients and heat for 1 minute more on HIGH. Set aside. Put the cod, a squeeze of lemon juice, and water into a casserole. Cover loosely and cook for 3-4 minutes on HIGH. Drain the fillets and top each one with the breadcrumb mixture. Heat through for 30 seconds on HIGH. Serve with lemon wedges.

Lychee Sole

PREPARATION TIME: 20 minutes

MICROWAVE COOKING TIME:
4-5 minutes

SERVES: 4 people

900g/2lbs sole fillets
225g/8oz lychees (canned or fresh),
  peeled
225g/8oz can pineapple chunks, 140ml/
  ¼ pint/½ cup juice reserved
Juice and rind of 2 limes
15-30g/½-1oz/1-2 tbsps sugar
15ml/½ fl oz/1 tbsp light soy sauce

10ml/2 tsps cornstarch/cornflour
2 green/spring onions, shredded
Salt and pepper

With a swivel peeler, peel strips off
the limes, and cut into thin slivers.
Cover well and set aside. Squeeze the
lime juice, and mix with the
pineapple juice, sugar, soy sauce and
constarch in a small, deep bowl. Fold
the fish fillets in half and place in a
large casserole, thinner ends of the
fillets towards the middle of the dish.
Pour over enough water to cover
1.5cm (½") of the sides of the fillets.
Cover the dish loosely and cook for

**This page: Lychee Sole. Facing
page: Sole Italienne (top) and
Halibut and Green Grapes
(bottom).**

2 minutes on HIGH. Set aside and
keep warm. Cook the sauce
ingredients for 2-3 minutes on
HIGH stirring often until thickened.
Add the cooking liquid from the fish,
strained. Stir in the pineapple
chunks, lychees, green/spring onions
and lime rind. Add a pinch of salt
and pepper and pour the sauce over
the fish. Serve with fried rice or chow
mein noodles.

Halibut and Green Grapes

PREPARATION TIME: 10 minutes

MICROWAVE COOKING TIME: 10-13 minutes

SERVES: 4 people

900g/2lbs halibut steaks
1 small bunch green seedless grapes
140ml/¼ pint/½ cup white wine
Lemon juice
200ml/6 fl oz/¾ cup heavy/double cream
5ml/1 tsp tarragon
Salt and pepper

Put the fish into a casserole and pour on the wine and lemon juice. Cook for 4-5 minutes on HIGH. Remove the fish from the casserole, cover and keep warm. Heat the wine for 2-3 minutes on HIGH to reduce by half. Cut the grapes in half if large, and add to the wine. Add the tarragon, salt and pepper, and cream. Heat through for 1 minute on HIGH. Pour over the fish to serve.

Halibut in Sesame Ginger Sauce

PREPARATION TIME: 20 minutes

MICROWAVE COOKING TIME: 6 minutes

SERVES: 4 people

4 halibut steaks
2 carrots, cut in Julienne strips
280ml/½ pint/1 cup water
45ml/1½ fl oz/3 tbsps ginger wine
60g/2oz/¼ cup light brown sugar
60g/2oz/¼ cup sesame seeds
30ml/2 tbsps chopped fresh ginger root
30ml/2 tbsps rice vinegar
10ml/2 tsps cornstarch/cornflour
Dash of sesame seed oil
Salt and pepper

Put the fish into a casserole with the ginger wine and water. Cover and cook for 2 minutes on HIGH. Put the carrots into a small bowl with 15ml/1 tbsp water. Cover loosely and cook for 1 minute on HIGH. Leave to stand while preparing the sauce. Combine the sugar, cornstarch,

ginger, sesame seed oil, rice vinegar, sesame seeds and cooking liquid from the fish. Cook for 4 minutes on HIGH, stirring often until thickened. Add the carrot, salt and pepper and pour over the fish to serve.

Sole Italienne

PREPARATION TIME: 15 minutes

MICROWAVE COOKING TIME: 6-8 minutes

SERVES: 4 people

8 sole fillets
120g/4oz Parma ham
140ml/¼ pint/½ cup white wine
15g/½ oz/1 tbsp butter or margarine
15g/½ oz/1 tbsp flour/plain flour
200ml/6 fl oz/¾ cup heavy/double cream
Pinch sage
Pinch thyme
Pinch chopped parsley
1 bay leaf
Salt and pepper

GARNISH
Fresh sage or bay leaves

Cut the ham into 1.5cm (½") strips. Wrap the ham strips lattice fashion around the fish and tuck the ends underneath. Put into a casserole with the bay leaf and wine. Cook for 3-4 minutes on HIGH. Remove the fish from the dish, cover and keep it warm. Discard the bay leaf. Melt the butter for 30 seconds on HIGH in a small casserole. Stir in the flour and fish cooking liquid, and add the thyme, parsley, sage, salt and pepper. Cook for 2 minutes on HIGH and stir in the cream. Cook for a further 1 minute on HIGH and spoon over the fish. Garnish with sage or bay leaves.

Fillets of Salmon with Peppercorn Sauce

PREPARATION TIME: 15 minutes

MICROWAVE COOKING TIME: 8-12 minutes

SERVES: 4 people

1 side of salmon, about 675-900g/ 1½-2lbs
30g/1oz/2 tbsps butter or margarine
280ml/½ pint/1 cup heavy/double cream
90ml/3 fl oz/⅓ cup dry vermouth
30ml/1 tbsp canned green peppercorns, rinsed and drained
Salt and pepper

Slice the salmon horizontally into very thin slices. Heat a browning dish for 3 minutes on HIGH. Drop in the butter and heat for 30 seconds on HIGH. Lay in the salmon slices and cook for 30 seconds each side. Cook the fish in several batches. Remove the cooked fish from the dish, cover it, and keep it warm. Pour the vermouth into the dish and add the peppercorns. Cook on HIGH for 2 minutes or until reduced by half. Add the cream, stir well, and cook for 2-3 minutes on HIGH until bubbling. Season with salt and pepper. Pour over the salmon scallops to serve. Serve with lightly cooked green/French beans or peapods/mangetout.

Fruits of the Sea

PREPARATION TIME: 15 minutes

MICROWAVE COOKING TIME: 5-9 minutes

SERVES: 4 people

900g/2 lbs mixture of:
    raw scallops, cut in half
    raw shrimp/prawns, peeled
    1 lobster tail, shelled and cut into 2.5cm (1") chunks
    sole fillets, cut into 5cm (2") chunks
    oysters, shelled
    mussels, shelled
280ml/½ pint/1 cup white wine
10ml/2 tsps cornstarch/cornflour
15ml/1 tbsp lemon juice
140ml/¼ pint/½ cup whole milk yogurt
30ml/1 oz/2 tbsps chopped chives
225g/8oz edible seaweed, soaked or cooked in 30ml/2 tbsps water
Salt and pepper

Facing page: Fruits of the Sea (top) and Fillets of Salmon with Peppercorn Sauce (bottom).

Cook all the seafood in the wine for 2-3 minutes on HIGH. Cook the seaweed with 30ml/1 fl oz/2 tbsps water for 1-2 minutes on HIGH. Mix the cornstarch and lemon juice. Remove the fish from the casserole and arrange on a serving dish with the seaweed. Combine the cornstarch and lemon juice with the cooking liquid from the seafood. Cook for 2-3 minutes on HIGH, stirring frequently until thickened. Add the yogurt and chives and heat through for 30 seconds on HIGH. Season with salt and pepper and pour over the seafood.

Salmon in Madeira

PREPARATION TIME: 15 minutes

MICROWAVE COOKING TIME: 8 minutes

SERVES: 4 people

4 salmon steaks, about 2.5cm (1") thick
225g/8oz mushrooms, stalks trimmed
5 sprigs fresh rosemary
280ml/½ pint/1 cup Rainwater Madeira
140ml/¼ pint/½ cup water
15g/½ oz/1 tbsp butter or margarine
15g/½ oz/1 tbsp flour/plain flour
Small pinch ground cloves
60ml/2 fl oz/¼ cup heavy/double cream.
Salt and pepper

Put the salmon steaks in a casserole with the Madeira. Strip the leaves off one sprig of rosemary and add to the salmon. Cover the dish loosely and cook for 5 minutes on HIGH. Add the mushrooms half way through the cooking time. Melt the butter in a small casserole for 2 minutes on HIGH until browning slightly. Add the flour and cook for 1 minute on HIGH. Stir in the cooking liquid from the fish and a pinch of cloves. Season with salt and pepper. Arrange the salmon and mushrooms on plates and pour over the Madeira sauce. Drizzle 15ml/1 tbsp cream over each salmon steak and garnish each with a sprig of fresh rosemary.

Curried Cod Nuggets

PREPARATION TIME: 15 minutes

MICROWAVE COOKING TIME: 7 minutes

SERVES: 4 people

900g/2 lbs cod, cut in 5cm (2") chunks
60ml/2 oz/¼ cup lime juice
200ml/6 fl oz/¾ cup water
30g/1oz/2 tbsps butter or margarine
30g/1oz/2 tbsps flour/plain flour
1 large onion, chopped
15g/1 tbsp curry powder
140ml/¼ pint/½ cup orange juice
2 oranges, peeled and segmented
2 tomatoes, peeled and seeded
Desiccated coconut

Combine the cod, lime juice and water in a large casserole. Cover loosely and cook on HIGH for 2 minutes. Set aside and keep warm. Melt the butter for 30 seconds on HIGH in a small, deep bowl. Add the

This page: Curried Cod Nuggets. Facing page: Halibut in Sesame Ginger Sauce (top) and Salmon in Madeira (bottom).

onion, cover loosely and cook for 1 minute on HIGH. Stir in the curry powder and cook for 1 minute on HIGH. Add the flour, orange juice and cooking liquid from the fish. Stir well and cook, uncovered, for 2-3 minutes. Stir often until the sauce is thick. Slice the tomatoes into thin strips and add to the sauce with the orange segments. Cook the sauce for 10 seconds on HIGH to heat the orange and tomato through. Pour the sauce over the cod nuggets and sprinkle with desiccated coconut.

Monkfish and Ribbons

PREPARATION TIME: 20 minutes

MICROWAVE COOKING TIME:
5-6 minutes

SERVES: 4 people

900g/2lbs monkfish tails
140ml/¼ pint/½ cup white wine
2 carrots, peeled
2 zucchini/courgettes, ends trimmed
1 large or 2 small leeks, washed and
   trimmed, retaining some green
140ml/¼ pint/½ cup heavy/double
   cream
30ml/2 tbsps chopped parsley
2.5ml/½ tsp ground oregano
1 bay leaf
Salt and pepper

Cut the monkfish tails into 1.5cm
(½″) rounds. Put the pieces into a
casserole with the wine and bay leaf.
Cover loosely and cook for 2
minutes on HIGH. Set aside and
keep warm. With a swivel vegetable
peeler, pare thin ribbons of carrot and
zucchini/courgettes. Cut the leeks in
half lengthwise and then into 1.5cm
(½″) strips. Put the vegetables into a
small casserole with 15ml/1 tbsp
water. Cover loosely and cook for 1
minute on HIGH. Set aside. Remove
the fish from the casserole and heat
the wine for 2-3 minutes on HIGH
to reduce. Pour in the cream, and add
the oregano, salt and pepper. Heat
through for 30 seconds on HIGH.
Pour the sauce over the fish and
sprinkle on the chopped parsley.
Surround with the vegetable ribbons
to serve.

Cod Steaks with Mushrooms

PREPARATION TIME: 15 minutes

MICROWAVE COOKING TIME:
5-7 minutes

SERVES: 4 people

4-8 cod steaks, depending on size
140ml/¼ pint/½ cup white wine
1 bay leaf
2 shallots, finely chopped
30g/1oz/2 tbsps butter
180g/6oz/1½ cups sliced mushrooms
15g/1 tbsp flour/plain flour
140ml/¼ pint/½ cup milk
5ml/1 tsp Worcestershire sauce
5ml/1 tsp chopped parsley
Salt and pepper

Put the cod and wine into a casserole
with the bay leaf and shallot. Cover
loosely and cook for 2 minutes on
HIGH. Leave covered and set aside.
Melt the butter in a small bowl for
30 seconds on HIGH. Add the
mushrooms. Cover loosely and cook
for 1 minute on HIGH to soften
slightly. Stir in the flour, milk and
Worcestershire sauce. Remove the
bay leaf from the fish and add the
fish cooking liquid to the sauce
ingredients. Cook, uncovered, for 2-3
minutes on HIGH, stirring often
until thickened. Add salt, pepper and
parsley. Pour over the cod to serve.

Sole Aurora

PREPARATION TIME: 15 minutes

MICROWAVE COOKING TIME:
6-7 minutes

SERVES: 4 people

900g/2lbs sole fillets
140ml/¼ pint/½ cup white wine
1 bay leaf

SAUCE
30g/1oz/2 tbsps butter or margarine
30g/1oz/2 tbsps flour/plain flour
280ml/½ pint/1 cup milk
Rind and juice of 1 orange
15ml/1 tbsp tomato purée/paste
Salt and pepper

GARNISH
4 tomatoes, peeled, seeded and cut into
   thin strips

Cook the fish with the wine and the
bay leaf for 3 minutes on HIGH in a
loosely covered casserole. Melt the
butter in a small, deep bowl for
30 seconds on HIGH. Add the flour,
milk, tomato paste, fish cooking

**Facing page: Monkfish and
Ribbons.**

liquid, salt and pepper. Cook for 2-3 minutes on HIGH, stirring frequently until thickened. Add the rind and juice of the orange and cook for 30 seconds more on HIGH. Pour the sauce over the fish and top with the tomato strips.

Sea Bass and Fennel

PREPARATION TIME: 15 minutes

MICROWAVE COOKING TIME: 23 minutes

SERVES: 4 people

1 sea bass, weighing 900g-1kg/2-2¼ lbs, cleaned and trimmed
2 bulbs Florentine fennel
4 oranges
Juice of 1 lemon
1 tbsp anise liqueur
430ml/¾ pint/1½ cups whole-milk yogurt
Salt
Coarsely ground pepper

GARNISH
Samphire
Orange slices

Squeeze the juice from one of the oranges and slice the others. Sprinkle the inside of the bass with salt and put it into a large, shallow casserole. Pour over the orange juice and lemon

This page: Sole Aurora (left) and Cod Steaks with Mushrooms (right). Facing page: Sea Bass and Fennel.

juice, cover and cook for 20 minutes on HIGH. Carefully lift out the fish and keep it warm. Cook the fennel in 30ml/2 tbsps water for 2 minutes on HIGH and set aside. Stir the liqueur, pepper and yogurt into the fish cooking liquid and heat through for 30 seconds on HIGH. Do not let the sauce boil. Peel the skin from the fish if desired and pour over the sauce. Garnish with the samphire and orange slices to serve. Prepare with other varieties of large whole fish if desired.

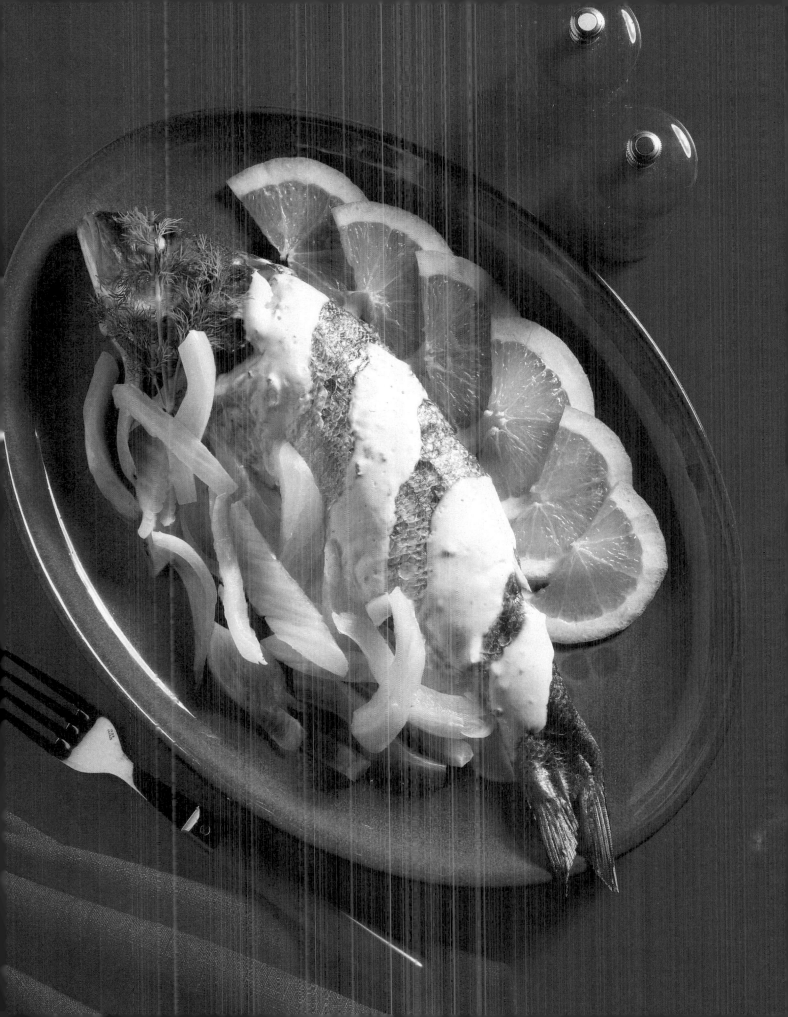

Microwave
MEAT & POULTRY

Microwave
MEAT & POULTRY

When you cook in a microwave oven you get far more for your meat money. Microwave roasting means less shrinkage and, contrary to popular belief, meat *will* brown. Leave a thin layer of fat on the roast/joint, or rub butter into a chicken or turkey and the high heat of the microwave oven will turn the fat golden brown. Alternatively, there are many marinades, bastes and coatings to give appetizing color to meat, poultry and game.

Because liquids evaporate much more slowly in a microwave oven, there will be more meat juices left to make good sauces and gravies. If you want, use a browning dish to brown the flour for gravies. Red wine, soy sauce, gravy browning and spices also give good color to brown sauces.

In general, stews and braises should be cooked on MEDIUM, regardless of what variety of meat is used. The highest setting in a microwave oven will toughen the cuts of meat used in stews and braises. When cooking small cuts of meat such as chops or steaks in a sauce, a medium setting is also recommended for a tender result. Stir-frying and pan-frying are both possible with a browning dish and the highest setting. Offal/variety meats cook very quickly, so a high setting suits them as well.

When roasting poultry and game birds, cover the legs and wings with foil to prevent them from drying out. Uncover for a portion of the cooking time and the whole bird will be evenly cooked. Depending on your oven, you may find that all roast meats need to be covered with foil on both ends for part of their cooking time. This is especially important for roasts/joints that are uneven in thickness.

Microwave roasts must be left to stand after cooking just like any roast meat. The standing time helps to finish off the cooking, so microwaved roast meat, poultry and game are usually covered for 5-15 minutes before carving.

Special microwave meat thermometers take the guesswork out of roasting, but times will vary from oven to oven. The following chart will serve as a quick reference, but is meant only as a guideline.

Time and Setting per 450g/1lb		
	HIGH	**MEDIUM**
Beef		
Rare	6-7 minutes	11-13 minutes
Medium	7-8 minutes	13-15 minutes
Well done	8-9 minutes	15-17 minutes
Chicken (whole)	6-8 minutes	9-11 minutes
Duck (whole)	6-8 minutes	9-11 minutes
Leg of Lamb	8-10 minutes	11-13 minutes
Pork	9-11 minutes	13-15 minutes
Veal	8-9 minutes	11-12 minutes
Steaks (7.5cm/1½" thick)		
Rare	9 minutes	
Medium rare	10 minutes	
Medium	12 minutes	
Well done	14 minutes	

There is also a method of roasting, Hazelnut Lamb is an example, which cuts down on the cooking time and depends on a longer standing time to finish cooking to the desired doneness. Also, meats and poultry can be roasted for part of their cooking time on HIGH and part on MEDIUM.

All the recipes were tested in both a conventional 700 watt microwave oven and a Combination microwave-convection oven with a maximum setting of 600 watts. The Combination oven does a superb job of roasting. It is nearly as fast as the conventional microwave oven, yet browns and crisps like a regular convection oven. These new ovens have a variety of settings, so it is best carefully to follow the instruction booklet that each manufacturer provides. Either way, the time saving is impressive, and the result delicious when a microwave oven is used on meat, poultry and game.

Microwave

MEAT & POULTRY

LAMB DISHES

Lamb Shanks with Leeks and Rosemary

PREPARATION TIME: 15 minutes

MICROWAVE COOKING TIME:
45 minutes

SERVES: 4 people

30ml/2 tbsps vegetable oil
900g-1kg/2-2¼ lbs lamb shanks
1 clove garlic, roughly chopped
2 sprigs fresh rosemary
280ml/½ pint/1 cup red wine
280ml/½ pint/1 cup beef stock
15g/1 tbsp butter
15g/1 tbsp flour
2-4 leeks, washed and thinly sliced
Salt and pepper

Heat the oil in a browning dish for 5 minutes on HIGH. Put in the lamb shanks and cook for 5 minutes on HIGH. Turn the lamb over and cook for further 5 minutes on HIGH. Add the garlic, rosemary, salt and pepper, wine and stock. Cover and cook on MEDIUM for 25 minutes. Melt the butter in a small bowl for 30 seconds on HIGH. Stir in the flour. Pour on the cooking juices from the lamb and stir well. Pour the sauce over the lamb and scatter over the sliced leeks. Cook a further 5 minutes on HIGH, until the leeks soften and the sauce has thickened. Remove the rosemary before serving.

Spiced Lamb Chops with Peaches

PREPARATION TIME: 15 minutes

MICROWAVE COOKING TIME:
20 minutes

SERVES: 4 people

4 lamb chops, fat slightly trimmed
30g/1oz/2 tbsps butter or margarine
15ml/1 tbsp ground allspice
15ml/1 tbsp ground ginger
15ml/1 tbsp brown sugar
Salt and pepper
225g/8oz sliced peaches, juice reserved
45ml/3 tbsps soy sauce
45ml/3 tbsps brown sugar
30ml/2 tbsps cider vinegar
5ml/1 tsp cornstarch/cornflour
10ml/2 tsps water

This page: Spiced Lamb Chops with Peaches (top) and Lamb Shanks with Leeks and Rosemary (bottom). Facing page: Orange Glazed Lamb with Haricot Beans.

Heat a browning dish for 5 minutes on HIGH. Drop in the butter and heat 30 seconds on HIGH. Mix 15ml/1 tbsp brown sugar with the spices, salt and pepper and rub into both sides of the chops. Fry the chops in the butter on HIGH for

2 minutes each side. Mix the peach juice with the soy sauce, remaining brown sugar, vinegar and additional salt and pepper. Pour over the chops and cover loosely. Lower the setting to MEDIUM and cook 10 minutes, turning the chops once and stirring the liquid frequently. Remove the chops and set aside to keep warm. Mix the cornstarch/cornflour with the water and stir into the hot liquid. Cook on HIGH for 1 minute, stirring frequently until the sauce is clear. Add the peaches to heat through for 30 seconds on HIGH and serve with the chops.

Lamb in Sour Cream Dill Sauce

PREPARATION TIME: 15 minutes

MICROWAVE COOKING TIME:
31 minutes

SERVES: 4 people

900g/2lbs leg of lamb, cut into 2.5cm/
    1 inch cubes
1 onion, sliced
1 bay leaf
15ml/1 tbsp dried dill or dill seed
430ml/¾ pint/1½ cups light stock
140ml/4 fl oz/½ cup white wine
45g/1½ oz/3 tbsps butter or margarine
45g/1½ oz/3 tbsps flour
30g/2 tbsps chopped fresh dill or 15g/
    1 tbsp dried dill
140ml/¼ pint/½ cup sour cream
Salt and pepper

Make sure all the fat is trimmed from the lamb. Put the lamb cubes, onion, bay leaf, dried dill or dill seed, salt, pepper, stock and wine into a casserole. Cover and cook on MEDIUM for 25 minutes. Set aside to keep warm. Melt the butter 30 seconds on HIGH. Stir in the flour and strain on the stock from the lamb. Stir well and cook for 5 minutes on HIGH, stirring frequently, until thickened. Add the dill, adjust the seasoning and stir in the sour cream. Pour over the lamb and heat through 1 minute on HIGH, without boiling. Serve with rice or pasta.

Orange Glazed Lamb with Haricot Beans

PREPARATION TIME: 15 minutes

MICROWAVE COOKING TIME:
24 minutes

SERVES: 4 people

2 racks/best-end necks of lamb

GLAZE
60g/2oz/¼ cup dark brown sugar
60ml/2 fl oz/¼ cup red wine
15ml/1 tbsp red wine vinegar
Juice and rind of 1 orange

ACCOMPANIMENT
450g/1lb canned haricot/navy beans or
    flageolets, drained
4 green/spring onions, chopped
60ml/2 fl oz/¼ cup dry white wine
Pinch thyme
Salt and pepper

Trim some of the fat from the lamb and score the remaining fat. Mix the glaze ingredients together and brush over the lamb. Put the lamb on a roasting rack. The bone ends may be covered with foil to protect them during the cooking. Cook on MEDIUM for 10 minutes. Raise the setting to HIGH and cook for 5 minutes, basting often during the whole of the cooking time. Leave to stand 5 minutes before carving. Cook for 20 minutes on the Combination setting of a microwave convection oven until the fat has browned. Mix the beans, wine, onions, thyme, salt and pepper together and cook 4 minutes on HIGH. Reheat any remaining glaze and pour over the lamb. Serve with the beans.

Peppercorn Lamb

PREPARATION TIME: 13 minutes

MICROWAVE COOKING TIME:
21-22 minutes

SERVES: 4 people

675g/1½ lbs lamb fillet or meat from the
    leg cut into 5mm/¼ inch slices
60g/2oz/4 tbsps butter or margarine

2 shallots, finely chopped
1 clove garlic, finely minced
45g/1½ oz/3 tbsps flour
5ml/1 tsp ground allspice
280ml/½ pint/1 cup beef stock
15ml/1 tbsp canned green peppercorns,
    rinsed and drained
2 caps pimento cut into thin strips
5ml/1 tsp tomato paste/purée
60ml/2 fl oz/¼ cup heavy/double cream
Salt and pepper

Heat a browning dish for 5 minutes on HIGH. Melt the butter for 1 minute on HIGH and add the slices of lamb. Cook for 2 minutes on HIGH, in 2 or 3 batches. Remove the meat and set aside. Cook the shallots and flour to brown slightly. Add the garlic, allspice, stock and tomato paste/purée. Season with salt and pepper and cook 2-3 minutes on HIGH, until starting to thicken. Add the lamb, cover and cook 10 minutes on MEDIUM, or until the lamb is tender. Add the peppercorns, pimento and cream and cook for 2 minutes on HIGH. Serve with rice.

Leg of Lamb with Aromatic Spices

PREPARATION TIME: 15 minutes

MICROWAVE COOKING TIME:
31 minutes, plus
5-15 minutes standing time

SERVES: 6-8 people

1.5kg/3lbs leg of lamb, fat completely
    trimmed off
140ml/¼ pint/½ cup stock

MARINADE
280ml/½ pint/1 cup plain yogurt
1 small piece fresh ginger root, grated
5ml/1 tsp crushed coriander seeds
1.25ml/¼ tsp cloves
5ml/1 tsp curry powder
5ml/1 tsp cumin
1.25ml/¼ tsp cardamom seeds, removed
    from the pods
1 clove garlic, minced
Salt and pepper

Facing page: Lamb in Sour Cream Dill Sauce (top) and Peppercorn Lamb (bottom).

SAUCE
Remaining marinade and stock
15ml/1 tbsp chopped fresh coriander
140ml/¼ pint/½ cup plain yogurt

Blend all the marinade ingredients together. In the lamb, make incisions with a sharp knife about 5cm/ 2 inches apart. Place the lamb in a shallow casserole. Push some of the marinade into each cut and spread the remaining marinade over the surface of the lamb. Cover and leave overnight in the refrigerator. Pour the stock into the casserole around the lamb. Cover the casserole loosely and cook on HIGH for 12 minutes, basting frequently. Turn the lamb over and cook a further 15 minutes, basting frequently. Leave the lamb to stand for 5 minutes in a covered dish if serving rare. For well-done or medium lamb leave it to stand for 15-20 minutes. Meanwhile heat the remaining marinade and stock for 3 minutes on MEDIUM. Stir in the yogurt and coriander leaves. Add more salt and pepper if necessary and heat through 1 minute on HIGH. Do not allow the sauce to boil. Serve with the carved lamb.

Hazelnut Lamb

PREPARATION TIME: 15 minutes

MICROWAVE COOKING TIME:
25-30 minutes, plus
5-15 minutes standing time

SERVES: 6-8 people

2kg/4½ lbs leg of lamb
1 clove garlic, finely minced
120g/4oz/1 cup dry breadcrumbs
120g/4oz/1 cup ground, roasted
*   hazelnuts*
30ml/2 tbsps chopped parsley
60g/2oz/¼ cup butter
Salt and pepper

Trim the fat off the lamb. Mix together the remaining ingredients, except the breadcrumbs. Spread the hazelnut paste over the surface of the lamb and press over the crumbs. Cook 25-30 minutes on MEDIUM. Increase the setting to HIGH for 2 minutes. Cook 40 minutes on a Combination setting of a microwave

convection oven. Leave the lamb to stand, loosely covered, 5 minutes before carving for rare. Leave 10-15 minutes if medium to well-done lamb is desired. Serve with minted new potatoes and peapods/mangetout.

Moroccan Lamb

PREPARATION TIME: 20 minutes

MICROWAVE COOKING TIME:
35 minutes

SERVES: 4 people

790g/1¾ lbs lamb fillet or meat from the
*   leg cut in 2.5cm/1 inch cubes*
1 clove garlic, minced
10ml/2 tsps ground cinnamon
1.25ml/¼ tsp ground cloves
1.25ml/¼ tsp ground cumin
10ml/2 tsps paprika

This page: Hazelnut Lamb. Facing page: Leg of Lamb with Aromatic Spices.

1 large red pepper
570ml/1 pint/2 cups light beef stock
340g/¾ lb okra, trimmed
120g/¼ lb/1 cup whole blanched
*   almonds*
60g/2oz/¼ cup currants
15ml/1 tbsp honey
15ml/1 tbsp lemon juice
Salt and pepper

Combine the lamb, garlic, spices, red pepper salt and pepper in a large casserole. Add the stock, cover the dish and cook on MEDIUM for 25 minutes. Add the okra, currants and almonds. Cook a further 5 minutes on MEDIUM. Remove the

meat and vegetables and almonds to a serving dish. Add the honey and lemon juice to the sauce and cook on HIGH for 5 minutes to reduce it slightly. Pour over the lamb and serve with rice.

Lamb Hot-Pot

PREPARATION TIME: 15 minutes

MICROWAVE COOKING TIME:
30 minutes

SERVES: 4 people

2 large onions, peeled and thinly sliced
30ml/2 tbsps oil
450g/1lb ground/minced lamb
30ml/2 tbsps chopped parsley
Pinch thyme
225g/8oz whole mushrooms
225g/8oz/1 cup canned tomatoes
30ml/2 tbsps Worcestershire sauce
3 potatoes, peeled and thinly sliced
1 red pepper, cut in rings
1 green pepper, cut in rings
Salt and pepper

**This page: Navarin of Lamb.
Facing page: Moroccan Lamb
(top) and Lamb Hot-Pot (bottom).**

GARNISH
Fresh bay leaves

In a large casserole, heat the oil for 30 seconds on HIGH. Put in the onions and cover the casserole loosely. Cook 5 minutes on HIGH to soften the onions. Add the lamb and thyme and cook 10 minutes on MEDIUM, mashing the lamb with a fork to break it up while it cooks. Add the mushrooms, tomatoes, parsley, salt and pepper and Worcestershire sauce. Arrange the slices of potato neatly on top of the lamb mixture and sprinkle with more salt and pepper. Cover the casserole and cook on MEDIUM for 15 minutes or until the potatoes are tender. Cook on a Combination

setting of a microwave convection oven for 15 minutes or until potatoes are cooked and slightly browned. Three minutes before the end of cooking time, arrange the pepper rings overlapping on top of the potatoes. Garnish with fresh bay leaves to serve.

Navarin of Lamb

PREPARATION TIME: 20 minutes

MICROWAVE COOKING TIME:
40 minutes

SERVES: 4 people

4 lamb chops
30ml/2 tbsps oil
30g/2 tbsps flour/plain flour
2 cloves garlic, finely minced
15ml/1 tbsp tomato paste/purée
280ml/½ pint/1 cup white wine
570ml/1 pint/2 cups stock
*2 sprigs fresh rosemary or 15ml/1 tbsp
  dried*
1 sprig fresh thyme or 5ml/1 tsp dried
Salt and pepper

GARNISH
2 carrots, cut lengthwise in quarters
*120g/4oz green/French beans, trimmed
  and cut in 5cm/2 inch pieces*
*8 small new potatoes, scrubbed but not
  peeled*
2 sticks celery, cut in 5cm/2 inch strips
12 small mushrooms, left whole
4 small turnips, peeled

Heat a browning dish 5 minutes on HIGH. Pour in the oil and put in the lamb chops. Cook 1 minute on HIGH. Turn the chops over and cook 2 minutes on HIGH on the other side. Remove the chops and stir in the flour, tomato purée/paste, wine, stock and garlic. Cook for 2 minutes on HIGH, stirring twice. Season with salt and pepper and return the chops to the dish or transfer the whole to a casserole. Cover and cook on MEDIUM for 15 minutes. Add the vegetables, except the beans and mushrooms, and cook 15 minutes further on MEDIUM. Add remaining vegetables 5 minutes before the end of cooking. Remove the herbs, if using fresh, and the bay leaf before serving.

PORK AND HAM

Glazed Ham and Spiced Peaches

PREPARATION TIME: 20 minutes

MICROWAVE COOKING TIME:
57 minutes, plus
5 minutes standing time

SERVES: 6-8 people

1.5kg/3lb ham/gammon, boneless and pre-cooked

GLAZE
30ml/2 tbsps Dijon mustard
120g/4oz/½ cup dark brown sugar
120g/4oz/1 cup dry breadcrumbs
Pinch powdered cloves
Pinch ginger

PEACHES
6 fresh peaches or 12 canned peach halves
120g/4oz/½ cup light brown sugar
5ml/1 tsp each ground cinnamon, cloves and allspice
140ml/¼ pint/½ cup water or canned peach juice
30ml/2 tbsps cider vinegar
12 walnut halves

If using fresh peaches, put them into a large bowl and cover with boiling water. Heat on HIGH for 3 minutes or until the water boils. Peel the peaches, cut in half and remove the stones. Mix the remaining ingredients for the peaches together and heat 2 minutes on HIGH, stirring frequently until the sugar dissolves. Add the peaches and cook 2 minutes on MEDIUM. Remove the peaches and cook the syrup a further 5 minutes on HIGH. Pour the syrup over the peaches and set them aside. Cover the ham with plastic wrap/cling film, or put into a roasting bag.

This page: Pork à l'Orange. Facing page: Glazed Ham and Spiced Peaches.

Cook on MEDIUM for 15 minutes per lb or ½ kg. Pour the glaze over during the last 10 minutes of cooking. Put a walnut half in the hollow of each peach. Let the ham stand 5 minutes before slicing. Serve either hot or cold with the peaches.

Pork à l'Orange

PREPARATION TIME: 15 minutes

MICROWAVE COOKING TIME:
24-25 minutes

SERVES: 4 people

30g/2 tbsps butter or margarine
675g/1½ lbs pork tenderloin/fillet cut in 1.25cm/½ inch slices
3 carrots, cut in 1.25cm/½ inch diagonal slices
3 small or 2 large leeks, washed and trimmed and cut in 1.25cm/½ inch diagonal slices
60g/2oz/¼ cup dried currants

1 clove garlic, finely minced
1 large onion, sliced
1 large green pepper, sliced
120g/4oz mushrooms, sliced
15ml/1 tbsp tomato paste/purée
30ml/2 tbsps molasses/treacle
225g/8oz canned tomatoes
1 bay leaf
Pinch Cayenne pepper
Salt and pepper

Melt the butter in a casserole for 30 seconds on HIGH and put in the pork pieces, garlic, onions and mushrooms. Cook 5 minutes on MEDIUM. Add the remaining ingredients and cook a further 5 minutes on MEDIUM, loosely covered. If the pork is not tender after 10 minutes, cook an additional 3 minutes on MEDIUM. Remove the bay leaf before serving.

Ginger Apricot Stuffed Pork

PREPARATION TIME: 15 minutes

MICROWAVE COOKING TIME:
33-34 minutes, plus
5 minutes standing time

SERVES: 6-8 people

1.5kg/3 lbs loin of pork, boned
570ml/1 pint/2 cups light stock
1 bay leaf
1 carrot, sliced

STUFFING
120g/4oz/¾lb dried apricots
30ml/2 tbsps green ginger wine
30ml/2 tbsps lemon juice
60ml/2 fl oz/¼ cup water
1 spring/green onion, finely chopped
Salt and pepper

SAUCE
280ml/½ pint/1 cup strained reserved
    stock from the pork
Apricot soaking liquid
30ml/1oz/2 tbsps butter or margarine
30ml/1oz/2 tbsps flour
Dash soy sauce

Mix the stuffing ingredients, except the onion, together in a bowl. Cover well and cook 1 minute on HIGH, then leave to stand to soften the

---

1.25ml/¼ tsp ground ginger
1 bay leaf
280ml/1½ pints/1 cup orange juice
60ml/2 fl oz/¼ cup orange liqueur
10ml/2 tsps cornstarch/cornflour
Salt and pepper

Heat a browning dish 5 minutes on HIGH. Drop in the butter and add the pork slices. Cook 2 minutes each side on HIGH. Cook the meat in 2 or 3 batches. Add the leeks, carrots, bay leaf, ginger, salt and pepper. Pour over the orange juice and cover the dish loosely. Cook 15 minutes on MEDIUM or until the pork and vegetables are tender. Add the currants during the last 3 minutes of cooking. Remove the pork and vegetables and keep them warm. Mix the liqueur and cornstarch/cornflour together and stir into the sauce. Cook, uncovered, 2 to 3

This page: Ginger Apricot Stuffed Pork. Facing page: Pork Creole (top) and Sausages, Apples and Cheese (bottom).

minutes on HIGH, stirring frequently until the sauce thickens and looks clear. Return the meat and vegetables to the sauce and stir carefully. Serve with rice.

Pork Creole

PREPARATION TIME: 15 minutes

MICROWAVE COOKING TIME:
13 minutes

SERVES: 4 people

15ml/1 tbsp butter
750g/1½ lbs lean pork shoulder or
    tenderloin/fillet cut into strips

apricots. Trim most of the fat from the pork. Turn the meat over and sprinkle the surface with pepper. Drain the apricots and reserve the juice. Spread the apricots evenly over the pork and sprinkle on the onion. Roll up the pork starting on the thickest side. Tie at even intervals with string. Place in a deep casserole with the bay leaf, stock and carrot. Cover well and cook 30 minutes on MEDIUM or until the pork is tender and no longer pink. Strain the stock and reserve it. Cover the pork and leave to stand 5 minutes before slicing. Melt the butter in a deep bowl for 30 seconds on HIGH. Stir in the flour and 280ml/½ pint/1 cup stock and the reserved apricot juice. Cook 2 to 3 minutes on HIGH to thicken. Add salt and pepper to taste and serve with the pork.

Speedy Ham Casserole

PREPARATION TIME: 10 minutes

MICROWAVE COOKING TIME: 6 minutes

SERVES: 4 people

225g/8oz cooked ham, cut in 1.25cm/ ½ inch strips
1 can concentrated cream of mushroom soup
1 can water chestnuts, drained and sliced
2 sticks celery, finely chopped
225g/8oz frozen, sliced green/French beans
30ml/1 fl oz/2 tbsps dry sherry
280ml/½ pint/1 cup light/single cream
Pinch thyme
Salt and pepper

TOPPING
1 can French-fried onions
or
60g/2oz/¼ cup seasoned breadcrumbs mixed with 5ml/1 tsp paprika

Mix all the ingredients, except the topping ingredients, together in a serving casserole. Cook 5 minutes on HIGH, stirring occasionally, or until the beans have cooked. Sprinkle on the topping and cook a further 1 minute on HIGH.

Sweet and Sour Ham

PREPARATION TIME: 20 minutes

MICROWAVE COOKING TIME: 2-3 minutes

SERVES: 4 people

450g/1lb cooked ham, cut into 1.25cm/ ½ inch cubes

SAUCE
60g/2oz/¼ cup brown sugar
60ml/2 fl oz/¼ cup rice vinegar
30ml/2 tbsps tomato ketchup
30ml/2 tbsps soy sauce
225g/8oz/1 can pineapple chunks/ pieces, drained and juice reserved
30g/1oz/2 tbsps cornstarch/cornflour
1 green pepper, sliced
2 green/spring onions, sliced diagonally
60g/2oz/½ cup blanched, whole almonds
3 tomatoes, quartered
Salt and pepper

Combine the sugar, vinegar, ketchup, soy sauce, cornstarch/cornflour and reserved pineapple juice and chunks. Add pepper, almonds, salt, pepper and ham. Cook 2-3 minutes on HIGH until the sauce clears and thickens. Add the tomatoes and green/spring onions and heat 30 seconds on HIGH. Serve with rice or crisp noodles.

Sausages, Apples and Cheese

PREPARATION TIME: 15 minutes

MICROWAVE COOKING TIME: 10-12 minutes

SERVES: 4 people

1 ring smoked sausage
4 medium cooking apples, cored and thinly sliced
30ml/2 tbsp brown sugar
30ml/2 tbsp flour
1 shallot, finely chopped
15ml/1 tbsp chopped sage
120g/4oz/1 cup shredded Cheddar cheese
Pinch salt and pepper

Toss the apples, brown sugar, flour,

sage and onion together. Slice the sausage in 1.25cm/½ inch diagonal slices and arrange on top of the apples. Cover loosely and cook on HIGH 5 to 7 minutes or until the apples are tender. Sprinkle over the cheese and cook 5 minutes on Medium to melt. Serve immediately.

Ham Loaf with Mustard Chive Sauce

PREPARATION TIME: 15 minutes

MICROWAVE COOKING TIME: 27-28 minutes, plus 5 minutes standing time

SERVES: 4 people

340g/12oz/¾ lb ground/minced, cooked ham
340g/12oz/¾ lb ground/minced pork
60g/2oz/½ cup dry breadcrumbs
140ml/¼ pint/½ cup milk
2 shallots, finely chopped
1 clove garlic, crushed
Salt and pepper

SAUCE
45g/1½ oz/3 tbsps butter or margarine
45g/1½ oz/3 tbsps flour/plain flour
30ml/2 tbsps Dijon mustard
280ml/½ pint/1 cup milk
140ml/¼ pint/½ cup light stock
30ml/2 tbsps chopped chives
Salt and pepper

Combine all the ingredients for the ham loaf and press into a glass loaf dish. Cook on HIGH for 5 minutes. Reduce setting to MEDIUM, cover with plastic wrap/cling film and cook 20-25 minutes, or until firm. Turn the dish after 10 minutes. Leave in the dish for 5 minutes before turning out to slice. Melt the butter for the sauce 30 seconds on HIGH. Stir in the flour and remaining ingredients, except for the chives. Cook 2-3 minutes on HIGH, stirring often until thick. Add the chives and serve with the ham loaf.

Facing page: Speedy Ham Casserole (top) and Sweet and Sour Ham (bottom).

Cranberry-Orange Ham Slices

PREPARATION TIME: 10 minutes

MICROWAVE COOKING TIME: 7-9 minutes

SERVES: 4 people

4 ham steaks
15g/1 tbsp butter or margarine

SAUCE
Juice and rind of 1 orange
225g/8oz whole cranberry sauce
60ml/2 fl oz/¼ cup red wine
5ml/1 tsp cornstarch/cornflour
1 bay leaf
Pinch salt and pepper

GARNISH
1 orange, sliced

Heat a browning dish 5 minutes on HIGH. Put in the butter and brown the ham 2 minutes on the first side and 1 minute on the other. Combine sauce ingredients in a small, deep bowl. Cook 1-2 minutes on HIGH, until the cornstarch/cornflour clears. Remove the bay leaf and pour over the ham to serve. Garnish with the orange slices.

Polynesian Ham Steaks

PREPARATION TIME: 20 minutes

MICROWAVE COOKING TIME: 9-10 minutes

SERVES: 4 people

4 ham steaks
15ml/1 tbsp oil
1 small fresh pineapple, sliced
1 papaya, sliced
2 bananas, peeled and sliced
1 fresh coconut, grated
280ml/½ pint/1 cup orange juice
Juice and grated rind of 1 lime
10ml/2 tsps cornstarch/cornflour
30ml/2 tbsps brown sugar

Heat a browning dish 5 minutes on HIGH. Add the oil to the dish and lay in the ham steaks. Cook 2 minutes on the first side and 1 minute on the other. Set the ham aside. Combine the orange juice, lime juice and rind, cornstarch/cornflour and sugar in a large bowl. Cook 1-2 minutes on HIGH, stirring frequently until thickened. Add the fruit and coconut and heat through 1 minute on HIGH. Pour over the ham steaks to serve.

Swedish Meatballs

PREPARATION TIME: 15 minutes

MICROWAVE COOKING TIME: 13-15 minutes

SERVES: 4 people

This page: Cranberry-Orange Ham Slices (top) and Polynesian Ham Steaks (bottom). Facing page: Ham Loaf with Mustard Chive Sauce.

MEATBALLS
225g./8oz ground/minced pork
225g./8oz ground/minced beef
225g./8oz ground/minced veal
2 shallots, finely chopped
60g/2oz/¼ cup dry breadcrumbs
Pinch ground cloves, nutmeg and allspice
60ml/2 fl oz/¼ cup milk
1 egg, beaten
Salt and pepper

SAUCE

30g/1oz/2 tbsps flour/plain flour
280ml/½ pint/1 cup milk
140ml/¼ pint/½ cup light/single cream
10ml/2 tsps fresh dill or 5ml/1 tsp dried dill
15ml/1 tsp lemon juice
5ml/1 tsp grated lemon rind
Salt and pepper

Combine all the meatball ingredients in a large bowl and mix very well. Shape into 2.5cm/1 inch balls and arrange in a large baking dish. Cook, uncovered, for 10 to 12 minutes on HIGH, or until firm and no longer pink. Rearrange the meatballs twice during cooking, bringing the ones from the edges of the dish to the middle. When the meatballs are cooked remove them to a serving dish to keep warm. Stir in the flour and add the milk, cream, dill and salt and pepper. Cook, stirring frequently, 3 to 5 minutes on HIGH. Add the lemon juice and rind and pour over the meatballs to serve.

Pork with Prunes and Apples

PREPARATION TIME: 15 minutes and 1 hour soaking time for prunes

MICROWAVE COOKING TIME: 26 minutes

SERVES: 4 people

4 pork chops
120g/4oz/½ cup prunes, stones removed
580ml/1 pint/2 cups tea
2 apples, peeled and sliced
5ml/1 tsp lemon juice
Pinch mace
Pinch thyme
30g/1oz/2 tbsps butter
30g/1oz/2 tbsps flour/plain flour
140ml/¼ pint/½ cup heavy/double cream

GARNISH

Parsley sprigs

Boil 580ml/1 pint/2 cups water in a covered bowl for 8 minutes on HIGH. Put in 2 tea bags and the prunes. Leave to soak 1 hour. Heat a browning dish 5 minutes on HIGH.

Melt the butter and brown the pork for 2 minutes on each side. Remove the chops and set aside. Add the flour to the dish and stir in well. Strain 280ml/½ pint/1 cup of the prune soaking liquid into the dish and add the lemon juice, mace, thyme, salt and pepper. Add the pork and cover the dish loosely. Cook 10 minutes on MEDIUM. Add the apples and prunes during the last 4 minutes of cooking. Stir in the cream and heat 1 minute on HIGH. Serve garnished with parsley sprigs.

Italian Pork Rolls

PREPARATION TIME: 20 minutes

MICROWAVE COOKING TIME: 24 minutes

SERVES: 4 people

4 pork escalopes or pork steaks
30g/1oz/2 tbsps vegetable oil

FILLING

60g/2oz/¼ cup ricotta cheese
60g/2oz salami, roughly chopped
120g/4oz/1 cup fresh breadcrumbs
120g/4oz/1 cup pimento stuffed olives, roughly chopped
60g/2oz/½ cup pistachio nuts
2 shallots, finely chopped
15ml/1 tbsp chopped basil
15ml/1 tbsp chopped parsley
Pinch oregano
Salt and pepper
1 egg, beaten

SALPICON

225g/8oz tomatoes, peeled, seeded and quartered
225g/8oz mushrooms, sliced
1 green pepper, cut in thin strips
1 onion, thinly sliced
60ml/2 fl oz/¼ cup dry white wine or vermouth
15ml/1 tbsp tomato paste/purée
Salt and pepper

Flatten the pork pieces with a meat mallet or rolling pin until very thin. Mix the filling ingredients together and spread evenly over the meat. Roll up, tucking in the sides, and fasten with a wooden pick/cocktail stick. Heat a browning dish for 5 minutes on HIGH. Add the oil and

place in the pork rolls in a circle. Cover loosely and cook on MEDIUM for 10 minutes. Rearrange the rolls twice to cook evenly. Cook a further 3 minutes on MEDIUM if the pork is still pink. Remove to a serving dish to keep warm. Cook the onion and the mushrooms in the meat juices for 3 minutes on HIGH. Add the wine, purée/paste, peppers, allspice, salt and pepper. Cook further 2 minutes on HIGH. Add the tomatoes and cook 1 minute on MEDIUM to heat through. Remove the wooden picks from the pork and serve it with the salpicon.

Pork with Plums and Port

PREPARATION TIME: 15 minutes

MICROWAVE COOKING TIME: 24-25 minutes

SERVES: 4 people

675g/1½ lbs pork tenderloin/fillet cut in 1.5cm/½ inch slices
30g/1oz/2 tbsps butter or margarine
30g/1oz/2 tbsps flour
1 bay leaf
2 whole cloves
280ml/½ pint/1 cup stock
140ml/¼ pint/½ cup port
450g/1 lb purple or red plums
Pinch sugar
5ml/1 tsp lemon juice

GARNISH

Chopped parsley

Heat a browning dish 5 minutes on HIGH. Melt the butter and put in the pork slices. Cook 2 minutes each side. Cook in 2 to 3 batches. Remove the pork and stir in the flour. Cook 2 minutes on HIGH, stirring frequently to brown the flour lightly and evenly. Stir in the stock and port and add the cloves, bay leaf, salt and pepper. Replace the meat and cover the dish loosely. Cook 10 minutes on MEDIUM. Cut the plums in half and

Facing page: Swedish Meatballs (top) and Pork with Prunes and Apples (bottom).

remove the stones. Cut in quarters if the plums are large. Add to the meat and cook 5 minutes further on MEDIUM. Taste the sauce and add sugar and/or lemon juice to taste. Remove the bay leaf and cloves. Sprinkle on the chopped parsley before serving.

Smoked Pork with Melon

PREPARATION TIME: 15 minutes

MICROWAVE COOKING TIME: 16 minutes

SERVES: 4 people

1 small, ripe melon
90g/3oz peapods/mangetout
4 smoked pork chops, fat trimmed
15ml/1 tbsp butter or margarine
Grated rind and juice or 1 orange
Salt and pepper
Chopped parsley or coriander

Scoop out the flesh of the melon in balls and set it aside. Spoon out any remaining flesh and blend with the orange juice, salt and pepper in a food processor. Add the orange rind. Trim the peapods/mangetout and cook 1 minute with 15ml/1 tbsp water in a covered bowl. Heat a

This page: Italian Pork Rolls. Facing page: Pork with Plums and Port (top) and Smoked Pork with Melon (bottom).

browning dish for 5 minutes on HIGH. Melt the butter and cook the chops 2 minutes each side on HIGH. Pour over the sauce and cook 5 minutes on MEDIUM. Add the reserved melon balls, peapods/mangetout and parsley or coriander. Heat 1 minute on HIGH before serving.

BEEF, VEAL AND OFFAL

Spinach and Ricotta Stuffed Veal

PREPARATION TIME: 25 minutes

MICROWAVE COOKING TIME: 34-35 minutes

SERVES: 6 people

900g-1.5kg/2-3lbs loin of veal, boned
   and trimmed
1 bay leaf
1 slice onion
280ml/½ pint/1 cup stock or water

STUFFING
450g/1lb fresh spinach, washed well
120g/4oz/½ cup ricotta cheese
1 egg, beaten
30g/2 tbsps pine nuts, roughly chopped
½ clove garlic, minced
5ml/1 tsp chopped basil
Grated nutmeg
Salt and pepper

SAUCE
Pan juices made up to 430ml/¾ pint/
   1½ cups with stock
30g/1oz/2 tbsps flour/plain flour
30g/1oz/2 tbsps butter or margarine
30ml/2 tbsps dry white wine
Salt and pepper

Cook the spinach with 15ml/1 tsp water for 2 minutes on HIGH, in a covered bowl. Drain well and chop roughly. Mix the remaining stuffing ingredients with the spinach and spread on one side of the veal. Roll up from the thicker end of the meat to the thin end. Tie at even intervals with string. Place in a casserole with 1 cup water or stock. Cover loosely and cook for 30 minutes on MEDIUM. Leave to stand 5 minutes before carving. Heat the butter 1 minute on HIGH and add the flour, stock, wine, salt and pepper. Stir to blend well and cook 2-3 minutes on HIGH, until thickened. Serve with the veal and a selection of vegetables.

This page: Spinach and Ricotta Stuffed Veal. Facing page: Veal Involtini (top) and Veal Ragout (bottom).

Liver Lyonnaise with Orange

PREPARATION TIME: 20 minutes

MICROWAVE COOKING TIME:
13-18 minutes

SERVES: 4 people

450g/1lb liver, sliced
45g/1½ oz/3 tbsps flour
30g/1oz/2 tbsps butter or margarine
1 onion, sliced
Rind and juice of 1 orange
140ml/¼ pint/½ cup stock
Pinch thyme
Salt and pepper

GARNISH
Orange slices
Chopped parsley

Heat a browning dish 5 minutes on HIGH. Melt the butter in the dish for 1 minute on HIGH. Dredge the liver in the flour and add to the butter in the dish. Cook the liver for 1 minute on HIGH. Turn over and cook 1 minute further on HIGH. Remove from the dish. Cook the onions 1 minute on HIGH. Peel 1 orange and cut the peel into very thin strips. Squeeze the juice and add to the liver along with the remaining ingredients. Cook 10-15 minutes on MEDIUM, until the liver is tender. Turn the slices over frequently during cooking. Serve garnished with the orange slices and chopped parsley.

Veal Involtini

PREPARATION TIME: 20 minutes

MICROWAVE COOKING TIME:
21-22 minutes

SERVES: 4 people

8 veal escalopes/cutlets
8 slices Parma ham
8 slices cheese
10ml/2 tbsps chopped sage
Salt and pepper
30ml/2 tbsps oil

SAUCE
1 400g/14oz can plum tomatoes
1 clove garlic, crushed

1 small onion, finely chopped
30ml/2 tbsps tomato purée
Pinch oregano
Pinch basil
Pinch sugar
1 bay leaf
Salt and pepper

Flatten the veal escalopes. Place on the ham and cheese and sprinkle on the sage, salt and pepper. Roll up, folding in the ends, and secure with wooden picks/cocktail sticks. Heat a browning dish 5 minutes on HIGH. Pour in the oil and heat 1 minute on HIGH. Add the veal rolls and cook 2 minutes, turning several times. Combine all the sauce ingredients in a deep bowl. Cook 3-4 minutes on HIGH. Remove bay leaf and blend in a food processor until smooth. Pour over the veal and cook, covered, on MEDIUM for 10 minutes. Serve with spinach.

Veal Ragout

PREPARATION TIME: 20 minutes

MICROWAVE COOKING TIME:
37-41 minutes, plus
5 minutes standing time

SERVES: 4 people

450g-900g/1½-2lbs veal shoulder or leg
*   cut in 2.5cm/1 inch cubes*
2 onions, sliced
225g/8oz mushrooms, quartered
60g/2oz/¼ cup butter or margarine
60g/2oz/¼ cup flour/plain flour
10ml/2 tsps thyme
1 bay leaf
1 clove garlic, minced
570ml/1 pint/2 cups beef stock
30ml/2 tbsps tomato paste/purée
Salt and pepper

ACCOMPANIMENT
225g/8oz/3 cups pasta
120g/4oz/1 cup grated cheese

Heat a browning dish 5 minutes on HIGH. Melt the butter 1 minute on HIGH. Brown the meat in 2 batches

Facing page: Liver Lyonnaise with Orange.

5ml/1 tsp coarsely crushed black
   peppercorns
10ml/2 tsps mustard seeds
2 crushed bay leaves
10ml/2 tsps dill
5ml/1 tsp crushed allspice berries
430ml/³⁄₄ pint/1½ cups water
6 carrots, peeled and quartered lengthwise
2 small rutabaga/swedes, peeled and cut
   into wedges
6-8 small potatoes, peeled and left whole
1 large head of white cabbage, cut into
   wedges

Put the corned/salt beef, water, herbs
and spices into a large, deep
casserole. Cover tightly and cook on
HIGH for 8 minutes, or until the
water boils. Reduce the setting to
MEDIUM and cook 30 minutes,
covered. Turn over the meat and add
the carrots, potatoes and rutabaga/
swedes. Re-cover the dish and cook a
further 30-40 minutes on MEDIUM.
Add the cabbage 15 minutes before
the end of cooking. Leave to stand
for 10 minutes before slicing the meat
across the grain. Serve with the
vegetables and some of the cooking
liquid.

Veal Parmesan with Courgettes/Zucchini

PREPARATION TIME: 20 minutes

MICROWAVE COOKING TIME:
17-22 minutes

SERVES: 4 people

4 veal escalopes/cutlets
4 courgettes/zucchini

COATING
30g/1 oz/2 tbsps seasoned breadcrumbs
45g/1½ oz/3 tbsps grated Parmesan
   cheese
1 egg, beaten
Salt and pepper

on HIGH for 3 minutes per batch.
Cook the onions and mushrooms for
2 minutes on HIGH. Remove the
meat and vegetables, and stir in the
flour. Cook the flour for 3 minutes to
brown slightly. Add the remaining
ingredients and return the meat and
the vegetables to the dish, or transfer
to a casserole, cover and cook on
MEDIUM 15 minutes. Put the pasta
in water and partially cover with
plastic wrap/cling film. Cook
6-10 minutes on HIGH, stirring
occasionally. Leave to stand 5
minutes and drain and rinse in hot
water. Remove the bay leaf from the
ragout. Arrange the pasta in a serving
dish and spoon the ragout into the
middle. Sprinkle on grated cheese
and heat 1 minute on HIGH to melt
the cheese before serving.

New England Boiled Dinner

PREPARATION TIME: 20 minutes

MICROWAVE COOKING TIME:
1 hour 8 minutes to 1 hour 18 minutes

SERVES: 6-8 people

900g-1.5kg/2-3lbs corned/salt beef
   brisket

**This page: New England Boiled
Dinner. Facing page: Veal
Parmesan with Courgettes/
Zucchini.**

SAUCE
1 400g/14oz can plum tomatoes
1 clove garlic, crushed
1 small onion, finely chopped
30ml/2 tbsps tomato purée/paste
Pinch oregano
Pinch basil
Pinch sugar
Pinch grated nutmeg
1 bay leaf
Salt and pepper

TOPPING
120g/4oz/1 cup mozzarella cheese
30g/2oz/¼ cup grated Parmesan cheese

Slice the zucchini/courgettes and cook 2 minutes on HIGH, with enough water to cover in a deep bowl. Mix the crumbs, Parmesan cheese, salt and pepper for the coating. Dip the veal in the egg and then in the breadcrumb coating. Put the veal into a shallow dish, cover loosely and cook 8-10 minutes. Do not turn the veal over, but rearrange once during cooking. Combine all the sauce ingredients in a deep bowl. Cook 3-4 minutes on HIGH. Arrange the courgette/zucchini slices in a serving dish, place the veal on top of the courgettes/zucchini and pour over the tomato sauce. Top with the mozzarella and Parmesan cheeses and cook 4-6 minutes on HIGH or Combination setting on a microwave convection oven. Serve immediately.

Beef Enchiladas

PREPARATION TIME: 20 minutes
MICROWAVE COOKING TIME: 12-14 minutes
SERVES: 4 people

225g/8oz package tortillas

SAUCE
1 onion, finely chopped
45ml/3 tbsps tomato purée/paste
1.2kg/1lb 10oz can tomatoes
1-2 small chili peppers, seeded and finely chopped
5ml/1 tsp ground coriander
1 bay leaf
Salt and pepper

FILLING
30ml/2 tbsps oil
225g/8oz minced/ground beef
1 clove garlic, finely minced
10ml/2 tsps ground cumin
1 green pepper, roughly chopped
12 black olives, stoned and chopped
Salt and pepper

GARNISH
1 avocado, sliced
120g/4oz/1 cup grated Cheddar or Monterey Jack cheese

If the tortillas are dry, brush them with water, cover in paper towels and heat 2 minutes on HIGH before rolling up. Combine all the sauce

This page: Risotto Stuffed Peppers (top) and Beef Enchiladas (bottom). Facing page: Chicken Livers and Walnut Pasta (top) and Kidney and Bacon Kebabs with Red Pepper Sauce (bottom).

ingredients in a deep bowl, cover the bowl loosely and cook 3 minutes on HIGH. Stir the sauce frequently to break up the tomatoes. If desired, blend the sauce until smooth in a food processor. Heat a browning dish for 3 minutes on HIGH. Pour in the oil and add the meat, breaking it up with a fork. Add the garlic and cumin and cook on HIGH for 3 minutes, breaking up the meat frequently. Add the green pepper and cook a further

minute on HIGH. Add the olives, salt and pepper. Roll up the filling in the tortillas and lay them in a shallow casserole, seam side down. Pour over the sauce and cook, uncovered, 1 minute on HIGH to heat through. Top with the avocado slices and cheese and heat 1 minute further on HIGH to melt the cheese.

Pepper Steak

PREPARATION TIME: 20 minutes

MICROWAVE COOKING TIME:
14 minutes

SERVES: 4 people

1 green pepper, sliced
1 red pepper, sliced
1 yellow pepper, sliced
900g/2lbs rump steak, cut in thin strips
30ml/2 tbsps oil
1 large onion, finely sliced
1 clove garlic
30ml/2 tbsps cornstarch/cornflour
30ml/2 tbsps soy sauce
30ml/2 tbsps dry sherry
430ml/¾ pint/1½ cups beef stock
1 small piece ginger root, grated
Salt and pepper

Heat a browning dish for 5 minutes on HIGH. Pour in the oil and add the strips of steak. Cook 2 minutes on HIGH. Add the onion, garlic and pepper slices. Mix the cornstarch/cornflour and the remaining ingredients and pour over the steak. Cook, uncovered, 7 minutes on HIGH or until the meat is cooked but the vegetables are still crisp. Serve with rice or chow mein noodles.

Filet Mignon with Mustard Peppercorn Hollandaise

PREPARATION TIME: 15 minutes

MICROWAVE COOKING TIME:
Steak 9 minutes rare
        10 minutes medium rare
        12 minutes medium
        14 minutes well done
Sauce 2 minutes

SERVES: 4 people

4 filet mignon/fillet steaks cut 7.5cms/
    1½ inches thick, brushed with oil on
    both sides

SAUCE
3 egg yolks
5ml/1 tbsp white wine vinegar
120g/4oz/½ cup butter
15ml/1 tbsp Dijon mustard
5ml/1 tsp green peppercorns
5ml/1 tsp chopped parsley
Salt and pepper

Heat a browning dish 5 minutes on HIGH. Cook the steak 2 minutes on one side and 2½ on the other for rare. For medium rare – 2 minutes on one side and 3½ minutes on the other. For medium – 3 minutes on one side and 4½ minutes on the other. For well done – 3 minutes on one side and 6 minutes on the other. Melt the butter 1 minute on HIGH. Mix the egg yolks, vinegar, salt and pepper in a glass measuring cup/jug. Beat in the butter and cook 15 seconds on HIGH and stir. Continue until the sauce thickens, about 2 minutes. Stir in the mustard, parsley and peppercorns. Serve with the steaks.

Kidney and Bacon Kebabs with Red Pepper Sauce

PREPARATION TIME: 20 minutes

MICROWAVE COOKING TIME:
9 minutes, plus
1 minute standing time

SERVES: 4 people

16 kidneys
8 strips bacon/streaky bacon
1 green pepper
60g/2oz/¼ cup butter or margarine

SAUCE
30ml/2 tbsps dry mustard
30ml/2 tbsps Worcestershire sauce
30ml/2 tbsps brown sauce/steak sauce
2 large caps pimento
Salt and pepper

Pierce the kidneys 2 or 3 times. Cut the kidneys in half through the middle and remove the cores with scissors. Wrap the kidneys in bacon and thread onto wooden skewers with the green pepper. Melt the butter for 1 minute on HIGH and brush over the kebabs. Blend the sauce ingredients together with any remaining butter in a food processor until smooth. Cook the sauce 2 minutes on HIGH. Put the kebabs on a roasting rack and cook 5 minutes on HIGH, turning once. Leave to stand 1 minute before serving. Brush with the cooking juices before serving with the sauce. Saffron rice may also be served.

Risotto Stuffed Peppers

PREPARATION TIME: 20 minutes

MICROWAVE COOKING TIME:
20 minutes

SERVES: 4 people

2 large or 4 small red, green or yellow
    peppers
30ml/2 tbsps oil
1 small onion, chopped
1 clove garlic, minced
120g/4oz/1 cup Italian risotto rice
60g/2oz/½ cup mushrooms
120g/4oz/1 cup roughly chopped salami
60g/2oz/¼ cup chopped black olives
225g/8oz canned tomatoes
1.25ml/¼ tsp basil
1.25ml/¼ tsp oregano
120g/4oz/1 cup mozzarella cheese,
    grated
Paprika
Salt and pepper

In a large casserole, cook the garlic, onion and mushrooms in the oil for 2 minutes on HIGH. Stir in the tomatoes, rice, herbs, salt and pepper. Cover the dish and cook on HIGH for 5 minutes. Stir in the meat and olives and leave to stand 5 minutes for the rice to continue cooking. If the peppers are small, cut 2.5cm/ 1 inch off the top to form a lid. Remove the core and seeds. If the peppers are large, cut in half lengthwise and remove the core and

Facing page: Filet Mignon with Mustard Peppercorn Hollandaise (top) and Pepper Steak (bottom).

seeds. Fill the peppers and place them in the casserole. Cover with plastic wrap/cling film and cook 8 minutes on HIGH, until the peppers are just tender. Top with the cheese and cook 2 minutes on MEDIUM to melt.

Veal Kidneys in Mustard Sauce

PREPARATION TIME: 20 minutes

MICROWAVE COOKING TIME: 12 minutes

SERVES: 4 people

2 veal kidneys
2 shallots, chopped
45g/1½ oz/3 tbsps butter or margarine
45g/1½ oz/3 tbsps flour
30ml/2 tbsps Dijon mustard
140ml/¼ pint/½ cup stock
140ml/¼ pint/½ cup light/single cream
140ml/¼ pint/½ cup dry white wine
15ml/1 tbsp capers
15ml/1 tbsp chopped chives
Salt and pepper

Remove the core from the kidneys and cut them into small pieces. Heat a browning dish for 5 minutes on HIGH. Melt the butter for 1 minute on HIGH and add the kidneys and the shallots. Cook 2 minutes on HIGH, stirring frequently. Add the flour, wine, stock, salt and pepper and cook a further 3 minutes on HIGH. Add the remaining ingredients and cook 2 minutes on HIGH. Serve immediately.

Sherried Sweetbreads

PREPARATION TIME: 20 minutes

MICROWAVE COOKING TIME: 17 minutes

SERVES: 4 people

450g/1lb lamb or veal sweetbreads, soaked in cold water
140ml/¼ pint/½ cup stock
60ml/4 tbsps/¼ cup dry sherry
120g/4oz mushrooms, sliced
220g/8oz small onions, peeled
60ml/4 tbsps/¼ cup heavy/double cream

Grated nutmeg
15ml/1 tbsp tomato purée/paste
30ml/2 tbsps chopped parsley
Salt and pepper

Drain the sweetbreads and pierce several times. Cover with fresh water and cook 3 minutes on HIGH. Drain and allow to cool slightly. Peel the outer membrane off the sweetbreads. Cut the sweetbreads in half if they are large. Put the sweetbreads into a casserole with the onions, mushrooms, sherry, stock, salt, pepper and nutmeg. Cook 8 minutes

This page: Sherried Sweetbreads (top) and Veal Kidneys in Mustard Sauce (bottom). Facing page: Roast Beef with Stuffed Courgettes/Zucchini and Tomatoes (bottom).

on HIGH, or until tender. Remove the onions, mushrooms and sweetbreads. Cook the liquid until well reduced, about 5 minutes on HIGH. Add the cream and tomato purée/paste and cook 1 minute on HIGH. Mix all the ingredients together in the sauce. Serve with rice or in puff pastry shells.

Chicken Livers and Walnut Pasta

PREPARATION TIME: 15 minutes

MICROWAVE COOKING TIME: 13 minutes

SERVES: 4 people

450g/1lb chicken livers, trimmed and pierced
60g/2oz/¼ cup butter or margarine
1 clove garlic
120g/4oz/½ cup walnuts, roughly chopped
280ml/½ pint/1 cup stock
4 spring/green onions
30ml/2 tbsps chopped parsley
1 red pepper, chopped
30ml/2 tbsps sherry
Salt and pepper
225g/8oz pasta, cooked

Heat a browning dish for 5 minutes on HIGH. Melt the butter for 1 minute on HIGH and add the liver. Cook for 2 minutes on HIGH and add the garlic, salt and pepper and stock. Cook 3 minutes on HIGH. Remove the livers from the stock and pour the stock into a food processor. Add the walnuts and blend until smooth. Chop the green/spring onions and add to the sauce with the parsley, red peppers, and sherry. Pour over the livers and heat 2 minutes on HIGH. Pour over pasta to serve.

Roast Beef with Stuffed Courgettes/Zucchini and Tomatoes

PREPARATION TIME: 20 minutes

MICROWAVE COOKING TIME:
Beef 14-21 minutes – rare
      16-24 minutes – medium
      18-27 minutes – well done
plus 10 minutes standing time

COMBINATION MICROWAVE CONVECTION TIME:
Beef 10-12 minutes – rare
      11-13 minutes – medium
      12-14 minutes – well done
Vegetables 13 minutes

SERVES: 6-8 people

900g-1.5kg/2-3lbs boneless beef roast/joint
6-8 tomatoes
6-8 courgettes/zucchini
60ml/4 tbsps chopped parsley
180g/6oz mushrooms, roughly chopped
60ml/4 tbsps chopped chives
60g/2oz/½ cup breadcrumbs
60g/2oz/1 cup grated cheese
Salt and pepper

Put the beef, fat side up, into a large casserole, cover loosely and cook for 14-21 minutes for rare, 16-24 minutes for medium, 18-27 minutes for well done on HIGH. Turn the beef over halfway through the cooking time. When cooked for the chosen amount of time cover with foil and leave to stand for 10 minutes before carving. The beef may also be cooked in a combination microwave and convection oven. Trim the ends of the courgettes/zucchini and cook, in enough water to cover, for 5 minutes on HIGH. Cut in half lengthwise and scoop out the flesh, leaving the shell intact. Chop the flesh roughly and mix with the chives, salt and pepper. Fill the shells and sprinkle on the grated cheese. Cut the tops from the round end of the tomatoes, scoop out the seeds and strain the juice. Mix the mushrooms, tomato juice, parsley, breadcrumbs, salt and pepper. Fill the tomatoes and replace the tops. Cook the courgettes/zucchini 5 minutes on HIGH and the tomatoes 3 minutes on HIGH, or until the vegetables are tender. Serve with the beef.

Beef Bourguignonne

PREPARATION TIME: 20 minutes

MICROWAVE COOKING TIME:
53 minutes, plus
10 minutes standing time

SERVES: 4 people

2 thick-cut slices bacon cut in 1.25cm/½ inch strips
675g-900g/1½lbs-2lbs chuck/braising steak cut in 2.5cm/1 inch cubes
1 clove garlic, minced
225g/8oz small onions
60g/4 tbsps flour/plain flour
280ml/½ pint/1 cup Burgundy
280ml/½ pint/1 cup beef stock
5ml/1 tsp tomato paste/purée
225g/8oz mushrooms, left whole
1 bay leaf
5ml/1 tsp thyme or majoram
Salt and pepper

Heat a browning dish for 5 minutes on HIGH. Add the bacon and cook 3 minutes on HIGH, stirring frequently until brown. Remove the bacon and add the meat. Cook 3 minutes on HIGH to brown slightly. Remove the meat and add the onions. Cook 2 minutes on HIGH. Stir in the flour, stock, wine and tomato purée/paste. Add the bay leaf, salt and pepper. Return the bacon and meat to the casserole and add the mushrooms. Cover and cook 40 minutes on MEDIUM, or until the meat is tender. Stir occasionally. Leave to stand for 10 minutes before serving. Serve with parsley potatoes.

Steak and Mushroom Pudding

PREPARATION TIME: 25 minutes

MICROWAVE COOKING TIME:
51-52 minutes, plus
10 minutes standing time

SERVES: 4 people

PASTRY
225g/8oz/2 cups flour/plain flour
10ml/2 tsps baking powder
120g/4oz shredded suet or ¼ cup butter or margarine
5ml/1 tsp salt
140ml/¼ pint/½ cup water

FILLING
225g/8oz whole mushrooms
450g/1lb braising/chuck steak
30ml/1oz/2 tbsps butter or margarine
30ml/1oz/2 tbsps flour
1 small onion, finely chopped
280ml/½ pint/1 cup beef stock
10ml/2 tsps chopped parsley
5ml/1 tsp thyme
Salt and pepper

Facing page: Steak and Mushroom Pudding (top) and Beef Bourguignonne (bottom).

Melt the butter in a deep bowl for
30 seconds on HIGH. Stir in the
flour and the stock and cook for
1-2 minutes on HIGH. Add the
remaining ingredients for the filling
and cover the bowl loosely. Cook for
35 minutes on MEDIUM.
Meanwhile, make the pastry. Sift the
flour and baking powder and salt into
a mixing bowl. Cut in the butter or
stir in the suet. Mix to a soft dough
with the water. Roll out ⅔ of the
dough and line a 1150ml/2 pint/
4 cup glass bowl, spoon in the filling
and dampen the edges of the pastry.
Roll out the remaining pastry for the
cover. Place it over the top of the
filling, pressing down the edges to
seal well. Make 2-3 cuts in the top to
let out the steam. Cover loosely with
plastic wrap/cling film and cook on
LOW for 15 minutes, turning the
bowl around several times. Leave to
stand for 10 minutes before turning
out.

Veal Escalopes with Vegetables

PREPARATION TIME: 20 minutes

MICROWAVE COOKING TIME:
20 minutes

SERVES: 4 people

4 veal escalopes/cutlets
30ml/2 tbsps oil
60g/2oz mangetout/peapods
2 carrots, peeled and thinly sliced
60g/2oz mushrooms, sliced
2 leeks, washed and thinly sliced
120g/4oz/1 cup low-fat soft cheese
140ml/¼ pint/½ cup dry white wine
15ml/1 tbsp lemon juice
15ml/1 tbsp chopped dill
Grated nutmeg
Salt and pepper

Heat a browning dish 3 minutes on
HIGH. Add the oil and heat 1 minute
on HIGH. Cook the veal for 8
minutes on HIGH. Add the
mushrooms halfway through the
cooking time. Combine the carrots
and the leeks with the wine in a
shallow dish and cook for 5 minutes
on HIGH. Add the mangetout/
peapods and cook a further 1 minute

on HIGH. Drain the vegetables and
reserve the liquid. Mix the cheese,
vegetable cooking liquid, lemon juice,
dill, nutmeg, salt and pepper in a
deep bowl. Heat for 1 minute on
HIGH, but do not allow the sauce to
boil. Combine with the drained
vegetables. Pour over the veal and
heat through 1 minute on HIGH
before serving.

Veal with Saffron Sauce

PREPARATION TIME: 20 minutes

MICROWAVE COOKING TIME:
26-27 minutes

SERVES: 4 people

4 veal chops
45g/1½ oz/3 tbsps butter or margarine
30g/1oz/2 tbsps flour/plain flour
2 shallots, finely chopped
1 red pepper, thinly sliced
140ml/¼ pint/½ cup white wine
140ml/¼ pint/½ cup light stock
140ml/¼ pint/½ cup light/single cream
Good pinch saffron
Salt and pepper

Heat a browning dish for 5 minutes
on HIGH. Melt the butter for
1 minute on HIGH and put in the
chops. Cook for 2 minutes on HIGH
per side. Remove the chops from the
dish and add the shallots. Cook for
1 minute on HIGH. Stir in the flour,
wine, stock, salt, pepper and saffron.

Cook 2-3 minutes on HIGH until thickened. Return the chops to the dish and add the sliced red pepper. Cover the dish or transfer to a covered casserole. Cook on MEDIUM for 15 minutes, or until the chops are tender. Remove the chops from the dish and stir in the cream. Pour the sauce over the chops to serve.

Veal Chops with Lemon and Thyme

PREPARATION TIME: 20 minutes

MICROWAVE COOKING TIME: 26-27 minutes

SERVES: 4 people

4 veal chops
60g/2oz/¼ cup butter or margarine
60g/2oz/¼ cup flour
1 clove garlic, minced
140ml/¼ pint/½ cup white wine
140ml/¼ pint/½ cup light stock
30ml/2 tbsps lemon juice
Salt and pepper

GARNISH
Sprigs of fresh thyme
Lemon slices

Heat a browning dish 5 minutes on HIGH. Melt the butter for 1 minute on HIGH. Put in the chops and cook 2 minutes on HIGH per side.

Facing page: Veal Chops with Lemon and Thyme (top) and Veal with Saffron Sauce (bottom). This page: Veal Escalopes with Vegetables.

Remove the chops from the dish and add the flour. Cook 1 minute to brown slightly. Stir in the wine, stock and lemon juice. Cook 2-3 minutes on HIGH until thickened. Season with salt and pepper and add a sprig of fresh thyme. Return the chops to the dish or transfer to a covered casserole. Cook on MEDIUM 15 minutes. Garnish with lemon slices and more fresh thyme.

POULTRY DISHES

Orange Glazed Duck

PREPARATION TIME: 15 minutes

MICROWAVE COOKING TIME:
40 minutes

SERVES: 3-4 people

2kg-2.5kg/4½-5lbs duckling
1 slice orange
1 slice onion
1 bay leaf
Salt

GLAZE
60ml/4 tbsps/¼ cup bitter orange
*   marmalade*
60ml/4 tbsps soy sauce
280ml/½ pint/1 cup chicken stock
10ml/2 tsps cornstarch/cornflour
Salt and pepper

GARNISH
Orange slices and watercress

Prick the duck all over the skin with a fork, brush some of the soy sauce over both sides of the duck and sprinkle both sides lightly with salt. Place the duck breast side down in a roasting rack. Cook 10 minutes on HIGH and drain well. Return the duckling to the oven, reduce the power to MEDIUM and continue cooking a further 15 minutes. Combine remaining soy sauce with the orange marmalade. Turn the duck breast side up and brush with the glaze. Continue cooking for 15 minutes on MEDIUM, draining away the fat often and brushing with the glaze. Remove the duck from the roasting rack and leave to stand, loosely covered with foil, for 5 minutes before carving. Alternatively, cook 20-25 minutes on Combination in a microwave convection oven. Drain all the fat from the roasting tin, but leave the pan juices. Combine the chicken stock, cornstarch/cornflour, salt, pepper and remaining glaze with the

This page: Orange Glazed Duck. Facing page: Turkey with Broccoli (top) and Turkey Tetrazzini (bottom).

Stuffed Turkey Leg

PREPARATION TIME: 20 minutes

MICROWAVE COOKING TIME: 33-34 minutes

SERVES: 4 people

1 large turkey leg, bone removed

STUFFING
2 slices white bread made into crumbs
120g/4oz cooked ham, finely minced
60g/2oz/½ cup shelled pistachio nuts
1 apple, cored and chopped
2 sticks celery, finely chopped
1 shallot, finely chopped
Pinch thyme
1 egg, beaten
Salt and pepper

SAUCE
15ml/1 tbsp dripping from turkey
30g/2 tbsps flour/plain flour
Pan juices
280ml/½ pint/1 cup chicken stock
30ml/2 tbsps dry sherry
Salt and pepper

GARNISH
1 bunch watercress

Combine all the stuffing ingredients and push into the cavity of the turkey leg, but do not overstuff. Close any openings with wooden picks/cocktail sticks. Prick the turkey skin lightly all over and put the turkey leg on a roasting rack. Cover loosely with greaseproof/wax paper and cook for 15 minutes on MEDIUM. Turn the turkey leg over and continue cooking on MEDIUM a further 15 minutes. Alternatively, cook 20 minutes on Combination in a microwave convection oven. When the turkey is tender and no longer pink, remove from the roasting rack and keep warm. Remove all but 15ml/1 tbsp of the fat from the roasting dish. Stir in the flour and add the chicken stock, sherry, salt and pepper. Transfer to a deep bowl if

pan juices and pour into a small, deep bowl. Cook 2-3 minutes on HIGH until thickened. Remove the onion, orange slice and bay leaf from the cavity of the duck and put in a bouquet of watercress. Surround the duck with orange slices and serve the sauce separately.

Lemon Pepper Chicken

PREPARATION TIME: 20 minutes

MICROWAVE COOKING TIME: 10 minutes

SERVES: 4 people

4 chicken breasts
Juice of 1 lemon
15ml/1 tbsp coarsely ground black pepper
Paprika
Salt

GARNISH
Lemon slices
Watercress

Heat 2 metal skewers in a gas flame or on an electric burner/hob. Skin the chicken breasts. Make a criss-cross pattern on the chicken flesh with the hot skewers. Place the chicken in a casserole and sprinkle over the paprika, pepper, lemon juice and salt. Cover the dish tightly and cook 10 minutes on MEDIUM. Pour the juices back over the chicken to serve. Garnish with the lemon slices and watercress.

This page: Stuffed Turkey Leg. Facing page: Lemon Pepper Chicken (top) and Lime and Chili Chicken (bottom).

desired and cook 3-4 minutes on HIGH, stirring frequently until thickened. Slice the stuffed turkey leg and pour over some of the sauce. Garnish with watercress and serve the remaining sauce separately.

Chinese Wings

PREPARATION TIME: 15 minutes

MICROWAVE COOKING TIME: 17 minutes

SERVES: 4 people

1.5kg/3lbs chicken wings
280ml/½ pint/1 cup hoisin sauce
  (Chinese barbecue sauce)
45g/1½ oz/3 tbsps sesame seeds
30ml/2 tbsps vegetable oil
15ml/1 tbsp sesame seed oil
225g/8oz mangetout/peapods
225g/8oz bean sprouts
Small piece grated fresh ginger root
Salt and pepper

Brush the chicken wings with the hoisin sauce and cook for 10 minutes on HIGH on a roasting rack. Baste the chicken wings often with the sauce while cooking. When the wings are cooked and well coated with sauce, sprinkle with sesame seeds and set aside. Heat the oil in a browning dish for 5 minutes on HIGH. Add the mangetout/peapods, bean sprouts, ginger, salt and pepper. Cook for 2 minutes on HIGH and add the sesame seed oil after cooking. Serve the Chinese wings with the stir-fried vegetables.

Lime and Chili Chicken

PREPARATION TIME: 20 minutes

MICROWAVE COOKING TIME: 12 minutes

SERVES: 4 people

4 chicken breasts, boned
2 limes
1 green chili pepper
90ml/6 tbsps/½ cup heavy/double
  cream
Salt and pepper
Pinch sugar

Heat 2 metal skewers in a gas flame or on an electric hob/burner. Skin the chicken breasts and make a pattern on the chicken flesh with the hot skewers. Squeeze 1 lime for juice. Peel and slice the other lime thinly. Remove the seeds from the chili pepper and slice it very thinly. Put the chicken into a casserole. Sprinkle over a pinch of sugar, the sliced chili pepper, salt, pepper and lime juice. Cover and cook 10 minutes on MEDIUM. Remove the chicken and keep warm. Stir the cream into the juices in the casserole. Cook 2 minutes on HIGH, stirring frequently. Pour over the chicken and garnish with the sliced lime.

Tandoori Poussins

PREPARATION TIME: 20 minutes, plus 1 hour to marinate

MICROWAVE COOKING TIME: 15 minutes

SERVES: 4 people

4 poussins

MARINADE
120g/4oz/½ cup chopped onion
1 small piece fresh ginger, grated
10ml/2 tsps ground coriander
10ml/2 tsps ground cumin
10ml/2 tsps paprika
5ml/1 tsp turmeric
5ml/1 tsp chili powder
280ml/½ pint/1 cup plain yogurt
Juice of 1 lime
2 chopped green chili peppers
30ml/2 tbsps chopped chives
Salt and pepper

ACCOMPANIMENT
1 head of lettuce, broken into leaves
4 tomatoes, cut in wedges
1 lemon, cut in wedges

Combine all the marinade ingredients together. Skin the poussins and cut them in half. Prick the flesh and rub in the marinade. Leave for 1 hour. Cook on HIGH or a Combination setting for 15 minutes, basting frequently with the marinade. Leave to stand, loosely covered, for 5 minutes before serving. Heat any remaining marinade on MEDIUM for 1 minute, but do not allow to boil. Pour over the chicken and serve on a bed of lettuce with lemon and tomato wedges.

Turkey with Broccoli

PREPARATION TIME: 20 minutes

MICROWAVE COOKING TIME: 13-14 minutes

SERVES: 4 people

4 turkey escalopes/cutlets
12 broccoli spears
140ml/¼ pint/½ cup chicken stock
1 bay leaf
Salt and pepper

SAUCE
45g/3 tbsps butter or margarine
45g/3 tbsps flour/plain flour
430ml/¾ pint/1½ cups milk
60g/2oz/½ cup Colby/Red Leicester
  cheese
Pinch Cayenne pepper
Salt and pepper
Paprika

Trim the broccoli, and divide evenly among the turkey escalopes/cutlets. Roll the turkey around the broccoli and lay the rolls in a casserole, seam side down. Pour over the chicken stock, sprinkle on salt and pepper and add the bay leaf. Cover and cook 10 minutes on MEDIUM. Leave to stand while preparing the sauce. Melt the butter for 30 seconds in a deep bowl. Stir in the flour and the milk. Add the salt, pepper, mustard, Cayenne pepper and cook until thickened, about 3-4 minutes on HIGH. Add the cheese and stir to melt. Transfer the turkey and broccoli rolls to a serving dish and pour some of the sauce over each one. Sprinkle on paprika and serve the rest of the sauce separately.

Facing page: Chinese Wings (top) and Tandoori Poussins (bottom).

appears to be drying out at any time during cooking, baste with oil and cover loosely with wax paper/greaseproof paper. Reserve 1 tbsp fat from the roasting pan and skim off the rest and discard. Reserve the pan juices. Mix the reserved fat with the flour and stir into the pan juices. Add the stock, wine, salt and pepper and cook 2-3 minutes until thickened. Stir in the chopped herbs and serve with the carved chicken.

Duck with Peaches

PREPARATION TIME: 20 minutes

MICROWAVE COOKING TIME: 9 minutes

SERVES: 4 people

2 whole duck breasts
60g/4 tosps/¼ cup butter
Salt and pepper

SAUCE
2 cans sliced peaches, drained and juice reserved
140ml/¼ pint/½ cup red wine
10ml/2 tsps cornstarch/cornflour
15ml/1 tbsp lime or lemon juice
1 bay leaf
Pinch cinnamon
Pinch nutmeg
15ml/1 tbsp whole allspice berries
60g/2oz/½ cup whole blanched almonds

Heat a browning dish for 5 minutes on HIGH. Melt the butter and put in the duck breasts. Brown the duck breasts 2 minutes on the skin side and 4 minutes on the other side. Remove from the dish and leave to stand while preparing the sauce. Mix the cornstarch/cornflour with the peach juice, red wine, lemon juice and the spices and bay leaf in a deep bowl. Cook on HIGH for 2-3 minutes until thickened. Remove the bay leaf and add the peaches. Slice the duck breast into thin slices. Pour the peach sauce over the duck breasts to serve.

This page: Herb Roasted Chicken. Facing page: Turkey Macadamia (top) and Duck with Peaches (bottom).

Herb Roasted Chicken

PREPARATION TIME: 25 minutes

MICROWAVE COOKING TIME: 26-33 minutes, plus 5-10 minutes standing time

SERVES: 4-6 people

1.5kg/3lbs roasting chicken
5ml/1 tsp each fresh thyme, basil, parsley, marjoram, chervil or tarragon
30ml/2 tbsps oil
Juice of 1 lemon
Salt and pepper

GRAVY
45g/1½ oz/3 tbsps flour/plain flour
Cooking juices from the chicken
430ml/¾ pint/1½ cups chicken stock
30ml/2 tbsps white wine
30ml/2 tbsps chopped mixed herbs as above
Salt and pepper

Chop the herbs finely. Loosen the skin of the chicken and stuff the herbs underneath. Prick the skin lightly and brush with the oil. Sprinkle over the lemon juice and pepper. Put onto a roasting rack breast-side down, and cook 30 minutes on MEDIUM, 25 minutes on HIGH and 30 minutes on a Combination setting. Turn the chicken halfway through cooking. Leave the chicken standing 5-10 minutes before carving. If the chicken

Spicy Tomato Chicken

PREPARATION TIME: 15 minutes

MICROWAVE COOKING TIME:
17 minutes, plus
5 minutes standing time

SERVES: 4 people

4 chicken breasts, skinned and boned
60ml/4 tbsps/¼ cup chicken stock or
    water
450g/1lb canned tomatoes
30ml/2 tbsps Worcestershire sauce
1 clove garlic, crushed
30ml/2 tbsps tomato purée/paste
30ml/2 tbsps cider vinegar
30g/1oz/2 tbsps light brown sugar or
    honey
1 small onion, finely chopped
1 bay leaf
Pinch allspice
Salt and pepper
GARNISH
4 tomatoes, skinned, seeded and cut into
    thin strips

Place the chicken in 1 layer in a large
casserole with the stock or water.
Cover tightly and cook on
MEDIUM for 10 minutes. Leave to
stand, covered, for at least ·5 minutes
while preparing the sauce. Combine
all the sauce ingredients with the
cooking liquid from the chicken in a
deep bowl. Cook, uncovered, for
7 minutes on HIGH, until the sauce
reduces and thickens. Remove the
bay leaf and blend the sauce in a food
processor until smooth. Arrange the
chicken breasts on a serving plate
and coat with the sauce. Add the
tomato strips and reheat for
30 seconds on HIGH before serving.

Chicken with Watercress Sauce

PREPARATION TIME: 15 minutes

MICROWAVE COOKING TIME:
12 minutes, plus
5 minutes standing time

SERVES: 4 people

4 large chicken breasts, skinned and
    boned
30ml/2 tbsps water
60ml/4 tbsps/¼ cup lemon juice

SAUCE
120g/4oz/1 cup low fat soft cheese
140ml/¼ pint/½ cup light/single cream
    or milk
1 large bunch watercress, well washed
    and drained
Salt and pepper
GARNISH
Lemon slices
Watercress

Place the chicken in one layer in a
large casserole. Pour over the water
and the lemon juice. Cover tightly
and cook 10 minutes on MEDIUM.
Leave to stand, covered, at least
5 minutes while preparing the sauce.
Combine the cheese and the cream
or milk with the chicken cooking
liquid and salt and pepper. Cook
1 minute on HIGH. Discard any
tough stalks from the watercress and
chop roughly. Add to the sauce and
cook 1 minute on HIGH. Blend the
sauce in a food processor until
smooth and a delicate green colour.
Coat over the chicken to serve.
Garnish with lemon slices and
watercress.

This page: Country Captain's
Chicken. Facing page: Chicken
with Watercress Sauce (top) and
Spicy Tomato Chicken (bottom).

Country Captain's Chicken

PREPARATION TIME: 20 minutes

MICROWAVE COOKING TIME:
36 minutes

SERVES: 4 people

1.5kg/3lbs chicken pieces
60g/4 tbsps butter
30ml/2 tbsps curry powder
1 clove garlic, minced
1 large onion, sliced
60g/2oz/½ cup blanched whole almonds
60g/2oz/½ cup golden raisins/sultanas
2 apples, peeled and diced
1 450g/16oz can tomatoes
30ml/2 tbsps tomato purée/paste
1 bay leaf
30ml/2 tbsps chopped coriander
    (optional)
Pinch sugar
Salt and pepper

GARNISH
Desiccated coconut

Heat a browning dish for 5 minutes on HIGH. Melt the butter and add the chicken pieces. Cook 15 minutes on both sides or cook in 2 batches for 7½ minutes each batch if necessary. Remove the chicken and add the onion, garlic and curry powder. Cook 1 minute on HIGH. Replace the chicken, skin side down, and add the sultanas/raisins, apples and almonds. Mix the tomatoes, tomato purée/paste, lime juice, coriander, bay leaf, sugar, salt and pepper together and pour over the chicken. Cook 15 minutes on HIGH, or until the chicken is tender and no longer pink. Turn the chicken over halfway through cooking. Remove the bay leaf and serve with rice and garnish with desiccated coconut.

Piquant Duck

PREPARATION TIME: 25 minutes

MICROWAVE COOKING TIME:
27 minutes

SERVES: 4 people

8 duck portions/pieces
60g/2oz/¼ cup butter
4 large cloves garlic, minced

SAUCE
60ml/2 fl oz/¼ cup vinegar
280ml/½ pint/1 cup dry white wine
45ml/3 tbsps Dijon mustard
30ml/2 tbsps tomato purée/paste
30ml/2 tbsps chives
1 red pepper, very thinly sliced
140ml/¼ pint/½ cup heavy/double cream
Salt and pepper

Heat a browning dish for 5 minutes on HIGH, melt the butter and add the duck pieces skin side down. Brown the duck for 5 minutes per side. Add the garlic and cover the dish tightly. Cook until the duck is tender, about 15 minutes on HIGH. Pour off all the fat and leave the duck covered while preparing the sauce. Combine all the sauce ingredients except the red pepper and the cream

in a deep bowl. Add the garlic and any juices from the duck. Cook for 10 minutes on HIGH until well reduced. Add the cream and the red pepper and cook a further 2 minutes on HIGH. Trim the duck pieces neatly and pour over the sauce to serve.

Turkey Macadamia

PREPARATION TIME: 20 minutes

MICROWAVE COOKING TIME:
18 minutes

SERVES: 4 people

4 turkey breast escalopes/cutlets
1 225g (8oz) can pineapple chunks/ pieces, juice reserved
4 spring/green onions, sliced
4 tomatoes, peeled, seeded and quartered
125g/4oz/1 cup macadamia nuts

SAUCE
30ml/2 tbsps soy sauce
280ml/½ pint/1 cup stock
30ml/2 tbsps vinegar
30ml/2 tbsps brown sugar
15ml/3 tsps cornstarch/cornflour
Reserved pineapple juice

Place the turkey breasts in a casserole dish and pour over the pineapple juice. Cover the dish tightly and cook 10-15 minutes on MEDIUM. Leave to stand while preparing the sauce. Drain the pineapple juice from the turkey and combine it in a deep bowl with the remaining sauce ingredients. Add the pineapple pieces and the macadamia nuts. Cook, uncovered, for 2-3 minutes on HIGH, stirring frequently until thickened. Immediately add the tomatoes and the onions to the hot sauce and pour over the turkey to serve.

Turkey Tetrazzini

PREPARATION TIME: 20 minutes

MICROWAVE COOKING TIME:
6-8 minutes

SERVES: 4-6 people

60g/2oz/¼ cup butter or margarine
60g/2oz flour/plain flour

120g/4oz mushrooms, sliced
1 clove garlic, crushed
2 sticks celery, sliced
280ml/½ pint/1 cup chicken stock
280ml/½ pint/1 cup milk
140ml/¼ pint/½ cup double/heavy cream
30ml/2 tbsps dry white wine or sherry
12 black olives, pitted and roughly chopped
225g/8oz cooked turkey, cut in cubes
225g/8oz spaghetti
Salt and pepper
60g/4 tbsps/¼ cup each seasoned breadcrumbs and Parmesan cheese

Cook spaghetti in enough water to cover for 12 minutes on HIGH. Stir frequently. Drain and set aside. Melt the butter 30 seconds on HIGH, and add mushrooms, garlic and celery. Cook 1 minute on HIGH. Stir in the flour and add milk, stock and wine or sherry. Cook, uncovered, until thickened, about 5 minutes on HIGH. Add the cream and the olives. Combine with the turkey and spaghetti and pour into a casserole. Sprinkle cheese and crumbs on top and cook 8-10 minutes on HIGH. Serve immediately.

Duck with Cherries

PREPARATION TIME: 20 minutes

MICROWAVE COOKING TIME:
9 minutes

SERVES: 4 people

2 whole duck breasts
60g/4 tbsps/¼ cup butter or margarine
Salt and pepper

SAUCE
2 cans dark, pitted cherries, drained and juice reserved
140ml/¼ pint/½ cup red wine
30ml/2 tbsps red wine vinegar
Grated rind and juice of 1 orange
10ml/2 tsps cornstarch/cornflour
1 bay leaf
1 sprig thyme
Pinch salt

Facing page: Duck with Cherries (top) and Piquant Duck (bottom).

Heat a browning dish 5 minutes on HIGH. Add the butter and put in the duck breasts. Brown the duck breasts 2 minutes on the skin side and 4 minutes on the other side. Remove the duck from the dish and keep warm. Mix the reserved cherry juice with the wine, vinegar, orange rind and juice, cornstarch/cornflour, bay leaf and thyme in a small bowl. Cook for 3 minutes on HIGH until thickened, stirring frequently. Add a pinch of salt and remove the bay leaf and thyme. Add the cherries to the sauce and slice the duck breasts into thin slices. Pour over the cherry sauce to serve.

Pecan Poussins

PREPARATION TIME: 25 minutes

MICROWAVE COOKING TIME: 35 minutes

SERVES: 4 people

4 poussins or Cornish game hens
60ml/4 tbsps/¼ cup Worcestershire
    sauce

STUFFING
6 slices white bread made into crumbs
225g/8oz cooked ham
4 green/spring onions, chopped
5ml/1 tsp thyme
1 egg, beaten
Salt and pepper

SAUCE
430ml/¾ pint/1½ cups brown stock
180g/6oz/⅔ cup light brown sugar
90ml/6 tbsps/⅓ cup cider vinegar
120g/4oz/1 cup chopped pecans

GARNISH
Watercress

Process the ham and bread in a food processor until finely chopped. Add the egg, salt, pepper and thyme and process once or twice to mix thoroughly. Stir in the onion by hand. Stuff the poussins and tie the legs together with string. Brush each poussin with Worcestershire sauce. Cook 15-20 minutes on HIGH or 20 minutes on a Combination setting. Leave to stand 5 minutes

before serving. Mix the sauce ingredients together and cook on HIGH, uncovered, for 10-15 minutes. The sauce should be reduced and of syrupy consistency. Pour over the poussins to serve and garnish with watercress.

Chicken Paprika

PREPARATION TIME: 20 minutes

MICROWAVE COOKING TIME: 32 minutes, plus 5 minutes standing time

SERVES: 4-6 people

1.5kg/3lbs chicken pieces
30g/1oz/2 tbsps butter
2 onions, sliced
30ml/2 tbsps paprika
1 clove garlic, finely minced
30ml/2 tbsps tomato purée/paste
1 450g/1lb can tomatoes
120g/4oz mushrooms
1 green pepper, thinly sliced
1 bay leaf
Salt and pepper

**This page: Chicken Paprika.
Facing page: Pecan Poussins.**

GARNISH
Sour cream

Melt the butter for 30 seconds on HIGH in a large casserole. Add the paprika, onions and garlic. Cook, uncovered, 2 minutes on HIGH. Lay the chicken pieces into the casserole skin-side down with the thickest portions to the outside of the dish. Combine the tomato paste/purée with the tomatoes, bay leaf, salt and pepper. Pour the tomato sauce over the chicken and cover the casserole tightly. Cook for 15 minutes on HIGH. Turn over the chicken pieces and scatter the mushrooms and the pepper slices on top. Cook a further 15 minutes, or until the chicken is tender and no longer pink. Leave to stand, covered, for 5 minutes. Top with sour cream before serving with pasta or potatoes.

MEAT & POULTRY

GAME DISHES

Quail with Artichokes and Vegetable Julienne

PREPARATION TIME: 25 minutes

MICROWAVE COOKING TIME: 19-21 minutes

SERVES: 4 people

8 quail
60g/4 tbsps/¼ cup butter or margarine
2 large artichokes, cooked
2 carrots, peeled
2 potatoes, peeled
2 leeks, washed

SAUCE
15ml/1 tbsps flour/plain flour
140ml/¼ pint/½ cup white wine
280ml/½ pint/1 cup double/heavy
   cream
30ml/2 tbsps Dijon mustard
Salt and pepper

GARNISH
Reserved artichoke leaves

Peel the leaves from the artichokes and remove the chokes. Set the leaves aside and cut the artichoke bottoms into thin slices. Cut the carrots, potatoes and leeks into julienne strips. Heat a browning dish for 5 minutes on HIGH. Melt the butter and add the carrots and potatoes. Cook on HIGH for 2 minutes. Add the leeks and artichoke bottoms and cook for a further 1 minute on HIGH. Remove the vegetables and set them aside. Add the quail to the butter in a dish and cook for 4-6 minutes on HIGH, turning frequently to brown lightly. Remove the quail from the dish and add the flour, white wine and Dijon mustard. Return the quail to the

dish, cover tightly and cook for 5 minutes on HIGH. Set the quail aside to keep warm. Add the cream and salt and pepper to the dish and stir well. Cook for 1 minute on HIGH to thicken slightly. Add the vegetables to the sauce and cook a further 1 minute on HIGH to heat

This page: Quail with Raspberries. Facing page: Quail with Apples and Calvados (top) and Quail with Artichokes and Vegetable Julienne (bottom).

through. Pour the sauce over the quail to serve and surround with the artichoke leaves.

Juniper Venison

PREPARATION TIME: 25 minutes

MICROWAVE COOKING TIME:
55 minutes, plus
10 minutes standing time

SERVES: 4 people

900g/2lbs venison, cut in 2.5cm/1 inch
cubes
60g/2oz/¼ cup butter or margarine
60g/2oz/¼ cup flour/plain flour
570ml/1 pint/2 cups beef stock
60ml/4 tbsps/¼ cup red wine
1 shallot, finely chopped
1 sprig rosemary
15ml/1 tbsp juniper berries
1 bay leaf
Salt and pepper

ACCOMPANIMENT
450g/1lb potatoes, peeled and cut into
small pieces
15g/1 tbsp butter or margarine
1 egg, beaten
Salt and pepper
Rowanberry jelly, redcurrant jelly or whole
cranberry sauce

Cook the potatoes in enough water to cover for 15 minutes on HIGH. Leave to stand for 5 minutes before draining and mashing. Season the potatoes with salt and pepper and add the butter. Beat in half the egg and pipe the mixture out into small baskets on a plate or a microwave baking sheet. Cook for 1 minute on HIGH and then brush with the remaining beaten egg and sprinkle with paprika. Cook a further 2 minutes on HIGH and set aside. Heat a browning dish for 5 minutes on HIGH. Melt the butter and brown the meat and the shallot for 4-6 minutes on HIGH. Remove the meat and shallot and stir in the flour, stock, red wine, salt, pepper, juniper berries, rosemary and bay leaf. Return the meat to the dish or transfer to a casserole. Cover and cook for 30 minutes on MEDIUM, stirring frequently. Remove the bay leaf and the sprig of rosemary before serving. Reheat the potato baskets for 30 seconds on HIGH and fill each with a spoonful of the jelly or cranberry sauce. Serve the potato

baskets with the venison. Garnish with fresh rosemary if desired.

Marmalade Venison

PREPARATION TIME: 15 minutes

MICROWAVE COOKING TIME:
40 minutes, plus
10 minutes standing time

SERVES: 4 people

900g/2lbs venison, cut in 2.5cm/1 inch
cubes
225g/8oz small onions, peeled and left
whole

This page: Juniper Venison (top)
and Marmalade Venison (bottom).
Facing page: Pheasant Alsacienne.

60g/2oz/¼ cup butter or margarine
60g/2oz/¼ cup flour
570ml/1 pint/2 cups beef stock
60ml/4 tbsps/¼ cup orange marmalade

GARNISH
Orange slices
Chopped parsley

Heat a browning dish for 5 minutes on HIGH. Melt the butter and add

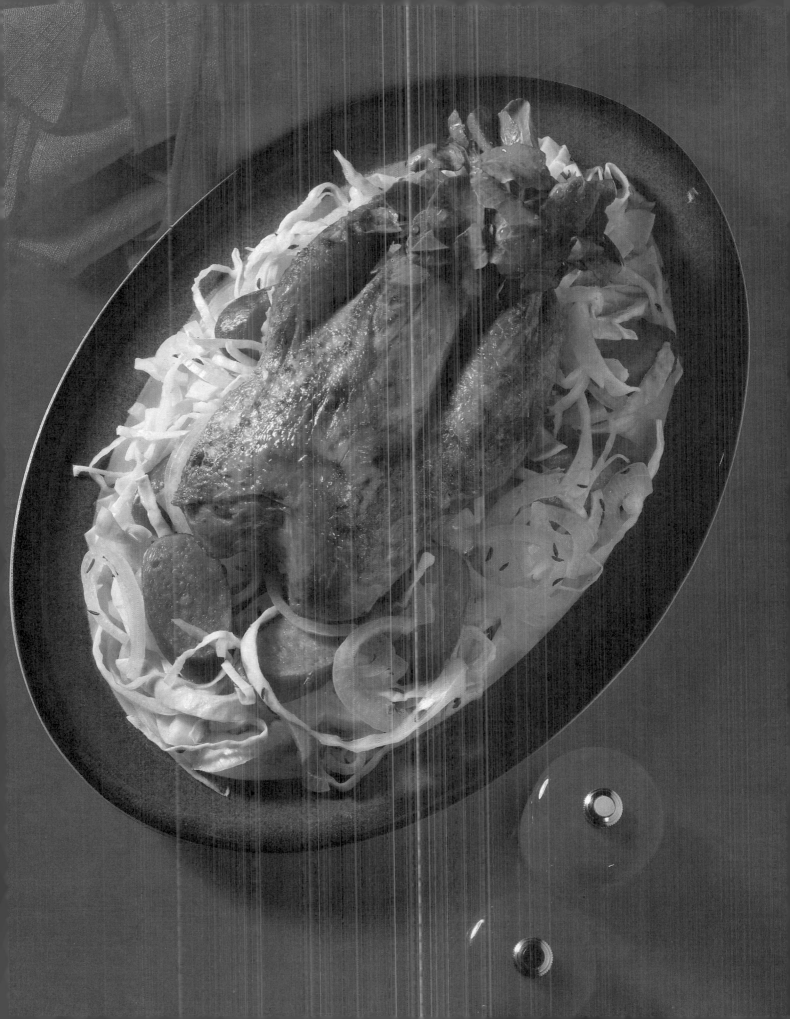

the venison. Cook 4-6 minutes on HIGH, stirring frequently. Remove the meat and add the onions. Cook 1-2 minutes on HIGH to brown slightly. Remove the onions and add the flour, stock and marmalade. Return the meat and the onions to the casserole, cover and cook 30 minutes on MEDIUM. Leave to stand 10 minutes before serving. Garnish with orange slices and sprinkle with chopped parsley before serving.

Garlic Roast Pigeon

PREPARATION TIME: 20 minutes

MICROWAVE COOKING TIME:
15 minutes, plus
5 minutes standing time

SERVES: 4 people

4 pigeons
60g/2oz/4 tbsps butter or margarine
12 cloves garlic, peeled
60ml/2 fl oz/¼ cup white wine
280ml/½ pint/1 cup chicken stock
1 bay leaf
1 sprig thyme
Salt and pepper

ACCOMPANIMENT
4 heads Belgian endive/chicory
280ml/½ pint/1 cup water and white wine mixed
Pinch sugar
Salt and pepper

Spread the butter on the pigeons and place them breast side up on a roasting rack with the cloves of garlic. Cook on HIGH or a Combination setting for 10 minutes. Leave the pigeons to stand for 5 minutes before serving. They may be served slightly pink. Meanwhile, mash the cloves of garlic and mix with the stock, wine, bay leaf and salt and pepper. Cook, uncovered, for 3 minutes to reduce the liquid. Purée the sauce until smooth. Cut the endive/chicory in half lengthwise and remove the cores. Put into a casserole dish with the wine and water mixed, sugar, salt and pepper. Cover loosely and cook for 2 minutes on HIGH. Drain and serve

around the pigeons. Pour the sauce over the pigeons and the endive to serve.

Pigeon Kebabs with Walnut Grape Pilaf

PREPARATION TIME: 20 minutes

MICROWAVE COOKING TIME:
14 minutes

SERVES: 4 people

3-4 pigeons, depending on size
8 strips of bacon/streaky bacon
30g/2 tbsps butter or margarine, melted

WALNUT GRAPE PILAF
180g/6oz/1½ cups brown rice
570ml/1 pint/2 cups stock and wine mixed
10ml/2 tsps thyme
120g/4oz/1 cup walnuts, chopped
1 small bunch purple or red grapes
Salt and pepper

Combine the rice with the stock and wine, salt, pepper and thyme in a large casserole. Cover loosely and cook for 10 minutes on HIGH. Cover completely and leave to stand 10 minutes for the rice to absorb the liquid. Add the chopped walnuts, cut the grapes in half and remove the seeds and add to the pilaf. Remove the breast meat from the pigeons and cut each breast half into 3 pieces. Thread onto skewers with the bacon. Brush each kebab with the melted butter or margarine and place on a roasting rack. Cook the kebabs 2 minutes per side. Set them aside, loosely covered, for 5 minutes before serving. Brush the kebabs with the cooking juices and serve on top of the pilaf.

Quail with Apples and Calvados

PREPARATION TIME: 20 minutes

MICROWAVE COOKING TIME:
17-19 minutes

SERVES: 4 people

8 quail
2 large apples, peeled and thinly sliced
60g/4 tbsps/¼ cup butter or margarine

SAUCE
15ml/1 tbsp flour/plain flour
140ml/¼ pint/½ cup white wine or cider
280ml/½ pint/1 cup double/heavy cream
60ml/4 tbsps/¼ cup Calvados or brandy
30ml/2 tbsps chopped parsley
Salt and butter

Heat a browning dish for 5 minutes on HIGH. Melt the butter and brown the quail for 4-6 minutes, turning often to brown evenly. Remove the quail and set aside. Add the sliced apples to the browning dish and cook for 2 minutes, turning over often to brown on both sides. If the apples are not browning sprinkle lightly with sugar. Remove the apples and set them aside. Stir the flour into the juices in the dish and add the white wine and the Calvados. Return the quail to the dish or transfer to a casserole. Cover the dish tightly and cook for 5 minutes on HIGH. Remove the quail and keep warm. Add the cream and the parsley to the dish with salt and pepper. Cook for 1 minute on HIGH. Add the apples to the sauce and pour over the quail to serve.

Pheasant Alsacienne

PREPARATION TIME: 20 minutes

MICROWAVE COOKING TIME:
28-30 minutes

SERVES: 4 people

2 pheasants, dressed
2 onion slices
2 sprigs thyme
30ml/2 tbsps oil

ACCOMPANIMENT
45g/3 tbsps butter
45g/3 tbsps flour
1 head white cabbage, shredded

Facing page: Pigeon Kebabs with Walnut Grape Pilaf (top) and Garlic Roast Pigeon (bottom).

2 apples, peeled and grated
30ml/2 tbsps caraway seeds
225g/8oz smoked sausage, sliced
280ml/½ pint/1 cup white wine
1 bay leaf
Salt and pepper

Prick the pheasants lightly all over the skin and brush with oil. Place the pheasants breast side down on a roasting rack, one at a time if necessary. Cook for 10 minutes on MEDIUM. Turn over and cook for a further 10 minutes on MEDIUM. Cook for 15 minutes on the Combination setting of a microwave convection oven, turning once. Cover and leave to stand while preparing the cabbage. Melt the butter in a large casserole for 30 seconds on HIGH. Add the flour and the wine and combine with the remaining ingredients. Cook for 8-10 minutes on HIGH, stirring frequently. Serve with the pheasants.

Wild Duck with Limes and Onions

PREPARATION TIME: 20 minutes

MICROWAVE COOKING TIME: 25 minutes

SERVES: 4 people

2 wild ducks
2 slices onion
2 bay leaves
60g/2oz/¼ cup butter or margarine

SAUCE
45g/1½ oz/3 tbsps flour/plain flour
Cooking juices from the duck
280ml/½ pint/1 cup stock
2 onions, finely sliced
Grated rind and juice of 1 lime
Pinch of sugar
Salt and pepper

GARNISH
Lime wedges

Prick the skin of the duck all over and rub with half of the butter. Put an onion slice and a bay leaf inside each duck. Put onto a roasting rack breast side down and cook for 5 minutes on MEDIUM. Turn the

ducks over and cook for 10 minutes further on MEDIUM. Cook on the Combination setting of a microwave convection oven for 16 minutes. Turn over after 8 minutes. Cover loosely and leave to stand for 5 minutes. Combine the pan juices with the remaining butter in a small bowl, and cook 30 seconds on HIGH to melt. Add the sliced onions, cover the dish loosely, and cook for 2 minutes on HIGH. Stir in the flour, stock, lime juice and grated rind. Add a pinch sugar, salt and pepper and cook a further 5 minutes on HIGH, or until thickened. Pour over the ducks to serve and surround with lime wedges.

Wild Duck with Blackcurrants and Port

PREPARATION TIME: 15 minutes

MICROWAVE COOKING TIME: 20-25 minutes

SERVES: 4 people

2 wild ducks
2 onion slices
2 sprigs thyme
30g/2 tbsps butter or margarine
450g/1lb can blackcurrants (if unavailable substitute other red berries or dark cherries)
15ml/1 tbsp red wine vinegar
140ml/¼ pint/½ cup port
15ml/1 tbsp cornstarch/cornflour
Pinch of salt and pepper

Prick the duck skin all over and rub each duck with the butter. Put a slice of onion and a sprig of thyme inside each duck and place them breast side down on a roasting rack. Cook on MEDIUM for 5 minutes. Turn over the ducks and cook a further 10 minutes on MEDIUM. Cook for 16 minutes on the Combination setting of a microwave convection oven. Turn halfway through the cooking time. Cover loosely and set aside for 5 minutes. Combine the blackcurrants with the port, vinegar, cornstarch/cornflour, pan juices from the duck, salt and pepper in a deep bowl. Cook, uncovered, for 5 minutes on HIGH or until thickened, stirring

frequently. Remove the onion and the thyme from the ducks and pour over the blackcurrant sauce to serve.

Quail with Raspberries

PREPARATION TIME: 15 minutes

MICROWAVE COOKING TIME: 9-11 minutes

SERVES: 4 people

8 quail
225g/8oz frozen raspberries
280ml/½ pint/1 cup red wine
15ml/1 tbsp red wine vinegar or raspberry vinegar
15g/1 tbsp sugar
1 sprig rosemary
15g/1 tbsp cornflour/cornstarch

GARNISH
Whole raspberries and watercress

Prick the quail lightly all over with a fork and rub with a bit of butter. Put the quail breast side down on a roasting rack in a circle with the thicker part of the quail pointing to the outside of the dish. Cook for 2 minutes on HIGH. Turn the quail over and cook for a further 3 minutes on HIGH. Cook for 6 minutes on the Combination setting of a microwave convection oven without turning. Cover loosely and set aside while preparing the sauce. Reserve 16 raspberries for garnish and combine the raspberries with the remaining sauce ingredients in a deep bowl. Cook for 4-6 minutes on HIGH, stirring frequently to break up the raspberries. When thickened, purée in a food processor until smooth. Strain to remove the raspberry seeds. Cut the quail in half and coat with the raspberry sauce. Garnish with the reserved whole raspberries and watercress to serve.

Dijon Rabbit with Capers

PREPARATION TIME: 15 minutes

MICROWAVE COOKING TIME: 34 minutes

SERVES: 4 people

8 rabbit quarters
45g/3 tbsps butter or margarine
45g/3 tbsps flour/plain flour
280ml/½ pint/1 cup stock
140ml/¼ pint/½ cup white wine
140ml/¼ pint/½ cup double/heavy
  cream
30ml/2 tbsps Dijon mustard
30ml/2 tbsps capers
15ml/1 tbsp chopped chives
Salt and pepper

Heat a browning dish for 5 minutes
on HIGH. Melt the butter and
brown the rabbit for 2 minutes on
each side. Remove the rabbit and add
the flour, stock, wine, salt, pepper
and mustard. Return the rabbit to
the dish or transfer to a casserole.
Cook, covered, for 25 minutes on
MEDIUM. Remove the rabbit from
the dish and add the capers, chives
and cream. Cook a further 2 minutes

on HIGH and pour over the rabbit
to serve. Serve with French/green
beans.

Pepper Rabbit and Mushrooms

PREPARATION TIME: 15 minutes

MICROWAVE COOKING TIME:
34 minutes

SERVES: 4 people

8 rabbit quarters
45g/3 tbsps butter or margarine
45g/3 tbsps flour/plain flour
2 shallots, finely chopped
280ml/½ pint/1 cup stock
140ml/¼ pint/½ cup white wine
225g/½ lb mushrooms, sliced
140ml/¼ pint/½ cup heavy/double
  cream

**Left: Pepper Rabbit and
Mushrooms (top) and Dijon
Rabbit with Capers (bottom).
Right: Wild Duck with Limes and
Onions (top) and Wild Duck with
Blackcurrants and Port (bottom).**

5ml/1 tsp coarsely ground black pepper
15ml/1 tbsp chopped parsley
Salt

Heat a browning dish for 5 minutes
on HIGH. Melt the butter and
brown the rabbit pieces and the
shallots for 1 minute per side on
HIGH. Add the stock, wine, pepper
and salt. Cook, covered, for
25 minutes on MEDIUM. Add the
mushrooms and cook a further
2 minutes on HIGH. Remove the
rabbit from the casserole and stir in
the cream and parsley. Pour the sauce
over the rabbit to serve.

Microwave
COOKING FOR 1&2

Do meals for singles or couples have to be uninspiring? Do people on their own have to rely on pre-prepared food for speed and convenience? Not when there is a microwave around. Small portions cook beautifully in practically the time it takes to open the package and read the cooking instructions. With a microwave oven there is no need to sacrifice variety for convenience.

Small packages of fresh vegetables and meat are readily available in supermarkets and specialty food stores. Even turkey and duck are available in manageable sizes for the small household. Cooking a dinner party for one special guest can be cheaper than dinner out. It can also be an occasion for experimenting with more elaborate preparations than you might want to attempt for large numbers.

However, leftovers come in handy, so don't shy away from cooking a whole turkey or a large piece of meat. Leftovers can be frozen and used as a basis for completely different meals later on. Small portions, well covered, will defrost in 2-3 minutes on a LOW or DEFROST setting. Soups can be kept refrigerated for up to two days and reheated on MEDIUM in about 2-5 minutes. Vegetable and flour-thickened soups can also be frozen, and then defrosted and reheated in about 10 minutes on a LOW or DEFROST setting, with frequent stirring. Meat, poultry and game stews and braises can be reheated as well, usually on MEDIUM for about 4-6 minutes. If frozen, they can be defrosted and reheated in about 12-15 minutes on LOW or DEFROST. Individual portions should be frozen in bags or containers that are suitable for reheating in microwave ovens or in individual serving dishes of the freezer-to-table variety.

All the recipes in this book were tested in an oven with a maximum power of 700 watts. Certain recipes were cooked in a combination microwave-convection oven, which combines the speed of microwave cooking with browning ability. However, any dish that requires browning can be placed under a preheated broiler or grill for a minute or two before serving. Also, toppings such as breadcrumbs, crushed cereals or cheeses can give an eye-pleasing finish to your very own brand of 'convenience' food.

SOUPS AND APPETIZERS

Confetti Spread and Sesame Crackers

PREPARATION TIME: 15 minutes

MICROWAVE COOKING TIME: 10-12 minutes

SERVES: 2 people

SPREAD
225g/8oz/1 cup cream cheese
2 strips bacon, diced
15g/1 tbsp chopped chives
Red pepper flakes
4 chopped black olives
Crushed garlic
60g/2oz/¼ cup chopped green and red
  peppers, mixed
30g/1oz/2 tbsps frozen corn
Salt and pepper

CRACKERS/BISCUITS
60g/2oz/¼ cup all-purpose flour/plain
  flour
60g/2oz/¼ cup wholewheat flour/
  wholemeal flour
45g/1½ oz/1½ tbsps butter
10ml/2 tsps sesame seeds
15-30ml/1-2 tbsps cold water
1 egg, beaten with a pinch of salt
Salt and pepper

Put the flours, salt and pepper into the bowl of a food processor. Cut the butter into small pieces and add to the flour. Process until the mixture looks like fine breadcrumbs. Add 1 tbsp sesame seeds and add the water with the machine running until the mixture forms a dough. Roll out thinly on a floured board and brush with the egg. Sprinkle on the remaining sesame seeds and cut into 2.5cm (1″) squares. Arrange into a circle on a large plate and cook on HIGH for 3-6 minutes until crisp.

Cool on a wire rack. Makes 12 crackers.
Heat a browning dish for 3 minutes and cook the diced bacon on HIGH for 1-2 minutes or until crisp. Drain on paper towels and allow to cool. Put the chopped peppers and corn into a small bowl and cover with water. Cover the bowl with pierced

This page: Confetti Spread with Sesame Crackers. Facing page: Oriental Kebabs.

plastic wrap and cook on HIGH for 2 minutes. Rinse with cold water and leave to drain dry. Put the cream cheese into a small bowl and heat for

30-40 seconds on MEDIUM to soften. Add the bacon, peppers and the remaining ingredients, and mix well. Serve with the sesame seed crackers. Unused peppers can be frozen.

Marinated Shrimp and Sour Cream Sauce

PREPARATION TIME: 15 minutes

MICROWAVE COOKING TIME: 5 minutes

SERVES: 2 people

225g/½ lb fresh large shrimp, shelled and cleaned

MARINADE
140ml/¼ pint/½ cup white wine
30ml/1oz/2 tbsps white wine vinegar
1 bay leaf
2 black peppercorns
1 whole allspice berry
2 whole cloves
2.5ml/½ tsp dill seeds
½ small onion, sliced
Salt

SAUCE
140ml/¼ pint/½ cup sour cream
30-45ml/2-3 tbsps strained reserved marinade
2.5ml/½ tsp chopped dill, fresh or dried
2.5ml/½ tsp grated horseradish
Salt and pepper

GARNISH
Lettuce leaves
Sprigs of fresh dill

Combine all the marinade ingredients in a 570ml/1 pint casserole and cover. Cook for 2-3 minutes on HIGH until boiling. Stir in the shrimp, cover, and cook on MEDIUM for 2 minutes. Allow to cool in the marinade. If using fresh dill, reserve 2 small sprigs for garnish and chop 2.5ml/½ tsp. Drain the marinade and mix with the sour cream, dill, horseradish, and salt and pepper. Arrange lettuce on serving plates, and place on the shrimp. Top with some of the sauce and the reserved dill. Serve remaining sauce separately.

Scallop Parcels with Curry Sauce

PREPARATION TIME: 15 minutes

MICROWAVE COOKING TIME: 3-4 minutes

SERVES: 2 people

6 large or 8 small scallops
1 small sweet red pepper
2 large mushrooms
30ml/1oz/2 tbsps white wine
5ml/1 tsp black pepper
1.5ml/¼ tsp salt
1.5ml/¼ tsp ground ginger
Garlic powder
15ml/1 tbsp oil
Whole fresh chives

SAUCE
15g/1 tbsp curry powder
140ml/¼ pint/½ cup plain yogurt
Juice of ½ a lime
2.5ml/½ tsp mango chutney
Salt and pepper

Mix the wine, salt, pepper, oil, ginger, and a pinch of garlic powder together well. Put in the scallops and turn them to coat evenly. Cut the pepper into pieces the size of the scallops. Cut the mushrooms into 5mm (¼") slices. Layer the pepper, mushrooms and scallops, and tie each parcel with 2 whole chives. Put the parcels on their sides onto a microwave roasting rack and cook on HIGH for 30 seconds. Turn every 30 seconds, ending with the parcels scallop-sides up. Cook for a total of 2-3 minutes, brushing frequently with the ginger basting liquid. Serve hot or cold, with the curry sauce.
Put the curry powder for the sauce onto a small plate and cook for 1 minute on HIGH. Allow to cool, and combine with the other ingredients. Serve with the scallops.

Oriental Kebabs

PREPARATION TIME: 20 minutes

MICROWAVE COOKING TIME: 5-6 minutes

SERVES: 2 people

90g/3oz ground/minced pork or beef
30g/1oz/2 tbsp breadcrumbs
5ml/1 tsp chopped onion
1 small can pineapple chunks
6 cherry tomatoes

BASTING MIXTURE
60ml/2oz/¼ cup honey
60ml/2oz/¼ cup soy sauce
60ml/2oz/¼ cup rice wine
15ml/1 tbsp sesame seed oil
5ml/1 tsp ground ginger
Pepper

SWEET AND SOUR SAUCE
Remaining basting mixture
15ml/1 tbsp ketchup
5ml/1 tsp cornstarch/cornflour
Reserved pineapple juice
15ml/1 tbsp cider vinegar
2.5ml/½ tsp garlic powder

Mix together the basting ingredients. Mix the meat, breadcrumbs, chopped onion and 1 tbsp of the basting mixture. Shape into 8 meatballs. Drain the can of pineapple and reserve the juice. Thread the meatballs onto wooden skewers, alternating with the pineapple chunks and tomatoes. Place the kebabs on a roasting rack and brush with the baste. Cook on HIGH for 3 minutes, turning and basting each minute. Combine the ingredients for the sauce, and cook on HIGH for 2-3 minutes until thickened. Stir every 30 seconds. Serve with the kebabs. For one person only, use half the amount of all the ingredients. Cook the kebabs for 2 minutes, and the sauce for 1-2 minutes.

Tomato and Basil Soup

PREPARATION TIME: 15 minutes

MICROWAVE COOKING TIME: 5 minutes

SERVES: 2 people

Facing page: Scallop Parcels with Curry Sauce (top) and Marinated Shrimp and Sour Cream Sauce (bottom).

700ml/1¼ pints/2 cups tomato sauce/
  tinned tomatoes, liquidized and sieved
280ml/½ pint/1 cup hot water
½ a beef bouillon stock cube, or 5ml/1 tsp
  instant beef bouillon granules
30ml/1oz/2 tbsps cream
30ml/1oz/2 tbsps red wine
1.25ml/¼ tsp cornstarch/cornflour
Pinch sugar
2 tbsps fresh basil leaves
2 tbsps parsley
½ clove garlic
30ml/1oz/2 tbsps olive oil
Salt and pepper

Mix the tomato sauce, water, beef
bouillon, sugar, and salt and pepper
together in a 1150ml/2 pint, 1 quart
casserole. Cover and cook for
2 minutes on HIGH. Mix the
cornstarch and wine together and stir
into the soup. Heat for 2 minutes on
HIGH, stirring every 30 seconds. Put
the basil leaves, parsley and garlic
into a blender and purée. Add the oil
in a thin, steady stream with the
machine running. Re-heat the soup
for 1 minute on HIGH, and stir in the
cream just before serving. Add the

basil mixture, and stir through the
soup.
To serve one person only, use half of
all the ingredients, and cook the soup
for a total of 2 minutes.

Consommé with Vegetable Noodles

PREPARATION TIME: 15 minutes

MICROWAVE COOKING TIME:
5 minutes

SERVES: 2 people

300g/10½ oz can condensed beef or
  chicken consommé
430ml/¾ pint/1½ cups water
1 bay leaf
15ml/½ oz/1 tbsp sherry
1 small zucchini/courgette
1 small carrot, peeled

Combine the consommé and the
water. Add the bay leaf and heat
through for 1 minute on HIGH. Cut
ends off the zucchini/courgette and
carrot, and using a swivel peeler, pare

the vegetables lengthwise into thin
strips. Add the carrot noodles to the
consommé, cover with pierced plastic
wrap, and cook on HIGH for
3 minutes. Add the zucchini/
courgette and cook for an additional
1 minute on HIGH. Stir in the sherry
before serving.

Cheesy Spinach Soup

PREPARATION TIME: 15 minutes

MICROWAVE COOKING TIME:
5 minutes

SERVES: 1 person

120g/4oz/½ cup frozen spinach
60g/2oz/½ cup shredded Red Leicester/
  Colby cheese
30ml/1oz/2 tbsps hot water
15g/½ oz/1 tbsp butter
15g/½ oz/1 tbsp flour/plain flour
½ a chicken bouillon/stock cube
15ml/1 tbsp chopped onion
280ml/½ pint/1 cup milk
Pinch of thyme
Pinch of nutmeg
Salt and pepper

Put the spinach, onion and water
into a small bowl and cover with
pierced plastic wrap. Cook for
1 minute on HIGH and set aside. Put
the butter into another bowl and
cook for 30 seconds on HIGH or
until melted. Add the flour, bouillon
cube, nutmeg, thyme, milk, and salt
and pepper. Cook on MEDIUM for
4 minutes or until thickened. Stir
frequently. Add the spinach and its
cooking liquid to the soup, and purée
in a food processor until smooth. Stir
in the cheese, reserving 1 tbsp.
Re-heat on MEDIUM for 1 minute.
Sprinkle the reserved cheese on top
to serve.
To serve 2 people, double the
ingredients and cook the soup for 5-6
minutes on MEDIUM.

**This page: Consommé with
Vegetable Noodles. Facing page:
Cheesy Spinach Soup (top) and
Tomato and Basil Soup (bottom).**

SNACKS

Italian Ham Sandwiches

| **PREPARATION TIME:** 10 minutes |
| **MICROWAVE COOKING TIME:** 4 minutes |
| **SERVES:** 2 people |

120g/¼ lb Parma, or other Italian ham
60g/2oz sliced Mozzarella cheese
4 mild Italian peppers
15g/½ oz/1 tbsp butter or margarine
Pinch garlic powder
Pinch of oregano
2 French rolls

Mix the butter, garlic and oregano. Split the rolls and spread the butter thinly on each of the cut sides. Layer the ham, peppers and cheese on the bottom half of the roll. Place the top on and press down. Place the sandwiches on a paper towel in the oven. Cook on MEDIUM for 4-5 minutes or until the cheese melts. Serve immediately.

Sloppy Joes

| **PREPARATION TIME:** 15 minutes |
| **MICROWAVE COOKING TIME:** 14 minutes |
| **SERVES:** 2 people |

225g/½ lb ground/minced beef or pork
1 small onion, finely chopped
60g/2oz/¼ cup chopped green pepper
280ml/½ pint/1 cup tomato sauce/ canned tomatoes

This page: Italian Ham Sandwiches (top) and Cheese and Mushroom Croissants (bottom). Facing page: Sausage and Sauerkraut Sandwiches (top) and Sloppy Joes (bottom).

2 tsps Worcestershire sauce
½ tsp dry mustard
1½ tsps cider vinegar
1 tsp brown sugar
Salt and pepper
2 Kaiser rolls or hamburger buns

Mix the meat and onion in a casserole and cook, uncovered, for 7 minutes on HIGH. Mash the meat with a fork several times while cooking, to break it up into small pieces. Strain off any fat. Add the remaining ingredients and stir well. Cover and cook for a further 5 minutes on HIGH, stirring occasionally. Wrap the rolls in paper towels and heat for 1-2 minutes on MEDIUM. Split and fill with the Sloppy Joe filling. Mixture freezes well.

Tacos

PREPARATION TIME: 15 minutes

MICROWAVE COOKING TIME: 6 minutes

SERVES: 2 people

4 taco shells
120g/¼ lb ground/minced beef
60g/2oz/¼ cup chopped onion
15g/½ oz/1 tbsp raisins
15g/½ oz/1 tbsp pine nuts
15g/½ oz/1 tbsp corn/sweetcorn
5ml/1 tsp chili powder
60ml/2oz/¼ cup tomato sauce/canned tomatoes
Salt and pepper

TOPPINGS
60g/2oz/½ cup grated cheese
140ml/¼ pint/½ cup sour cream
120g/4oz/½ cup chopped tomatoes
60g/2oz/1 cup shredded lettuce
1 chopped avocado

Put the beef and onion into a 1150ml/2 pint/1 quart casserole. Break the meat up well with a fork. Cover and cook for 2 minutes on HIGH, stirring occasionally to break into small pieces. Drain any fat from the meat and add salt and pepper, chili powder, corn, nuts, raisins and tomato sauce. Cover and cook on MEDIUM for 4 minutes. Spoon into the taco shells and serve with the various toppings.

Sausage and Sauerkraut Sandwiches

PREPARATION TIME: 10 minutes

MICROWAVE COOKING TIME: 1½ minutes

SERVES: 2 people

4 slices rye bread, light or dark
120g/¼ lb smoked sausage (kielbasa or bratwurst), thinly sliced
4 slices Muenster or Tilsit cheese
90g/3oz/½ cup drained sauerkraut
30g/1oz/2 tbsps butter or margarine

DRESSING
15ml/1 tbsp spicy brown mustard
2 tbsps mayonnaise
7.5ml/1½ tsps chopped dill pickle

Melt the butter for 30 seconds on HIGH in a small bowl. Mix dressing and spread on both sides of the bread slices. Layer on the sauerkraut, sausage and cheese. Heat a browning dish for 5 minutes on HIGH. Brush 1 side of the bread with melted butter and place the sandwich in the dish. Cook for 15 seconds, or until golden brown. Turn over and brush the other side with butter and cook that side for 20-30 seconds or until the bread is browned and the cheese melted. Serve hot.

Cheese and Mushroom Croissants

PREPARATION TIME: 15 minutes

MICROWAVE COOKING TIME: 3 minutes

SERVES: 1 person

1 croissant or crescent roll
5ml/1 tsp butter
2.5ml/½ tsp flour/plain flour
2 mushrooms, sliced
60g/2oz/¼ cup Gruyère cheese
60ml/2oz/¼ cup milk
15ml/½ oz/1 tbsp white wine
2.5ml/½ tsp Dijon mustard
Nutmeg
Salt and pepper

Split the top of the croissant, taking care not to cut through to the bottom or the ends. Melt 2.5ml/½ tsp butter in a small bowl for 15 seconds on HIGH. Add the mushrooms and cook for 30 seconds on HIGH and set aside. Melt the remaining butter in a 570ml/1 pint measure. Stir in the flour and add the milk and wine gradually. Add a pinch of nutmeg, mustard and salt and pepper. Cook on HIGH for 1 minute or until thick. Stir in the cheese and spoon into the croissant. Top with the mushrooms and heat through for 1 minute on MEDIUM. Serve immediately.

Pizza Muffins

PREPARATION TIME: 10 minutes

MICROWAVE COOKING TIME: 2 minutes

SERVES: 1 person

1 English muffin, split
30ml/2 tbsps tomato paste
30ml/1oz/2 tbsps water
1 green/spring onion, sliced
1.25ml/¼ tsp oregano
Pinch garlic powder
60g/2oz/¼ cup pepperoni or Italian salami, chopped, or 4 anchovies
2-3 Italian olives, stoned and halved
5ml/1 tsp capers
45g/1½ oz/⅓ cup grated Mozzarella cheese
15g/½ oz/1 tbsp Parmesan cheese
Salt and pepper

Mix the tomato paste with the water, salt and pepper, onion, oregano and garlic powder, and spread on the muffin halves. Arrange the sausage or a cross of anchovies on top. Add the olives and capers and sprinkle on the Mozzarella cheese. Sprinkle on the Parmesan cheese last and put the pizzas on a paper towel, then cook for 1½-2 minutes on HIGH. Turn the pizzas once or twice during cooking. For 2 people, double the ingredients and cook for 4-4½ minutes on HIGH.

Facing page: Tacos.

Vegetable Pockets

PREPARATION TIME: 10 minutes

MICROWAVE COOKING TIME:
4-5 minutes

SERVES: 2 people

1 piece wholewheat pitta bread
15ml/½ oz/1 tbsp olive oil
5ml/1 tsp lemon juice
1 tomato, roughly chopped
1 red onion, thinly sliced or 2 green/spring
    onions, sliced
1 green pepper, thinly sliced
60g/2oz/1 cup fresh spinach leaves
2.5ml/½ tsp chives
15ml/1 tbsp fresh basil leaves, if available
1 small zucchini/courgette, thinly sliced
6 black olives, stoned
30g/1oz/¼ cup crumbled feta cheese
Salt and pepper

Cut the pitta bread in half and open
out the pockets. Mix the lemon juice
and oil together with the salt and
pepper. Toss the cheese, tomato,
vegetables, herbs and olives together
in the dressing. Fill the pockets with
the vegetables and heat for 4-5
minutes on MEDIUM. Serve
immediately.

Tuna Melt

PREPARATION TIME: 10 minutes

MICROWAVE COOKING TIME:
2 minutes

SERVES: 1 person

1 English muffin, split
1 small can white tuna
30ml/2 tbsps cottage cheese
30ml/2 tbsps mayonnaise
1 stick celery, chopped
5ml/1 tsp chopped parsley
10ml/2 tsps chopped chives
2.5ml/½ tsp lemon juice
Alfalfa sprouts
30g/1oz/¼ cup grated Colby/Red
    Leicester cheese
Salt and pepper

Mix together the tuna, cottage
cheese, mayonnaise, celery, parsley,
chives, and salt and pepper. Taste and
add lemon juice if desired. Put alfalfa
sprouts on the muffin halves and

spoon on the tuna mixture. Top with
the cheese and heat for 1 minute on
MEDIUM. Increase the heat to
HIGH and heat for 1 minute further,
turning once or twice during cooking.
Serve immediately.

Pocketful of Shrimp

PREPARATION TIME: 10 minutes

MICROWAVE COOKING TIME:
2-4 minutes

SERVES: 2 people

1 piece pitta bread, cut in half
60g/2oz/½ cup bean sprouts
120g/4oz/½ cup cooked shrimp, peeled
    and de-veined
15ml/1 tbsp chili sauce
30ml/1oz/2 tbsps mayonnaise
2.5ml/½ tsp horseradish

This page: Pizza Muffins (top) and
Tuna Melt (bottom). Facing page:
Pocketful of Shrimp (top) and
Vegetable Pockets (bottom).

1 stick celery, chopped
1 ripe avocado, peeled and thickly sliced
15ml/1 tbsp lemon juice
Salt and pepper

Cut the pitta bread in half and open
a pocket in each half. Toss the
avocado slices in lemon juice and
place them in the sides of the
pockets. Fill each pocket with bean
sprouts. Mix the shrimp, chili sauce,
mayonnaise, horseradish, salt, pepper
and chopped celery together. Put on
top of the bean sprouts and heat
through for 2-4 minutes on
MEDIUM. Serve immediately.

Microwave
COOKING FOR 1 & 2

EGG AND CHEESE

Piperade

PREPARATION TIME: 10 minutes

MICROWAVE COOKING TIME:
6 minutes, plus 1 minute standing time

SERVES: 1 person

30ml/1 tbsp finely chopped onion
7.5gm/¼ oz/½ tbsp butter
½ cap pimento, finely chopped
1 tomato
Pinch garlic powder
2 eggs
Pinch oregano
Salt and pepper

Put 570ml/1 pint/2 cups water into a bowl and cover with pierced plastic wrap. Heat for 3 minutes on HIGH or until boiling. Put in the tomato and leave for 30 seconds. Peel and seed the tomato, and chop roughly. Put the butter into a medium-sized bowl with the garlic powder and onion. Cook on HIGH for 3 minutes. Add the pimento, tomato and oregano. Cook on HIGH for 1 minute. Beat the eggs, salt and pepper together, and add to the bowl. Cook on HIGH for about 2 minutes, stirring every 30 seconds, or until the eggs are softly scrambled. Leave to stand for 1 minute before serving. Serve on buttered toast or English muffins, or with French bread.

Sunrise Scramble

PREPARATION TIME: 15 minutes

MICROWAVE COOKING TIME:
5 minutes, plus 1 minute standing time

SERVES: 1 person

30g/1oz/2 tbsps ham, finely chopped
2 eggs
15g/½ oz/1 tbsp butter
15g/½ oz/1 tbsp grated cheese
30g/1oz/¼ cup mushrooms, sliced
1 tomato
15ml/1 tbsp chopped parsley
Salt and pepper

Put the butter into a small bowl, add the mushrooms, and cook for 2 minutes on HIGH or until soft. Drain away any excess liquid. Add the ham, and cook for 1 minute on HIGH. Cut the tomato in quarters, but leave attached at the base. Heat for 1 minute on HIGH, and keep warm. Beat the eggs and add the cheese, parsley, and salt and pepper. Add the eggs to the bowl with the ham and mushrooms, and cook for 2 minutes on HIGH, stirring every 30 seconds until softly scrambled. Leave to stand for 1 minute. Fill the tomato with the egg mixture and serve.

Spinach and Cheese Layered Quiche

PREPARATION TIME: 20 minutes

MICROWAVE COOKING TIME:
11-14 minutes, plus 6 minutes standing time

SERVES: 2 people

PASTRY
60g/2oz/⅓ cup all-purpose flour
60g/2oz/⅓ cup wholewheat/wholemeal flour
60g/2oz/¼ cup margarine
30g/1oz/2 tbsps shortening
60ml/2oz/¼ cup ice cold water
Pinch of salt

FILLING
60g/2oz/½ cup shredded Gruyère or Swiss cheese
3 eggs
60ml/2oz/¼ cup half and half/single cream
60g/2oz/¼ cup chopped frozen spinach, well drained
Nutmeg
Cayenne pepper or Tabasco
Salt and pepper

Put the flours, salt, margarine and shortening into the bowl of a food processor and work until the mixture resembles fine breadcrumbs. With the machine running, add the water gradually until the dough holds together. It may not be necessary to add all the water. Roll out the pastry on a floured board to 3mm (⅛") thick, and put into an 18cm (7") pie plate. Trim the edge and flute. Refrigerate for 10 minutes. Mix the eggs, cheese, half and half/cream and salt and pepper together well. Divide the mixture in half: add the spinach and pinch of nutmeg to one half, and a pinch of Cayenne pepper or a dash of Tabasco to the other. Prick the base of the pastry with a fork and cook on HIGH for 2-3 minutes or until it starts to crisp. Pour in the cheese mixture and cook for 4 minutes on MEDIUM, or until softly set. Leave to stand for 1 minute. Pour on the spinach mixture and cook for a further 7-10 minutes or until the center is softly set. Leave to stand for 6 minutes before serving.

Facing page: Sunrise Scramble (top) and Piperade (bottom).

Niçoise Eggs

PREPARATION TIME: 10 minutes

MICROWAVE COOKING TIME:
9 minutes

SERVES: 2 person

2 eggs
4 tomatoes, peeled, seeded and chopped
5ml/1 tsp butter
2 mushrooms, chopped
30ml/1oz/2 tbsps white wine
15ml/1 tbsp capers
4 black olives, stoned and sliced
2 anchovies, chopped
15ml/1 tbsp tarragon
Pinch of paprika
Salt and pepper
*30g/1oz/¼ cup Gruyère or Swiss cheese,
    grated*

**This page: Italian Fondue (left)
and Niçoise Eggs (right). Facing
page: Tuna and Tomato Quiche
(top) and Spinach and Cheese
Layered Quiche (bottom).**

Put the butter into a small casserole
and melt for 30 seconds on HIGH.
Add the chopped mushrooms,
tarragon and half the wine, and cook
for 2 minutes on HIGH. Add the
remaining ingredients except the
cheese, eggs and paprika, and cook
for 1-2 minutes on HIGH. Divide the
tomato mixture into 2 custard cups/
ramekin dishes and make a well in
the center. Put an egg into the center
of the mixture in each cup. Pierce the
yolk with a sharp knife. Pour over the
remaining wine. Cook for 3 minutes

on HIGH or until the white is set
and yolk is still soft. Sprinkle on the
cheese and paprika and cook for
1 minute on LOW to melt the
cheese.

Italian Fondue

PREPARATION TIME: 10 minutes

MICROWAVE COOKING TIME:
5 minutes

SERVES: 1 person

*120g/4oz/1 cup shredded Mozzarella
    cheese*
*60g/2oz/½ cup shredded mild Cheddar
    cheese*
5ml/1 tsp cornstarch/cornflour
90ml/3oz/⅓ cup red wine

15ml/1 tbsp tomato paste
5ml/1 tsp dry vermouth
½ clove garlic, crushed
2.5ml/½ tsp basil
2.5ml/½ tsp oregano
1 French roll, cut into cubes, or broccoli
    flowerets, carrot sticks and celery sticks

Toss the cheese and cornstarch to mix. Put the wine into a deep bowl and cook on MEDIUM for 1-2 minutes, or until it begins to bubble – do not allow it to boil. Add the remaining ingredients except the bread (or vegetables), and stir well to blend completely. Cook for a further 2-3 minutes on MEDIUM, or until the cheese melts. Stir every few seconds. If the mixture begins to boil, reduce the setting to LOW. Serve with the bread cubes or vegetables. Re-heat on LOW if necessary. Serve as an appetizer/starter or as an entrée with a tossed salad.
To serve 2 people, double the ingredients. Cook the wine for 2-3 minutes on MEDIUM, and the cheese and other ingredients for 3-4 minutes on MEDIUM.

Tuna and Tomato Quiche

PREPARATION TIME: 20 minutes

MICROWAVE COOKING TIME:
18 minutes, plus 6 minutes standing time

SERVES: 2 people

PASTRY
120g/4oz/⅔ cup all-purpose/plain flour
60g/2oz/¼ cup margarine
30g/1oz/2 tbsps shortening
30ml/1 tbsp paprika
Pinch of salt
60ml/2oz/¼ cup ice cold water

FILLING
1 can (about 180g/6oz) white tuna,
    drained and flaked
3 eggs
2 tomatoes, peeled
60g/2oz/½ cup shredded Cheddar
    cheese
60ml/2oz/¼ cup half and half/single
    cream
15ml/1 tbsp chopped green/spring onion
Salt and pepper

TOPPING
15ml/1 tbsp dry, seasoned breadcrumbs
30g/1oz/2 tbsps grated Parmesan cheese

Put the flour, salt, paprika, margarine and shortening into the bowl of a food processor and work until the mixture resembles fine breadcrumbs. With the machine running, add the water gradually until the dough holds together. It may not be necessary to add all the water. Roll out the pastry on a floured board to 3mm (⅛″) thick and put into an 18cm (7″) pie plate. Trim the edge and flute. Refrigerate for 10 minutes. Beat the eggs with the salt, pepper and half and half/single cream. Add the cheese, onion and tuna. Cut the tomatoes into quarters and take out the seeds. Prick the base of the pastry and cook on HIGH for 2-3 minutes, or until starting to crisp. Pour the filling into the pastry shell and decorate the top with the tomatoes. Cook on MEDIUM for 10-15 minutes. Mix the topping ingredients and sprinkle over the top of the quiche 5 minutes before the end of baking. Left-over quiche can be refrigerated for up to 2 days. Eat cold or re-heat on MEDIUM for 2 minutes.

Ham, Broccoli and Pineapple au Gratin

PREPARATION TIME: 15 minutes

MICROWAVE COOKING TIME:
10-12 minutes

SERVES: 2 people

To serve 1 person, make full quantity sauce and cut all other ingredients to half quantity. Cook the mushrooms for 30 seconds on HIGH and the broccoli for 3 minutes on HIGH. Once assembled, cook for 2-3 minutes on MEDIUM. Left-over cheese sauce can be frozen, or kept in the refrigerator for 2 days. Bring to room temperature, re-heat on MEDIUM for 1-2 minutes to serve the sauce.

Asparagus and Tomato Omelette

PREPARATION TIME: 15 minutes

MICROWAVE COOKING TIME: 15 minutes

SERVES: 2 people

4 eggs, separated
120g/4oz/½ cup chopped asparagus, fresh or frozen
30ml/1oz/2 tbsps water
2 tomatoes, peeled, seeded and chopped
45g/1½ oz/⅓ cup Gruyère cheese, grated
90ml/3oz/⅓ cup milk
15g/½ oz/1 tbsp butter or margarine
5ml/1 tsp flour/plain flour
Salt and pepper

Put the asparagus and water into a 570ml/1 pint casserole. Cover and cook for 5-6 minutes on HIGH. Beat the egg yolks, milk, flour, and salt and pepper together. Beat the egg whites until stiff but not dry and fold into the yolks. Melt the butter in a 23cm (9") pie plate for 30 seconds on HIGH. Pour the omelette mixture onto the plate and cook on MEDIUM for 7 minutes or until set. Lift the edges of the omelette to allow the uncooked mixture to spread evenly. Sprinkle with the cheese, and spread on the asparagus and chopped tomato. Fold over and cook for 1 minute on LOW to melt the cheese. Serve immediately.

4 slices cooked ham
8 broccoli spears
30g/1oz/¼ cup sliced mushrooms
15g/½ oz/1 tbsp butter
4 pineapple rings, drained
30ml/1oz/2 tbsps water
Pinch of salt
5ml/1 tsp dark brown sugar

SAUCE
15g/½ oz/1 tbsp flour/plain flour
15g/½ oz/1 tbsp butter
1.25ml/¼ tsp dry mustard
140ml/¼ pint/½ cup milk
30g/1oz/2 tbsps shredded Cheddar cheese
Salt and pepper

TOPPING
30g/1oz/¼ cup dry seasoned breadcrumbs

Put 15g/½ oz/1 tbsp butter in a small bowl and cook for 30 seconds on HIGH. Add the mushrooms and cook for 1 minute on HIGH and set aside. Put the broccoli spears into a casserole with the water and a pinch of salt. Cover and cook for 4 minutes on HIGH. Leave covered while preparing the sauce. In a 570ml/1 pint/2 cup measure, melt 15g/1oz/1 tbsp butter for 30 seconds on HIGH. Stir in the flour, mustard, salt and pepper. Add the milk gradually and cook on HIGH for 1-2 minutes, stirring frequently until thick. Stir in the cheese. Put 2 broccoli spears on each ham slice, stalks towards the middle, and top each with the mushrooms. Roll up and put seam-side down in a baking dish. Arrange pineapple rings on each side and sprinkle with the dark brown sugar. Coat the cheese sauce over the broccoli and ham rolls and top with the crumbs. Cook on MEDIUM for 3-4 minutes or until hot. Serve immediately.

This page: Ham, Broccoli, and Pineapple au Gratin. Facing page: Asparagus and Tomato Omelette.

Egg Foo Yung

PREPARATION TIME: 15 minutes

MICROWAVE COOKING TIME:
10 minutes

SERVES: 2 people

CRAB PATTIES
*120g/4oz/½ cup frozen crabmeat,
  defrosted*
15ml/1 tbsp chopped green pepper
*15ml/1 tbsp chopped green onion/spring
  onion*

30g/1oz/¼ cup chopped mushrooms
1 small clove garlic, crushed
60g/2oz/½ cup beansprouts
2 eggs, beaten
1.25ml/¼ tsp ground ginger
Salt and pepper

SAUCE
140ml/¼ pint/½ cup chicken bouillon
5ml/1 tsp sherry
15ml/1 tbsp soy sauce
5ml/1 tsp oyster sauce (optional)
2.5ml/½ tsp brown sugar
10ml/2 tsps cornstarch/cornflour

Beat the eggs in a medium-sized bowl and stir in the remaining ingredients for the patties. Cook on HIGH for 2 minutes, stirring frequently, until softly set. Heat a browning dish on HIGH for 5 minutes. Pour the mixture into the hot dish in 140ml/¼ pint/½ cup amounts, and cook for about 30 seconds per side on HIGH. Cover and keep warm. Combine the sauce ingredients in a 570ml/1 pint/2 cup measure and cook for 1-2 minutes, stirring frequently until clear and thickened. Pour over the patties and serve immediately.

RICE, PASTA AND GRAINS

Bulgur and Spicy Lamb

PREPARATION TIME: 20 minutes

MICROWAVE COOKING TIME: 26 minutes

SERVES: 2 people

120g/4oz/1 cup bulgur wheat
280ml/½ pint/1 cup water
1 small onion, finely chopped
120g/4oz/¼ lb ground/minced lamb
2.5ml/¼ tsp oil
225g/8oz/1 cup canned plum tomatoes
5ml/1 tsp cumin
1.25ml/¼ tsp cinnamon
5ml/1 tsp chopped mint
30g/1oz/2 tbsps raisins
30g/1oz/2 tbsps almonds, chopped
60ml/2oz/¼ cup yogurt
1 egg
Salt and pepper
1 bay leaf

Put the bulgur and water into a 2 quart casserole with a pinch of salt. Cover and cook on HIGH for 5 minutes, and leave covered while preparing the rest of the ingredients. Heat a browning dish for 5 minutes on HIGH. Put in the oil, add the onion and lamb, breaking the latter up into small pieces with a fork. Add the cumin, cinnamon, and salt and pepper. Return the dish to the oven and cook for 5 minutes on HIGH, stirring frequently. Add the tomatoes, mint, bay leaf, and salt and pepper. Cover and cook for 5 minutes on HIGH. Add the raisins and almonds, and leave to stand. Drain the bulgur wheat well, pressing to remove excess moisture. Mix with the egg and yogurt. Add salt and pepper and put half the bulgur in the bottom of a baking dish. Spread with the lamb filling and cover with another layer of bulgur. Cook uncovered for 5-6 minutes on MEDIUM. Leave to stand, to firm up, for 5 minutes before serving. Serve with a cucumber and yogurt salad.

Facing page: Egg Foo Yung. This page: Polenta with Pepper and Leek Salad (top) and Bulgur and Spicy Lamb (bottom).

To serve 1 person, prepare the full quantity casserole and divide into two. One of the casseroles may be frozen.

Sausage Risotto

PREPARATION TIME: 15 minutes

MICROWAVE COOKING TIME: 29 minutes

SERVES: 2 people

60g/2oz/½ cup Italian rice, uncooked
30g/1oz/¼ cup broken, uncooked
*   spaghetti*
1 Italian sausage, mild or hot
15ml/1 tbsp oil
1 small onion, finely sliced
½ clove garlic, crushed
60g/2oz/½ cup quartered mushrooms
2 tomatoes, peeled and seeded
7.5ml/1½ tsps chopped parsley
2.5ml/½ tsp basil
280ml/½ pint/1 cup beef bouillon
60g/2oz/¼ cup Parmesan cheese
Salt and pepper

Remove sausage meat from casing. Heat a browning dish for 5 minutes on HIGH. Add the oil and sausage. Cook for 4 minutes on HIGH, breaking up the sausage meat with the fork. Add the onion, garlic and mushrooms, and cook for 2 minutes more on HIGH, stirring frequently. Put the contents of the browning dish into a 1150ml/2 pint/1 quart casserole and add the rice, spaghetti, basil, salt and pepper, and beef bouillon. Cover and cook for 15 minutes on HIGH. Stir in the parsley and chopped tomatoes, and leave to stand 3 minutes before serving. Sprinkle with Parmesan cheese.

Tri-colored Tagliatelle and Vegetables

PREPARATION TIME: 10 minutes

MICROWAVE COOKING TIME: 12 minutes, plus 2 minutes standing time

SERVES: 1 person

60g/2oz tagliatelle or fettucini (mixture of red, green and plain)
½ a small sweet red pepper, cut into 5mm (¼") strips
½ a small onion, thinly sliced
60g/2oz/½ cup broccoli flowerets
30g/1oz/2 tbsps butter
1 small clove garlic, crushed
7.5ml/1½ tsps dried rosemary (or 1 sprig fresh)
Grated Parmesan cheese
Salt and pepper

Put the pasta into a large bowl and cover with water. Cook for 6 minutes on HIGH. Leave to stand for 2 minutes. Rinse in hot water and leave to drain. If using fresh pasta, cut the cooking time in half. Put 15g/½ oz/ 1 tbsp butter into a medium-sized

This page: Sausage Risotto. Facing page: Tri-colored Tagliatelle and Vegetables.

bowl and add the broccoli, onion and red pepper strips. Cover with pierced plastic wrap and cook for 1-2 minutes on HIGH. Toss with the pasta and keep warm. Melt the remaining butter with the crushed garlic and rosemary for 30 seconds on HIGH in a small bowl or custard cup/ramekin dish. Strain the butter onto the pasta and vegetables and discard the rosemary and garlic. Season with salt and pepper. Heat the pasta through on MEDIUM for 2 minutes. Toss with

Parmesan cheese and serve. For 2 people, double all the ingredients. Cook the pasta for 10 minutes on HIGH if using dried, and 5 minutes on HIGH if using fresh. Cook the broccoli, onion and red pepper for 2-3 minutes on HIGH.

Polenta with Pepper and Leek Salad

PREPARATION TIME: 15 minutes

MICROWAVE COOKING TIME: 12 minutes, plus 5 minutes standing time

SERVES: 2 people

120g/4oz/½ cup yellow cornmeal
420ml/¾ pint/1½ cups water
15ml/1 tbsp finely chopped onion
30g/1oz/¼ cup shredded Mozzarella cheese
60g/2oz/¼ cup Parmesan cheese
Salt and pepper

SALAD
1 red pepper
1 large or 2 small leeks

DRESSING
15ml/1 tbsp vinegar
30ml/2 tbsps oil
2.5ml/½ tsp dry mustard
1.25ml/¼ tsp sugar
1.25ml/¼ tsp fennel seeds, crushed
1.25ml/¼ tsp marjoram

Mix the cornmeal, salt and pepper, onion and water in a large bowl. Cook for 6 minutes on HIGH. Add the Mozzarella, cover and leave to stand for 5 minutes. Spread into a square pan and sprinkle the top with the Parmesan cheese. Refrigerate, and when ready to use, cut into squares and heat for 1 minute on HIGH before serving. Slice the pepper into 5mm (¼") strips. Trim off the dark green tops of the leeks and slice the white part into quarters. Mix the dressing ingredients together and put the vegetables into a 1 pint casserole. Pour over the dressing and mix together well. Cover and cook for 5 minutes on MEDIUM. Serve warm with the polenta.

Barley Ring with Turkey Filling

PREPARATION TIME: 20 minutes

MICROWAVE COOKING TIME: 31 minutes, plus 5 minutes standing time

SERVES: 2 people

120g/4oz/1 cup pearl barley
850ml/1½ pints/3 cups water
1 egg, beaten
60g/2oz/½ cup whole cranberries
2.5ml/½ tsp sugar
Grated rind and juice of half an orange
60g/2oz/½ cup chopped walnuts
30g/1oz/2 tbsps butter or margarine
1 shallot
90g/3oz/¾ cup mushrooms, sliced
225g/8oz/½ lb uncooked boned turkey, cut into 2.5cm (1") pieces
15g/½ oz/1 tbsp flour/plain flour
140ml/¼ pint/½ cup chicken bouillon/ stock
30ml/2 tbsps parsley
140ml/¼ pint/½ cup cream
Salt and pepper

Put the barley into a large bowl with the water and a pinch of salt. Cover with pierced plastic wrap and cook for 20 minutes on HIGH, stirring once. Leave to stand, covered, for at least 5 minutes. Combine the cranberries, sugar and orange juice in a small bowl. Cook uncovered for 1-2 minutes on HIGH. Drain the barley well, and fold in the parsley, cranberries, walnuts, orange rind and beaten egg. Press into a 570ml/ 1 pint/2 cup microwave ring-mold. Put the butter into a 570ml/1 pint/ 2 cup casserole and cook for 30 seconds on HIGH to melt. Add the turkey, shallot and mushrooms. Cover and cook for 2 minutes on HIGH, stirring every 30 seconds. Sprinkle on the flour and stir in well. Add the stock and cream and blend well. Season, cover and cook for an additional 3 minutes on HIGH, stirring every 30 seconds until thickened. Keep warm. Re-heat the barley ring covered with pierced plastic wrap for 3 minutes on HIGH. Turn it out and fill the center with the turkey.
To serve one person, cut all the

ingredients to half quantity, and omit the egg. Serve the barley as a pilaff topped with the turkey filling.

Indian Pilaff

PREPARATION TIME: 15 minutes

MICROWAVE COOKING TIME: 30 minutes

SERVES: 2 people

60g/2oz/½ cup long-grain rice (basmati, if available)
30g/1oz/¼ cup almonds, toasted
1 small onion, sliced
15ml/1 tbsp oil
30g/1oz/2 tbsps peas
2 okra, sliced
30g/1oz/2 tbsps coconut
30g/1oz/2 tbsps golden raisins
280ml/½ pint/1 cup chicken bouillon
15ml/1 tbsp lemon juice
15ml/1 tbsp curry powder
15ml/1 tbsp chopped parsley
2.5ml/½ tsp dried red pepper flakes
Salt and pepper

Heat a browning dish for 5 minutes on HIGH. Sprinkle on the almonds and return the dish to the oven. Cook on HIGH for 3 minutes, stirring the almonds every 30 seconds until golden brown. Remove the almonds from the dish and allow to cool. Add the oil to the browning dish and stir in the sliced onion. Return to the oven and cook for 2 minutes on HIGH or until golden brown. Add the curry powder and cook for 1 minute on HIGH. Put the onion into a casserole and add the rice, pepper flakes, coconut, chicken bouillon and lemon juice. Cover and cook on HIGH for 3 minutes until boiling. Reduce the setting to MEDIUM, add the raisins and cook for 12 minutes. Add the peas, okra and parsley 2 minutes before the end of the cooking time. Sprinkle with toasted almonds before serving. (One serving may be kept in the refrigerator for 2 days. Re-heat for 2-3 minutes on MEDIUM.)

Facing page: Barley Ring with Turkey Filling.

Fried Rice

PREPARATION TIME: 15 minutes

MICROWAVE COOKING TIME:
12 minutes

SERVES: 2 people

60g/2oz/½ cup quick-cooking rice
200ml/6oz/¾ cup water
3 dried Chinese mushrooms
2 green/spring onions, sliced
60g/2oz/¼ cup shrimp, peeled and de-
   veined
Small piece ginger root
Small can sliced bamboo shoots or lotus
   root
1 egg
7.5ml/1½ tsps soy sauce
2.5ml/½ tsp sesame oil
1 tbsp vegetable oil
Salt and pepper

Put the mushrooms into a bowl with
enough water to cover. Cover with
pierced plastic wrap and cook for
3 minutes on HIGH. Leave to stand
until softened. Put the rice, water and
a pinch of salt in a 150ml/2 pint/
1 quart casserole. Cover and cook on
HIGH for 2½ minutes. Leave to
stand while preparing the other
ingredients. Drain and slice the
mushrooms. Slice the ginger into thin
slivers. Beat the egg with the soy
sauce. Heat a browning dish for
5 minutes on HIGH, pour in the
vegetable oil and quickly add the
mushrooms, bamboo shoots, ginger,
and half the onion. Stir and return to
the oven, and cook for 1 minute on
HIGH. Mix the rice with the egg, soy
sauce and sesame oil, and stir into
the mixture in the browning dish.
Cook, uncovered, for 3 minutes on
HIGH, stirring every 30 seconds
until the egg sets. Add the shrimp
after 2 minutes. Serve garnished with
the remaining green onion.

Clam Shells in Saffron Sauce

PREPARATION TIME: 15 minutes

MICROWAVE COOKING TIME:
16 minutes, plus 5 minutes
standing time

SERVES: 2 people

120g/4oz/1½ cups wholewheat
225g/8oz/1 cup canned whole clams,
   liquid reserved
30ml/2 tbsps chopped parsley
1-2 tomatoes, peeled, seeded and cut into
   5mm (¼″) strips
1 shallot, finely chopped
15ml/1 tbsp saffron
15g/½ oz/1 tbsp butter
7ml/½ tbsp flour/plain flour
140ml/¼ pint/½ cup heavy/double
   cream
Reserved clam juice, made up to 140ml/

¼ pint/½ cup with water if necessary
30ml/1oz/2 tbsps white wine
Salt and pepper

Put the pasta shells into a large bowl
with enough hot water to cover.
Cook for 8 minutes on HIGH and
leave to stand for 5 minutes. Rinse
under hot water and leave in cold
water. Melt the butter in a small bowl
on HIGH for 30 seconds. Stir in the
flour and add the clam juice gradually. Add the wine, shallot and
saffron and cook, covered with

SAUCE

345g/12oz/1½ cups canned plum
  tomatoes
15ml/1 tbsp oil
60g/12oz/½ cup sliced mushrooms
½ clove garlic, crushed
1.25ml/¼ tsp basil
Pinch ground allspice
5ml/1 tsp tomato paste
1 bay leaf
Salt and pepper

FILLING

120g/4oz/½ cup frozen chopped spinach,
  defrosted
60g/2oz/¼ cup pepperoni sausage,
  skinned and chopped
120g/4oz/1 cup ricotta cheese
60g/2oz/¼ cup grated Parmesan cheese
  (plus extra for serving if desired)
Nutmeg
Salt and pepper

Put the cannelloni or large shell pasta into a large, shallow casserole, and pour over enough hot water to cover. Cook for 8 minutes on HIGH. Leave to stand for 5 minutes. Rinse in hot water and leave standing in cold water. Put the oil into a 1 quart casserole and heat for 30 seconds on HIGH. Add the mushrooms and garlic and cook for 1 minute on HIGH. Add the remaining sauce ingredients, cover, and cook for 5 minutes on HIGH. Stir well and mash the tomatoes to break them up. Meanwhile drain the pasta well. Mix the filling ingredients together and fill the pasta. Put the pasta into a small casserole dish and pour over the tomato sauce. Cook on HIGH for 5 minutes to heat through. Serve with additional Parmesan cheese. To serve one person, halve the quantity of each ingredient. Cook the sauce for 3 minutes total in a smaller casserole or bowl. Alternatively, prepare this recipe in full and freeze one half for later use.

Facing page: Indian Pilaff (top) and Fried Rice (bottom). This page: Clam Shells in Saffron Sauce (top) and Cannelloni Stuffed with Spinach, Cheese and Pepperoni (bottom).

pierced plastic wrap, for 3 minutes on HIGH until thickened. Stir every 30 seconds. Stir in the cream and cook for 1 minute on HIGH. Mix in the clams, parsley, and salt and pepper. Cover and cook for 2 minutes on HIGH to heat through. Add the tomato strips and cook for 1 minute on MEDIUM. Pour over the pasta and serve immediately. To serve 1 person, cut the quantity of all the ingredients by half. Cook the sauce for half of the recommended time.

Cannelloni Stuffed with Spinach, Cheese and Pepperoni

PREPARATION TIME: 15 minutes

MICROWAVE COOKING TIME:
19 minutes, plus 5 minutes standing time

SERVES: 2 people

6-8 (depending on size) cannelloni or large shell pasta

Microwave
COOKING FOR 1 & 2

FISH AND SEAFOOD

Stuffed Trout

PREPARATION TIME: 15 minutes

MICROWAVE COOKING TIME:
5 minutes

SERVES: 1 person

1 whole rainbow trout, cleaned
1 shallot, finely chopped
120g/4oz/½ cup frozen chopped spinach,
    thawed
Pinch of nutmeg
90g/3oz/¼ cup flaked crabmeat
15g/½ oz/1 tbsp chopped hazelnuts
1 cap pimento, chopped
30ml/1oz/2 tbsps heavy/double cream
15ml/½ oz/1 tbsp lemon juice
Paprika
Salt and pepper

Put the spinach, nutmeg and shallot
into a small bowl. Cover with
pierced plastic wrap and cook for
1 minute on HIGH to soften the
shallot. Stir in the crab, nuts, paprika,
salt, pepper, pimento and cream.
Trim the tail and fins of the trout,
and spoon the stuffing into the
cavity. Sprinkle with lemon juice and
cook in a shallow baking dish
covered with pierced plastic wrap for
4 minutes on HIGH. Peel the skin off
the body of the trout, but leave on
the head and tail. Garnish with
lemon if desired.

Salmon Steaks Bernaise

PREPARATION TIME: 10 minutes

MICROWAVE COOKING TIME:
4-5 minutes

SERVES: 1 person

1 salmon steak
15ml/½ oz/1 tbsp lemon juice
Salt and pepper
SAUCE
2 egg yolks
5ml/1 tsp tarragon or white wine vinegar
5ml/1 tsp lemon juice
5ml/1 tsp chopped tarragon
5ml/1 tsp chopped parsley
Cayenne pepper
60g/2oz/¼ cup butter, melted

**This page: Portuguese Seafood
Stew. Facing page: Salmon Steaks
Bernaise (top) and Stuffed Trout
(bottom).**

Have a bowl of ice water ready.
Combine the egg yolks, vinegar,
lemon juice and herbs in a 570ml/
1 pint glass measure. In a small bowl,
melt the butter for 1 minute on
HIGH until very hot. Whisk it into
the egg yolks. Cook on HIGH for 15

seconds and whisk again. Repeat the process until the sauce is thick: this usually takes about 2 minutes. Put immediately into the bowl of ice water to stop the cooking. Add the Cayenne pepper, and salt if necessary. If the sauce begins to curdle, put the measure immediately into ice water and beat vigorously. Put the fish into a small baking dish with salt and pepper and lemon juice. Cover with pierced plastic wrap and cook on MEDIUM for 2-3 minutes. Leave to stand, covered, while making the sauce.

Flounder with Avocado

PREPARATION TIME: 15 minutes

MICROWAVE COOKING TIME: 8 minutes

SERVES: 2 people

225g/½ lb flounder fillets, skinned
1 small ripe avocado
30ml/1oz/2 tbsps cream cheese
5ml/1 tsp chives
Juice of 1 lime (or of half a lemon)
15ml/½ oz/1 tbsp white wine
5ml/1 tsp butter
2.5ml/½ tsp flour/plain flour
140ml/¼ pint/½ cup heavy/double
*   cream*
Salt and pepper

GARNISH
Reserved chives
Reserved avocado slices

Reserve 2-4 thin slices of avocado and brush with the lemon or lime juice. Mash the rest of the avocado with the cream cheese, chives, salt and pepper, and 5ml/1 tsp lime or lemon juice. Spread the filling over the fish and fold each fillet in half. Put the fillets in a shallow casserole and pour over the wine and remaining juice. Cover with pierced plastic wrap and cook for 6 minutes on MEDIUM. Keep warm. In a small bowl, melt the butter for 30 seconds on HIGH and stir in the flour. Strain on the cooking liquid from the fish and add the cream. Cook, uncovered, for 2 minutes on HIGH until thickened. Remove the fish to

serve on plates and pour some of the sauce over each fillet. Garnish with the reserved avocado slices and chives.

Lemon and Almond Sole

PREPARATION TIME: 10 minutes

MICROWAVE COOKING TIME: 11 minutes

SERVES: 2 people

2 whole sole fillets
1 lemon
30g/1oz/2 tbsps butter
60g/2oz/½ cup almonds
30g/1oz/¼ cup cornflake crumbs
2-4 parsley sprigs
Salt and pepper

Cut 4 thin slices from the lemon and squeeze the rest for juice. Cut 2 circles of baking parchment/unwaxed paper and grease with 15g/½ oz/ 1 tbsp butter. Lay on the fillets of fish and sprinkle over the lemon juice, salt and pepper. Seal up the parcels by twisting the open edges of the paper together. Cook for 5 minutes on MEDIUM. Heat a browning dish on HIGH for 4 minutes and add the remaining butter. Stir in the almonds and cook for 2 minutes, stirring frequently until brown. Stir in the cornflake crumbs. Open the parcels to serve and spoon on the almond topping. Garnish with reserved lemon slices and parsley.

Portuguese Seafood Stew

PREPARATION TIME: 15 minutes

MICROWAVE COOKING TIME: 11 minutes

SERVES: 2 people

3 tomatoes, chopped
½ a green pepper, chopped
½ cup canned clams, in shells if possible,
*   and liquid*
1 cod fillet (about 120g/¼ lb), cut into
*   5cm (2") pieces*
1 red snapper fillet (about 120g/¼ lb), cut
*   into 5cm (2") pieces*

4 large raw shrimp/prawns, peeled and
*   de-veined, or 60g/2oz/½ cup small*
*   shrimp/prawns*
½ a clove garlic, chopped
60g/2oz/¼ cup chopped onion
2 tbsps olive oil
5ml/1 tsp tomato paste
30ml/1 tbsp chopped parsley
6 chopped black olives
140ml/¼ pint/½ cup white wine
1 potato, cut into 2.5cm (1") pieces
Salt and pepper

Put the cod and snapper into a casserole. Put the olive oil into another casserole with the onion and garlic and heat for 1 minute on HIGH. Add the potatoes, liquid from the clams, and the wine. Cover and cook for 6 minutes on HIGH. Stir in the tomato paste, add the fish and peppers, and cook for 2 minutes on HIGH. Add the shrimp and cook a further minute on HIGH. Add the tomatoes, clams and olives and cook for another minute on HIGH. Season, and garnish with chopped parsley.

Macadamia Fillets

PREPARATION TIME: 10 minutes

MICROWAVE COOKING TIME: 5 minutes

SERVES: 2 people

2 sole or flounder fillets
1 small can pineapple chunks
¼ of a green pepper, cut into 5mm (¼")
*   strips*
1 green/spring onion, shredded
30g/1oz/⅓ cup Macadamia nuts,
*   roughly chopped*

SAUCE
Reserved pineapple juice
15ml/½ oz/1 tbsp honey
10ml/2 tsps soy sauce
15ml/½ oz/1 tbsp vinegar
1.25ml/¼ tsp dry mustard
1 tsp cornstarch/cornflour

Facing page: Flounder with Avocado (top) and Lemon and Almond Sole (bottom).

Drain the pineapple and set aside the chunks. Mix the juice and the other sauce ingredients together in a bowl. Add the green pepper and cook uncovered for 1-2 minutes on HIGH or until thickened, stirring every 30 seconds. Add the pineapple chunks, nuts and onions, and set aside. Put the fish into a shallow casserole, thinner portion towards the center of the dish. Cover with pierced plastic wrap, and cook for 2 minutes on HIGH. Allow to stand for 30 seconds. Remove carefully to serving dishes. Coat with the Macadamia sauce. Serve with fried rice or stir-fried vegetables.

This page: Shrimp and Broccoli au Gratin. Facing page: Macadamia Fillets.

Shrimp and Broccoli au Gratin

| **PREPARATION TIME:** 10 minutes |
| **MICROWAVE COOKING TIME:** 6 minutes |
| **SERVES:** 2 people |

120g/4oz/1 cup broccoli flowerets
225g/½ lb large cooked shrimp, peeled and de-veined
30g/1oz/2 tbsps Parmesan cheese
15g/½ oz/1 tbsp dry breadcrumbs
5ml/1 tsp paprika

SAUCE
30g/1oz/2 tbsps Cheddar cheese
15g/½ oz/1 tbsp butter
15g/½ oz/1 tbsp flour/plain flour
140ml/¼ pint/½ cup milk
Pinch of dry mustard
Pinch of Cayenne pepper
Salt and pepper

Melt 15g/1 tbsp butter in a small

140ml/¼ pint/½ cup heavy/double cream

Melt the butter in a 570ml/1 pint casserole for 30 seconds on HIGH and add the shallot. Cook for 1 minute on HIGH, add the flour, white wine and saffron, and stir well to mix. Add the scallops (cut in half if large) and cook for 1-2 minutes on HIGH. Stir in the cream, parsley and pepper, and cook for a further 2 minutes on HIGH. Serve on parsley rice.

Lobster in Sherry Cream

PREPARATION TIME: 20 minutes

MICROWAVE COOKING TIME: 4 minutes

SERVES: 2 people

1 whole large lobster, boiled; or 1 large lobster tail
60g/2oz/½ cup sliced mushrooms
2.5ml/½ tsp celery salt
140ml/¼ pint/½ cup heavy/double cream
30ml/1oz/2 tbsps sherry
2.5ml/½ tsp butter
2.5ml/½ tsp flour/plain flour
60g/2oz/½ cup Gruyère cheese
Paprika
Pepper

Crack the lobster claws and remove the meat. Remove the meat from the tail, and combine. Reserve the empty tail shell to cook in if desired. Melt the butter for 15 seconds on HIGH, and add the mushrooms. Cook for 1 minute on HIGH and add the flour, sherry cream, celery salt, and pepper. Cook for 2 more minutes on HIGH until thick, stirring frequently. Add the lobster and spoon into the shell, or a baking dish. Sprinkle on the cheese and plenty of paprika. Cook for 2 minutes on HIGH. Serve immediately.

bowl for 30 seconds on HIGH. Stir in the flour, mustard and Cayenne pepper. Add the milk gradually until smooth. Cook for 1-2 minutes on HIGH, stirring every 30 seconds. Add salt and pepper and stir in the Cheddar cheese. Cover and set aside. Put the broccoli in a small bowl with 30ml/1oz/2 tbsps water. Cover with pierced plastic wrap and cook for 3 minutes on HIGH until almost tender. In individual dishes or 1 large baking dish, scatter over the broccoli and shrimp. Coat over the sauce, and sprinkle on the Parmesan cheese, crumbs and paprika. Heat through for 1-2 minutes on HIGH before serving.

Scallops in Saffron Cream

PREPARATION TIME: 10 minutes

MICROWAVE COOKING TIME: 8 minutes

SERVES: 2 people

340g/12oz/2 cups uncooked scallops (or 180g/6oz/1 cup, if very large)
1 shallot, finely chopped
1 small red pepper cut into 5mm (¼") strips
5ml/1 tsp parsley
5ml/1 tsp saffron
140ml/¼ pint/½ cup white wine
25g/¾ oz/1½ tbsps butter
25g/¾ oz/1½ tbsps flour/plain flour

This page: Scallops in Saffron Cream (top) and Lobster in Sherry Cream (bottom). Facing page: Orange Glazed Lamb Chops with Glazed Vegetables.

MEAT, POULTRY AND GAME

Orange Glazed Lamb Chops with Glazed Vegetables

PREPARATION TIME: 20 minutes

MICROWAVE COOKING TIME: 14 minutes

SERVES: 2 people

2 lamb shoulder chops
140ml/¼ pint/½ cup orange juice
10ml/2 tsps dark corn syrup
2.5ml/½ tsp red wine vinegar or cider
  vinegar
2.5ml/½ tsp cornstarch/cornflour
15ml/½ oz/1 tbsp water
15ml/½ oz/1 tbsp oil
1 carrot, cut into thick barrel shapes
1 turnip, quartered
60g/2oz/½ cup small onions
1 small potato, quartered
15g/½ oz/1 tbsp butter
Salt and pepper

GARNISH
Orange slices

Heat a browning dish for 5 minutes on HIGH. Put in the oil and chops and cook for 2 minutes on HIGH, turning once, until lightly browned on both sides. Transfer the chops to a casserole dish. Melt the butter and add the vegetables. Cook for 5 minutes on HIGH, stirring frequently to brown evenly. Add to the casserole dish with the chops. De-glaze the browning dish with the orange juice and vinegar, scraping any sediment off the base of the dish. Stir in the corn syrup, salt and pepper, and pour over the chops and vegetables. Cover with pierced plastic wrap and cook on MEDIUM for 6 minutes, or until chops are cooked as much as desired. The chops may be served slightly pink. Remove the chops and vegetables from the casserole and dissolve the cornstarch/cornflour in the water. Stir into the liquid in the casserole and cook, uncovered, for 1 minute on HIGH or until boiling and clear. Pour over the chops and vegetables and garnish with orange slices.

To serve 1 person, reduce the quantity of each ingredient by half, but cook for the same length of time.

warm vegetable salad instead of the red cabbage garnish.
To serve 1 person, prepare the complete recipe and use half. The other half will freeze well.

Spicy Steak Kebabs

PREPARATION TIME: 10 minutes, plus 1 hour to marinate meat

MICROWAVE COOKING TIME: 6 minutes

SERVES: 2 people

225g/8oz/½ lb sirloin steak, cut into 4cm (1½") cubes
1 leek, white part only
4 large mushrooms
4 cherry tomatoes
½ green pepper, sliced into 2.5cm (1") squares

MARINADE
30ml/1oz/2 tbsps oil
15ml/½ oz/1 tbsp lemon juice
½ clove garlic, crushed
1.25ml/¼ tsp ground cumin
1.25ml/¼ tsp ground coriander
1.25ml/¼ tsp gravy browning
Pinch Cayenne pepper
Salt and pepper

Mix the marinade ingredients together and put in the steak cubes, turning to coat evenly. Leave for 1 hour. Thread the meat and vegetables onto wooden skewers. Do not pack the ingredients too tightly together. Put on a roasting rack and cook on MEDIUM for about 6 minutes, turning and basting frequently until cooked as much as desired. Put remaining marinade into a smaller dish and cook for 2-3 minutes on HIGH until syrupy. Serve on a bed of rice. Pour the sauce over the cooked kebabs.
To serve one person, prepare only half of each ingredient, but cook for the same length of time.

Pheasant in Gin

PREPARATION TIME: 15 minutes

MICROWAVE COOKING TIME: 22 minutes

SERVES: 2 people

1 small pheasant, dressed (about 675-790g/1½-1¾ lbs)
1 apple, peeled and chopped
60ml/2oz/¼ cup gin
5ml/1 tsp juniper berries
2.5ml/½ tsp rosemary
30ml/1oz/2 tbsps chicken bouillon
15g/½ oz/1 tbsp butter
7.5g/1½ tsps flour/plain flour
225g/8oz/1½ cups shredded red cabbage

Heat a browning dish for 5 minutes on HIGH. Put in the butter and, when foaming, add the pheasant. Cook for 3 minutes to lightly brown all sides of the pheasant, turning four times while cooking. Transfer to a medium-sized deep casserole and set aside. Add flour to the dish and scrape up any sediment. Cook for 1 minute to lightly brown the flour. De-glaze the pan with chicken bouillon and add the casserole with the remaining ingredients except the cabbage. Cover and cook for 10 minutes or until the pheasant is tender. It may be served slightly pink. During the last 3 minutes, add the red cabbage. Can be served with the

**This page: Spicy Steak Kebabs.
Facing page: Pheasant in Gin.**

Stuffed Chicken Breasts in Lemon Tarragon Cream

PREPARATION TIME: 15 minutes

MICROWAVE COOKING TIME: 18 minutes

SERVES: 2 people

2 boned chicken breast halves, skinned
5g/1 tsp butter
60g/2oz/½ cup finely chopped
    mushrooms
90g/3oz package/carton cream cheese
30ml/1oz/2 tbsps white wine
15ml/½ oz/1 tbsp lemon juice
Salt and pepper

SAUCE
15g/½ oz/1 tbsp butter
7.5g/½ tbsp flour/plain flour
Juice of ½ lemon
140ml/¼ pint/½ cup chicken stock
60ml/2oz/¼ cup heavy/double cream
2.5ml/½ tsp chopped tarragon, fresh or
    dried
Salt and pepper

GARNISH
Lemon slices

Cut a pocket along the thicker side of each chicken breast half. Melt 15g/1 tbsp butter for 30 seconds on HIGH in a small bowl. Add the white wine, salt and pepper, and mushrooms. Cook, uncovered, for 2 minutes on HIGH to soften the mushrooms. Cook for an additional 1 minute to evaporate liquid if excessive. Mix with the cream cheese and fill the pockets of the chicken. Put the breasts into a small casserole and sprinkle over the lemon juice and about 15ml/½ oz/1 tbsp water. Cover and cook for about 12 minutes on MEDIUM or until white and firm. Keep warm. In a small bowl melt 1 tbsp butter for 30 seconds on HIGH. Stir in the flour and add the stock and lemon juice gradually. Pour in any cooking liquid from the chicken and add the cream and tarragon. Cook for 1-2 minutes on HIGH, stirring every 30 seconds until thickened. Add salt and pepper. Spoon over the chicken breasts to serve and garnish with lemon slices. Serve with French peas or zucchini/courgette rolls.

To serve one person, reduce the quantity of each ingredient by half. Cook the mushroom filling for the same length of time, and the filled chicken breasts for 10 minutes on MEDIUM. Cook the sauce for about 1 minute on HIGH.

Chicken, Ham and Cheese Rolls with Mustard Sauce

PREPARATION TIME: 15 minutes

MICROWAVE COOKING TIME: 9 minutes

SERVES: 1 person

1 chicken breast half, skinned and boned
1 thin slice cooked ham
1 thin slice Swiss cheese
5ml/1 tsp chopped capers
5ml/1 tsp butter
30g/1oz/2½ tbsps cornflake crumbs
1.25ml/¼ tsp paprika
Salt and pepper

SAUCE
15g/½ oz/1 tbsp butter or margarine
15g/½ oz/1 tbsp flour/plain flour
140ml/¼ pint/½ cup milk
45ml/1½ oz/3 tbsps dry white wine
5ml/1 tsp Dijon mustard
5ml/1 tsp salad mustard
Salt and pepper

Place the chicken breast between 2 pieces of waxed/greaseproof paper and flatten with a meat mallet to about 3mm (⅛"). Lay the cheese on top of the slice of ham. Sprinkle on the capers, and roll up, folding in the sides, and fasten with wooden picks/cocktail sticks. Melt 5ml/1 tsp butter for 30 seconds on HIGH. Combine the cornflake crumbs with the paprika and salt and pepper on a sheet of waxed/greaseproof paper. Brush the chicken with the melted butter and then roll in the crumbs to coat. Push the crumb coating into the surface of the chicken. Put the chicken seam side down into a small casserole dish and cook, uncovered, on MEDIUM for 2 minutes. Turn over, cook for a further 1 minute on MEDIUM, and keep warm while

preparing the sauce. Melt 2.5ml/½ tbsp butter for 30 seconds on HIGH in a small bowl. Stir in the flour and add the milk and wine gradually. Stir in the mustards and salt and pepper. Cook, uncovered, for 1-2 minutes on HIGH, stirring every 30 seconds until thickened. Keep warm. Re-heat the chicken on HIGH for 2 minutes and serve with the sauce.

To serve 2 people, double all the ingredients. Cook the chicken for 4 minutes on MEDIUM and the sauce for 2-3 minutes on HIGH. Re-heat the chicken on HIGH for 2 minutes.

Rabbit with Olives

PREPARATION TIME: 15 minutes

MICROWAVE COOKING TIME: 23-28 minutes

SERVES: 2 people

2 rabbit pieces (hind- or fore-quarters)
30g/1oz/2 tbsps butter
10g/2 tsps flour/plain flour
1 shallot, chopped
60ml/2oz/¼ cup dry vermouth
60ml/2oz/¼ cup beef bouillon
60g/2oz/½ cup whole mushrooms
1.25ml/¼ tsp oregano
1.25ml/¼ tsp thyme
15ml/1 tbsp wholegrain mustard
12 stoned green olives, left whole
60ml/2oz/¼ cup heavy/double cream
Salt and pepper

Soak the rabbit overnight to whiten the meat, in enough water to cover, with a squeeze of lemon juice and a pinch of salt. Heat a browning dish for 5 minutes on HIGH. Melt the butter and cook the rabbit pieces for 2 minutes on HIGH, turning over after 1 minute to brown both sides. Remove from the dish to a 570ml/1 pint casserole. Add the mushrooms and shallot to the browning dish with the flour. Cook for 1 minute on HIGH to brown lightly. De-glaze the pan with the bouillon and pour the

Facing page: Chicken, Ham and Cheese Rolls with Mustard Sauce (top) and Stuffed Chicken Breasts in Lemon Tarragon Cream (bottom).

contents over the rabbit. Add the
vermouth, herbs, mustard, and salt
and pepper. Cover and cook on
MEDIUM for 15-20 minutes, or until
the rabbit is tender. After 10 minutes,
add the olives and cream. Serve with
rice or noodles.
To serve one person, half the
complete recipe will freeze well.

Devilled Cornish Hen with Golden Rice Stuffing

PREPARATION TIME: 20 minutes

MICROWAVE COOKING TIME:
16 minutes

SERVES: 1 person

1 Cornish game hen/poussin (about
    675g/1½ lbs)
30g/1oz/¼ cup quick-cooking rice
90ml/3oz/⅓ cup hot water
1 shallot, finely chopped
½ cap pimento, diced
15g/½ oz/1 tbsp chopped pecans
Pinch saffron
30ml/1oz/2 tbsps bottled steak sauce/
    brown sauce
15g/½ oz/1 tbsp butter
2.5ml/½ tsp paprika
2.5ml/½ tsp dry mustard
2.5ml/½ tsp chili powder
5ml/1 tsp sugar
Pinch Cayenne pepper
60ml/2oz/¼ cup chicken bouillon
Salt and pepper

GARNISH
Small bunch watercress or parsley

Put the rice, saffron, shallot and hot
water into a 570ml/1 pint casserole,
cover, and cook on HIGH for
2 minutes or until the rice is tender
and has absorbed all the color from
the saffron. Add the pimento and
pecans, and allow to cool slightly.
Stuff the hen with rice. Mix together
the spices, salt and pepper, and sugar.
Melt 15g/½ oz/1 tbsp butter for 30
seconds on HIGH and brush it over
the hen. Rub the spices over all
surfaces of the hen. Close the cavity
with wooden picks and place the hen,
breast-side down, on a roasting rack.
Combine remaining melted butter
with the steak/brown sauce and any

remaining spices. Cook the hen for
5 minutes on HIGH and baste with
the steak/brown sauce mixture. Turn
breast-side up, cook for 5 minutes
on HIGH, and baste. Cook for
2 minutes more, or until the juices
run clear. Leave to stand for
5 minutes before serving. Add the
chicken bouillon to the remaining
sauce mixture, re-heat for
1-2 minutes on HIGH and pour over
the hen to serve. Garnish with
watercress or parsley.
To serve 2 people, double all
quantities. Add 5 minutes to the
cooking time for the hens.

This page: **Rabbit with Olives
(top) and Venison Bourguignonne
(bottom). Facing page: Devilled
Cornish Hen with Golden Rice
Stuffing.**

Venison Bourguignonne

PREPARATION TIME: 15 minutes

MICROWAVE COOKING TIME:
36 minutes, plus 15 minutes standing
time

SERVES: 2 people

225g/½ lb venison from the leg
1 thick-cut slice bacon, cut into 5mm (¼")
    pieces
60g/2oz/½ cup small onions
30g/1oz/¼ cup mushrooms, quartered
½ clove garlic, crushed
15g/½ oz/1 tbsp butter
15g/½ oz/1 tbsp flour/plain flour
90ml/3oz/⅓ cup red wine
200ml/6oz/¾ cup beef bouillon
5ml/1 tsp tomato paste
1 bay leaf
5ml/¼ tsp thyme
Salt and pepper

Melt the butter for 30 seconds on
HIGH in a large casserole. Add the
onion, bacon, mushrooms and garlic,
and cook for 1 minute on HIGH until
slightly brown. Remove from the
casserole and set aside. Add the
venison and cook for 2-3 minutes on
HIGH, stirring occasionally to brown
slightly. Sprinkle on the flour, and
cook for a further minute on HIGH.
Stir in the wine, bouillon and tomato
paste. Add the thyme and bay leaf
and cover the casserole. Cook,
stirring occasionally, for 15 minutes
on MEDIUM. Add the remaining
ingredients, re-cover the casserole,
and cook for another 15 minutes
on MEDIUM. Leave to stand for
15 minutes before serving. Serve
with boiled potatoes or noodles.
To serve one person, cook the full
recipe, use half and the other half will
freeze well.

Fiery Duck

PREPARATION TIME: 15-20 minutes,
plus 30-60 minutes to marinate duck

MICROWAVE COOKING TIME:
8 minutes, plus 1 minute standing time

SERVES: 2 people

½ a duck breast, boned and skinned –
    about 225g/½ lb. If duck parts are
    unavailable, cut a whole duck into
    quarters and freeze the leg portions.
½ a small red pepper, sliced into 5mm
    (¼") strips
2 sticks celery, thinly sliced
120g/4oz/1 cup beansprouts
2 green/spring onions, sliced
60g/2oz/½ cup roasted cashew nuts

2.5-5ml/½-1 tsp Szechuan pepper, or
    crushed dried chili peppers
2.5ml/½ tsp cornstarch/cornflour
60ml/2oz/¼ cup chicken bouillon

MARINADE
10ml/2 tsps rice or cider vinegar
10ml/2 tsps soy sauce
10ml/2 tsps sherry
10ml/2 tsps sesame seed oil
Pinch ground ginger
½ clove crushed garlic
Salt and pepper

Remove the skin and bone from the
breast portions and cut the duck into
thin strips. Combine the marinade
ingredients in a medium-sized bowl
and stir in the duck pieces. Cover the
bowl and chill for 30-60 minutes.
Drain the duck, reserving the
marinade, and mix the cornstarch/
cornflour, bouillon and Szechuan or
chili pepper with the marinade. Put
the duck into a large casserole and
pour over sauce. Stir to mix, cover
the dish and cook for 10 minutes on
MEDIUM, stirring occasionally. Add
the red pepper and celery to the
casserole and cook for a further
2 minutes on HIGH. Stir in the
cashews, onions and beansprouts.
Serve with fried rice or crisp noodles.
Best prepared for 2 people.

Turkey Korma (Mild Curry)

PREPARATION TIME: 15 minutes

MICROWAVE COOKING TIME:
10 minutes

SERVES: 1 person

1 turkey leg
30g/1oz/2 tbsps chopped onion
5ml/1 tsp oil
7.5g/1½ tsps butter or margarine
7.5ml/½ tbsp curry powder
5ml/1 tsp paprika
5ml/1 tsp ground coriander
25g/¾ oz/1½ tbsps flour/plain flour
140ml/¼ pint/½ cup chicken bouillon
15g/½ oz/1 tbsp golden raisins
15g/½ oz/1 tbsp roasted cashew nuts or
    shelled pistachio nuts
10ml/2 tsps unsweetened coconut

60ml/2oz/¼ cup plain yogurt
Salt and pepper

Skin and bone the turkey leg and cut
the meat into 2.5cm (1") pieces. Use
half and freeze the other half for use
later. Heat the oil in a large casserole
for 30 seconds on HIGH. Add the
butter and, when melted, add the
onion, turkey and spices. Cook for 3
minutes on HIGH to cook the spices.
Add the flour and bouillon and stir
to mix well. Cover the casserole and
cook for 5 minutes on HIGH, stirring
frequently until the turkey is tender.
Add the raisins, coconut, nuts, salt,
pepper and yogurt. Leave to stand,
covered, for 1 minute. Serve with rice
and chutney.
To serve 2 people, use the whole
turkey leg and double all other
ingredients. Cook the casserole for 8
minutes on HIGH.

Ham Steaks with Mango Sauce

PREPARATION TIME: 10 minutes

MICROWAVE COOKING TIME:
13 minutes

SERVES: 2 people

2 fully cooked ham slices (about 120g/
    ¼ lb each)
15g/½ oz/1 tbsp butter

SAUCE
1 ripe mango, peeled and thinly sliced
2.5ml/½ tsp ground ginger
Juice of half a lime
2.5ml/½ tsp soy sauce
Pinch Cayenne pepper
1.25ml/¼ tsp cornstarch/cornflour
90ml/3oz/⅓ cup orange juice

Cut the ham slices around the
outside at 5cm (2") intervals, 5mm
(¼") in from the edge, to stop them
from curling. Reserve 4 thin slices of
mango and purée the rest in a food
processor with the remaining sauce
ingredients. Heat a browning dish on

Facing page: Fiery Duck (top) and
Turkey Korma (Mild Curry)
(bottom).

HIGH for 5 minutes. Put in the butter and the ham steaks and cook for 1 minute on HIGH. Turn the ham steaks once to brown both sides. Remove the ham from the dish to a casserole and pour over the puréed sauce ingredients. Cook, uncovered, for about 5 minutes on MEDIUM, or until the sauce has thickened. If necessary, remove the ham and keep warm while cooking the sauce for a further 2 minutes on HIGH. Garnish with the reserved mango slices. Serve with sesame stir-fry.

To serve one person, use 1 ham slice and 7.5g/½ tbsp butter. Use full quantity sauce ingredients and cook for the same length of time as for 2 people.

Beef Roulades

PREPARATION TIME: 20 minutes

MICROWAVE COOKING TIME: 19 minutes

SERVES: 2 people

*4 pieces rump steak, cut thin and
    flattened
1 dill pickle, cut into quarters lengthwise
2 green/spring onions, trimmed and cut
    in half lengthwise
15ml/1 tbsp oil*

SAUCE
*60g/2oz/½ cup mushrooms, quartered
7.5g/1½ tsp butter or margarine
10ml/2 tsps flour
1.25ml/¼ tsp thyme
1 bay leaf
180ml/5oz/⅔ cup beef bouillon
15ml/½ oz/1 tbsp red wine
Salt and pepper
Gravy browning (if necessary)*

GARNISH
Buttered spinach pasta

Roll each of the beef slices around a quarter of the dill pickle and half a green/spring onion. Sprinkle with pepper and fasten with wooden picks/cocktail sticks. Heat a browning dish on HIGH for 5 minutes. Put in the oil and add the roulades. Cook for 8 minutes, turning frequently. Remove from the dish and set aside in a casserole dish.

Add the butter to the dish and allow to melt. Add the mushrooms and cook for 1 minute on HIGH. Stir in the flour and cook for 2 minutes to brown lightly. Add the bouillon, wine, thyme and bay leaf, scraping any sediment off the surface of the browning dish. Add gravy browning for extra color if necessary. Season, and pour over the roulades. Cover the dish and cook for 12 minutes on MEDIUM. Test the meat with a knife and if not tender, cook for a further 3 minutes on HIGH. Serve with the pasta or French peas.

To serve one person, prepare only half the quantity of each ingredient and cook the roulades in the sauce for about 10 minutes on MEDIUM. Alternatively, the full quantity recipe freezes well.

Mexican Pork Casserole

PREPARATION TIME: 15 minutes

MICROWAVE COOKING TIME: 28 minutes

SERVES: 2 people

*225g/8oz/½ lb boneless pork loin, cut
    into 2.5cm (1") cubes*

peppers, cover, and cook on MEDIUM for 17 minutes, or until the pork loses its pink color. Add the beans and heat for 2 minutes on MEDIUM. Serve with tortilla chips if desired.
To serve 1 person, prepare full quantity casserole, and freeze half.

Veal Chops in Peppercorn Cream Sauce

PREPARATION TIME: 15 minutes
MICROWAVE COOKING TIME: 25 minutes
SERVES: 2 people

2 loin veal chops
15g/½ oz/1 tbsp butter or margarine
140ml/¼ pint/½ cup heavy/ double cream
60ml/2oz/¼ cup chicken bouillon
30ml/½ oz/2 tbsps brandy
15ml/1 tbsp green peppercorns, dried (or packed in brine, drained and rinsed)
½ cap pimento, diced
2 black olives, stoned and sliced thinly
Salt and pepper

Remove some of the fat from the outside of the chops. Heat a browning dish on HIGH for 5 minutes. Put in the butter or margarine and the chops. Cook for 3 minutes on HIGH, turning once, until both sides are lightly browned. Remove the chops to a casserole. Deglaze the dish with the bouillon and add the brandy, salt and pepper. Pour the sauce over the chops, cover with pierced plastic wrap, and cook on MEDIUM for 15 minutes or until the chops are tender. Add the peppercorns, pimento and olives during the last 3 minutes of cooking time. If the chops are not tender after 15 minutes, cook for an additional 2 minutes on MEDIUM. Add the cream and cook 1 minute on HIGH. Serve with zucchini/courgette rolls, leeks Provençale, or French peas.
To serve 1 person, cut the quantities of each ingredient by half and cook for the same length of time.

90g/3oz/½ cup canned garbanzo beans/ chickpeas
90g/3oz/½ cup canned kidney beans
30g/1oz/¼ cup chopped sweet red pepper
30g/1oz/¼ cup chopped green pepper
½ small chili pepper, finely chopped
30g/1oz/¼ cup chopped onion
15g/½ oz/1 tbsp flour/plain flour
10ml/2 tsps oil
200ml/6oz/¾ cup beef bouillon/stock
15ml/1 tbsp instant coffee
½ clove garlic, crushed
1.25ml/¼ tsp ground cumin
1.25ml/¼ tsp ground coriander

GARNISH
Tortilla chips

Facing page: Veal Chops in Peppercorn Cream Sauce (top) and Ham Steaks with Mango Sauce (bottom). This page: Mexican Pork Casserole (top) and Beef Roulades (bottom).

Heat a browning dish for 5 minutes on HIGH. Put in the oil and add the pork cubes. Cook for 2 minutes on HIGH, stirring frequently, until slightly browned. Add the cumin, coriander, garlic, onion and flour, and cook for 1-2 minutes on HIGH. Dissolve the instant coffee in the bouillon/stock and add to the casserole, stirring well. Add the

VEGETABLES

Corn on the Cob with Flavored Butters

PREPARATION TIME: 10 minutes

MICROWAVE COOKING TIME:
8 minutes

SERVES: 2 people

2 ears of corn
45g/1½ oz/3 tbsps butter with a choice
of:
2.5ml/½ tsp wholegrain mustard, or
2.5ml/½ tsp tomato purée and
1.25ml/¼ tsp basil, or
2.5ml/½ tsp garlic powder and
1.25ml/¼ tsp parsley, or
2.5ml/½ tsp chili powder

Clean the husks and silk from the ears/cobs of corn and wrap each in plastic wrap, or put into a roasting bag and seal tightly. Cook for about 8 minutes, turning once. Mix the butter with one or more of the flavoring choices and serve with the hot corn.

Leeks Provençale

PREPARATION TIME: 10 minutes

MICROWAVE COOKING TIME:
8 minutes

SERVES: 2 people

3 leeks, washed, trimmed and cut into
5cm (2″) pieces
1 small clove garlic, finely chopped
2 tomatoes, chopped
15ml/1 tbsp oil
30ml/2 tbsps white wine
2.5ml/½ tsp thyme
15ml/1 tbsp chopped parsley
Salt and pepper

Put the oil into a 1150ml/2 pint/ 1 quart casserole, and add the leeks and garlic, tossing to coat. Cook, uncovered, for 3 minutes on HIGH, stirring occasionally. Add the herbs,

This page: Corn on the Cob with Flavored Butters. Facing page: French Peas (top) and Leeks Provençale (bottom).

white wine, salt and pepper, and cover and cook for a further 5 minutes on HIGH. Add the tomatoes and cook for 1 minute on HIGH. Serve immediately.

To serve one person, use 1 large or 2 small leeks and half of each of the other ingredients. Cook the leeks for 2 minutes on HIGH and after adding the other ingredients, cook for a further 3-4 minutes on HIGH. Add the tomatoes and cook for 1 minute on HIGH.

Eggplant/Aubergine Niramish

PREPARATION TIME: 20 minutes

MICROWAVE COOKING TIME: 17 minutes

SERVES: 2 people

1 eggplant/aubergine
30g/1oz/2 tbsps butter
1 clove garlic, finely chopped
1 small onion, chopped
1 small potato, diced
1 small carrot, diced
30g/1oz/¼ cup peas
225g/8oz/1 cup canned tomatoes, chopped and juice reserved
5ml/1 tsp flour/plain flour
30g/1oz/¼ cup raisins
30g/1oz/¼ cup pine nuts or chopped almonds
15ml/1 tbsp chopped coriander leaves or parsley
1.25ml/¼ tsp ground coriander
1.25ml/¼ tsp ground cumin
1.25ml/¼ tsp turmeric
1.25ml/¼ tsp fenugreek
1.25ml/¼ tsp ground ginger
Cayenne pepper
Paprika
Salt and pepper

GARNISH
60ml/2oz/¼ cup plain yogurt
Parsley or coriander leaves

Cut the eggplant/aubergine in half lengthwise and score the flesh lightly. Sprinkle with salt and leave to stand for 20 minutes. The salt will draw out any bitterness. Rinse the eggplant well and pat dry. Melt the butter for 30 seconds on HIGH in a large

casserole. Add the spices and cook for 2 minutes on HIGH. Add the onion, garlic, carrots and potatoes. Cover and cook for 3 minutes on HIGH. Stir in the flour and add the tomato juice and pulp and chopped coriander or parsley. Cover the bowl and cook on HIGH for a further 5 minutes or until vegetables are just tender. Add the raisins, nuts and peas. Put the eggplant in another casserole, cover, and cook for 5 minutes on HIGH. Scoop out the flesh and reserve the skins. Mix the eggplant with the vegetable filling and fill the skins. Sprinkle with paprika and cook for 3 minutes on HIGH. Serve immediately. Top with a spoonful of yogurt and garnish with sprigs of parsley or coriander.

To serve 1 person, prepare the full quantity, serve one half and freeze the other.

French Peas

PREPARATION TIME: 10 minutes

MICROWAVE COOKING TIME: 6-10 minutes

SERVES: 2 people

225g/8oz/1½ cups peas, fresh or frozen
4 leaves Romaine/cos lettuce
60g/2oz/½ cup parsley or chervil sprigs
120g/4oz/½ cup small onions, peeled
5ml/1 tsp sugar
15g/½ oz/1 tbsp butter
15g/½ oz/1 tbsp flour/plain flour
2 sticks celery, diced
140ml/¼ pint/½ cup chicken bouillon/ stock
Salt and pepper

If using fresh peas, shell them and combine with the celery, onions, half the bouillon/stock, salt and pepper, and sugar in a 1150ml/2 pint/1 quart casserole. Cover and cook for 7 minutes on HIGH until almost tender. Add the lettuce and parsley (or chervil) and cook for a further 2 minutes on HIGH. Set aside. (If using frozen peas, combine the lettuce and parsley at the beginning and cook for a total of 5 minutes.) Melt the butter in a small bowl for 30 seconds on HIGH. Add the flour and remaining stock, and cook,

uncovered, for 1 minute on HIGH. Stir into the peas, and serve. Best cooked for 2 people.

Stuffed Potatoes

PREPARATION TIME: 15 minutes

MICROWAVE COOKING TIME: 18 minutes, plus 5 minutes standing time

SERVES: 1 person

1 large baking potato
10ml/2 tsps chopped chives
30ml/1oz/2 tbsps milk
2 strips bacon
30ml/1oz/2 tbsps sour cream
15g/½ oz/1 tbsp crumbled blue cheese
15g/½ oz/1 tbsp shredded/grated Cheddar cheese
15ml/1 tbsp dry seasoned breadcrumbs
Paprika
Salt and pepper

Heat a browning dish for 5 minutes on HIGH. Put in the bacon and cook for 2-3 minutes on HIGH, or until crisp. Crumble the bacon and set it aside. Pierce the potato skin several times with a fork. Put the potato on a plate and cook on HIGH for 5 minutes, or until soft. Turn over after 2 minutes. Cover it tightly in foil and leave it to stand for 5 minutes. Cut the potato in half lengthwise and scoop out the flesh, reserving the shells. Heat the milk for 30 seconds on HIGH, add to the potato with the sour cream and beat well. Add the chives, salt and pepper, bacon and blue cheese, and spoon into the potato shells. Sprinkle on the Cheddar cheese, crumbs and paprika. Cook on MEDIUM for 3 minutes and increase the setting to HIGH for 1 minute. Serve immediately.

For two people, use the full quantity recipe for a side dish, or double the quantity of each ingredient. Cook the potatoes for 7 minutes on HIGH, and the filled potato shells for 4 minutes on MEDIUM and 1 minute on HIGH.

Facing page: Eggplant/Aubergine Niramish (top) and Stuffed Potatoes (bottom).

Zucchini/Courgette Rolls

PREPARATION TIME: 15 minutes

MICROWAVE COOKING TIME:
8 minutes

SERVES: 2 people

1 large zucchini/courgette
1 carrot, cut into 8cm (3") sticks
1 green pepper, cut into 12mm (½") slices
2 green/spring onions, shredded
* lengthwise*
Small bunch of whole fresh chives
1.25ml/¼ tsp herbs (thyme or basil)
15g/½ oz/1 tbsp butter
Juice of half a lemon
Salt and pepper

Trim the end of the zucchini/
courgette and cut lengthwise into
very thin slices. Spread evenly over
the bottom of a large casserole. Pour
on the lemon juice, cover, and cook
for 1 minute to soften. Remove and
set aside. In the same casserole, cook
the carrot, covered, for 3 minutes on
HIGH. Add the pepper and cook for
a further 2 minutes on HIGH. Add
the onion. Sprinkle with herbs and
salt and pepper. Divide the
vegetables evenly and place on top of
the zucchini/courgette slices, twisting
the ends of the zucchini around the
piles of vegetables. Tie at both ends
with the chives. Melt the butter in a
small bowl for 30 seconds on HIGH.
Pour the butter over the vegetables in
the casserole, cover, and heat
through for 1-2 minutes on HIGH
before serving. Best cooked for 2
people.

Sesame Stir-fry

PREPARATION TIME: 15 minutes

MICROWAVE COOKING TIME:
7 minutes

SERVES: 2 people

30ml/2 tbsps oil
60g/2oz/¼ lb pea pods/mangetout
1 stick celery, sliced
2 ears baby corn, cut in half lengthwise
60g/2oz/¼ cup water chestnuts, sliced
30g/1oz/¼ cup mushrooms, sliced
120g/4oz/1 cup beansprouts
1 green/spring onion, diagonally sliced

120g/4oz/1 cup Chinese cabbage,
* shredded*
2.5ml/½ tsp chopped ginger root
1 small sweet red pepper, thinly sliced
15g/½ oz/1 tbsp cornstarch/cornflour
30ml/2 tbsps soy sauce
15ml/1 tbsp sherry
2.5ml/½ tsp sesame seed oil
15g/½ oz/1 tbsp sesame seeds
60ml/2oz/¼ cup water

Heat a browning tray for 5 minutes
on HIGH. Put in 30ml/2 tbsps of oil
and add all the vegetables except the
Chinese cabbage and green onion.
Toss in the oil and add the ginger and
sesame seeds. Cook on HIGH for
4 minutes. Add the Chinese cabbage
and beansprouts and cook for
1 minute more on HIGH. Combine

**This page: Zucchini/Courgette
Rolls.
Facing page: Sesame Stir-fry.**

the cornstarch, sherry, soy sauce,
water and sesame seed oil in a small
bowl. Cook on HIGH for 2 minutes,
or until clear. Pour over the vegetables and toss to coat before serving.
To serve one person, cut the ingredient quantities by half and cook the
vegetables for 3 minutes on HIGH.
Add the cabbage and beansprouts
and cook for 30 seconds on HIGH.
Cook the sauce ingredients for
2 minutes on HIGH.

Warm Vegetable Salad

PREPARATION TIME: 20 minutes

MICROWAVE COOKING TIME:
5 minutes

SERVES: 2 people

60g/2oz/¼ cup shredded red cabbage
60g/2oz/¼ cup green beans
30g/1oz/¼ cup sliced mushrooms
4 green/spring onions, trimmed
1 hard-boiled egg
Shredded lettuce

DRESSING
25ml/1½ tbsps oil
15ml/1 tbsp vinegar
15ml/1 tbsp Dijon mustard
2.5ml/½ tsp caraway seeds
Salt and pepper

Mix the dressing ingredients together
thoroughly. Chop the white of the egg
and push the yolk through a strainer.
Put the cabbage, beans, onions and
mushrooms into a 570ml/1 pint
casserole with 15ml/1 tbsp water and
cook, covered, for 5 minutes. Add
the lettuce and dressing during the
last minute of cooking, and toss well.
Serve garnished with the egg.
For one person, reduce the ingredient
quantities by half, except for the egg.
Cook the vegetables for 3-4 minutes
before adding the lettuce and
dressing.

Lima Beans, Carrots and Bacon with Mustard

PREPARATION TIME: 15 minutes

MICROWAVE COOKING TIME:
11 minutes

SERVES: 2 people

120g/4oz/1 cup Lima beans
120g/4oz/1 cup sliced carrots
2 strips bacon
15ml/1 tbsp Dijon mustard
25g/¾ oz/1½ tbsps butter
Salt and pepper

Heat a browning dish for 5 minutes
on HIGH. Cook the bacon for
1-2 minutes on HIGH or until crisp.
Crumble the bacon and set it aside.

Put the beans into a 570ml/1 pint
casserole with 30ml/1oz/2 tbsps
water and cook for 1 minute on
HIGH. Peel off the outer skin if
desired and set the beans aside. Put
the carrots into the casserole with
2 tbsps water. Cook, uncovered, for
2 minutes on HIGH. Add the peeled
beans to the casserole and cook for
1 minute more on HIGH. Drain and
keep warm. Add the bacon to the
beans and carrots. In a small bowl,
melt the butter for 30 seconds on

**This page: Warm Vegetable Salad
(top) and Lima Beans, Carrots and
Bacon with Mustard (bottom).
Facing page: Raspberry
Meringues.**

HIGH. Add the salt and pepper, and
beat in the mustard until the sauce
holds together. Pour over the vegetables and toss to serve.
For one person, cut the quantity of
each ingredient by half and cook for
half the stated time.

DESSERTS

Raspberry Meringues

PREPARATION TIME: 15 minutes

MICROWAVE COOKING TIME: 1 minutes

SERVES: 2 people

MERINGUES
1 egg white
120g/4oz/1 cup powdered/icing sugar
2.5ml/½ tsp raspberry flavoring
2 drops red food coloring

FILLING
140ml/¼ pint/½ cup cream, whipped
120g/4oz/1 cup fresh or frozen raspberries
30ml/½ oz/2 tbsps raspberry liqueur
Sugar

GARNISH
Powdered/icing sugar
Cocoa

Put the egg white into a bowl and stir with a fork. Stir in the powdered/icing sugar, adding enough to make a firm, pliable dough. Add the coloring and flavoring with the powdered/icing sugar. Roll to 1.5cm (½") thick on a board sprinkled with powdered/icing sugar. Cut into 5cm (2") heart shapes or rounds and place 10cm (4") apart on a microwave baking sheet lined with wax/greaseproof paper. If making heart shapes, have the points towards the middle. Cook for 1 minute on HIGH until firm and dry. Combine the raspberries, liqueur and sugar to taste. When the meringues are cool, fill with some of the raspberries and sandwich 2 of the meringues together with cream. Sprinkle the tops with powdered/icing sugar and cocoa. Serve remaining raspberries separately.

thickened. Stir in the kirsch. Serve the pudding warm with the sauce, and whipped cream or ice cream if desired.

Oranges in Caramel Sauce

PREPARATION TIME: 15 minutes

MICROWAVE COOKING TIME: 4 minutes

SERVES: 1 person

1 orange
45g/1½ oz/3 tbsps brown sugar
60ml/2oz/¼ cup water
5ml/1 tsp Grand Marnier
2.5ml/½ tsp cornstarch/cornflour
1.25ml/¼ tsp lemon juice

Peel the orange, removing all the white pith. Set aside the whole orange and scrape all the pith off the peel. Cut the orange peel into thin strips. Mix the brown sugar, water and lemon juice and heat for 2 minutes on HIGH. Stir occasionally to help dissolve the sugar. Mix the cornstarch/cornflour and the liqueur and stir into the sugar syrup. Cook for 1 minute on HIGH to thicken. Add the orange peel to the hot sauce and pour over the orange. Heat through for 1 minute on HIGH, turning once. Serve immediately.

Cherry and Almond Bread Pudding

PREPARATION TIME: 15 minutes

MICROWAVE COOKING TIME: 9-14 minutes

SERVES: 2 people

60g/2oz/¼ cup chopped, unblanched almonds
1 egg
200ml/6oz/¾ cup light cream
90g/3oz/1½ cups brioche, cut into 5cm (2″) cubes
1.25ml/¼ tsp cinnamon
45g/1½ oz/3 tbsps sugar
90g/3oz/½ cup pitted dark, sweet cherries, canned, and juice reserved

SAUCE
140ml/¼ pint/½ cup reserved cherry juice
1.25ml/¼ tsp cornstarch/cornflour
15ml/1 tbsp cherry brandy or kirsch
1.25ml/¼ tsp almond extract/essence

Heat a browning dish for 5 minutes on HIGH. Put in the almonds and cook on HIGH for about 3 minutes, stirring every 30 seconds until golden brown. Combine the egg and cream. Beat in the sugar and cinnamon, and stir in the bread cubes and cherries. Pour into a 570ml/1 pint casserole and cook for 5-10 minutes on HIGH, or until the center is just set. Leave to stand for 2 minutes before serving. Combine the juice, extract and cornstarch. Cook on HIGH for 1 minute, stirring once or twice until

Cranberry Crisp

PREPARATION TIME: 10 minutes

MICROWAVE COOKING TIME: 11-12 minutes

SERVES: 2 people

FILLING
140ml/¼ pint/½ cup orange juice or cranberry juice
120g/4oz/1 cup fresh cranberries
10ml/2 tsps sugar
10ml/2 tsps cornstarch/cornflour
1.25ml/¼ tsp cinnamon

This page: Oranges in Caramel Sauce. Facing page: Cherry and Almond Bread Pudding (top) and Cranberry Crisp (bottom).

TOPPING
225g/8oz/¾ cup crunchy oatmeal cereal
30g/1oz/2 tbsps butter or margarine
15g/½ oz/1 tbsp flour/plain flour
30ml/1oz/2 tbsps honey

Combine the filling ingredients in a small casserole or individual dishes and cook on HIGH for 3-4 minutes, or until the mixture thickens. Stir twice during cooking and set aside. Toss the flour and cereal together. Melt the butter and mix in. Sprinkle over the top of the cranberry filling and cook for 4 minutes on HIGH. Drizzle over the honey and cook for a further 4 minutes on HIGH. Serve warm, with whipped cream.

Black Velvet and White Lace

PREPARATION TIME: 25 minutes

MICROWAVE COOKING TIME:
5 minutes

SERVES: 2 people

BLACK VELVET
120g/4oz/½ cup unsalted butter
60g/2oz/¼ cup sugar
2 eggs, separated
120g/4oz/4 squares cooking chocolate
15g/½ oz/1 tbsp instant coffee dissolved
  in 30ml/1oz/2 tbsps boiling water

WHITE LACE
120g/¼ lb white chocolate

Soften the butter in a medium-sized bowl for 20 seconds on HIGH. Add sugar and beat until light and fluffy. Add the egg yolks one at a time, beating between each addition until the mixture is light and lemon-colored. Melt the chocolate with the strong coffee mixture for 2 minutes on MEDIUM. Whisk the egg whites until stiff but not dry. Beat the warm chocolate into the egg yolks quickly and heat 2 minutes on MEDIUM, stirring every 30 seconds. Fold in the egg whites. Refrigerate until firm. Put the white chocolate into a small bowl and melt on MEDIUM for 1-2 minutes, stirring once. Fill a small pastry piping bag fitted with a writing tube/nozzle. Pipe out a lacy pattern

onto wax/bakewell paper and refrigerate to harden. To serve, scoop out spoonfuls of the mousse into bowls or onto plates. Pour over 15ml/1 tbsp of coffee liqueur if desired. Carefully peel off the white chocolate lace patterns and use to decorate the black velvet mousse.

Brown Sugar Bananas

PREPARATION TIME: 10 minutes

MICROWAVE COOKING TIME:
3½ minutes

SERVES: 2 people

2 bananas
30g/1oz/2 tbsps butter or margarine
60g/2oz/4 tbsps brown sugar
Grated rind and juice of 1 lemon
60g/2oz/¼ cup whole pecans
30ml/1oz/2 tbsps dark rum

Peel the bananas and cut in half lengthwise. Brush all surfaces with lemon juice to prevent browning. Melt the butter in a baking dish for 30 seconds on HIGH. Add the lemon juice and rind. Add the bananas and cook on MEDIUM for 2 minutes until heated through. Remove the bananas and keep them warm. Stir in the sugar and cook for 1 minute on HIGH, stirring frequently until bubbling. Add the pecans and rum, and pour over the bananas to serve.

Orange Creams

PREPARATION TIME: 15-20 minutes

MICROWAVE COOKING TIME:
5 minutes

SERVES: 2 people

30ml/1oz/2 tbsps orange juice
200ml/6oz/¾ cup milk
2 eggs, beaten
60g/2oz/¼ cup sugar
Ground ginger
1 tangerine
1 egg white
Granulated sugar

Peel the tangerine, removing all the white pith. Leave the membranes around each segment. Beat the egg white lightly and dip in the segments. Roll in the granulated sugar and put on wax/greaseproof paper to set. Heat the milk on HIGH for 2 minutes in a 570ml/1 pint/2 cup measure, do not allow the milk to boil. Add the orange juice. Mix the eggs, sugar, ginger and a pinch of salt. Beat well and gradually add the milk. Pour into 2 custard cups/ramekin dishes, and put them into a baking dish with hot water to come 5mm (¼") up the outsides of the cups/ dishes. Cover the baking dish loosely with plastic wrap and cook for 3 minutes on LOW. If softly set, remove from the oven and allow to cool. If still liquid, cook for 1½ minutes more on LOW, watching carefully. Serve warm or cold with the frosted tangerines.

Grenadine and Lemon Pears

PREPARATION TIME: 15 minutes

MICROWAVE COOKING TIME:
15-20 minutes

SERVES: 2 people

2 fresh pears, approximately equal size
Juice and peel of 1 lemon
280ml/½ pint/1 cup Grenadine syrup
140ml/¼ pint/½ cup light corn syrup
60ml/2oz/¼ cup water

GARNISH
Mint leaves

Mix the corn syrup, water and Grenadine syrup and cook for 5 minutes on HIGH. Peel the lemon and cut the peel into very thin strips. Squeeze the juice from the lemon and mix with the syrup. Peel the pears and leave whole. Leave the stem attached, but remove the eye on

Facing page: Orange Creams (top) and Brown Sugar Bananas (bottom).

the base. Put the pears into a small, deep bowl, big enough for them to stand upright in. Pour over the syrup and cover the bowl with pierced plastic wrap. Cook for 5 minutes on HIGH. Lower the setting to MEDIUM and cook 5 minutes, or until tender. If not tender after 5 minutes, cook for a further 5 minutes on MEDIUM. Remove the pears from the syrup and re-boil the syrup for 5 minutes on HIGH to reduce. Stir in the peel and coat over the pears. Garnish with the mint leaves, and serve hot or cold with whipped cream.

This page: Black Velvet and White Lace. Facing page: Grenadine and Lemon Pears.

Microwave
VEGETARIAN
COOKING

The microwave oven has a brilliant way with vegetables. Fast cooking times mean vegetables keep their fresh colour and crisp texture. Low evaporation means vegetables need very little water to cook, so they keep their nutrients. Fresh vegetables cook as quickly as frozen vegetables do by conventional methods, and frozen vegetables are cooked beautifully in almost the blink of an eye.

Vegetarian diets are losing their "cranky" image as more people turn to that way of eating because of weight and nutrition consciousness. The humble dried bean or lentil has an abundant supply of protein to add to our diets, with the added plus of more fibre than many other protein foods.

The microwave method of rehydrating pulses – dried peas, beans and lentils – eliminates overnight soaking. Just cover the dried pulses with water and bring them to the boil, which usually takes about 10 minutes on the highest setting. After that, allow the pulses to boil for 2 minutes. Leave them standing, covered, in the hot water for 1 hour and they will be ready to cook according to your recipe. Dried pulses usually take about an hour to cook. If that doesn't seem like convenience cooking, remember that conventional methods would take twice as long. It is essential, though, that dried peas, beans and lentils are thoroughly cooked. Eating insufficiently cooked pulses can be dangerous.

Vegetarian menus have suffered from the image that they are composed solely of nut cutlets. I have always found that unfair, since well seasoned cutlets are a delicious alternative to meat and a good addition to a healthy diet. Nut cutlets, escalopes and croquettes are very easy to cook in a microwave oven with the use of a browning dish. Be creative with shapes, too, because nut mixtures hold up better in a microwave oven than they do when fried or baked conventionally.

When organising the recipes into chapters, I was amazed to find just how many recipes could fit easily in several different categories. Pulses can be used in salads, appetizers or entrées. Main courses can be cut down and used as appetizers and appetizers can be expanded to main-meal-sized portions. Even desserts and puddings can be based on vegetables. Which all goes to prove that, vegetarian or not, we can all enjoy more creative meals thanks to the versatility of vegetables.

Microwave
VEGETARIAN

APPETIZERS

Tomato and Tarragon Creams with Sweetcorn Salad

PREPARATION TIME: 25 minutes

MICROWAVE COOKING TIME: 9-10 minutes

SERVES: 4 people

400g/14oz plum tomatoes, canned
30ml/2 tbsps tomato purée/paste
1 onion, finely chopped
5ml/1 tsp chopped tarragon
1 bay leaf
Salt and pepper
225g/8oz low fat or cream cheese
2 eggs
280ml/½ pint/1 cup whipped cream
15g/½ oz/1 tbsp gelatine or agar-agar
45ml/3 tbsps water and lemon juice
    mixed
Salt and pepper

SALAD
225g/8oz/baby corn-on-the-cob
1 green pepper, cut in thin strips
4-6 tomatoes, peeled, seeded and cut in
    strips
4-6 spring/green onions, shredded
45ml/3 tbsps salad oil
15ml/1 tbsp white wine vinegar
5ml/1 tsp white wine vinegar
5ml/1 tsp Dijon mustard
5ml/1 tsp chopped fresh tarragon
Lettuce leaves

GARNISH
Whole tarragon leaves

Sprinkle the gelatine on top of the water and lemon juice in a small ramekin/custard cup. If using agar-agar in leaf form, dissolve with the water or lemon juice in a small cup. Combine the tomatoes, onion,

tarragon, bay leaf, tomato purée/paste, salt and pepper in a deep bowl. Cook, uncovered, 5 minutes on HIGH. Sieve the pulp and set it aside to cool. Beat the eggs and cheese together until smooth. Add the

This page: **Tomato and Tarragon Creams with Sweetcorn Salad.** Facing Page: **Danish Egg Salad (top) and Pasta and Asparagus Salad (bottom).**

cooled tomato pulp. Melt the gelatine or agar-agar for 30 seconds on HIGH. Pour into the tomato mixture and stir well. Set briefly over ice and stir constantly until beginning to thicken. Fold in the cream and adjust the seasoning. Brush 4 ramekin dishes/custard cups lightly with oil and spoon in the tomato mixture. Chill until firm. Put the corn into a large bowl with enough hot water to cover. Cover loosely and cook for 3-4 minutes on HIGH until tender. After 2-3 minutes add the pepper strips. Remove the vegetables with a slotted spoon and rinse under cold water. Set aside to drain. Put the tomatoes into the same water and cook 30 seconds on HIGH. Put into cold water immediately. Remove the skins, cut in half and scoop out the seeds. Slice the flesh into thin strips. Mix the oil, vinegar, tarragon, salt and pepper and combine with the vegetables. Add the spring/green onions just before serving. Arrange lettuce leaves on serving plates and carefully turn out the tomato creams. It may be necessary to dip the moulds briefly into hot water to loosen. Decorate the creams with whole tarragon leaves and serve surrounded with the corn salad.

Danish Egg Salad

PREPARATION TIME: 20 minutes

MICROWAVE COOKING TIME: 7 minutes

SERVES: 4 people

4 eggs
30ml/2 tbsps cream
30g/1oz/2 tbsps butter or margarine
225g/8oz/1 cup frozen peas, thawed
1 cucumber, cut into 1.25cm/½ inch dice
6 sticks of celery, diced
3 spring onions, chopped
30ml/2 tbsps chopped dill
120g/4oz/1 cup diced cheese
280ml/½ pint/1 cup sour cream
60ml/2 fl oz/¼ cup mayonnaise
Paprika
Salt and pepper
1 head Chinese cabbage/leaves, shredded

Beat the eggs and cream together with salt and pepper. Heat a browning dish 5 minutes on HIGH, melt the butter or margarine for 1 minute on HIGH. Pour in half the egg mixture and cook the omelette on one side for 1 minute on HIGH. Turn over and cook a further 1 minute. Cook the egg in two batches. Cook the peas for 1 minute on HIGH with 2 tbsps water. Rinse under cold water and drain to dry. Mix the sour cream, mayonnaise, dill, salt and pepper together. Reserve 30ml/ 2 tbsps dressing and mix the remaining dressing with the peas, celery, cheese and cucumber. Arrange the Chinese cabbage/leaves on serving plates. Pile on the salad. Cut the omelettes into strips and arrange on top. Drizzle the remaining dressing over the omelette strips and sprinkle with paprika.

Warm Salad with Avocado, Grapes, Blue Cheese and Walnuts

PREPARATION TIME: 20 minutes

MICROWAVE COOKING TIME: 1-2 minutes

SERVES: 4 people

1 head curly endive
1 head Belgian endive (chicory)
1 head radicchio
1 small bunch lambs lettuce or watercress
1 head Chinese leaves/cabbage
1 head leaf or iceberg lettuce
4 tbsps chopped fresh herbs
120g/4oz/1 cup walnuts
120g/4oz/1 cup blue cheese crumbled
1 large or 2 small avocados
1 small bunch purple/black grapes

DRESSING
90ml/6 tbsps walnut oil and grapeseed oil mixed
30ml/2 tbsps lemon vinegar or white wine vinegar and lemon juice mixed
Pinch sugar

Tear the curly endive, Belgian endive, radicchio and lettuce into small pieces. If using lambs lettuce separate the leaves. If using watercress remove any thick stalks. Shred the Chinese leaves/cabbage and peel and slice the avocado. Cut the grapes in half and remove any seeds/pips. Combine all the salad ingredients in a large bowl. Mix the salad dressing ingredients and toss with the salad. Arrange on individual salad plates and heat each plate for 1-2 minutes on HIGH before serving.

Pasta and Asparagus Salad

PREPARATION TIME: 15 minutes

MICROWAVE COOKING TIME: 11 minutes plus 8 minutes standing time

SERVES: 4 people

120g/4oz tagliatelle/fettuccine
450g/1lb asparagus, trimmed and cut into 5cm/2 inch pieces
2 courgettes/zucchini, cut into 5cm/ 2 inch sticks
1 lemon, peeled and segmented
30g/2 tbsps chopped parsley
30g/2 tbsps chopped marjoram
Grated rind and juice of 1 lemon
90ml/3 fl oz/⅓ cup salad oil
Pinch sugar (optional)
Salt and pepper
1 head lettuce
1 head Belgian endive (chicory)

Put the pasta into a large bowl with 570ml/1 pint/2 cups hot water, a pinch of salt and 5ml/1 tsp oil. Cook 6 minutes on HIGH and leave to stand in the water for 8 minutes. Drain and leave to cool completely. Cook the asparagus in 140ml/ ¼ pint/½ cup water for 5 minutes on HIGH or until tender. Add the courgettes/zucchini after 3 minutes cooking time. Rinse under cold water and drain. Combine the pasta, asparagus, courgettes/zucchini, parsley, marjoram and lemon segments in a large bowl. Mix the lemon rind, juice, oil, salt and pepper together to blend well. Pour over the

Facing page: Warm Salad with Avocado, Grapes, Blue Cheese and Walnuts.

combined ingredients and toss to coat. Arrange lettuce and endive on serving plates and pile on the salad to serve.

Eggs Primavera

PREPARATION TIME: 20 minutes

MICROWAVE COOKING TIME: 12-14 minutes

SERVES: 4 people

4 eggs
120g/4oz peapods/mangetout
2 large carrots
225g/8oz asparagus
1 small cauliflower
4 spring onions/green onions
1 small head Chinese leaves/cabbage, shredded

DRESSING
280ml/½ pint/1 cup yogurt
1 ripe avocado
140ml/¼ pint/½ cup cream

Put 570ml/1 pint/2½ cups water in a shallow dish with 15ml/1tbsp vinegar and 5ml/1 tsp salt. Heat the water on HIGH for 3-4 minutes or until boiling. Break the eggs one at a time into a cup and slide them into the water. Pierce the yolks once with a small knife or skewer. Cover the dish loosely and cook for 2-3 minutes on MEDIUM. When the whites are set lift the eggs out of the dish and put them immediately into a bowl of cold water. Trim the asparagus spears and cut them into 5cm/2 inch pieces. Separate the head of cauliflower into individual flowerets. Put the asparagus into a casserole with 30ml/2 tbsps water. Cook for 5 minutes on HIGH. After 1 minute add flowerets of cauliflower. Three minutes before the end of cooking time add the mangetout/peapods and the carrots, cut into ribbons with a vegetable peeler. Leave the vegetables to stand, covered, for 1 minute and then rinse under cold water and dry well. Slice the spring/green onions and add to the rest of the vegetables. Pile the Chinese leaves/cabbage onto 4 individual plates. Put the mixed vegetables on top. Drain the poached eggs well and put 1 egg on top of each

salad. Peel the avocado and combine with the yogurt in a food processor and purée until smooth. Stir in the cream and season with salt and pepper. Coat some of the dressing over each egg and serve the rest separately.

Red Pepper Pâté in Lemon Shells

PREPARATION TIME: 20 minutes

MICROWAVE COOKING TIME: 8-9 minutes

SERVES: 4 people

4 lemons, cut in half
6 red peppers, cored, seeded and cut in pieces
60ml/2 fl oz/4 tbsps white wine
1 bay leaf
450g/1lb cream cheese
½ chili pepper, finely chopped
Pinch ground oregano
Salt
Pinch sugar (optional)

This page: Red Pepper Pâté in Lemon Shells. Facing page: Oeufs à la Russe (top) and Eggs Primavera (bottom).

GARNISH
8 thin slices of red pepper
8 small fresh bay leaves
Chinese cabbage/leaves, shredded

ACCOMPANIMENT
Melba or hot buttered toast

Scoop out the pulp from the lemon. Squeeze the juice and set it aside. Trim a slice from the bottom of each lemon half so that they stand upright. Combine peppers, wine and bay leaf in a medium size casserole. Cover and cook 8-10 minutes on HIGH until very soft. Remove the bay leaf and purée the peppers and wine in a food processor. Add the cream cheese, chili pepper, oregano, salt, lemon juice and sugar (if using). Process until smooth. Adjust the seasoning and pipe or spoon the pâté into the lemon shells. Chill briefly

aside. Chop the mushroom stalks and combine with the walnuts, pimento, chives, mustard, salt, pepper and breadcrumbs. Add any cooking liquid from the mushrooms and the beaten egg. Mound the filling onto the mushroom caps. Cook on MEDIUM for 6-8 minutes until the filling is set. Mix the topping ingredients and spoon onto the mushroom filling. Cook a further 2 minutes on MEDIUM or 3 minutes on a combination setting of a microwave convection oven. Serve immediately. The cheese topping may be sprinkled lightly with paprika before the final cooking if desired.

Spinach-Stuffed Artichoke Hearts

PREPARATION TIME: 25 minutes

MICROWAVE COOKING TIME: 19-20 minutes

SERVES 4 people

4 globe artichokes
450g/1lb fresh spinach, stalks removed and well washed
1 shallot finely chopped
1 egg, beaten
140ml/¼ pint/½ cup heavy/double cream
2 slices bread, made into crumbs
15g/½ oz/1 tbsp butter or margarine
Nutmeg
Cayenne pepper
Salt

TOPPING
60g/2oz/½ cup grated Cheddar cheese
60ml/4 tbsps heavy/double cream

Cut all of the top leaves off the artichokes. Trim the remaining leaves down to the thickest part. Cut out as much of the choke as possible. Cover the artichokes with water and cook in a covered casserole for 7-8 minutes on HIGH. Drain well and remove any remaining choke. Trim the remaining leaves down further until

This page: Spinach-Stuffed Artichoke Hearts (top) and Stuffed Mushrooms (bottom). Facing page: Aubergine/Eggplant Caviar (top) and Avocado, Tomato and Mozzarella on Garlic Toast (bottom).

before serving. Garnish each with a slice of red pepper and one bay leaf. Arrange on a bed of Chinese cabbage/leaves. Serve with hot buttered toast or melba toast.

Stuffed Mushrooms

PREPARATION TIME: 15 minutes

MICROWAVE COOKING TIME: 8-11 minutes

SERVES: 4 people

4 very large or 8 medium-size mushrooms
30g/2 tbsps butter
3 slices white bread, made into crumbs
120g/4oz/1 cup chopped walnuts
3 pimento caps, chopped
1 egg, beaten
1 small bunch chives, snipped
15ml/1 tbsp Dijon mustard
Salt and pepper

TOPPING
30g/1oz/2 tbsps cream cheese
15g/½ oz/1 tbsp grated Gruyère or Cheddar cheese
90ml/3 fl oz/⅓ cup heavy/double cream
Pinch cayenne pepper

Melt the butter in a large, shallow dish. Remove the stalks from the mushrooms and set them aside. Cook the whole mushroom caps for 2 minutes on HIGH, remove and set

only the thick, edible part remains. Cook the spinach in the water that clings to the leaves on HIGH for 5 minutes. Melt the butter 30 seconds on HIGH in a small bowl. Cook the shallot for 1 minute until softenend. Combine with the spinach, breadcrumbs, egg, cream, nutmeg, cayenne pepper and salt. Mound the filling onto the artichoke bottoms. Arrange in a circle and cook 5 minutes on MEDIUM or until set. Mix the topping ingredients together and spoon onto the spinach filling. Cook a further 2 minutes on MEDIUM to melt the cheese, or for 3 minutes on a combination setting in a microwave convection oven. Sprinkle lightly with more grated nutmeg before serving.

Courgette/Zucchini and Carrot Terrine

PREPARATION TIME: 20 minutes

MICROWAVE COOKING TIME: 17 minutes plus 10 minutes standing time

SERVES: 4-6 people

6-8 large, green cabbage leaves
340g/12oz low fat cheese
4 slices bread, made into crumbs
2 eggs
140ml/¼ pint/½ cup cream, lightly whipped
1 bunch chives, snipped
Salt and pepper
1-2 carrots, cut in strips
1-2 courgettes/zucchini, cut in strips

SAUCE
280ml/½ pint/1 cup sour cream or plain yogurt
140ml/¼ pint/½ cup mayonnaise
2 tomatoes, peeled, seeded and cut in small dice
30ml/2 tbsps chopped parsley
15ml/1 tbsp lemon juice or white wine
Pinch sugar (optional)
Salt and pepper

Trim the spines of the cabbage leaves to make them thinner. Place the leaves in a shallow dish with 30ml/ 2 tbsps water and a pinch of salt. Cover the dish loosely and cook for 1 minute on HIGH. Line a 450g/1lb loaf dish with the cabbage leaves. Mix together the cheese, breadcrumbs, eggs, cream, chives and salt and pepper. Cook the carrots in 30ml/2 tbsps water for 5 minutes on HIGH. Add the courgettes after 3 minutes cooking time. Drain and dry both vegetables very well. Put a quarter of the mixture into the bottom of the loaf dish on top of the cabbage leaves. Place on 1 layer of carrots and cover with another quarter of the cheese mixture. Place on a layer of courgettes and repeat the process until all the mixture and the vegetables are used. Wrap over the overlapping cabbage leaves. Cover the dish with the cling film/ plastic wrap, pierce several times to release the steam. Put into the microwave oven with a small dish of hot water and cook for 10 minutes on MEDIUM. Allow to cool in the dish. Combine the sauce ingredients. Slice the terrine and arrange on lettuce leaves or watercress. Spoon over some of the sauce and serve the rest separately.

Aubergine/Eggplant Caviar

PREPARATION TIME: 20 minutes

MICROWAVE COOKING TIME: 7-9 minutes

SERVES: 4 people

1 large or 2 small aubergines/eggplants
60ml/4 tbsps oil
Juice of ½ lemon
1 clove garlic, minced
Pinch cayenne pepper
Salt

GARNISH
2 hard boiled eggs
1 small onion, finely chopped
30g/2 tbsps chopped parsley
4-8 slices French bread, toasted

Remove the stem from the eggplant/ aubergine, cut it in half and lightly score the flesh. Sprinkle with salt and leave to stand for 30 minutes to draw out any bitterness. Rinse and pat dry. Put into a covered casserole and cook on HIGH for 7-9 minutes. Allow to cool and cut into small pieces. Combine in a food processor with the garlic, lemon juice, salt and pepper. Blend until smooth. Pour the oil gradually through the feedtube with the machine running. Adjust the seasoning and chill. Sieve the egg yolk and finely chop the white. To serve, pile the aubergine/eggplant caviar on top of the French bread toast and sprinkle on the onion, egg and parsley.

Oeufs à la Russe

PREPARATION TIME: 20 minutes

MICROWAVE COOKING TIME: 35-40 minutes plus 10 minutes standing time

SERVES: 4 people

4 eggs
3 beetroot/beets
120g/4oz mushrooms
4 sticks celery
2-3 potatoes, depending on size
15ml/1 tbsp butter or margarine
180g/6oz fresh spinach

DRESSING
430ml/¾ pint/1½ cups sour cream
5ml/1 tsp white wine vinegar
2.5ml/½ tsp sugar
1 bunch chives, chopped
Salt and pepper

Poach the eggs as for Eggs Primavera. Leave in cold water until ready to use. Put the beetroot/beets into a deep bowl with 140ml/¼ pint/½ cup water and a pinch of salt. Cover the bowl loosely with cling film/plastic wrap and cook on HIGH for 12-16 minutes, stirring once or twice. Remove the beetroot/beets from the bowl and set aside to stand 10 minutes before peeling. Rinse out the bowl and add the potatoes cut in 1.25cm/½ inch dice. Add 140ml/ ¼ pint/½ cup water and a pinch of

Facing page: Broccoli and Hazelnut Terrine (top) and Courgette/ Zucchini and Carrot Terrine (bottom).

salt and cover the bowl loosely with cling film/plastic wrap. Cook the potatoes on HIGH for 8-10 minutes, stirring once. Leave to stand while preparing the rest of the salad. Heat the butter in a small bowl for 30 seconds on HIGH and add the mushrooms, quartered, and the celery, cut in small dice. Cook for 1 minute on HIGH, stirring occasionally. Drain the potatoes and add them to the celery and mushrooms. Leave to cool. Combine the dressing ingredients and set them aside. Wash the spinach leaves well and dry and shred them finely. Add 60ml/2 fl oz/¼ cup of the dressing to the potatoes, celery and mushrooms and stir to coat. Add the beetroot/ beets and stir very carefully. Pile the salad onto the spinach and top each salad with 1 drained poached egg. Coat the remaining dressing over each egg before serving.

Avocado, Tomato and Mozzarella on Garlic Toast

PREPARATION TIME: 15 minutes

MICROWAVE COOKING TIME: 9 minutes

SERVES: 4 people

4 slices French or Vienna bread, sliced
   1.25cm/½ inch thick, on the diagonal
60g/2oz/4 tbsps butter or margarine
15ml/1 tbsp oil
1 clove garlic, crushed
2-4 beefsteak tomatoes
1-2 ripe avocados
120g/4oz mozzarella cheese, sliced
30ml/2 tbsps capers
30ml/2 tbsps salad oil
10ml/2 tsps lemon juice
2.5ml/½ tsp oregano
Salt and pepper

Heat a browning dish for 5 minutes on HIGH. Add the oil, butter and garlic. Put in the bread slices, two at a time if necessary. Brown for 1 minute on HIGH and turn over. Cook another 1 minute on HIGH and set on paper towels to drain. Peel the avocados, remove the stones and slice. Slice the tomatoes and the

cheese and arrange on top of the bread slices, alternating with the avocado slices. Scatter over the capers. Mix the oil, lemon juice, oregano, salt and pepper and spoon on top. Heat 2 minutes on MEDIUM to melt the cheese. Serve immediately.

Salad of Wild Mushrooms and Artichokes

PREPARATION TIME: 20 minutes

MICROWAVE COOKING TIME: 9-11 minutes

SERVES: 4 people

2-3 globe artichokes, depending on size
1 slice lemon
1 bay leaf
6 black peppercorns
225g/8oz oyster mushrooms (other
   varieties of wild mushrooms may be
   substituted)
30ml/2 tbsps oil
1 head radicchio (red or Italian lettuce)
1 head iceberg or leaf lettuce
1 bunch watercress
1 small bunch fresh chives, snipped

DRESSING
90ml/6 tbsps oil
30ml/2 tbsps white wine vinegar
15ml/1 tbsp Dijon mustard
Salt and pepper

GARNISH
Fresh chervil or dill

Trim the tips of the artichoke leaves. Put the artichokes into a large bowl with the lemon, bay leaf, peppercorns and enough water to cover. Cook 7-8 minutes or until the bottom leaf pulls away easily. Drain upside-down. Remove the stalks and slice the mushrooms thickly. Cook for 1-2 minutes in 30ml/2 tbsps oil and set aside. Tear the radicchio and lettuce into small pieces. Add the watercress leaves and toss together with the chives. Mix the salad dressing ingredients together until very well blended. Remove the leaves of the artichokes and arrange them on 4 plates. Top with the radicchio and watercress. Remove the chokes from

the artichoke hearts and discard. Cut the artichoke hearts into thin slices and combine with the mushrooms. Toss with half of the dressing, spoon equal amounts over the salads. Reheat each for 1 minute on HIGH. Garnish with the chervil and serve the remaining dressing separately.

Broccoli and Hazelnut Terrine

PREPARATION TIME: 20 minutes

MICROWAVE COOKING TIME: 10 minutes plus 10 minutes standing time

SERVES: 4-6 people

6-8 large or 12-14 small whole spinach
   leaves
450g/1lb broccoli
1 shallot, finely chopped
180g/6oz/¾ cup low fat cheese
4 slices bread, made into fine crumbs
2 eggs
280ml/½ pint/1 cup cream, lightly
   whipped
120g/4oz/1 cup coarsely chopped,
   roasted hazelnuts
Pinch nutmeg
Pinch thyme
Salt and pepper

SAUCE
280ml/½ pint/1 cup mayonnaise
140ml/¼ pint/½ cup plain yogurt
Grated rind and juice of 1 lemon
Pinch cayenne pepper
Salt

Trim away any coarse stalks from the spinach but leave the leaves whole. Wash them well and put them into a shallow dish with a pinch of salt. Loosely cover the dish and cook for 1 minute on HIGH with only the water that clings to the leaves. Remove from the dish and press on paper towels to drain. Line a 450g/1lb loaf dish with the spinach leaves and set aside. Chop the broccoli finely. Mix the eggs, cheese, cream, breadcrumbs, shallot, thyme, nutmeg and salt and pepper together. Stir in the broccoli and the hazelnuts. Spoon the mixture into the loaf dish on top of the spinach leaves and pack down well.

Fold the spinach leaves over on top of the mixture. Cover the dish with 2 layers of cling film/plastic wrap, pierced several times to let out steam. Put a ramekin/custard cup of water into the microwave oven with the terrine and cook on MEDIUM for 10 minutes or until just barely set. Allow to cool in the dish. Mix the sauce ingredients together. Turn the terrine out of the dish and slice. Arrange on lettuce leaves or

This page: Salad of Wild Mushrooms and Artichokes.

radicchio (red or Italian lettuce) and spoon over some of the sauce. Serve the remaining sauce separately.

VEGETABLE SOUPS

Cream of Watercress Soup

PREPARATION TIME: 20 minutes

MICROWAVE COOKING TIME:
12-13 minutes plus 5 minutes
standing time

SERVES: 4 people

2 medium potatoes, cut in even-size
  pieces
3 bunches watercress, well washed and
  root ends removed
1 litre/1¾ pints/3½ cups vegetable stock
Juice of ½ lemon
1.25ml/¼ tsp ground nutmeg
280ml-430ml/½-¾ pint/1-1½ cups
  single/light cream
Salt and pepper

GARNISH
120ml/4 tbsps heavy/double cream
Reserved watercress leaves

Put the stock and the potatoes into a
large bowl with a pinch of salt.
Partially cover and cook for 10
minutes on HIGH or until the
potatoes are tender. Allow to stand
for 5 minutes. Add the lemon juice,
salt, pepper, watercress and nutmeg
and purée in a food processor until
smooth. Stir in the cream and
process once more. Heat 2-3 minutes
on HIGH before serving. Garnish
with a swirl of cream and the
reserved watercress leaves.

Tomato and Dill Bisque

PREPARATION TIME: 20 minutes

MICROWAVE COOKING TIME:
7½ minutes

SERVES: 4 people

900g/2lbs tomatoes
850ml/1½ pints/3 cups vegetable stock
30ml/2 tbsps tomato purée/paste
1 onion, peeled and chopped
2 sprigs fresh dill
Salt and pepper
10ml/2 tsps chopped fresh dill
140ml/¼ pint/½ cup double/heavy
  cream

This page: Beetroot and Sour
Cream Soup with Horseradish.
Facing page: Tomato and Dill
Bisque (top) and Cream of
Watercress Soup (bottom).

GARNISH
1 slice tomato
4 small sprigs fresh dill
60ml/2 fl oz/¼ cup plain yogurt

Cut half of 1 cucumber into small dice and set aside. Peel the other half and the remaining 2 cucumbers and chop them roughly. Place the cucumbers in a large bowl with the stock and salt and pepper. Remove the mint leaves from the stalks and add the stalks to the cucumbers. Cover the bowl loosely and cook 6 minutes on HIGH or until the cucumbers are tender. Remove the mint stalks and purée the soup in a food processor. Strain if desired and add the cream and cucumber dice. Re-heat for 2 minutes on HIGH. Chop the mint leaves just before serving and add to the soup. Garnish with yogurt.

Sweetcorn and Red Pepper Soup

PREPARATION TIME: 20 minutes

MICROWAVE COOKING TIME: 14 minutes plus 5 minutes standing time

SERVES: 4 people

4 medium potatoes, cut in even-size pieces
570ml/1 pint/2 cups vegetable stock
225g/8oz/1½ cups corn/sweetcorn
1 bay leaf
15ml/1 tbsp butter or margarine
1 red chili pepper
1 large, sweet red pepper
1 onion, chopped
Salt and pepper
570ml/1 pint/2 cups milk

GARNISH
Chopped parsley

Pour the stock into a large bowl and add the potatoes, bay leaf and a pinch of salt. Partially cover and cook 10 minutes on HIGH or until the potatoes are tender. Leave to stand for 5 minutes and remove the bay leaf. Purée until smooth. Melt the butter 30 seconds on HIGH and

Cut the tomatoes in half, remove the seeds and strain the juice into a large bowl. Add the onion, sprigs of dill, tomato purée/paste, halved tomatoes, salt, pepper and stock. Partially cover and cook on HIGH for 7 minutes or until the tomatoes have broken down and the onions are soft. Remove the sprigs of dill and pour the soup into a food processor. Purée the soup until smooth, and strain to remove any tomato skins. Adjust the seasoning and add a pinch of sugar if necessary to bring out the tomato flavour. Stir in the cream and chopped dill and re-heat for 30 seconds on HIGH. Garnish each serving with a spoonful of yogurt, a tomato strip and a sprig of fresh dill.

Cream of Cucumber Soup with Mint

PREPARATION TIME: 20 minutes

MICROWAVE COOKING TIME: 7-8 minutes plus 5 minutes standing time

SERVES: 4 people

3 large cucumbers (seedless variety)
1 litre/1¾ pints/3½ cups vegetable stock
2-3 sprigs mint
280ml/½ pint/1 cup single/light cream
Salt and pepper

GARNISH
Cucumber dice
60ml/2 fl oz/¼ cup plain yogurt

This page: Sweetcorn and Red Pepper Soup. Facing page: Cream of Cucumber Soup with Mint (top) and Fresh Pea Soup with Thyme (bottom).

cook the onion, pepper, and chili pepper for 2 minutes on HIGH. Add to the puréed potato along with the corn/sweetcorn and milk. Cook 2 minutes on HIGH and adjust the seasoning. Garnish with chopped parsley.

Purée of Asparagus Soup

PREPARATION TIME: 15 minutes

MICROWAVE COOKING TIME: 11 minutes plus 5 minutes standing time

SERVES: 4 people

1340g/3lbs asparagus
1 litre/1¾ pints/3½ cups vegetable stock
1.25ml/¼ tsp ground mace
280ml/½ pint/1 cup single/light cream
Salt and pepper

GARNISH
140ml/¼ pint/½ cup whipped cream, unsweetened
Ground mace

Trim the thick ends of the asparagus and chop the spears to even-sized pieces. Place in a large bowl with the stock, mace, salt and pepper. Partially cover and cook 10 minutes on HIGH or until the asparagus is soft. Leave to stand for 5 minutes. Purée in a food processor and strain if desired. Add the cream and heat 1 minute on HIGH. Garnish each serving with a spoonful of whipped cream and sprinkle with mace.

Fresh Pea Soup with Thyme

PREPARATION TIME: 20 minutes

MICROWAVE COOKING TIME: 7-13 minutes

SERVES: 4 people

1.8kg/4lbs fresh peas, shelled (1.3kg/3lbs frozen peas may be substituted)
1 litre/1¾ pints/3½ cups vegetable stock
2 sprigs fresh thyme
280ml/½ pint/1 cup single/light cream
Salt and pepper

GARNISH
140ml/¼ pint/½ cup heavy/double cream
Reserved peas

Place the peas in a large bowl with the stock, thyme, salt and pepper. Partially cover and cook for 10 minutes on HIGH or until the peas are soft. If using frozen peas, cook for 5 minutes on HIGH. Leave to stand for 5 minutes. Remove the thyme and discard. Remove about 60g/ 4 tbsps peas to reserve for garnish. Purée the remaining peas and stock in a food processor until smooth. Strain the soup if desired. Stir in the cream and adjust the seasoning. Add the reserved peas and re-heat 2-3 minutes on HIGH. Before serving, swirl a spoonful of cream through each bowl.

Beetroot and Sour Cream Soup with Horseradish

PREPARATION TIME: 20 minutes

MICROWAVE COOKING TIME: 22-23 minutes plus 10 minutes standing time

SERVES: 4 people

225g/8oz turnips, peeled and cut in even-size pieces
450g/1lb beetroot/beets
1 litre/1¾ pints/3½ cups vegetable stock
1 bay leaf
Salt and pepper
280ml/½ pint/1 cup sour cream
15ml/1 tbsp grated fresh or bottled horseradish

GARNISH
Chopped chives
Reserved sour cream

Cook unpeeled beetroot/beets in a large bowl, covered, with 60ml/ 2 fl oz/¼ cup stock for 10 minutes on HIGH. Leave to stand for 10 minutes before peeling. Pre-cooked or canned beetroot may be substituted. Cut into small pieces and return to the bowl with the turnips, remaining stock, bay leaf, salt and pepper. Partially cover the bowl and cook for a further 10 minutes on HIGH. Remove the bay leaf and purée the soup in a food processor until smooth. Reserve 60ml/4 tbsps sour cream and add the rest to the soup along with the horseradish. Heat 2-3 minutes on MEDIUM. Do not allow the soup to boil. Serve topped with sour cream and chopped chives.

Lettuce Cream Soup with Coriander

PREPARATION TIME: 20 minutes

MICROWAVE COOKING TIME: 15-16 minutes plus 5 minutes standing time

SERVES: 4 people

2 medium-sized potatoes, cut into even-size pieces
1 litre/1¾ pints/3½ cups vegetable stock
2 small heads lettuce, washed and shredded
2.5ml/½ tsp ground coriander
280ml-430ml/½-¾ pint/1-1½ cups single/light cream
Salt and pepper

GARNISH
Reserved shredded lettuce
Chopped parsley

Place the potatoes, stock and a pinch of salt in a large bowl. Partially cover the bowl and cook 10 minutes on HIGH or until the potatoes are tender. Add the lettuce, reserving about a quarter for garnish. Add the coriander and pepper and cook a further 3 minutes on HIGH. Leave to stand 5 minutes before blending in a food processor until smooth. Add 280ml/½ pint/1 cup cream (add more cream if the soup is too thick). The soup should be the consistency of lightly-whipped cream. Add the reserved shredded lettuce and parsley and re-heat for 2-3 minutes on HIGH.

Facing page: Lettuce Cream Soup with Coriander (top) and Purée of Asparagus Soup (bottom).

Mushroom and Sherry Cream Soup

PREPARATION TIME: 20 minutes

MICROWAVE COOKING TIME:
9-11 minutes plus 5 minutes standing time

SERVES: 4 people

900g/2lbs mushrooms, chopped
5-6 slices bread, crust removed
700ml/1¼ pints/2½ cups vegetable stock
1 sprig fresh thyme
1 bay leaf
½ clove garlic, crushed (optional)
430ml/¾ pint/1½ cups light/single cream
60ml/2 fl oz/¼ cup sherry
Salt and pepper

GARNISH
140ml/¼ pint/½ cup whipped cream
Grated nutmeg

Combine the mushrooms, bread, stock, thyme, bay leaf, salt, pepper and garlic (if using) in a large bowl. Partially cover and cook on HIGH for 7-8 minutes. Leave to stand for 5 minutes. Remove the thyme and the bay leaf and purée in a food processor until smooth. If the soup is not thick enough, add 1-2 slices more bread with the crusts removed. Add the sherry and process once more. Re-heat 2-3 minutes on HIGH. Garnish each bowl with a spoonful of whipped cream and a sprinkling of nutmeg.

Purée of Leek and Potato Soup

PREPARATION TIME: 20 minutes

MICROWAVE COOKING TIME:
12 minutes plus 5 minutes standing time

SERVES: 4 people

3 medium-size potatoes, cut in even-size pieces
4 leeks, depending on size
1 litre/1¾ pints/3½ cups vegetable stock
1 bay leaf
2 sprigs thyme
1.25ml/¼ tsp ground nutmeg

Salt and pepper
280-430ml/½-¾ pint/1-1½ cups single/ light cream

Wash leeks well and shred the light green portion of 1 of the leeks and reserve. Slice the remaining leeks and combine with the potatoes in a large bowl. Pour on the stock and add the bay leaf, thyme and a pinch of salt. Partially cover the bowl and cook on HIGH for 10 minutes or until the potatoes and leeks are tender. Leave to stand for 5 minutes. Remove the bay leaf and thyme and purée the soup in a food processor until smooth. Add the nutmeg, pepper

This page: Purée of Leek and Potato Soup (top) and Mushroom and Sherry Cream Soup (bottom). Facing page: Spring Vegetable Soup.

and 280ml/½ pint/1 cup cream. Process again and add more cream if the soup is too thick. It should be the consistency of lightly whipped cream. Put the reserved leek into a small dish with 30ml/2 tbsps water and cook for 2 minutes on HIGH. Drain and garnish the soup with a spoonful of sour cream and the reserved leek strips.

Purée of Carrot Soup

PREPARATION TIME: 20 minutes

MICROWAVE COOKING TIME:
16-17 minutes

SERVES: 4 people

1340g/3lbs carrots, scraped and grated
1 litre/1¾ pints/3½ cups vegetable stock
2-3 sprigs rosemary
280ml/½ pint/1 cup milk or light/single
 cream
Salt and pepper

GARNISH
140ml/¼ pint/½ cup unsweetened
 whipped cream
Chopped parsley

Combine the carrots, rosemary, salt, pepper and stock in a large bowl. Partially cover and cook 15 minutes on HIGH or until the carrots are very tender. Remove the rosemary and purée the soup in a food processor. Add the milk or cream and process until smooth. Adjust the seasoning and re-heat 1-2 minutes on HIGH before serving. Top with spoonfuls of whipped cream and chopped parsley.

Spring Vegetable Soup

PREPARATION TIME: 25 minutes

MICROWAVE COOKING TIME:
30 minutes plus 15-20 minutes
standing time

SERVES: 4-6 people

VEGETABLE STOCK
225g/8oz carrots, roughly chopped
6 sticks celery, roughly chopped
1 turnip, roughly chopped (optional)
3 onions, chopped and the peel of 1
 reserved for colour
1 tomato, quartered and seeded
3 parsley stalks
1 whole clove
1 bay leaf
1 blade mace
2 sprigs thyme or other fresh herbs
6 black peppercorns
Pinch salt
1150ml/2 pints/4 cups water

SOUP
1 litre/1¾ pint/3½ cups vegetable stock
1 head green cabbage, shredded
120g/4oz asparagus cut in 2.5cm/1 inch
 pieces
120g/4oz French/green beans cut in
 2.5cm/1 inch pieces
3 carrots, cut in 5cm/2 inch strips
120g/4oz fresh or frozen peas
1 large red pepper, thinly sliced
3 spring/green onions, sliced
60ml/2 fl oz/¼ cup white wine, optional
Salt and pepper

Combine all the ingredients for the stock in a large bowl. Half cover the bowl with cling film/plastic wrap and cook 15 minutes on HIGH. The stock will boil, so the bowl must be deep enough to contain it. Allow to stand for 15-20 minutes before straining. The stock will keep up to 3 days in the refrigerator or frozen in

This page: Purée of Carrot Soup. Facing page: French/Green Beans with Lemon Herb Sauce (top) and Asparagus Tied with Fresh Herbs (bottom).

ice cube trays for convenience. To prepare the soup, pour the measured stock into a large bowl. If using fresh peas add them to the stock and partially cover the bowl. Cook the peas for 5 minutes on HIGH. Add the carrots and cook a further 5 minutes on HIGH. Add the beans, asparagus and cabbage and cook for 5 minutes further on HIGH. Add the onions, peppers and wine after 2 minutes cooking time. If using frozen peas, add them with the onions and peppers. Season with salt and pepper to taste before serving. If preparing the soup in advance, re-heat it for 5-6 minutes on HIGH before serving.

SIDE DISHES

French/Green Beans with Lemon Herb Sauce

PREPARATION TIME: 10 minutes

MICROWAVE COOKING TIME: 7 minutes

SERVES: 4 people

450g/1lb French /green beans
60ml/4 fl oz/¼ cup water
Salt

SAUCE
280ml/½ pint/1 cup low fat soft cheese
   or fromage blanc
60-140ml/2 fl oz-¼ pint milk
30g/1oz/1 cup watercress leaves, and
   thin stalks
30ml/2 tbsps chopped fresh herbs
Juice and grated rind of ½ lemon
Salt and pepper

Combine the beans, water and salt in a casserole dish and cover loosely. Cook on HIGH for 4 minutes, stirring once or twice. Leave to stand while preparing the sauce. Heat the milk for 3 minutes on HIGH. If using low fat soft cheese, use the greater quantity of milk. Combine with the remaining ingredients, except the lemon rind, in a food processor and work until well blended. Drain the beans and pour over the sauce. Sprinkle on the lemon rind, and toss just before serving.

Asparagus Tied with Fresh Herbs

PREPARATION TIME: 15 minutes

MICROWAVE COOKING TIME: 14 minutes

SERVES: 4 people

900g/2lb asparagus spears
8 sprigs of fresh thyme or marjoram or
   8 chives

SAUCE
3 egg yolks
180g/6oz/¾ cup butter
30ml/2 tbsps white wine
Squeeze of lemon juice

5ml/1 tsp chopped thyme, marjoram or
   chives
Salt and pepper

Trim the thick ends of the asparagus
and place the spears in a shallow
dish. Add 140ml/¼ pint/½ cup water
and cover the dish loosely. Cook on
HIGH for 10 minutes. Drain and
keep warm. In a small, deep bowl,
heat the wine and butter for 2
minutes on HIGH. Remove from the
oven and gradually beat in the egg
yolks. Cook on HIGH 10 seconds
and then stir. Repeat the process
until the sauce thickens, which takes
about 2 minutes. Add the lemon
juice, chopped herbs, salt and pepper.
Tie up 4 bundles of asparagus with
the chosen herbs. Serve the
asparagus with the sauce.

Broccoli with Toasted Sunflower Seeds

PREPARATION TIME: 10 minutes

MICROWAVE COOKING TIME:
4½-5½ minutes

SERVES: 4 people

450g/1lb broccoli
30g/2 tbsps butter or margarine
120g/4oz/1 cup toasted, salted sunflower
   seeds
Pepper
5ml/1 tsp lemon juice (if desired)

Trim the ends of the broccoli stalks
and separate into even-sized pieces.
Place in a large casserole or shallow
dish with 60ml/2 fl oz/¼ cup water.
Cover loosely and cook 4-5 minutes
on HIGH. Melt the butter for
30 seconds on HIGH, stir in the
sunflower seeds and add pepper and
lemon juice. Drain the broccoli and
sprinkle over the sunflower seeds to
serve.

Broccoli and Cauliflower Mold with Salsa

PREPARATION TIME: 25 minutes

MICROWAVE COOKING TIME:
7½ minutes

SERVES: 4-6 people

1 small head cauliflower
225g/8oz broccoli

DRESSING
45ml/3 tbsps oil
15ml/1 tbsp wine vinegar
5ml/1 tsp ground mustard
½ clove garlic, minced
Salt and pepper

SALSA
4-5 tomatoes, depending on size
1 green pepper, chopped
15ml/1 tbsp oil
1 green chili pepper, finely chopped
5ml/1 tsp cumin seed or ground cumin
4 spring onions, finely chopped
Salt and pepper

This page: Broccoli and
Cauliflower Mold with Salsa.
Facing page: Broccoli with Toasted
Sunflower Seeds (top) and Brussels
Sprouts and Hazelnuts (bottom).

Divide the cauliflower into flowerets
and trim down any long, thick stalks.
Trim the broccoli stalks to within
5cm/2 inches of the flowerets and
combine with the cauliflower in a
deep bowl. Add 30ml/2 tbsps water
and a pinch of salt. Cover loosely
and cook 3 minutes on HIGH. Mix
the dressing ingredients together
thoroughly. Drain the vegetables well
and pour the dressing over the
vegetables while still warm. Arrange
the vegetables in a deep 570ml/
1 pint/2 cup bowl, alternating the

2 vegetables. Press lightly to push the vegetables together. Leave the vegetables to cool in the bowl and then refrigerate. Put the tomatoes in a bowl of very hot water. Microwave 30 seconds on HIGH. Put the tomatoes into cold water and then peel and chop roughly. Heat the oil in a large bowl for 30 seconds on HIGH. Add the green pepper, chili pepper and cumin. Cook for 2 minutes on HIGH. Stir in the tomatoes, onions, salt and pepper and leave to cool. Turn out the vegetables carefully onto a serving plate and spoon the salsa around the base. Serve cold. Both the mold and the salsa may be prepared several hours in advance. If left overnight, the broccoli may discolour the cauliflower.

Vegetable Stir Fry with Tofu

PREPARATION TIME: 20 minutes

MICROWAVE COOKING TIME:
7½ minutes

SERVES: 4 people

60ml/2 fl oz/¼ cup oil
Blanched whole almonds
225g/8oz tofu
4 spears broccoli
120g/4oz peapods/mangetout
120g/4oz bean sprouts
120g/4oz baby corn-on-the-cob
1 red pepper, sliced
60g/2oz/½ cup water chestnuts, sliced
1 clove garlic, minced
140ml/¼ pint/½ cup vegetable stock
10ml/2 tsps cornstarch/cornflour
60ml/2 fl oz/4 tbsps soy sauce
Dash sherry
Dash sesame oil
Salt and pepper
4 spring onions/green onions, sliced

Heat a browning dish for 5 minutes on HIGH. Add the oil and fry the almonds for 5 minutes, stirring often to brown evenly. Remove the almonds from the dish and set them aside. Cut out the broccoli flowerets and reserve. Slice the stalks diagonally. If the corn cobs are large cut in half lengthwise. Cook the

broccoli and the corn together for 1 minute on HIGH. Add the garlic, red pepper, peapods/mangetout, water chestnuts and the broccoli flowerets. Mix the soy sauce, sesame oil, sherry, stock, and cornstarch/cornflour together. Pour over the vegetables and cook 1 minute on HIGH. Add the bean sprouts, almonds, spring/green onions and the tofu, cut in small cubes. Cook 30 seconds on HIGH. Serve immediately.

Vegetables Mornay

PREPARATION TIME: 25 minutes

MICROWAVE COOKING TIME:
24-28 minutes

SERVES: 4-6 people

225g/8oz new potatoes, scrubbed but not
    peeled
125g/8oz button or pickling onions,
    peeled
15g/1 tbsp butter
Pinch sugar
2-3 carrots, cut in strips
2 parsnips, cut in strips
120g/4oz mangetout/peapods
120g/4oz button mushrooms
30g/2 tbsps butter
Salt

SAUCE
45g/3 tbsps butter
45g/3 tbsps flour
5ml/1 tsp dry mustard
Pinch cayenne pepper
570ml/1 pint/2 cups milk
120g/4oz/1 cup Cheddar cheese,
    shredded
Salt and pepper
Nutmeg

Cook the new potatoes in 60ml/ 2 fl oz/¼ cup water with a pinch of salt for 8-10 minutes on HIGH in a deep, covered dish. Leave to stand 5 minutes. Cook the carrots and parsnips together in 60ml/2 fl oz/ ¼ cup water in a covered dish for 6 minutes on HIGH. Combine the onions with the sugar and 15g/1 tbsp butter in a deep bowl. Cook, covered, for 7 minutes on HIGH. Stir twice while cooking. Melt the remaining butter for the vegetables

and add the mangetout/peapods and mushrooms. Cook for 2 minutes on HIGH. Leave all the vegetables covered while preparing the sauce. Melt the butter for 1 minute on HIGH in a glass measure. Stir in the flour, mustard and cayenne pepper. Gradually whisk in the milk and add the salt and pepper. Cook for 3-4 minutes on HIGH, whisking after 1 minute, until the sauce has thickened and is bubbling. Stir in the cheese to melt. Arrange the vegetables on a serving dish, keeping each different vegetable in a separate pile. Coat with some of the sauce and sprinkle on nutmeg. Serve remaining sauce separately.

Brussels Sprouts and Hazelnuts

PREPARATION TIME: 20 minutes

MICROWAVE COOKING TIME:
20-21 minutes

SERVES: 4 people

60g/2oz/½ cup hazelnuts
450g/1lb Brussels sprouts
30g/2 tbsps butter or margarine
Salt and pepper

Put the nuts into a small, deep bowl. Cover with hot water and heat 3 minutes on HIGH. Leave to soak for 10 minutes. Drain and rub off the skins. Leave the nuts to dry. Heat a browning dish 5 minutes on HIGH and drop in the butter. Add the nuts and cook 5 minutes on HIGH, stirring every 30 seconds to brown the nuts evenly. Cook the Brussels sprouts with 30ml/2 tbsps water and a pinch of salt in a lightly covered bowl or a cooking bag. Cook for 7-8 minutes on HIGH or until tender. Drain and combine with the nuts and butter.

Facing page: Vegetable Stir Fry with Tofu.

Ginger Sesame Carrots

PREPARATION TIME: 10 minutes

MICROWAVE COOKING TIME:
7½-10½ minutes

SERVES: 4-6 people

900g/2lb carrots, sliced diagonally
30g/1oz/2 tbsps butter or margarine
30g/1oz/2 tbsps brown sugar
7.5ml/1½ tsps ground ginger or 1 small
*   piece fresh ginger, grated*
30g/1oz/¼ cup sesame seeds
Dash soy sauce
Dash sesame oil
Salt and pepper

Place the carrots in a casserole dish
with 60ml/2 fl oz/¼ cup water. Add
a pinch of salt, cover and cook on
HIGH for 7-10 minutes. Leave to
stand while melting the butter for
30 seconds on HIGH. Stir in the
brown sugar, ginger, sesame seeds,
sesame oil, soy sauce, salt and pepper.
Add 15-30ml/1-2 tbsps of the
cooking liquid from the carrots to
the sesame-ginger mixture. Stir in the
carrots to coat with the sauce.

Pommes Noisettes

PREPARATION TIME: 15 minutes
plus overnight refrigeration

MICROWAVE COOKING TIME:
14-15 minutes

SERVES: 4-6 people

450g/1lb potatoes, scrubbed but not
*   peeled*
30ml/2 tbsps water
30g/1oz/2 tbsps butter
Salt and pepper
60g/2oz/½ cup grated Gruyère cheese
60g/2oz/½ cup ground browned
*   hazelnuts*
Chopped parsley

Prick the potato skins with a fork.
Put the potatoes and water into a
covered dish and cook 12 minutes on
HIGH until tender. Drain the
potatoes and cut in half. Scoop out
the pulp and mash with a fork or
potato masher. Beat in the butter,
salt, pepper and cheese. Allow to
cool and then refrigerate until cold.

Shape into 2.5cm/1 inch balls. Roll
the potatoes in the nuts. Place in a
circle on a baking sheet or serving
dish and heat 2-3 minutes on HIGH.
Sprinkle with chopped parsley before
serving.

Dilled White Cabbage

PREPARATION TIME: 10 minutes

MICROWAVE COOKING TIME:
8 minutes plus 5 minutes
standing time

SERVES: 4-6 people

This page: **Vegetable Mornay.**
Facing page: **Ginger Sesame Carrots
(top) and Pommes Noisettes
(bottom).**

1 medium head white cabbage or Dutch
*   cabbage, shredded*
30g/2 tbsps butter or margarine
Pinch sugar
30ml/2 tbsps dill seed
30ml/2 tbsps white wine vinegar
30ml/2 tbsps chopped fresh dill
Salt and pepper

Place the cabbage in a large casserole or bowl with 30ml/2 tbsps water and the remaining ingredients except the chopped fresh dill. Cover loosely and cook 8 minutes on HIGH, stirring twice. Leave to stand, covered, 5 minutes before serving. Sprinkle with the fresh dill.

Beets with Sour Cream and Dill

PREPARATION TIME: 20 minutes

MICROWAVE COOKING TIME: 13-17 minutes plus 10 minutes standing time

SERVES: 4 people

4-8 beetroot/beets, depending on size
280ml/½ pint/1 cup sour cream
2.5ml/1 tsp grated fresh horseradish
1 small bunch dill
Salt and pepper

Place raw beets, unpeeled, in 140-280ml/¼-½ pint/½-1 cup water depending on the number of beets. Use a casserole or a bowl covered with pierced cling film/plastic wrap. Cook 12-16 minutes. Leave to stand 10 minutes before peeling. If using pre-cooked beets, just peel them and heat through 1 minute on HIGH. Slice into 6mm/¼ inch slices. Arrange in a serving dish. Mix the sour cream, horseradish, dill, salt and pepper together. Spoon over the beets and heat through 30 seconds to 1 minute on HIGH. Do not allow the sour cream to boil. Garnish with a few sprigs of fresh dill and serve immediately.

Sweet and Sour Red Cabbage with Apple

PREPARATION TIME: 15 minutes

MICROWAVE COOKING TIME: 9-10 minutes plus 5 minutes standing time

SERVES: 4-6 people

30g/2 tbsps butter or margarine
1 medium head red cabbage, shredded
1 small onion, finely chopped

1 apple, cored and chopped
30g/2 tbsps brown sugar
30ml/2 tbsps red wine vinegar
140ml/¼ pint/½ cup water
Pinch cinnamon
Salt and pepper
GARNISH
15g/1 tbsp butter or margarine
1 apple, cored and chopped
Chopped parsley

Melt the butter or margarine in a deep casserole dish for 30 seconds on HIGH. Add all the remaining ingredients except the garnish and cover with pierced cling film/plastic wrap. Cook on HIGH for 8 minutes. Leave to stand, covered, 5 minutes while preparing the garnish. Melt the butter or margarine 30 seconds on HIGH in a small bowl. Add the apple and cook 1 minute on HIGH, uncovered, to partially soften. Toss with the parsley and sprinkle on top of the cabbage.

This page: Beets with Sour Cream and Dill. Facing page: Sweet and Sour Red Cabbage with Apple (top) and Dilled White Cabbage (bottom).

Creamed Spring/Green Onions

PREPARATION TIME: 10 minutes

MICROWAVE COOKING TIME: 5 minutes

SERVES: 4 people

2 bunches spring/green onions
15g/½ oz/1 tbsp butter or margarine
Salt and pepper
280ml/½ pint/1 cup low fat soft cheese or fromage blanc
5ml/1 tsp chopped basil
5ml/1 tsp chopped parsley
140ml/¼ pint/½ cup milk

Wash the onions, barely remove the root ends and trim off about 5cm/2 inches off the green tops. Melt butter in a casserole for 30 seconds on HIGH. Add the onions, salt, pepper and cover loosely with cling film/plastic wrap. Cook 3 minutes on HIGH. Remove the onions and keep covered in a serving dish. Add the cheese, herbs, milk, salt and pepper to the casserole and stir together well. Cook 1 minute on HIGH. Add the onions and heat through 30 seconds on HIGH. Serve immediately.

Spinach and Ricotta Pâté in Red Pepper Cups

PREPARATION TIME: 20 minutes

MICROWAVE COOKING TIME: 6-8 minutes

SERVES: 4 people

4 medium-size sweet red peppers
900g/2lb fresh spinach, washed with stalks removed
450g/1lb ricotta, cottage or cream cheese
45ml/3 tbsps milk
1 small clove garlic, crushed
60g/2oz/½ cup chopped pine-nuts or walnuts
1.25ml/¼ tsp ground nutmeg
Squeeze lemon juice
Salt and pepper

GARNISH
Whole pine-nuts

ACCOMPANIMENTS
Lettuce
Buttered toast or rolls

Cook the spinach for 4 minutes on HIGH in a loosely covered bowl. Cook in the moisture that clings to the leaves. Rinse under cold water, drain very well and chop finely. Mix with the cheese and milk and add the garlic, nuts, nutmeg, lemon juice, salt and pepper. Cut about 5cm/2 inches off the tops of the peppers. Remove the stems and chop the flesh finely. Remove the cores and seeds from the peppers. Place the whole and chopped peppers into a large bowl or casserole and cover with hot water. Cook for 2-3 minutes on HIGH, and rinse immediately under cold water. Drain the whole peppers upside-down on paper towels. Drain the chopped peppers well and add to the spinach pâté. Fill the drained pepper cups with the spinach mixture. Arrange on serving plates with the lettuce leaves and top with whole pine-nuts. Serve with hot buttered toast or rolls.

Ratatouille

PREPARATION TIME: 35 minutes

MICROWAVE COOKING TIME: 14 minutes

SERVES: 4-6 people

30ml/2 tbsps oil
1 onion, sliced
1 aubergine/eggplant
2 courgettes/zucchini
1 green pepper
1 red pepper

This page: Creamed Spring/Green Onions (top) and Spinach with Blue Cheese and Walnuts (bottom). Facing page: Ratatouille.

120g/4oz mushrooms, sliced
1 clove garlic, crushed
10ml/2 tsps chopped fresh basil
5ml/1 tsp chopped parsley
15ml/1 tbsp tomato purée/paste
1 bay leaf
30ml/2 tbsps white wine
Salt and pepper

Cut the aubergine/eggplant in half, score the flesh lightly and sprinkle with salt. Leave on paper towels for ½ hour to draw out any bitterness. Heat the oil in a casserole for 30 seconds on HIGH. Add the onion and garlic and cook 2 minutes on HIGH. Wash the aubergine/eggplant and dry it well. Slice it thinly and slice the courgettes/zucchini and peppers and add to the onions. Cook 5 minutes on HIGH, loosely covered. Add the herbs, bay leaf, tomato purée/paste, wine, salt and pepper and cook a further 5 minutes on HIGH. Add the mushrooms and tomatoes and cook 2 minutes on HIGH. Remove the bay leaf before serving.

Spinach with Blue Cheese and Walnuts

PREPARATION TIME: 15 minutes
MICROWAVE COOKING TIME: 4½ minutes
SERVES: 4-6 people

900g/2lb fresh spinach, washed with
    stalks removed
30g/1oz/2 tbsps butter or margarine
Nutmeg
Salt and pepper

This page: Spinach and Ricotta Pâté in Red Pepper Cups. Facing page: Red Lentil and Mushroom Loaf.

120g/4oz/1 cup coarsely chopped
    walnuts
120g/4oz/1 cup crumbled blue cheese

Place spinach in a large bowl with a pinch of salt. Cover the bowl loosely and cook in the water that clings to the leaves. Microwave on HIGH for 4 minutes. Press between 2 plates to drain thoroughly. Melt the butter in a serving dish for 30 seconds on HIGH. Add the spinach, pepper, nutmeg, walnuts and cheese and toss together to serve.

Microwave VEGETARIAN

RECIPES WITH PULSES

Red Lentil and Mushroom Loaf

PREPARATION TIME: 20 minutes

MICROWAVE COOKING TIME:
25-28 minutes plus the indicated
standing times

SERVES: 4-6 people

180g/6oz/1 cup red lentils, picked over
   and washed
340ml/12oz/1½ cups vegetable stock or
   water
1 clove garlic, finely chopped
15ml/1 tbsp chopped parsley
15ml/1 tbsp chopped tarragon
90g/3oz mushrooms, coarsely chopped
120g/4oz/½ cup cream cheese
1 egg plus 30ml/2 tbsps heavy/double
   cream
Salt and pepper

QUICK TOMATO SAUCE
1 400g/14oz can tomatoes
15ml/1 tbsp tomato purée/paste
5ml/1 tsp dry tarragon
Pinch sugar
Salt and pepper
15ml/1 tbsp chopped fresh tarragon

Cover the lentils with water and leave to stand overnight or microwave 10 minutes to boil the water. Allow the lentils to boil 2 minutes further on HIGH. Allow to stand 1 hour. Combine the lentils with stock or fresh water in a large bowl. Partially cover the bowl and cook 10-12 minutes on HIGH or until the lentils are very soft. Check the amount of liquid and add more if necessary as the lentils cook. Allow to stand for 5 minutes. Mash to a thick purée. Beat the eggs and cream together and add to the purée. Stir in the remaining ingredients and press into a lightly greased loaf dish. Cover with cling film/plastic wrap pierced several times. Cook on MEDIUM for 7-8 minutes until firm around the edges but soft in the middle. Leave to stand 5-10 minutes to firm. May be served hot with the sauce or cold. To prepare the sauce combine all the ingredients except the fresh tarragon. Cook, uncovered, 8 minutes or until thickened. Purée in a food processor and strain to remove the seeds if desired. Add the chopped fresh tarragon and serve with the red lentil and mushroom loaf.

Beans Bourguignonne

PREPARATION TIME: 20 minutes

MICROWAVE COOKING TIME:
1 hour 43 minutes plus indicated
standing times

SERVES: 4 people

225g/8oz/2 cups field beans (other dark
    coloured beans may be substituted)
45ml/3 tbsps oil
4 carrots
225g/8oz small onions, peeled and left
    whole
225g/8oz mushrooms, quartered
140ml/¼ pint/½ cup vegetable stock
280ml/½ pint/1 cup red wine
1 bay leaf
5ml/1 tsp chopped thyme
10ml/2 tsps chopped parsley
45g/3 tbsps butter or margarine
4 slices wholemeal/whole-wheat bread,
    crusts removed

Cover the beans with water and
leave to stand overnight or
microwave for 10 minutes on HIGH
to bring to the boil. Allow the beans
to boil for 2 minutes. Leave to stand
for 1 hour before using. Cover with
fresh water and add the bay leaf and
a pinch of salt. Loosely cover the
dish and cook on MEDIUM for
45 minutes. Leave to stand for
10 minutes before draining. Heat a
browning dish for 5 minutes on
HIGH. Pour in the oil and add the
carrots, onions and mushrooms.
Cook on HIGH for 2 minutes,
stirring frequently to brown slightly.
Remove the vegetables from the
browning dish and add 45g/3 tbsps
butter or margarine. Heat the butter
for 1 minute on HIGH and put in the
bread, cut into triangles. Brown the
croutes 1 minute on HIGH and turn
over. Brown the other side for
1 minute on HIGH and drain on
paper towels. Put the beans into a
casserole with the vegetable stock
and the red wine. Cover the
casserole and cook an additional
15 minutes on HIGH or until the
beans are almost tender. Add the
carrots, onions, mushrooms, thyme,
parsley and additional salt and
pepper. Re-cover the casserole and
cook a further 15-20 minutes on
HIGH or until the vegetables and the

beans are completely tender. Leave to
stand for 15 minutes before serving.
Re-heat the bread for 1 minute on
MEDIUM. Remove the bay leaf and
the beans and transfer them to a
serving dish and surround with the
croutes to serve.

Red Beans Creole

PREPARATION TIME: 20 minutes

MICROWAVE COOKING TIME:
1 hour 23 minutes plus standing
times indicated in the recipe

SERVES: 4 people

180g/6oz/1 cup red kidney beans
180g/6oz/1½ cups long-grain rice
30g/2 tbsps butter or margarine
1 green pepper, cut in strips
3-4 tomatoes, peeled, seeded and cut in
    strips

**This page: Red Beans Creole.
Facing page: Chickpea and Pepper
Casserole (top) and Beans
Bourguignonne (bottom).**

120g/4oz mushrooms, sliced
4 spring/green onions, chopped
30ml/2 tbsps chopped parsley
Cayenne pepper
Ground nutmeg
1 bay leaf
Salt and pepper

Cover the beans with water and
leave overnight, or microwave 10
minutes to boil the water. Allow the
beans to boil for 2 minutes. Leave to
stand 1 hour. Cover with fresh water
and add a pinch of salt and the bay
leaf. Cook on MEDIUM for 55
minutes to 1 hour. Allow to stand
10 minutes before draining. The
beans must be completely cooked.

Save the cooking liquid to use as stock in other recipes if desired. Place rice in a large bowl or casserole dish, add 570ml/1 pint/2 cups water and a pinch of salt. Cook about 10 minutes on HIGH. Leave to stand for 5 minutes before draining. Heat the butter or margarine 30 seconds on HIGH in a casserole dish, and add the pepper strips and mushrooms. Cook for 2 minutes, stirring once. Stir in the cayenne pepper, nutmeg, salt, pepper, rice and beans. Cook 1 minute on HIGH. Add the spring/green onions, parsley and tomatoes and cook a further 30 seconds on HIGH.

Chickpea and Pepper Casserole

PREPARATION TIME: 20 minutes

MICROWAVE COOKING TIME:
51 minutes to 1 hour 6 minutes

SERVES: 4 people

225g/8oz/1⅓ cups chickpeas (garbanzo beans)
30ml/2 tbsps oil
1 large onion, sliced
1 green pepper, sliced
1 red pepper, sliced
1 clove garlic, minced
10ml/2 tsps chopped parsley
5ml/1 tsp chopped mint
2.5ml/½ tsp ground cumin
Salt and pepper
4 tomatoes, seeded and cut in strips

ACCOMPANIMENT
1 cucumber, thinly sliced
280ml/½ pint/1 cup yogurt
Salt and pepper

Leave the chickpeas to soak in water overnight or use the microwave rehydrating method. Cover with fresh water and add a pinch of salt. Cover the bowl and cook 45 minutes to 1 hour until tender. Drain and reserve the liquid. Heat the oil 30 seconds on HIGH. Add the onion, peppers, garlic and cumin. Cook 1 minute on HIGH. Add the chickpeas and half the cooking liquid. Cook a further 5 minutes on HIGH. Add parsley, mint, tomatoes, and

season with salt and pepper. Cook 30 seconds on HIGH. Combine the accompaniment ingredients and serve with the casserole.

Vegetable Cassoulet

PREPARATION TIME: 20 minutes

MICROWAVE COOKING TIME:
1 hour 40 minutes plus indicated standing times

SERVES: 4 people

225g/8oz/2 cups haricot/navy beans
60ml/2 fl oz/¼ cup oil
2 cloves garlic, minced
2 small leeks, cut in 2.5cm/1 inch pieces
3 carrots, cut in 2.5cm/1 inch chunks
4 sticks celery, cut in 2.5cm/1 inch pieces
2 parsnips, halved, cored and cut in 2.5cm/1 inch pieces
2 turnips, peeled and cut in 2.5cm/1 inch pieces
120g/4oz mushrooms, quartered
15ml/1 tbsp Worcestershire sauce
1 bay leaf
15ml/1 tbsp marjoram, chopped
430ml/¾ pint/1½ cups vegetable stock
Salt and pepper

TOPPING
30g/2 tbsps butter or margarine
60g/2oz/½ cup dry breadcrumbs

Heat a browning dish for 5 minutes on HIGH. Melt the butter for the topping and add the crumbs. Stirring frequently, cook on HIGH for 2-3 minutes until the crumbs are golden brown and crisp. Set them aside. Add the oil to the browning dish and heat for 1 minute on HIGH. Add all of the vegetables and cook 2 minutes on HIGH to brown. Stir frequently. Remove the vegetables from the browning dish and de-glaze the dish with the vegetable stock. Stir to remove any sediment from browning the vegetables. Cover the beans with water and leave to soak overnight or microwave for 10 minutes to bring the water to the boil. Allow the beans to boil for 2 minutes. Leave them to stand for 1 hour. Drain the beans and put them into the casserole dish with the garlic, bay leaf, Worcestershire sauce, marjoram,

salt and pepper. Add half the stock, cover and cook for 1 hour on HIGH. Add more stock as necessary during cooking. The mixture should be fairly thick at the end of the cooking time. Add the vegetables and re-cover the dish. Cook an additional 15-20 minutes on HIGH, adding more stock if necessary. When the beans are tender and most of the liquid has been absorbed, sprinkle on the brown crumbs and cook for 5 minutes on HIGH. Leave the cassoulet to stand for 15 minutes before serving. The cassoulet may be prepared in advance and refrigerated. Re-heat 2-3 minutes on HIGH. Add the crumbs and cook a further 5 minutes on HIGH before serving.

Chinese Black Bean Casserole

PREPARATION TIME: 20 minutes

MICROWAVE COOKING TIME:
1 hour 33 minutes plus indicated standing time

SERVES 4 people

450g/1lb black beans
1 small piece fresh ginger root, grated
1 clove garlic, minced
10ml/2 tsps 5-spice powder
1 piece star anise
6-8 sticks celery
1 small can water chestnuts, drained and sliced
90ml/3 fl oz/⅓ cup sherry
15ml/1 tbsp soy sauce
5ml/1 tsp sesame seed oil

GARNISH
120g/4oz bean sprouts
4 spring/green onions shredded

Cover the beans with water and leave to stand overnight, or microwave on HIGH for 10 minutes to boil the water. Allow the beans to boil for 2 minutes and leave to stand for 1 hour before using. If using salted

Facing page: Chinese Black Bean Casserole (top) and Vegetable Cassoulet (bottom).

Chinese black beans, soak in cold water for ½ hour and drain. Cut the cooking time in half. Cover the beans with water and add the grated ginger, star anise, 5-spice powder and garlic. Add a pinch of salt and pepper and loosely cover the bowl. Cook for 1 hour on HIGH, stirring occasionally. Add the celery and cook a further 15 minutes on HIGH. Add the sherry, soy sauce and sesame oil and cook a further 5 minutes on HIGH. If a lot of liquid remains, continue to cook until the liquid is absorbed. Add the water chestnuts just before serving and cook 1 minute on HIGH to heat through. Garnish with the bean sprouts and shredded spring/green onion to serve.

Butter Bean, Lemon and Fennel Salad

PREPARATION TIME: 15 minutes

MICROWAVE COOKING TIME:
1 hour 12 minutes plus standing times indicated in the recipe

SERVES: 4 people

225g/8oz/2 cups butter beans
1 large bulb Florentine fennel, thinly sliced
Juice and rind of 1 lemon
60ml/4 tbsps oil
Pinch sugar
Salt and pepper

Cover the beans with water and leave overnight, or microwave 10 minutes to boil the water and allow the beans to boil for 2 minutes. Leave to stand for 1 hour. Cover with fresh water and add a pinch of salt. Cook on MEDIUM for 55 minutes to 1 hour. The beans must be cooked all the way through. Allow to stand for 10 minutes before draining. Boil 570ml/1 pint/2 cups water for 10 minutes on HIGH. Reserve the green tops of the fennel and blanch the sliced bulb in the water for 2 minutes on HIGH. Drain thoroughly. Pare the rind from the lemon and scrape off any white pith. Cut the rind into very thin strips and squeeze the juice from the lemon. Mix with the oil, pinch sugar, salt and

pepper. Chop the fennel tops and add to the dressing. Pour over the drained beans and fennel slices. Toss to coat thoroughly. Serve on a bed of lettuce or radicchio.

Black-Eyed Bean/Pea and Orange Salad

PREPARATION TIME: 20 minutes

MICROWAVE COOKING TIME:
1 hour plus 10 minutes standing time

SERVES: 4 people

225g/8oz/1½ cups black-eyed beans/
* peas*
1 bay leaf
1 slice onion
Salt

SALAD
4 oranges
Small handful fresh basil leaves
30ml/2 tbsps chopped parsley
6 black olives, pitted
1 large bunch watercress

DRESSING
Juice and rind of 1 orange
75ml/5 tbsps oil
4 spring/green onions, chopped
Salt and pepper

Cover the beans with water and leave overnight, or microwave for 10 minutes to boil the water. Allow the beans to boil for 2 minutes. Leave to stand for 1 hour. Cover with fresh water and add a pinch of salt, the bay leaf and the slice of onion. Cook on MEDIUM for 55 minutes to 1 hour. Allow to stand 10 minutes before draining. Mix the oil and the juice and grated rind of 1 orange with the basil leaves, chopped, chopped parsley, chopped spring/green onions and salt and pepper. Pour the dressing over the beans and add the black olives, sliced, and toss. Peel and segment the remaining four oranges. Chop the segments of two of the oranges and add those to the bean salad. Arrange the watercress on 4 individual plates and pile on the bean salad. Arrange the remaining orange segments on the plates and serve immediately.

Curried Lentils

PREPARATION TIME: 25 minutes

MICROWAVE COOKING TIME: 36 minutes plus 5-10 minutes standing time

SERVES: 4 people

225g/8oz lentils, brown or green
60g/2oz/¼ cup butter or margarine
1 large onion, chopped
1 clove garlic, chopped
1 red or green chili pepper, finely chopped
5ml/1 tsp cumin
5ml/1 tsp coriander
5ml/1 tsp turmeric
2.5ml/½ tsp cinnamon
2.5ml/½ tsp nutmeg
60g/2oz/½ cup whole blanched almonds
570ml/1 pint/2 cups vegetable stock
Salt and pepper
Desiccated coconut
Coriander leaves

APPLE AND CUCUMBER RELISH
2 apples, cored and chopped
60g/2oz/½ cup raisins
120g/4oz/1 cup chopped cucumber
60ml/2 fl oz/¼ cup mango chutney

SPICED BANANAS
2 bananas, sliced
30g/2 tbsps butter or margarine
Pinch nutmeg
Pinch cinnamon
15ml/1 tbsp brown sugar
15ml/1 tbsp lemon juice
Garam masala

TOMATO AND ONION RELISH
2 tomatoes, chopped
1 green pepper, chopped

1 small onion, chopped
Juice of ½ lemon
10ml/2 tsps oil
Pinch cayenne pepper
Salt

Cover the lentils with water and leave to soak overnight. Alternatively microwave 10 minutes to boil the water and allow the lentils to boil 2 minutes. Leave to stand for 1 hour. Melt the butter for 1 minute on HIGH in a large casserole dish. Add the onion, garlic, chili pepper and spices. Cook 4 minutes on MEDIUM. Drain the lentils and add to the casserole with the vegetable stock. Cover and cook on HIGH for 30 minutes until the lentils are tender. Allow to stand 5-10 minutes before serving. Heat a browning dish for 3 minutes on HIGH. Melt the

Facing page: Butter Bean, Lemon and Fennel Salad (top) and Black-Eyed Bean/Pea and Orange Salad (bottom). This page: Curried Lentils.

butter and add the sliced bananas. Cook 30 seconds on HIGH on one side and turn over. Cook a further 30 seconds and sprinkle with the spices and the lemon juice. Sprinkle with garam masala just before serving. Combine the ingredients for the apple and cucumber relish and those for the tomato and onion relish and serve the accompaniments with the curried lentils. Sprinkle the lentils with desiccated coconut and garnish with coriander leaves before serving.

MAIN COURSES

Curried Vegetables

PREPARATION TIME: 20 minutes

MICROWAVE COOKING TIME:
17 minutes

SERVES: 4 people

2 medium-size potatoes, peeled and cut
    into 2.5cm/1 inch chunks
3 carrots, cut into 2.5cm/1 inch chunks
3 courgettes/zucchini, sliced
120g/4oz okra, stems trimmed
60g/2oz mushrooms, quartered
2 tomatoes, quartered
1 large onion, sliced
45ml/3 tbsps oil
1 clove garlic, minced
1 red or green chili pepper, minced after
    removing the seeds
30ml/2 tbsps flour
5ml/1 tsp ground cumin
5ml/1 tsp ground coriander
5ml/1 tsp turmeric
10ml/2 tsps mustard seed
2.5ml/½ tsp paprika
Pinch ground cloves
Bay leaf
570ml/1 pint/2 cups vegetable stock or
    vegetable cooking liquid and water
140ml/¼ pint/½ cup natural yogurt
Salt and pepper

GARNISH

Chopped coriander leaves

Cook the potatoes and carrots
together in a large, covered casserole.
Add just enough salted water to
cover the vegetables. Cook on HIGH
for 8 minutes. Add the courgettes/
zucchini and okra after 6 minutes
cooking. Leave the vegetables to
stand, covered, for 5 minutes.
Reserve the quartered tomatoes and
mushrooms. Heat the oil for 1 minute
on HIGH and add the onion, garlic,
chili pepper and mushrooms. Cook

for 1 minute on HIGH. Stir in the
flour and spices and cook a further
1 minute on HIGH. Add the liquid
gradually, stirring until smooth. Add
the bay leaf, salt and pepper and
cook 5 minutes on HIGH, stirring
frequently after 1 minute. When
thickened, remove the bay leaf and
add the cooked vegetables and the
quartered tomatoes. Heat through
1 minute on HIGH. Serve with rice
and chutney. The accompaniments
from the Curried Lentil recipe may
also be served.

This page: Pasta, Peas and Peppers.
Facing page: Gratin of Vegetable
Oliver (top) and Curried Vegetables
(bottom).

Pasta, Peas and Peppers

PREPARATION TIME: 20 minutes

MICROWAVE COOKING TIME:
10 minutes plus 10 minutes
standing time

SERVES: 4 people

*225g/8oz/3 cups plain and whole-wheat
   pasta shells, mixed*
225g/8oz/1 cup frozen peas
1 green pepper, shredded
1 yellow pepper, shredded
1 red pepper, shredded
4 spring/green onions, shredded
120g/4oz grated Parmesan cheese

DRESSING
140ml/¼ pint/½ cup oil
60ml/2 fl oz/¼ cup white wine vinegar
15ml/1 tbsp Dijon mustard
10ml/2 tsps poppy seeds
10ml/2 tsps chopped parsley
5ml/1 tsp chopped thyme
Salt and pepper

Cook the pasta 6 minutes in a large bowl with 570ml/1 pint/2 cups salted water. Leave to stand, covered, 10 minutes before draining. Cook the peas and peppers in 30ml/2 tbsps water for 2 minutes. Drain and allow to cool, uncovered. Mix the dressing ingredients together until well blended. Pour over the pasta, add the cheese and toss to coat the pasta well. Add the peas, peppers and spring/green onions and toss again to mix all the ingredients before serving.

Pasta-Stuffed Cabbage Leaves

PREPARATION TIME: 20 minutes
MICROWAVE COOKING TIME:
29 minutes plus 10 minutes
standing time
SERVES: 4 people

1 head cabbage, white or green

FILLING
120g/4oz/¾ cup soup pasta
1 hard boiled egg, finely chopped
*60g/2oz/½ cup walnuts, roughly
   chopped*
15ml/1 tbsp chopped chives
30ml/2 tbsps chopped parsley
5ml/1 tsp chopped marjoram
Salt and pepper

SAUCE
1 450g/1lb can tomatoes
15ml/1 tbsp oil
120g/4oz mushrooms, sliced

1 small onion, diced
1 green pepper, diced
30ml/2 tbsps tomato purée/paste
1 bay leaf
Pinch sugar
Salt and pepper

Place the pasta in a large bowl with 570ml/1 pint/2 cups salted water and cook for 5 minutes on HIGH. Leave to stand, covered, 10 minutes before draining. Put the cabbage leaves in a large bowl or roasting bag with 30ml/1 fl oz/2 tbsps water with a pinch of salt. Cook 3-4 minutes on HIGH. Lay flat on paper towels to drain. Heat the oil for 30 seconds on HIGH. Add the onions and peppers for the sauce and cook 1 minute on HIGH. Add the remaining sauce ingredients and cook 8 minutes on HIGH. Combine the drained pasta with the remaining filling ingredients and spoon on to the cabbage leaves. Roll up the leaves, tucking in the ends, and lay them in a serving dish. Pour over the sauce and cook on MEDIUM for 8 minutes. Serve immediately.

Gratin of Vegetables Oliver

PREPARATION TIME: 20 minutes
MICROWAVE COOKING TIME:
12-13 minutes
SERVES: 4 people

TOPPING
*120g/4oz/½ cup butter or margarine
   melted*
*225g/8oz/1 cup chopped, pitted black
   olives*
120g/4oz/1 cup dry breadcrumbs
*180g/6oz/1½ cups shredded Cheddar
   cheese*
120g/4oz/1 cup chopped walnuts
10ml/2 tsps chopped fresh basil
Pinch cayenne pepper

VEGETABLES
4 courgettes/zucchini, sliced
1 bunch broccoli
4 carrots, sliced
225g/8oz French/green beans
2 red peppers, sliced
8 spring/green onions, sliced
Salt and pepper

Melt the butter for the topping for 30 seconds on HIGH. Stir in the remaining ingredients and set aside. Cook the carrots in 60ml/4 tbsps water with a pinch of salt for 8 minutes. After 5 minutes add the courgettes/zucchini, broccoli and beans. Add the peppers and spring/green onions 1 minute before the end of cooking time. Drain the vegetables and arrange in a serving dish. Sprinkle lightly with salt and pepper and sprinkle over the topping ingredients. Bake 4 minutes on MEDIUM or 5 minutes on a combination setting in a microwave convection oven. Serve immediately.

Watercress-Stuffed Potatoes

PREPARATION TIME: 25 minutes
MICROWAVE COOKING TIME:
27-29 minutes plus 5 minutes
standing time
SERVES: 4 people

4 large baking potatoes
140ml/¼ pint/½ cup milk
120g/4oz mushrooms, sliced
1 shallot, chopped
15g/1 tbsp butter or margarine
4 eggs
1 bunch watercress

SAUCE
45g/1½ oz/3 tbsps butter or margarine
30g/1oz/2 tbsps flour
Pinch dry mustard
Pinch cayenne pepper
280ml/½ pint/1 cup milk
60g/2oz/½ cup grated cheese
Salt and pepper

GARNISH
30g/1oz/¼ cup grated cheese
Reserved watercress

Wash and prick the potato skins several times with a fork. Bake the potatoes 10-12 minutes on HIGH. Wrap them in foil and leave to stand 5 minutes. Pour 1150ml/2 pints/ 4 cups hot water into a large, shallow dish. Add 15ml/1 tbsp vinegar and 5ml/1 tsp salt. Heat the water 5 minutes on HIGH or until boiling.

reserving 4 sprigs for garnish. Add the chopped watercress to the potatoes and beat in the hot milk. Add salt and pepper to taste and pipe or spoon the potatoes on top of the cheese sauce in the potato shells. Sprinkle on cheese and cook for 3 minutes on HIGH to heat through and melt the cheese. Alternatively, heat 5 minutes on a combination setting in a microwave convection oven. Garnish with the watercress and serve immediately.

Mushroom Croquettes with Green Peppercorn Sauce

PREPARATION TIME: 25 minutes
MICROWAVE COOKING TIME: 16-17 minutes
SERVES: 4 people

120g/4oz/1 cup finely chopped
   mushrooms
90g/3oz/1¾ cups fresh breadcrumbs
30g/1oz/2 tbsps butter or margarine
1 shallot, finely chopped
30g/1oz/2 tbsps flour
140ml/¼ pint/½ cup milk
5ml/1 tsp chopped parsley
5ml/1 tsp chopped thyme
1 beaten egg
Salt and pepper

COATING
Remaining beaten egg
Dry breadcrumbs
30-60ml/2-4 tbsps oil for frying

SAUCE
15g/1 tbsp butter or margarine
1 shallot, finely chopped
15g/1 tbsp flour
30ml/2 tbsps vermouth or white wine
280ml/½ pint/1 cup heavy/double
   cream
30ml/2 tbsps green peppercorns, drained
   and rinsed
1 small cap pimento, diced
Salt and pepper

Melt the butter for the croquettes for 1 minute on HIGH. Add the shallot and the mushrooms and cook 30

Break the eggs into a cup and slide them, one at a time into the water. Prick the yolks once with a sharp knife or skewer. Cook on MEDIUM for 3 minutes. Remove from the dish and place in enough cold water to cover them. Melt the 15g/1 tbsp butter in a small bowl for 30 seconds on HIGH. Add the mushrooms and shallot. Cook for 1 minute on HIGH and set aside. Melt the butter for the sauce for 30 seconds on HIGH in a glass measure. Add the flour, mustard, and cayenne pepper. Stir in the milk gradually and cook 3

This page: Pasta-Stuffed Cabbage Leaves (top) and Watercress-Stuffed Potatoes (bottom).

minutes on HIGH. Stir after 1 minute. Add the cheese and stir to melt. Cut a slice off the top of each potato and scoop out the pulp, leaving a border inside the skin. Fill with the mushrooms and top with one of the drained eggs. Spoon over the cheese sauce. Mash the potato and heat the milk for 2 minutes on HIGH. Chop the watercress leaves and thin stalks in a food processor,

1 shallot, finely chopped
30g/1oz/2 tbsps flour
140ml/¼ pint/½ cup milk
5ml/1 tsp chopped parsley
5ml/1 tsp chopped thyme
1 beaten egg
Salt and pepper

COATING
Beaten egg
Dry breadcrumbs
30-60ml/2-4 tbsps oil for frying

SAUCE
280ml/½ pint/1 cup heavy/double
    cream
15ml/1 tbsp pear brandy
60g/2oz/½ cup grated Parmesan cheese
Coarsely ground black pepper
Salt

GARNISH
4 small, ripe, unpeeled pears, halved and
    cored
Lemon juice
8 fresh sage leaves

Melt the butter for the escalopes for
1 minute on HIGH. Add the shallot
and cook 30 seconds on HIGH. Stir
in the flour and add the milk
gradually. Cook for 2 minutes on
HIGH until thickened. Add the
remaining escalope ingredients and
half the beaten egg. Spread the
mixture into a square pan and chill
until firm. Cut the mixture into
8 equal pieces and flatten into thin
patties. Coat with the remaining egg
and dry breadcrumbs, shaking off the
excess. If the patties become difficult
to handle, chill for 10 minutes in the
refrigerator before coating with egg
and crumbs. Heat a browning dish
for 5 minutes on HIGH and pour in
the oil. Heat for 30 seconds on
HIGH, put in the escalopes and
cover the dish. Cook for 2-3 minutes
on HIGH, turning over halfway
through the cooking time. Drain the
escalopes on paper towels. Boil the
cream and brandy for 6 minutes on
HIGH in a glass measure. Stir in the

seconds on HIGH. Stir in the flour
and add the milk gradually. Cook for
2 minutes on HIGH until thickened.
Add the remaining croquette
ingredients and half the beaten egg.
Spread the mixture into a square pan
and chill until firm. Cut the mixture
into 16 equal pieces and shape into
small ovals. Coat with the remaining
egg and press on the dry crumbs,
shaking off the excess. Heat a
browning dish for 5 minutes on
HIGH and pour in the oil. Heat for
30 seconds on HIGH and put in the
croquettes. Cover and cook 3-4
minutes on HIGH, turning over after
2 minutes. Drain on paper towels.
Heat the butter for the sauce for
30 seconds on HIGH in a small, deep
bowl. Add the shallot, finely
chopped and cook for 30 seconds on
HIGH. Stir in the flour, vermouth or
white wine and the cream. Season

lightly with salt and pepper and cook
for 3-4 minutes on HIGH, stirring
frequently. Add the green
peppercorns and the pimento
1 minute before the end of cooking
time. Arrange the croquettes in a
serving dish and pour over the sauce
to serve.

Hazelnut Escalopes with Pear Brandy Cream Sauce

PREPARATION TIME: 25 minutes
MICROWAVE COOKING TIME: 17-18 minutes
SERVES: 4 people

120g/4oz/1 cup ground hazelnuts
60g/2oz/1⅓ cups fresh breadcrumbs
30g/1oz/2 tbsps butter or margarine

**This page: Walnut Cutlets with
Three Pepper Salpicon. Facing
page: Mushroom Croquettes with
Green Peppercorn Sauce (top) and
Hazelnut Escalopes with Pear
Brandy Cream Sauce (bottom).**

cheese and pepper. Taste and add salt if desired. Heat for 30 seconds on HIGH to melt the cheese. Place a spoonful of the sauce on each of 4 serving plates. Brush the cut sides of the pears with lemon juice and arrange on the plates with the sage leaves. Place on the cutlets and spoon over some of the sauce to serve. Hand the rest of the sauce separately.

Walnut Cutlets with Three Pepper Salpicon

PREPARATION TIME: 25 minutes

MICROWAVE COOKING TIME: 17-18 minutes

SERVES: 4 people

CUTLETS
120g/4oz/1 cup walnuts, ground
60g/2oz/1⅓ cups fresh breadcrumbs
5ml/1 tsp chopped parsley
5ml/1 tsp chopped thyme
30g/1oz/2 tbsps butter or margarine
1 shallot, finely chopped
30g/1oz/2 tbsps flour
140ml/¼ pint/½ cup milk
1 beaten egg
Salt and pepper

COATING
Remaining beaten egg
Dry breadcrumbs
30-60ml/2-4 tbsps oil for frying

SALPICON
30g/1oz/2 tbsps butter or margarine
1 small onion, thinly sliced
15g/1 tbsp flour
Juice of 1 lemon
90ml/3oz/⅓ cup vegetable stock
1-2 green peppers, sliced
1-2 red peppers, sliced
1-2 yellow peppers, sliced
Pinch cayenne pepper
10ml/2 tsps capers
Salt and pepper

Melt the butter for the cutlets for 1 minute on HIGH. Add the shallot and cook 30 seconds on HIGH. Stir in the flour and add the milk gradually. Cook for 2 minutes on HIGH until thickened. Add the remaining cutlet ingredients and half the beaten egg. Spread the mixture into a square pan and chill until firm. Cut the mixture into 8 equal portions and shape into cutlets or patties. Coat with the remaining egg and the dry breadcrumbs, shaking off the excess. Heat a browning dish for 5 minutes on HIGH. Pour in the oil and heat 30 seconds on HIGH. Put in the cutlets, cover the dish and cook 3-4 minutes on HIGH, turning over after 2 minutes. Drain on paper towels. Heat the butter for the salpicon 30 seconds on HIGH in a casserole. Add the onion and cook for 1 minute on HIGH. Stir in the flour and add the lemon juice and stock and cook for 1 minute on HIGH until very thick. Add the peppers and capers and cook a further 3 minutes on HIGH. Add the cayenne pepper, salt and pepper and serve with the cutlets.

Pasta Primavera

PREPARATION TIME: 20 minutes

MICROWAVE COOKING TIME: 14 minutes plus 10 minutes standing time

SERVES: 4 people

450g/1lb/6 cups pasta shapes, or noodles
225g/8oz asparagus
120g/4oz French/green beans
60g/2oz mushrooms, sliced
2 carrots
3 tomatoes peeled, seeded and cut in strips
6 spring/green onions
30ml/2 tbsps chopped parsley
10ml/2 tsps chopped tarragon
140ml/¼ pint/½ cup heavy/double cream
Salt and pepper

Cook the pasta 6 minutes on HIGH in 1150ml/2 pints/4 cups hot water with a pinch of salt and 15ml/1 tbsp oil. Cover and leave to stand 10 minutes before draining. Leave to drain completely. Slice the asparagus diagonally, leaving the tips whole. Cut the beans and carrots diagonally into thin slices. Cook the carrots and asparagus in 30ml/2 tbsps water for 4 minutes on HIGH, loosely covered. Add the beans and mushrooms and cook an additional 2 minutes on HIGH. Add to the drained pasta and stir in the cream, salt and pepper. Cook 1 minute on HIGH to heat the pasta. Add the tomatoes, onions, herbs and toss gently. Cook an additional 1 minute on HIGH. Serve immediately with grated cheese if desired.

Aubergine/Eggplant Rolls

PREPARATION TIME: 25 minutes

MICROWAVE COOKING TIME: 20-23 minutes

SERVES: 4 people

2-3 aubergines/eggplants, depending on size, sliced 1.25cm/½ inch thick
45ml/3 tbsps oil, or more as needed, for frying
120g/4oz/1 cup grated mozzarella cheese

SAUCE
1 450g/1lb can plum tomatoes
30ml/2 tbsps tomato purée/paste
1 onion, finely chopped
Pinch sugar
Pinch oregano
1 bay leaf
2 parsley stalks
Salt and pepper

FILLING
225g/8oz ricotta cheese
120g/4oz pitted black olives, chopped
60g/2oz/¼ cup grated Parmesan cheese
60g/2oz/¼ cup pine-nuts
15ml/1 tbsp white wine
1 clove garlic, finely minced
5ml/1 tsp each chopped parsley and basil
Pinch nutmeg
Salt and pepper

Facing page: Pasta Primavera. This page: Aubergine/Eggplant Rolls.

Lightly score the slices of aubergine/eggplant on both sides and sprinkle with salt. Leave on paper towels to stand for 30 minutes to draw out any bitterness. Combine all the sauce ingredients in a small, deep bowl. Cook, uncovered, for 8 minutes on HIGH. Remove the bay leaf and parsley stalks and purée in a food processor. Strain to remove the seeds if desired. Rinse the aubergine/ eggplant and pat dry. Heat a browning dish for 5 minutes on HIGH. Pour in the oil and heat for 1 minute on HIGH. Add the aubergine/eggplant slices and brown for 1 minute per side. Cook in 2 or 3 batches if necessary and add more oil if needed. Drain on paper towels. Mix the filling ingredients and fill half of each aubergine/eggplant slice. Fill the bottom of a large, shallow baking dish with half the sauce. Fold the aubergine/eggplant slices in half and place on top of the sauce. Spoon over the remaining sauce, cover the dish loosely with cling film/plastic wrap and cook 3 minutes on HIGH. Sprinkle on the cheese and cook, uncovered, a further 2-3 minutes on MEDIUM. Alternatively, coat with sauce and sprinkle on the cheese and cook for 8 minutes on a combination setting of a microwave convection oven.

Vegetable Moussaka

PREPARATION TIME: 55 minutes

MICROWAVE COOKING TIME: 29 minutes

SERVES: 4 people

2 potatoes, peeled and sliced
1 aubergine/eggplant
120g/4oz mushrooms sliced
2 courgettes/zucchini
4 tomatoes, peeled and sliced
1 green pepper, sliced

TOMATO SAUCE
15ml/1 tbsp oil
1 onion, finely chopped
1 clove garlic, minced
1 400g/14oz can tomatoes
15ml/1 tbsp tomato purée/paste
1.25ml/¼ tsp ground cinnamon
1.25ml/¼ tsp ground cumin
Salt and pepper
Pinch of sugar

EGG SAUCE
30g/2 tbsps butter or margarine
30g/2 tbsps flour
280ml/½ pint/1 cup milk
1 egg, beaten
60g/2oz/½ cup feta cheese
Nutmeg
Salt and pepper

Cut the aubergine/eggplant in half and lightly score the cut surface. Sprinkle with salt and leave to stand for ½ hour. Put the potatoes into a roasting bag, seal and cook 10 minutes on HIGH. Heat the oil for the tomato sauce 30 seconds on HIGH. Add the onions and garlic and cook 1 minute on HIGH. Add the remaining ingredients and cook a further 6 minutes on HIGH. Wash the aubergine/eggplant well and dry. Slice it thinly and cook in 30ml/ 2 tbsps oil for 2 minutes on HIGH in a covered dish. Remove the slices

and drain. Add the mushrooms to the dish and cook for 2 minutes on HIGH. Remove and set aside. Add the green pepper and the courgettes/ zucchini and cook for 1 minute on HIGH. Layer the vegetables, starting with the aubergine/eggplant and ending with the potatoes. Spoon the tomato sauce over each layer except the potatoes. Cook the butter for the egg sauce for 30 seconds on HIGH. Stir in the flour, nutmeg, salt and pepper. Add the milk gradually and cook for 3 minutes on HIGH, stirring after 1 minute. Add the cheese and egg and stir well to blend. Pour over the potatoes and cook 4 minutes on HIGH or 5 minutes on a combination setting in a microwave convection oven, or until set.

This page: Sweet and Sour Nuggets. Facing page: Vegetable Moussaka (top) and Mushrooms Florentine (bottom).

Sweet and Sour Nuggets

PREPARATION TIME: 25 minutes

MICROWAVE COOKING TIME: 15½-16½ minutes

SERVES: 4 people

60g/2oz/½ cup ground almonds
60g/2oz/½ cup finely chopped water chestnuts
30g/1oz/2 tbsps butter or margarine
1 shallot, finely chopped
30g/1oz/2 tbsps flour

5ml/1 tsp chopped parsley
5ml/1 tsp ground ginger
140ml/¼ pint/½ cup milk
1 beaten egg
Salt and pepper

COATING
Remaining beaten egg
Dry breadcrumbs
Sesame seeds
30-60ml/2-4 tbsps oil for frying

SWEET AND SOUR SAUCE
60g/2oz/¼ cup brown sugar
60ml/2 fl oz/¼ cup vinegar
30ml/2 tbsps tomato ketchup
30ml/2 tbsps soy sauce
1 225g/8oz can pineapple chunks/pieces
30g/2 tbsps cornstarch/cornflour
1 green pepper
2 green/spring onions, sliced
1 small can bamboo shoots

ACCOMPANIMENT
225g/8oz bean sprouts

Melt the butter for the nuggets for 1 minute on HIGH. Add the shallot and cook 30 seconds on HIGH. Stir in the flour and add the milk gradually. Cook for 2 minutes on HIGH until thickened. Add the remaining nugget ingredients and half the beaten egg. Spread the mixture into a square pan and chill until firm. Shape the mixture into an even number of 2.5cm/1 inch balls. Coat with the remaining egg and the dry breadcrumbs and sesame seeds, shaking off the excess. Heat a browning dish for 5 minutes on HIGH and pour in the oil. Put in the nuggets and cover the dish. Cook for 3-4 minutes on HIGH, turning frequently. Drain on paper towels. Combine the sugar, vinegar, ketchup, soy sauce, pineapple juice and cornstarch/cornflour in a small, deep bowl. Cook for 2-3 minutes on HIGH until thickened, stirring frequently. Add the peppers and onions and cook 1 minute on HIGH. Add the pineapple pieces and the bamboo shoots and cook a further 30 seconds on HIGH. Place the bean sprouts in a serving dish and heat 1 minute on HIGH. Put the nuggets in the middle. Coat over with the sweet and sour sauce to serve.

Japanese Steamer

PREPARATION TIME: 20 minutes

MICROWAVE COOKING TIME: 13 minutes

SERVES: 4 people

3 packages tofu, drained
16 dried black mushrooms, soaked and stems removed
120g/4oz small mushrooms
8 baby corn-on-the-cob
1 small diakon (mooli) radish, sliced
1 bunch fresh chives, left whole
120g/4oz buckwheat noodles or other variety Japanese noodles
1 package dried sea spinach
1 lemon, sliced

SAUCE
1 small piece fresh ginger root, grated
140ml/¼ pint/½ cup soy sauce
60ml/4 tbsps vegetable stock
15ml/1 tbsp sherry or white wine
5ml/1 tsp cornstarch/cornflour

Cover the noodles with 570ml/1 pint/2 cups water and a pinch of salt. Cook on HIGH for 6 minutes and leave to stand, covered, for 10 minutes before using. Put the mushrooms and spinach into 2 separate bowls, fill both bowls with water and leave the spinach to soak. Put the mushrooms into the microwave oven and heat for 5 minutes on HIGH and set aside. Put the small mushrooms and the baby corn-on-the-cob into a small bowl with 15ml/1 tbsp water. Cover the bowl with pierced cling film/plastic wrap and cook for 2 minutes on HIGH and set aside. Combine all the ingredients for the sauce in a glass measure. Cook on HIGH for 3 minutes or until thickened. Stir after 1 minute. Slice the tofu into 1.25cm/½ inch slices. Drain the black mushrooms and remove the stalks. Drain the noodles and arrange in 4 separate serving dishes. Add the spinach, tofu, whole black mushrooms and small mushrooms, baby ears of corn, radish slices, and lemon slices. Pour some of the sauce over each serving and garnish with the fresh chives. Heat the dishes through for 1 minute on HIGH and serve the remaining sauce separately.

Mushrooms Florentine

PREPARATION TIME: 20 minutes

MICROWAVE COOKING TIME: 17 minutes

SERVES: 4 people

60g/2oz/¼ cup butter or margarine
450g/1lb large mushrooms
900g/2lb fresh spinach, stalks removed and leaves washed
2 shallots, finely chopped
4 tomatoes, peeled, seeded and diced
Salt and pepper
Nutmeg

SAUCE
45g/3 tbsps butter or margarine
45g/3 tbsps flour
570ml/1 pint/2 cups milk
180g/6oz/1½ cups grated Cheddar cheese
2.5ml/½ tsp dry mustard
Pinch cayenne pepper
Salt and pepper
60g/2oz/¼ cup Parmesan cheese, grated
Paprika

Place the washed spinach in a large bowl or a roasting bag with a pinch of salt. Cover or seal and cook 4 minutes in the water that clings to the leaves. Set aside. Melt the butter in a large casserole for 30 seconds on HIGH. Cook the mushrooms for 3 minutes on HIGH, turning often. Remove the mushrooms and set them aside. Add the shallots to the butter in the bowl, cover, and cook 2 minutes on HIGH. Chop the spinach roughly and add to the shallots with the tomato, salt, pepper and nutmeg. Place in the bottom of the casserole dish and arrange the mushrooms on top. Melt the butter for the sauce 1 minute on HIGH. Stir in the flour, mustard, salt, pepper and a pinch of cayenne pepper. Add the milk gradually, beating until smooth. Cook, uncovered, 4 minutes on HIGH, stirring twice after 1 minute's cooking. Add Cheddar cheese and stir to melt. Coat over the mushrooms and spinach and sprinkle the Parmesan and paprika on top. Cook 3 minutes until bubbling.

Facing page: Japanese Steamer.

Escalopes d'Aubergines au Fromage

PREPARATION TIME: 25 minutes

MICROWAVE COOKING TIME: 14-15 minutes

SERVES: 4 people

1 large or 2 small aubergines/eggplants
Seasoned flour for coating
45ml/3 tbsps oil for frying

TOPPING

15g/1 tbsp butter
2 shallots, finely chopped
10ml/2 tsps chopped tarragon
10ml/2 tsps chopped chervil
225g/8oz cream cheese
120g/4oz/1 cup grated Gruyère or Swiss
   cheese
180ml/6 fl oz/¾ cup heavy/double
   cream
Dry breadcrumbs

VEGETABLES

12 small new potatoes
8 baby carrots
4 small turnips
4 small fresh beets
8 spring/green onions
4 very small courgettes/zucchini
120g/4oz French/green beans, trimmed
120g/4oz mangetout/peapods, trimmed
120g/4oz/½ cup butter, melted
Chopped parsley

Slice the aubergines/eggplants into 8 2.5cm/1 inch thick slices. Score the slices lightly on both sides and sprinkle with salt. Leave to stand for 30 minutes to draw out any bitterness. Melt the butter for the topping for 30 seconds on HIGH. Add the shallot and cook for 2 minutes. Cool and mix with the other topping ingredients, except the dry breadcrumbs, and set aside. Cook the vegetables in 60ml/2 fl oz/ ¼ cup salted water as follows:–
new potatoes for 10 minutes
baby carrots for 10 minutes
fresh beets for 8-9 minutes
turnips for 8 minutes
spring/green onion for 2-3 minutes
French/green beans for 2-3 minutes
courgettes/zucchini for 2-3 minutes
mangetout/peapods for 2-3 minutes.
Cook the vegetables in a loosely covered casserole and keep the

beetroot separate. Melt the butter for 1 minute on HIGH and pour over the vegetables. Sprinkle the carrots and the new potatoes with chopped parsley. Leave the vegetables covered while preparing the aubergines/ eggplants. Rinse the aubergines/ eggplants well and pat dry. Mix the flour with salt and pepper and lightly coat the aubergine/eggplant slices. Heat a browning dish for 5 minutes on HIGH. Pour in the oil and put in the aubergine/eggplant slices. Cover the dish and cook for 2-3 minutes, turning halfway through the cooking time. Remove the aubergines/ eggplants from the browning dish and drain them on paper towels. Place them in a clean casserole or on a plate and top each slice with a spoonful of the cheese mixture. Sprinkle on the dry breadcrumbs and

This page: Escalopes d'Aubergines au Fromage. Facing page: Pasta Spirals with Walnuts and Gorgonzola (top) and Forester's Pasta (bottom).

cook on MEDIUM for 2 minutes. Arrange on serving plates with the vegetables.

Macaroni, Cheese and Tomato Squares

PREPARATION TIME: 15 minutes

MICROWAVE COOKING TIME: 14 minutes plus 10 minutes standing time

SERVES: 4 people

225g/8oz/3 cups macaroni
60g/2oz/¼ cup butter or margarine

60g/2oz/4 tbsps flour
Pinch dry mustard
Pinch cayenne pepper
850ml/1½ pints/3 cups milk
120g/4oz/1 cup grated Cheddar cheese
Salt and pepper
2 tomatoes

Put the macaroni into a large bowl with 1150ml/2 pints/4 cups salted water. Cook on HIGH for 6 minutes and leave to stand, covered, for 10 minutes before draining. Melt the butter for 1 minute on HIGH and stir in the flour, mustard, cayenne pepper, salt and pepper. Add the milk gradually and cook for 3-4 minutes on HIGH, stirring after 1 minute. Add the cheese to the sauce and stir to melt. Drain the macaroni well and mix it with half of the sauce. Press the macaroni mixture into a 20cm/ 8 inch square pan and chill until firm. Dilute the remaining sauce with 280ml/½ pint/1 cup milk. When the macaroni mixture is firm, cut it into 8 squares and remove from the tin. Place on a serving dish and slice the tomatoes, putting 1 slice on top of each square. Reheat the sauce for 1 minute on HIGH and pour over the macaroni squares. Reheat the squares on a serving dish for 2 minutes on HIGH. Serve immediately.

Forester's Pasta

PREPARATION TIME: 15 minutes

MICROWAVE COOKING TIME: 18 minutes plus 10 minutes standing time

SERVES: 4 people

450g/1lb spinach and plain tagliatelle/ fettucine
2 carrots, shredded
90ml/3oz oyster or wild mushrooms
30g/2 tbsps butter or margarine
1 clove garlic
30ml/2 tbsps chopped herbs such as thyme, parsley and sage
180ml/½ pint/1 cup heavy/double cream
Salt and pepper
60g/2oz fresh Parmesan cheese, ungrated

Place the pasta in a large bowl with 1150ml/2 pints/4 cups hot water, a

pinch of salt and 15ml/1 tbsp oil. Cook for 6 minutes on HIGH. Cover and leave to stand 10 minutes before draining. Rinse in hot water and leave to dry. Heat a browning dish 5 minutes on HIGH. Melt the butter 1 minute and add the garlic and carrots. Cook 1 minute on HIGH. The garlic should brown slightly. Add the mushrooms and cook 1 minute further on HIGH. Add the herbs, cream, salt and pepper and cook 2 minutes on HIGH. Toss with the pasta. Use a cheese slicer or a knife to shave off thin slices of Parmesan cheese to serve on top.

Stuffed Vine Leaves

PREPARATION TIME: 25 minutes

MICROWAVE COOKING TIME: 26-34 minutes

SERVES: 4 people

1 package vine leaves

FILLING
180g/6oz/1½ cups rice
1 onion, finely chopped
60g/2 tbsps butter or margarine
120g/8oz/1 cup black olives, stoned and chopped
1 green pepper, chopped
120g/4oz/1 cup pine-nuts
120g/4oz/1 cup feta cheese, crumbled
30g/2 tbsps chopped parsley
5ml/1 tsp ground coriander

TOMATO SAUCE
1 400g/14oz can tomatoes
15ml/1 tbsp tomato purée/paste
1 onion, finely chopped
15ml/1 tbsp oil
1 clove garlic
1.25ml/¼ tsp cinnamon
1.25ml/¼ tsp ground cumin
Salt and pepper

If the vine leaves are packed in brine, soak them in cold water for 30 minutes before using. Cook the rice 8-10 minutes in 570ml/1 pint/2 cups water with a pinch of salt. Leave the rice to stand, covered, for 5 minutes. Melt the butter for 30 seconds on HIGH and add the onion, pepper and coriander. Cook for 2 minutes on HIGH. Stir in the drained rice,

cheese, parsley, salt and pepper. Fill the leaves and roll them up, tucking in the ends. Arrange the leaves in a baking dish and set aside while preparing the sauce. Heat the oil for the sauce 30 seconds on HIGH and add the onion and garlic and cook for 1 minute on HIGH. Add the remaining ingredients and cook 6 minutes on HIGH. Leave to stand for 5 minutes before pouring over the vine leaves. Cook the vine leaves for 16 minutes on HIGH. Garnish with more chopped parsley if desired.

Pasta Spirals with Walnuts and Gorgonzola

PREPARATION TIME: 15 minutes

MICROWAVE COOKING TIME: 12 minutes plus 10 minutes standing time

SERVES: 4 people

450g/1lb pasta spirals
450g/1lb Gorgonzola cheese
120g/4oz/1 cup walnut halves
280ml/½ pint/1 cup heavy/double cream
Coarsely ground pepper

GARNISH
2 ripe figs
4 sprigs fresh thyme

Place the pasta in a large bowl with 1150ml/2 pints/4 cups hot water, a pinch of salt and 15ml/1 tbsp oil. Cook for 6 minutes on HIGH. Cover and leave to stand for 10 minutes before draining. Rinse in hot water and leave to dry. Combine the cream and crumbled cheese in a deep bowl. Cook on MEDIUM for 4 minutes until the cheese melts. Do not stir too often. Add the walnut halves and the coarsely ground pepper. Taste, and add salt if desired. Pour over the pasta in a serving dish and toss to coat. Cut the figs in half and then in half again. Put one half fig on each plate with a sprig of thyme to garnish.

Facing page: Stuffed Vine Leaves (top) and Macaroni, Cheese and Tomato Squares (bottom).

Microwave
VEGETARIAN
DESSERTS

Avocado Creams

PREPARATION TIME: 25 minutes
plus setting time

MICROWAVE COOKING TIME:
11½ minutes

SERVES: 4-6 people

2 eggs, separated
60g/2oz/4 tbsps sugar
430ml/¾ pint/1½ cups milk
2.5ml/½ tsp pistachio flavouring
15g/½ oz/1 tbsp gelatine or agar-agar
45ml/3 tbsps water and lemon juice
    mixed
1 large ripe avocado, well mashed
280g/½ pint/1 cup whipped cream

DECORATION
Pistachio nuts
Grated chocolate
Reserved whipped cream

Sprinkle the gelatine or agar-agar
onto the liquid and leave it to soak.
Beat the egg yolks and sugar together
until thick and lemon coloured. Heat
the milk for 5 minutes on HIGH
until almost boiling. Gradually stir
the milk into the eggs. Return to the
microwave oven in a large glass
measure. Heat for 6 minutes on
LOW, whisking every 2 minutes until
the mixture thickens. Have a bowl of
iced water ready. Place the measure in
the water to stop the cooking, and
any time during cooking that the
mixture seems about to curdle. Mash
the avocado in a food processor until
very smooth, combine with the
custard and add the flavouring.
Allow to cool. Melt the gelatine or
agar-agar for 30 seconds on HIGH.
Stir into the custard. Chill in the iced
water until beginning to thicken,
stirring constantly. Remove from the
iced water while beating the egg
whites until stiff but not dry. Fold
into the custard with half of the
whipped cream. Pour into the serving
dish and chill until set. Decorate with
the remaining cream piped into
rosettes, pistachio nuts and grated
chocolate.

Pumpkin Pecan Pudding

PREPARATION TIME: 15 minutes

MICROWAVE COOKING TIME:
19-23 minutes

SERVES: 4-6 people

60g/2oz/½ cup chopped pecans
30g/1oz/2 tbsps butter or margarine
225g/8oz/2 cups canned pumpkin
2.5ml/1 tsp ground cinnamon
2.5ml/½ tsp ground ginger
Pinch ground cloves
Pinch nutmeg
90g/3oz/⅓ cup cream cheese
90ml/3 fl oz/⅓ cup evaporated milk
3 eggs
120g/4oz/½ cup sugar

DECORATION
140ml/¼ pint/½ cup whipped cream
Preserved/crystallised ginger, sliced
Angelica, cut in thin strips

Heat the butter for 30 seconds on
HIGH. Stir in the pecans and cook a
further 1 minute on HIGH. In a deep
bowl, beat the remaining ingredients
together until smooth. Add the
buttered pecans. Cook on HIGH for
3 minutes, stirring halfway through.
Reduce the setting to MEDIUM and
cook 15-20 minutes or until
thickened. Pour into a large serving
dish or individual ramekins/custard
cups. Leave to stand at least
15 minutes before serving, or chill
and decorate with piped cream and
slices of ginger and angelica.

Halva of Carrots and Cashews

PREPARATION TIME: 15 minutes

MICROWAVE COOKING TIME:
20 minutes

SERVES: 4-6 people

1kg/2lbs carrots, peeled and shredded
280ml/½ pint/1 cup heavy/double
    cream
180g/6oz/¾ cup dark brown sugar
30ml/2 tbsps honey
60g/2oz/¼ cup raisins
60g/2oz/¼ cup butter or margarine
10ml/2 tsps ground coriander
5ml/1 tsp ground cinnamon
Pinch saffron
120g/4oz/1 cup chopped, unsalted,
    roasted cashews

DECORATION
Candied violets
Silver leaf or silver argentées/balls
Desiccated coconut

Cook the carrots, milk, sugar, honey
and spices in a large bowl for 15
minutes on HIGH. Cook uncovered.
Add the butter, raisins, nuts and
cook for 5 minutes on HIGH, stirring
frequently until thick. It may be
necessary to add 2-3 more minutes
cooking time to thicken. Allow the
mixture to cool and pile onto serving
dishes. Decorate with violets, silver
leaf or argentées/balls and coconut.
Serve warm or chilled with cream if
desired.

**Facing page: Halva of Carrots and
Cashews (top), Avocado Creams
(center) and Pumpkin Pecan
Pudding (bottom).**

Microwave
LOW CALORIE

Microwave
LOW CALORIE

A slimmer's life is difficult enough without having to suffer the temptations of hours spent in the kitchen. A microwave oven makes dieting that little bit easier by limiting the time you spend in preparing the food, as well as keeping all those irresistible aromas, and consequently your taste buds, under control.

On its own, of course, the microwave cannot magically produce low calorie meals. Cooked in a microwave, however, low calorie recipes seem particularly appetising, as the food retains much of its texture and colours remain bright and attractive. Somehow, the lack of rich ingredients becomes less noticeable. Perhaps of even greater interest to those watching their waistline is the fact that the microwave system of cooking requires little or no use of fat, since food is unlikely to stick to the container.

The ingredients in the selected recipes have all been carefully chosen to keep the calorie count down, but this does not mean that all the more exciting foods have been cut out. With a little skilful management, a judicious mix of low-rated foods together with a minimal quantity of high-calorie

ingredients can, in combination, produce mouthwatering dishes – a rosette of cream is only 15 calories.

Generally speaking, vegetables and salads are low in calories while foods containing fats and sugars are more fattening. But even the more fattening foods, eaten in moderation, have their place in your diet.

Calorie counts and the number of servings are given with each of the featured recipes, and if the recipe is stretched to serve more people, the total calories per serving will be further reduced.

Cooking times can be influenced by a variety of factors and those given should be used as a guide. Remember that you can always add extra cooking time, but overcooking cannot be rectified.

To cover the food in a microwave use either vented cling film/plastic wrap or a lid, but note that these covers should never be tight fitting unless specifically stated.

Always refer to the manufacturer's handbook for specific instructions on the use of the microwave oven.

SOUPS

Beetroot Soup

PREPARATION TIME: 10 minutes

MICROWAVE COOKING TIME:
25 minutes

MAKES: Approximately 1150ml/
2 pints/5 cups

TOTAL CALORIES: 330

450g/1lb/2 or 3 raw medium beetroots/
   beets
1 medium onion
850ml/1½ pints/3¾ cups hot stock
30ml/2 tbsps cider vinegar
1.25ml/¼ tsp bay leaf powder
140ml/¼ pint/⅔ cup skimmed milk
Salt
Freshly ground black pepper
1 small cucumber, finely diced
30ml/2 tbsps natural low fat yogurt

Peel the beetroots/beets and onion
and put into a large bowl with the
stock, vinegar and bay leaf powder.
Cover and cook for 20 minutes on
HIGH until the beetroots are tender.
Cut up the vegetables and purée in a
blender with as much of the liquid as
is needed. Pour back into the bowl
with the remaining liquid, add the
milk and season to taste with salt and
pepper. Stir in the cucumber, cover
and cook for 5 minutes on HIGH.
Remove from the microwave and stir
in the yogurt.

Chicken and Vermicelli Soup

PREPARATION TIME: 5 minutes

MICROWAVE COOKING TIME:
15 minutes

MAKES: 1150ml/2 pints/5 cups

TOTAL CALORIES: 500

285g/10oz raw chicken, skinned and
   diced
1150ml/2 pints/5 cups hot chicken stock
30ml/2 tbsps fresh lemon juice

This page: Chicken and Vermicelli
Soup (top) and Mulligatawny Soup
(bottom). Facing page: Beetroot
Soup (top) and Mushroom Soup
(bottom).

Salt
Freshly ground black pepper
30g/1oz/2 nests vermicelli
15ml/1 tbsp chopped chives

Put the chicken into a large bowl and pour in sufficient stock to cover. Cook uncovered for 6 minutes on HIGH. Add the remaining stock and lemon juice and season to taste with salt and pepper. Cook uncovered for 4 minutes or until boiling. Stir in the vermicelli and cook for 5 minutes, stirring once during cooking, until the chicken and vermicelli are tender. Garnish each portion with chopped chives.

Mulligatawny Soup

PREPARATION TIME: 5 minutes
MICROWAVE COOKING TIME: 8-9 minutes
MAKES: 700ml/1¼ pints/2½ cups
TOTAL CALORIES: 295

75g/3oz mixed diced vegetables
330ml/11½ fl oz can vegetable juice
425ml/15 fl oz can ready-to-serve consommé
1.25ml/¼ tsp ground coriander
1.25ml/¼ tsp ground cardamom
1.25ml/¼ tsp ground turmeric
Pinch ground cloves
15g/½ oz/2 tbsps slivered/flaked almonds, browned

Combine the vegetables, vegetable juice, consommé and spices in a large bowl. Cover and cook for 8-9 minutes on HIGH until the vegetables are tender and the soup is hot. Pour into individual bowls and garnish with the browned almonds.

Mushroom Soup

PREPARATION TIME: 10 minutes
MICROWAVE COOKING TIME: 17 minutes
MAKES: 1 litre/1¾ pints/4¼ cups
TOTAL CALORIES: 162

225g/8oz/2 cups button mushrooms
1 small onion, peeled and quartered

½ small clove garlic, peeled and crushed
1.25ml/¼ tsp dried rosemary
850ml/1½ pints/3¾ cups hot chicken stock
30ml/2 tbsp soured cream
Salt
Freshly ground black pepper

Slice and set aside two or three mushrooms. Cut up the remainder and purée in a blender with the onion, garlic, rosemary and 570ml/1 pint/2½ cups of the stock. Pour into a large bowl, cover and cook for 15 minutes on HIGH, stirring occasionally. Stir in the remaining stock and season to taste with salt and pepper. Cover and cook for 2 minutes on HIGH, stirring once during cooking. Stir in the soured cream. Garnish each portion with slices of raw mushroom.

Fish Chowder

PREPARATION TIME: 20 minutes
MICROWAVE COOKING TIME: 26-27 minutes
MAKES: 1150ml/2 pints/5 cups
TOTAL CALORIES: 685

675g/1½ lbs whole whitefish (including head and bones)
1 bay leaf
280ml/½ pint/1¼ cups water
Squeeze lemon juice
5ml/1 tsp anchovy essence
2 slices rindless bacon
1 medium potato
1 medium onion
Salt
Freshly ground black pepper
225g/8oz canned tomatoes
15ml/1 tbsp chopped parsley
75g/3oz/1 cup peeled cooked shrimp/prawns

Remove head, skin and all bones from the fish, and put them into a large bowl. Add the bay leaf, water and lemon juice. Cook uncovered for 6-7 minutes on HIGH until boiling. Reduce the setting to DEFROST/35% and cook uncovered for 10 minutes. Set aside. Meanwhile dice the bacon and peel and dice the potato and onion. Put them into a

large bowl. Cover and cook the bacon and vegetables for 5 minutes on HIGH, stirring occasionally. Strain in the fish liquor and season to taste with salt and pepper. Roughly cut up the fish and stir into the mixture. Add the tomatoes and their juice, the parsley and shrimp/prawns and cook uncovered for 5 minutes on HIGH, stirring two or three times during cooking.

Tomato and Leek Soup

PREPARATION TIME: 10 minutes
MICROWAVE COOKING TIME: 11-13 minutes
MAKES: 1½ litres/2½ pints/1½ quarts
TOTAL CALORIES: 212

2 large leeks, trimmed, washed and finely sliced
570ml/1 pint/2½ cups boiling water
570ml/1 pint/2½ cups tomato juice
Dash Worcestershire sauce
1.25ml/¼ tsp celery seeds
Shake garlic powder
Salt
Freshly ground black pepper
4 tomatoes, skinned and sliced

Put the leeks and water into a large bowl, cover and cook for 5-6 minutes on HIGH. Remove half the leeks with a slotted spoon and set aside. Purée the remaining leeks and cooking liquid in a blender. Pour back into the bowl and add the tomato juice, Worcestershire sauce, celery seeds and garlic powder. Cover and cook for 3-4 minutes on HIGH until hot, stirring once during cooking. Season to taste with salt and pepper. Stir in reserved leeks and sliced tomatoes, cover and cook for 3 minutes on HIGH, stirring once during cooking. Ladle into individual serving dishes.

Facing page: Tomato and Leek Soup.

Stir and cook for a further 2-3 minutes. Season to taste with salt and pepper. Garnish each portion with watercress leaves.

Lettuce Soup

PREPARATION TIME: 5-10 minutes

MICROWAVE COOKING TIME: 13-14 minutes

MAKES: 1¼ litres/2 pints/5 cups

TOTAL CALORIES: 285

2 medium butterhead/cabbage lettuces, rinsed and trimmed
15g/½ oz/1 tbsp low calorie margarine
½ bunch scallions/spring onions, trimmed and finely sliced
15ml/1 tbsp all-purpose/plain flour
570ml/1 pint/2½ cups hot water
1 vegetable stock/bouillon cube, crumbled
280ml/½ pint/1¼ cups skimmed milk
Salt
Freshly ground black pepper
Grated nutmeg
1 small carrot, scraped and cut into julienne strips

Coarsely shred the lettuce. Put the margarine into a large bowl with the scallions/spring onions. Cover and cook for 3 minutes on HIGH. Add lettuce, cover and cook for 5 minutes on HIGH. Blend the flour with 2 tbsps cold water and stir into the lettuce mixture, then add half of the hot water and the stock/bouillon cube. Cover and cook for 3 minutes on HIGH. Purée in a liquidiser/blender, then pour back into the bowl. Stir in the milk and remaining water. Season to taste with salt and pepper and add a dash of grated nutmeg. Reheat for 2-3 minutes on HIGH, stirring once during cooking. Garnish with the carrot strips.

Watercress Soup

PREPARATION TIME: 10 minutes

MICROWAVE COOKING TIME: 13-21 minutes

MAKES: 900ml/1½ pints/4 cups

TOTAL CALORIES: 480

2 bunches watercress
570ml/1 pint/2½ cups home-made chicken stock
30g/1oz wholemeal/whole-wheat flour
30g/1oz/¼ cup butter
280ml/½ pint/1¼ cups skimmed milk
Salt
Freshly ground black pepper

Rinse the watercress and discard any coarse stalks. Reserve a few leaves for garnish and put the remaining watercress into a large bowl with 280ml/½ pint/1½ cups of the stock. Cover and cook for 3-6 minutes on HIGH until the liquid boils, then cook for a further 8-10 minutes on HIGH until the watercress is tender. Meanwhile, blend the flour and butter together in a small bowl to form a paste. Beat the butter paste, a little at a time, into the boiling mixture. Purée in a blender with the remaining stock, pour back into the bowl and stir in the milk. Cook uncovered for 2 minutes or until bubbles appear around the edges.

This page: Fish Chowder. Facing page: Lettuce Soup (top) and Watercress Soup (bottom).

Microwave
LOW CALORIE

EGG AND CHEESE

Tacos Mexicana

PREPARATION TIME: 10 minutes

MICROWAVE COOKING TIME:
2 minutes

SERVES: 4 people

TOTAL CALORIES: 962

120g/4oz Edam/Monterey Jack cheese,
* grated*
2 red or green bottled chilis, seeds
* removed and finely sliced*
60g/2oz can red kidney beans, rinsed and
* well drained*
450g/1lb bean sprouts
8 taco shells
Green or red pepper and onion rings to
* garnish (optional)*

Mix the cheese, chilis, beans and
bean sprouts together and pile into
the taco shells. Place the tacos close
together and curved side down in a
small, shallow dish and cook
uncovered for 2 minutes on HIGH.
Serve immediately.

Eggs Dolmades

PREPARATION TIME: 15 minutes

MICROWAVE COOKING TIME:
4-5 minutes

SERVES: 4 people

TOTAL CALORIES: 565

1 medium cabbage/butterhead lettuce
4 hard-boiled eggs, finely chopped/
* minced*
60g/2oz/¼ cup cooked long grain rice
30ml/2 tbsps low calorie mayonnaise
Salt
Freshly ground black pepper

Trim and wash the lettuce leaves. Pat
dry or spin. Pile the leaves eight at a
time in the microwave and cook
uncovered for 30 seconds on HIGH
until slightly softened. Remove with
a fish slice and repeat with another
batch of leaves. Mix together the
eggs, rice and mayonnaise and season
to taste with salt and pepper. Layer
two lettuce leaves together and place
a little of the egg mixture in the
middle. Roll up, tucking in the sides

This page: Tacos Mexicana. Facing
page: Eggs Dolmades (top) and
Tuna Scramble (bottom).

to form a parcel. Repeat with the
remaining leaves and filling. Arrange
the lettuce parcels smooth side up in
a small, shallow dish and cook
uncovered for 3-4 minutes on HIGH,
giving the dish a half turn halfway
through cooking. Baste with the
juices and serve hot or cold.

Eve's Rarebit

PREPARATION TIME: 5 minutes

MICROWAVE COOKING TIME:
2 minutes

SERVES: 4 people

TOTAL CALORIES: 842

120g/4 oz Edam/Monterey Jack cheese,
    grated
1 small onion, peeled and very finely
    chopped/minced
1 medium carrot, peeled and grated
15ml/1 tbsp bran
2 eggs
2.5ml/½ tsp mustard powder
30ml/2 tbsps skimmed milk
Salt
Freshly ground black pepper
4 thin slices bread, toasted

Thoroughly mix the cheese, onion,
carrot, bran, eggs, mustard and milk
together and season with the salt and
pepper. Cook uncovered for 2
minutes on HIGH until thickened,
beating every 30 seconds. Pile on to
the toast and brown under the grill/
broiler if desired.

Eggs Benedict on Wilted Watercress

PREPARATION TIME: 10 minutes

MICROWAVE COOKING TIME:
11-12 minutes

SERVES: 6 people

TOTAL CALORIES: 1004

2 bunches watercress
60g/2oz/¼ cup low calorie margarine
8 eggs
30ml/2 tbsps lemon juice
Salt
White pepper

Wash the watercress, remove and
discard the thick stalks, and pat the
leaves dry. Put the margarine in a
small bowl and heat uncovered for

**This page: Eggs Benedict on Wilted
Watercress. Facing page: Almond
and Pepper Timbale (top) and Eve's
Rarebit (bottom).**

Almond and Pepper Timbale

PREPARATION TIME: 5 minutes

MICROWAVE COOKING TIME:
15-19½ minutes

SERVES: 4 people

TOTAL CALORIES: 755

¼ green pepper, finely diced
1 medium onion, peeled and finely
    chopped/minced
120ml/8 tbsps skimmed milk
4 eggs, beaten
60g/2oz Edam/Monterey Jack cheese,
    grated
Salt

Freshly ground black pepper
25g/1oz flaked/slivered almonds,
    browned

Spread the pepper and onion in a
570ml/1 pint/2½ cup straight-sided
soufflé dish. Cover and cook for
2½-3½ minutes on HIGH until the
vegetables are cooked. Stir in the
milk and, without covering, cook for
30 seconds to 1 minute until the milk
is steaming but not boiling. Mix in
the eggs and cheese and lightly
season. Cover and cook for 12-15
minutes on LOW, giving the dish a
half turn once during cooking.
Garnish with the almonds and
serve hot.

30 seconds on HIGH until melted. Beat two of the eggs and mix with the lemon juice, then whisk into the melted margarine and season with salt and pepper. Cook uncovered for 45 seconds to one minute on HIGH, whisking every 10 seconds until the sauce thickens sufficiently to coat the back of a spoon. Do not overcook or the sauce will curdle. Cover and set aside. Break the remaining six eggs into individual greased poachers or ramekin dishes. Cover each loosely with cling film/plastic wrap and arrange in a circle in the microwave. Cook for 8-9 minutes on LOW until the white is just set, giving each dish a half turn halfway through cooking. Arrange the watercress leaves on a micro-proof serving dish and cook, uncovered, for 1 minute on HIGH to warm and wilt. Arrange the eggs on the watercress, coating them with the sauce. Serve immediately.

Whole-Wheat Vegetable Quiche

PREPARATION TIME: 20 minutes

MICROWAVE COOKING TIME: 21-23 minutes

SERVES: 4 people

TOTAL CALORIES: 873

90g/3oz/¾ cup wholemeal/whole-wheat flour
15g/½ oz/¼ cup bran
60g/2oz/¼ cup low calorie margarine
30ml/2 tbsps cold water
1 small red pepper, cored, seeded and diced
120g/4oz courgettes/zucchini, diced
2 spring onions/scallions, trimmed and finely sliced
1 tomato, skinned and chopped
2 eggs
15ml/1 tbsp skimmed milk
Salt
Pepper

Put the flour and bran in a bowl and rub in the margarine. Add the water and mix to form a wet dough. Put into a 16cm/6½ inch shallow dish and press out to form a pie case. Cook uncovered for 4 minutes on

HIGH, turning the dish every minute. Set aside. Put the diced pepper in a bowl, cover and cook for 2 minutes on HIGH. Add the courgettes/zucchini and onions, then cover and cook for 3 minutes on HIGH. Spread the cooked vegetables and the tomato in the base of the pastry case. Beat the eggs and milk together thoroughly and season with salt and pepper, pour over the vegetables and cook uncovered for 12-14 minutes on LOW, or until set. Give the dish a turn occasionally during cooking. Serve hot or cold.

Tuna Scramble

PREPARATION TIME: 10 minutes

MICROWAVE COOKING TIME: 8-9 minutes

SERVES: 4 people

TOTAL CALORIES: 815

1 small onion, peeled and finely chopped/minced
6 eggs, beaten
6 large tomatoes, skinned and chopped
Salt
Freshly ground black pepper
1 210g/7oz can tuna in brine, drained and flaked

Put the onion in a bowl, cover and cook for 4-5 minutes on HIGH until tender, stirring occasionally. Thoroughly mix in the eggs and tomatoes and season with salt and pepper. Cook uncovered for 3 minutes on HIGH, stirring every minute until the mixture is moistly scrambled. Gently mix in the tuna and continue cooking for 1 minute, stirring gently halfway through the cooking period. Serve on thinly sliced toast if desired.

Cottage Cheese and Chervil Cocottes

PREPARATION TIME: 5 minutes

MICROWAVE COOKING TIME: 5-6 minutes plus standing time

SERVES: 4 people

TOTAL CALORIES: 370

225g/8oz cottage cheese
1 egg
2 spring onions/scallions, finely sliced
2.5ml/½ tsp dried chervil or 10ml/2 tsp fresh chervil
10ml/2 tsp freshly chopped parsley
Pinch ground mace
Salt
Pepper
30ml/2 tbsps soured cream

Mix the cottage cheese, egg, onion, chervil, parsley and mace to a smooth paste in the blender. Season to taste with salt and pepper. Divide the mixture between four individual ramekins, cover each with cling film/plastic wrap and cook for 5-6 minutes on LOW until just set. Leave to stand for 3 minutes, then uncover and pour a little cream on each. Serve hot or cold.

Soufflé Omelette

PREPARATION TIME: 10 minutes

MICROWAVE COOKING TIME: 7-11 minutes plus standing time

SERVES: 2 people

TOTAL CALORIES: 350

5ml/1 tsp vegetable oil
Non-stick vegetable parchment
190g/6¼ oz can pimentos, drained and puréed
5ml/1 tsp tomato purée/paste
15ml/1 tbsp pine kernels, finely grated
Salt
Freshly ground black pepper
3 eggs, separated
45ml/3 tbsp cold water

Brush a little of the oil round the edge and in the base of a 22cm/9 inch shallow, round dish and line the base with a disc of non-stick vegetable parchment. Mix the puréed pimentos, tomato purée/paste, nuts and seasoning in a small bowl, and cook uncovered for 1-2 minutes on HIGH, stirring occasionally. Cover and keep warm. Using grease-free

Facing page: Whole-Wheat Vegetable Quiche.

This page: Soufflé Omelette. Facing page: Cottage Cheese and Chervil Cocottes (top) and Egg, Bacon and Tomato Pots (bottom).

beaters, whisk the egg whites until stiff. In another large bowl whisk the egg yolks and water, with salt and pepper to taste. Stir in one tablespoon of the egg white, then gently fold in the remainder. Pour the egg mixture into the prepared dish and cook uncovered for 5-8 minutes on LOW until just set. Give the dish a quarter turn every minute during cooking. Leave to stand for 1 minute, then turn out onto a flame-proof dish and gently fold the omelette over. Lightly brown under the grill/broiler. Reheat the sauce for 1 minute on HIGH, then pour over the omelette. Serve immediately.

Egg, Bacon and Tomato Pots

PREPARATION TIME: 8 minutes	
MICROWAVE COOKING TIME: 20-23½ minutes	
SERVES: 4 people	
TOTAL CALORIES: 745	

4 large beef/Moroccan tomatoes
5ml/1 tsp cornstarch/cornflour
2.5ml/½ tsp bottled fruity sauce
5ml/1 tsp tomato purée/paste
Salt
Freshly ground black pepper
2 bacon rashers/slices, rind and outside fat removed
4 eggs, beaten together

Cut off a thick slice from the stalk end of the tomatoes. Scrape out all the pulp into a bowl, making sure that the tomatoes are well drained. Cover and cook for 3 minutes on HIGH, then press through a sieve into another bowl and discard the pips. Stir in the cornstarch/cornflour, sauce and tomato purée/paste and season to taste with salt and pepper. Cook uncovered for 1-2 minutes on HIGH, stirring occasionally until the mixture thickens. Dice the bacon and spread out on a saucer covered with absorbent kitchen paper. Cook for 30 seconds on HIGH. Arrange the tomato shells open side up in a shallow dish, three-quarters fill with the beaten egg and top with the bacon. Cover and cook for 10 minutes on LOW. Carefully stir the egg and bacon filling, then cook uncovered for 5-7 minutes on LOW. Remove from the microwave, then reheat the sauce, covered, for 30 seconds to 1 minute on HIGH. Pour over the tomatoes and serve hot.

FISH AND SEAFOOD

Quenelles Poche au Crème de Tomates

PREPARATION TIME: 10-15 minutes

MICROWAVE COOKING TIME: 21-22 minutes

SERVES: 4 people

TOTAL CALORIES: 645

450g/1lb pike or whitefish fillet
1 bay leaf
1 spring onion/scallion, peeled and sliced
1 blade mace
140ml/¼ pint/⅔ cup water
3 thin slices white bread, crusts removed
45ml/3 tbsp skimmed milk
2 egg whites
Salt
Pepper
Pinch grated nutmeg
1 430ml/15 fl oz/2 cup can low calorie tomato soup
Freshly chopped parsley to garnish (optional)

Skin the fish and remove any bones. Cut up the skin and place with the bones, bay leaf, onion, mace and water in a bowl. Cook uncovered for 2-3 minutes on HIGH or until boiling. Reduce the setting and cook for 10 minutes on LOW. Strain the liquor and make up to 90ml/6 tbsp with water if necessary. If the liquor exceeds this quantity, continue cooking on FULL POWER until it is reduced. Cut up the fish and purée in the food processor with the bread coarsely torn, the milk, egg whites and fish liquor. Season with salt, pepper and nutmeg. Pour the soup into a large, shallow dish and cook uncovered for 2-3 minutes on HIGH until hot, stirring occasionally. Divide the fish mixture into eight oval shapes using two tablespoons and place well spaced out into the hot soup. Cover and cook for 6 minutes on HIGH, repositioning the fish quenelles halfway through cooking. Serve hot, garnished with parsley if desired.

Cutlets, Sauce Champignon

PREPARATION TIME: 10 minutes

MICROWAVE COOKING TIME: 18-20 minutes

SERVES: 4 people

TOTAL CALORIES: 794

10ml/2 tsp corn oil
1 medium onion, peeled and finely chopped/minced
1 garlic clove, skinned and crushed
10ml/2 tsp cornstarch/cornflour
140ml/¼ pint/⅔ cup dry white wine
30ml/2 tbsps tomato purée/paste
1.25ml/¼ tsp mixed dry herbs
Salt
Freshly ground black pepper
225g/8oz mushrooms, sliced
4 225g/8oz cod steaks
Low calorie sweetener

Combine the oil, onion and garlic in a bowl, cover and cook for 3 minutes on HIGH until the onion is soft. Stir in the cornstarch/cornflour, wine, tomato purée/paste and herbs and season with salt and pepper. Cook uncovered for 2 minutes on HIGH, then beat thoroughly with a whisk. Stir in the mushrooms and cook uncovered for 5-6 minutes on HIGH, stirring occasionally until the mushrooms are tender and the sauce is thick. Cover and set aside. Arrange the cod steaks in a shallow dish, the thin ends towards the centre. Cover and cook for 6-7 minutes on HIGH until the fish is cooked. Spoon the juices into the mushroom mixture, adjust seasoning to taste, adding a drop of liquid sweetener. Pour the sauce over the fish and, without covering, reheat on HIGH for 2 minutes. Serve hot.

Fish Pie

PREPARATION TIME: 10 minutes

MICROWAVE COOKING TIME: 10-12 minutes

SERVES: 4 people

TOTAL CALORIES: 1030

1 tbsp vegetable oil
30g/1oz/¼ cup flour
225ml/8 fl oz/1 cup skimmed milk
Salt
Pepper
450g/1lb whitefish fillets, skinned
4 slightly undercooked hard boiled eggs
15ml/1 tbsp capers, chopped

Stir the oil and flour together in a medium bowl and cook for 30 seconds on HIGH. Beat in the milk and cook uncovered for 1 minute on HIGH. Beat, then cook for a further 1½-2 minutes on HIGH, beating every 30 seconds. Season to taste with salt and pepper. Arrange half the fish in a round or square dish, cover with a layer of sliced eggs, then spoon over half the sauce. Repeat the

Facing page: Cutlets, Sauce Champignon.

layers, then top with a sprinkling of capers. Cook uncovered for 5-6 minutes on HIGH, turning the dish every 2 minutes until the fish is cooked. Brown under the grill/ broiler if the dish is flameproof.

Fresh Salmon Steaks Royale

PREPARATION TIME: 5 minutes

MICROWAVE COOKING TIME: 11-15 minutes

SERVES: 4 people

TOTAL CALORIES: 1373

4 225g/6oz fresh salmon steaks
Salt
Freshly ground black pepper
10ml/2 tsp crushed dill weed
2 scallops, washed and sliced
60g/2oz cooked, shelled prawns/shrimp
15g/½ oz lumpfish caviar

Season the salmon with salt and pepper and sprinkle one side of the steaks with the dill weed. Arrange herb side down in a single layer, the thicker parts towards the outside in a large, shallow dish. Cover with non-stick baking parchment and cook for

This page: **Fresh Salmon Steaks Royale. Facing page: Quenelles Poche au Crème de Tomates (top) and Fish Pie (bottom).**

9-12 minutes on LOW. Transfer the salmon steaks to a hot serving dish. Stir the scallops and prawns/shrimp into the juices remaining in the dish. Cover tightly and cook for 2-3 minutes on LOW until the scallops are opaque. Arrange the scallops and prawns/shrimp on top of the salmon and sprinkle with caviar.

Curried Prawns/Shrimp

PREPARATION TIME: 5 minutes

MICROWAVE COOKING TIME:
8-9 minutes

SERVES: 4 people as a starter

TOTAL CALORIES: 560

5ml/1 tsp vegetable oil
1 small shallot, peeled and finely
    chopped/minced
7.5ml/1½ tsp garam masala
⅛ tsp Cayenne pepper
Pinch salt
Pinch freshly ground black pepper
225g/8oz/1 cup shelled, cooked,
    prawns/shrimp
¼ red pepper, cut into thin strips
15ml/1 tbsp water
180g/6oz/1 cup cooked long grain rice
15ml/1 tbsp low fat natural yogurt

Combine the oil, shallot, garam
masala, Cayenne, salt and pepper in a
medium bowl. Cover and cook for
2 minutes on HIGH. Drain the
prawns/shrimp if freshly thawed and
stir into the mixture. Cover and set
aside. Put pepper strips and water in
a dish, cover and cook for 2 minutes
on HIGH. Drain and set aside.
Arrange a border of rice on one large
or four small micro-proof serving
dishes. Place in the microwave and
heat for 2-2½ minutes on HIGH.
Heat the prawn/shrimp mixture for
2-2½ minutes on HIGH, stirring once
during cooking. Stir the yogurt into
the hot prawns/shrimp, then spoon
into the centre of the rice. Garnish
with a lattice of pepper strips and
serve immediately.

Lemon Poached Trout

PREPARATION TIME: 5 minutes

MICROWAVE COOKING TIME:
16-18 minutes

SERVES: 4 people

TOTAL CALORIES: 985

1 small onion, peeled and finely chopped/
    minced
1 celery stalk, finely chopped/minced
1 leek, trimmed, washed and thinly sliced
1 bay leaf

2.5ml/½ tsp lemon thyme
4 black peppercorns
140ml/¼ pint/⅔ cup medium white
    wine
15ml/1 tbsp fresh lemon juice
Salt
4 225g/8oz trout, gutted and cleaned
15ml/1 tbsp cornstarch/cornflour
60ml/4 tbsps/¼ cup water
Lemon and cucumber slices to garnish

Combine the onion, celery, leek, bay
leaf, lemon thyme, peppercorns, wine
and lemon juice in a large bowl.
Cover and cook for 5 minutes on
HIGH. Add salt to taste. Leave to
cool. Arrange the fish in a single layer

**This page: Folded Flounder in
Pernod Sauce. Facing page: Curried
Prawns/Shrimp (top) and Lemon
Poached Trout (bottom).**

in a large, shallow dish and strain in
the liquid. Cover and cook for
8 minutes on HIGH, basting
occasionally with the juices. Remove
the two outer fish. Cover and cook
the remaining fish for 2 minutes on
HIGH, then remove from the dish.
Peel off the skin and remove the
heads from the fish if desired. Blend
the cornstarch/cornflour with the
water, stir into the liquid remaining

in the dish and cook uncovered for 1-2 minutes on HIGH, stirring halfway through cooking. When the sauce thickens pour over the fish and garnish with lemon and cucumber slices cut into triangles.

Folded Flounder in Pernod Sauce

PREPARATION TIME: 5 minutes

MICROWAVE COOKING TIME: 25-29 minutes

SERVES: 4 people

TOTAL CALORIES: 604

225g/8oz bulb fennel, trimmed and shredded
140ml/¼ pint/⅔ cup skimmed milk
15ml/1 tbsp Pernod
Salt
Freshly ground black pepper
4 120g/4oz plaice/flounder fillets, skinned if preferred
1 egg yolk
15ml/1 tbsp cold water
Green fennel sprigs to garnish

Put the fennel in a bowl, cover and cook for 4-5 minutes on HIGH until soft, stirring once during cooking. Without uncovering, set aside. Put the milk and Pernod in a suitable shallow dish and cook uncovered for 2½-3 minutes on HIGH or until boiling. Reduce the setting and cook for 5 minutes on LOW. Season the fish with salt and pepper and fold each fillet in half. Arrange slightly overlapping in the liquid in the dish. Cover and cook for 10-12 minutes on LOW until the fish is just cooked. Arrange the shredded fennel on a suitable micro-proof serving dish. Using two fish slices place the fish on top of the fennel. Pour the remaining liquor into a bowl. Blend the egg yolk and water together, mix into the liquid and cook uncovered for 2½-3 minutes on HIGH, beating every 15-20 seconds until the sauce thickens to the consistency of thin cream. Do not overcook or the sauce will curdle. Lightly cover the fish and fennel and reheat for 1 minute on HIGH, then pour the sauce over the fish and garnish with fennel sprigs.

Luxury Seafood Shells

PREPARATION TIME: 10 minutes

MICROWAVE COOKING TIME: 4½-5½ minutes

SERVES: 4 people

TOTAL CALORIES: 765

4 90g/3oz plaice/flounder fillets, skinned
10ml/2 tsp lemon juice
120g/4oz/½ cup cooked shelled prawns/shrimp
4 scallops, washed and cut into quarters
90g/3oz crabmeat
15g/½ oz/1 tbsp butter
Salt
Freshly ground black pepper
Pinch grated nutmeg
Cayenne pepper

Cut the fish lengthwise into 2.5 cm/1 inch wide strips, sprinkle with lemon juice and roll up. Arrange the fish rolls, prawns/shrimp and scallops in four individual shells and top with the crabmeat. Put the butter, salt, pepper and nutmeg in a small jug and heat uncovered for 30 seconds on HIGH until melted. Pour over the fish and sprinkle with Cayenne. Arrange the shells in a circle in the microwave and cover each with a disc of non-stick vegetable parchment. Cook for 2-3 minutes on HIGH, give the dishes a half turn then continue cooking for 2-3 minutes on HIGH until the fish and scallops are cooked. Do not overcook.

Smoked Trout Mousse

PREPARATION TIME: 10 minutes

MICROWAVE COOKING TIME: 1 minute

MAKES: Approximately 570ml/1 pint/2½ cups

SERVES: 4-8 people)

TOTAL CALORIES: 450

225g/8oz smoked trout (weight after skinning and boning)
1 small shallot, peeled and quartered
140ml/¼ pint/⅔ cup low fat natural yogurt
1.25ml/¼ tsp grated mace
Salt

Freshly ground black pepper
60ml/4 tbsps/¼ cup water
15g/½ oz envelope gelatine
2 egg whites
Orange or lemon slices to garnish

Make sure that all the bones have been removed, then liquidise/blend the fish with the shallot, yogurt and mace, seasoning sparingly with salt and pepper. Put the water in a jug and heat uncovered for 30 seconds on HIGH. Sprinkle the gelatine over the surface, then stir and cook for 20 seconds on HIGH. Stir until the gelatine has dissolved. Leave to cool for 5 minutes, then pour gradually into the puréed fish, beating continuously. Whisk the egg whites until stiff and fold into the fish mixture. Pour into a mould and chill until set. Garnish with orange or lemon slices.

Mackerel in Gooseberry Sauce

PREPARATION TIME: 15 minutes

MICROWAVE COOKING TIME: 14-15 minutes

SERVES: 4 people

TOTAL CALORIES: 1570

225g/8oz/1¼ cups gooseberries, fresh or frozen
120ml/4 fl oz water
5ml/1 tsp grated lemon zest
5ml/1 tsp caster sugar
Low calorie sweetener to taste
Freshly ground black pepper
4 285g/10oz mackerel, cleaned and heads removed

Top and tail the gooseberries if necessary and put them into a bowl with the water, lemon zest and sugar. Cook for 5-6 minutes, stirring once during cooking until the gooseberries are soft. Purée in the blender, then rub through a sieve/strainer. Add

Facing page: Luxury Seafood Shells (top) and Smoked Trout Mousse (bottom).

sweetener to taste. Season the mackerel and arrange in a single layer in a large, shallow dish. Cover with non-stick vegetable parchment or a lid and cook for 4 minutes on HIGH. Reposition, putting the two fish on the outside in the middle. Cover and cook for a further 3 minutes on HIGH. Pour the gooseberry sauce over and cook uncovered for 2 minutes on HIGH, or until the fish is cooked.

Smoky Fish Kebabs

PREPARATION TIME: 10 minutes

MICROWAVE COOKING TIME: 4-7 minutes

SERVES: 8 people

TOTAL CALORIES: 550 excluding rice

450g/1lb thick smoked cod fillet, skinned
180g/6oz cucumber
16 pearl baby onions
4 tomatoes
8 wooden skewers
120g/4oz long grain rice cooked in saffron (optional)

Cut the fish into sixteen cubes. Cut the cucumber into eight 1cm/½ inch slices, then cut each slice in half again. Halve the tomatoes. Thread each skewer in the following order – cucumber, fish, onion, tomato, onion, fish, cucumber. Arrange the skewers on a shallow dish or plate and cook for 4-7 minutes on HIGH, repositioning halfway through the cooking time.

Fillets Stälhammer

PREPARATION TIME: 15 minutes

MICROWAVE COOKING TIME: 10-11 minutes

SERVES: 4-6 people

TOTAL CALORIES: 972

1 large leek, trimmed, rinsed and finely sliced
12 spring onions/scallions, trimmed, rinsed and finely sliced
105ml/6 tbsps white wine

1 210g/7oz can shrimp
Pinch saffron
10ml/2 tsp arrowroot
60ml/4 tbsps cold water
Salt
Freshly ground black pepper
1 125g/4oz can mussels
450g/1lb whitefish fillet
2 tomatoes, skinned and sliced
Chopped parsley to garnish

Put the leek and spring onions/scallions in a medium bowl with the wine, the drained liquor from the shrimp and the saffron. Stir

This page: Smoky Fish Kebabs (top) and Fillets Stälhammer (bottom). Facing page: Middle European Gratinee.

thoroughly, then cover and cook for 5 minutes on HIGH, stirring once during cooking, until the vegetables are tender. Mix the arrowroot and water together and season with salt and pepper. Stir into the vegetables, cover and cook for 1-2 minutes on HIGH, stirring frequently until the

sauce thickens. Drain the mussels, discarding their liquor, rinse and drain. Add the mussels and shrimps to the vegetable mixture. Arrange the fish fillets in a single layer in a shallow dish and season with salt and pepper. Top with the tomato slices. Pour the sauce over, then cover the dish and cook for 4 minutes on HIGH, giving the dish a half turn halfway through cooking. Sprinkle with the parsley and serve hot.

Middle European Gratinee

PREPARATION TIME: 15 minutes

MICROWAVE COOKING TIME: 14-16 minutes

SERVES: 4 people

TOTAL CALORIES: 842

1 medium onion, peeled and finely chopped/minced
6 medium tomatoes, skinned and chopped
5ml/1 tsp dry basil
Salt
Freshly ground black pepper
450g/1lb whitefish fillet, skinned
450g/1lb courgettes/zucchini rinsed, topped and tailed and thinly sliced
60g/2oz Edam/Monterey Jack cheese
30ml/2 tbsps fresh breadcrumbs

Put the onion into a bowl, cover and cook for 1 minute on HIGH. Stir in the tomatoes and basil and season with salt and pepper. Arrange layers of fish, onion mixture and courgettes/zucchini in a shallow dish, finishing with a layer of courgettes/zucchini. Cover and cook for 10 minutes on HIGH, turning the dish three times during cooking. Mix the cheese and breadcrumbs together and sprinkle over the courgette/zucchini. Without covering, cook for 3-5 minutes on HIGH or until the fish and courgettes/zucchini are cooked. If the dish is flameproof brown under the grill/broiler.

This page: Mackerel Gooseberry Sauce. Facing page: Welsh Ham Rolls.

MEAT AND POULTRY

Welsh Ham Rolls

PREPARATION TIME: 12 minutes

MICROWAVE COOKING TIME:
12-14 minutes

SERVES: 4-6 people

TOTAL CALORIES: 688

450g/1lb leeks, washed, trimmed and
   finely sliced
140ml/¼ pint/⅔ cup salted water
Freshly ground black pepper
180g/6oz/¾ cup cottage cheese
2 spring onions/scallions, trimmed and
   finely sliced
1 egg
6 30g/1oz even shaped, lean, cooked ham
   slices

Put the leeks and water into a
casserole. Cover and cook for
6 minutes on HIGH. Without
draining, purée in the liquidiser or
food processor. Season with pepper
and add salt if necessary. Spread the
purée in a shallow oval dish, and
cook for 2-3 minutes on HIGH.
Thoroughly mix the cottage cheese,
spring onions/scallions with the egg
and pile a border of the mixture
along one edge of each ham slice.
Roll up and arrange on top of the
purée. Cover and cook for 4-6
minutes on HIGH. Serve hot.

Chicken Indienne

PREPARATION TIME: 2 minutes
plus marinating time

MICROWAVE COOKING TIME:
9-11 minutes

SERVES: 4 people

TOTAL CALORIES: 614

60ml/4 tbsps/¼ cup low fat natural
   yogurt
15ml/1 tbsp curry paste
1.25ml/¼ tsp salt
4 120g/4oz boneless chicken breasts
Fresh coriander leaves to garnish

In a shallow micro-proof dish
combine the yogurt, curry paste and
salt. Add the chicken breasts, turning
the pieces until all are well coated.
Cover and refrigerate for 12 hours,
turning the chicken pieces over

30ml/2 tbsp dry sherry
30ml/2 tbsp tomato purée/paste
30ml/2 tbsp Tamari sauce
10ml/2 tsp clear honey

Separate the ribs and trim away
excess fat. Rub with salt and pepper.
In a large dish combine the vinegar,
sherry, tomato purée/paste, Tamari
sauce and honey. Add the ribs and
turn them until they are well coated.
Cover the dish and leave to marinate
in a cool place for 3-4 hours, turning
the ribs occasionally. Pile the ribs on
a rack in a shallow dish. Cover with
non-stick paper and cook for 5
minutes on HIGH. Reposition and
brush with marinade. Cover and
cook for 5 minutes on HIGH,
brushing with any remaining
marinade. Cover and cook for
20 minutes on LOW until the meat
is cooked. Serve hot.

Bombay Chicken Salad

PREPARATION TIME: 8 minutes plus marinating time	
MICROWAVE COOKING TIME: 5-6 minutes	
SERVES: 4-8 people	
TOTAL CALORIES: 1070	

450g/1lb boneless raw chicken
Grated zest and juice of one lemon and
    grated zest and juice of one lime
30ml/2 tbsps garam masala
4 dessert apples
½ head/bunch celery, finely sliced
10 spring onions/scallions, finely sliced
4 fresh dates, stoned and finely sliced
280ml/½ pint/1¼ cups low fat natural
    yogurt
Salt
Freshly ground black pepper

Dice the chicken and put into a bowl
with the citrus zest and juices. Mix in
the garam masala thoroughly. Cover
and leave to stand for 20 minutes,
stirring once. Cover and cook for

occasionally. Cover with non-stick
baking parchment and cook for
4 minutes on HIGH. Reposition and
turn the chicken pieces over and
cook for 3 minutes or until the
chicken is cooked. Transfer the
chicken breasts to a serving plate and
keep warm. Stirring frequently, cook
the remaining sauce uncovered for
2-4 minutes on HIGH until slightly
reduced. Spoon the sauce over the
chicken. Garnish with fresh coriander
leaves and serve with a tomato and
onion salad.

Barbecued Spare Ribs

PREPARATION TIME: 10 minutes	
MICROWAVE COOKING TIME: 30 minutes	
SERVES: 4 people	
TOTAL CALORIES: 360	

8 pork spare ribs, total weight
    approximately 900g/2lb
Salt
Freshly ground black pepper
30ml/2 tbsp vinegar

**This page: Barbecued Spare Ribs.
Facing page: Bombay Chicken
Salad (top) and Chicken Indienne
(bottom).**

5-6 minutes on HIGH, stirring once during cooking until the chicken is cooked. Cool rapidly. Drain away surplus juices. Core and dice the apples and mix into the chicken with the remaining ingredients. Season to taste. Chill for one hour before serving. Not suitable for freezing.

Turkey Fillet en Papillote

PREPARATION TIME: 15 minutes

MICROWAVE COOKING TIME:
6 minutes plus standing time

SERVES: 4 people

TOTAL CALORIES: 575

450g/1lb raw turkey breast fillet, about
    1cm/½ inch thick
120g/4oz button mushrooms, sliced
Salt
Freshly ground black pepper
1 large red pepper, cored, seeded and cut
    into rings
Paprika

Cut the fillet into four even pieces. Slash each piece vertically in three places part way through, and insert mushroom slices into these slits. Season with salt and pepper. Put each piece onto a sheet of non-stick baking parchment. Top each turkey piece with two pepper rings and sprinkle with paprika. Wrap each parcel separately, making sure that the turkey portion is completely enclosed. Secure with wooden pick/cocktail stick if necessary. Arrange the parcels in a circle in the microwave and cook for 6 minutes on HIGH, repositioning halfway through cooking time. Leave wrapped for 5 minutes. Open the parcels and baste the turkey with the juices. Re-wrap and add extra cooking time if necessary. Serve hot.

Chinese Meatballs

PREPARATION TIME: 10 minutes

MICROWAVE COOKING TIME:
6 minutes

SERVES: 4 people

TOTAL CALORIES: 1050

450g/1lb/2 cups lean raw minced/
    ground beef
30ml/2 tbsps bran
1 egg
Grated zest and juice of 1 lemon
15ml/1 tbsp tomato purée/paste
15ml/1 tbsp French/Dijon mustard
Salt
Freshly ground black pepper
450g/1lb/8 cups bean sprouts, rinsed
    and drained
1 small red pepper, seeded, cored and
    diced
1 large carrot, peeled and cut into thin
    strips
15ml/1 tbsp dark soy sauce

Mix together the meat, bran, egg, lemon juice and zest, tomato purée/paste and mustard. Season with salt and pepper. Form into sixteen balls and arrange in a shallow dish. Cover and cook for 5-6 minutes on HIGH, repositioning the meatballs once during cooking. Meanwhile, pat the bean sprouts dry in a clean cloth, then combine with the diced pepper and carrot strips. Arrange in nests in individual dishes. Put three or four meatballs in the centre of each nest. Sprinkle with soy sauce and serve immediately.

Chicken and Ham Stuffed Mushrooms

PREPARATION TIME: 10 minutes

MICROWAVE COOKING TIME:
6½ minutes

SERVES: 4 as a main course or
6 as a starter

TOTAL CALORIES: 395

8 7.5cm/3 inch open flat mushrooms
90g/3oz cooked minced/ground chicken
30g/1oz lean cooked ham, finely chopped
1 egg, separated
2 spring onions/scallions, finely sliced
Salt
Freshly ground black pepper
1.25ml/¼ tsp cornstarch/cornflour
30ml/2 tbsps soured cream
Paprika
Spring onions/scallions to garnish

Remove and finely chop the mushroom stalks, then mix with the chicken, ham, egg yolk and onions and season with salt and pepper. Beat egg white until stiff and fold in. Arrange the mushroom caps dark side up in a shallow dish. Pile the filling on the mushrooms and cook uncovered for 6 minutes on HIGH until the mushrooms are tender. Remove to a hot serving dish. Mix together the cornstarch/cornflour and cream and stir into the juices remaining in the dish. Cook uncovered for 30 seconds on HIGH. (Do not overcook or the cream will curdle.) Pour a little sauce on each mushroom, sprinkle with paprika and garnish with spring onions/scallions. Serve immediately.

Saucy Meatloaf

PREPARATION TIME: 5 minutes

MICROWAVE COOKING TIME:
11 minutes plus standing time

SERVES: 4 people

TOTAL CALORIES: 960

225g/8oz/2 cups lean raw minced/
    ground beef
225g/8oz/2 cups lean raw minced/
    ground pork
120g/4oz carrots, peeled and grated
1 egg
60g/2oz chives, chopped or 30ml/2 tbsps
    dried chives
15ml/1 tbsp finely chopped celery
30ml/2 tbsp bottled fruity sauce
Salt
Freshly ground black pepper
Parsley sprigs, chives and carrot flowers to
    garnish

Mix together the beef, pork, carrot, egg, chives, celery and 1 tbsp of the fruity sauce. Season with salt and pepper. Press the mixture into a 19 x 9 x 5cm/7 x 3½ x 2 inch/1½ pint glass, loaf-shaped dish. Cook uncovered for 10 minutes on HIGH,

Facing page: Chicken and Ham Stuffed Mushrooms.

turning occasionally. Drain away fat. Cover and leave to stand for 10 minutes. Turn out onto a dish or non-stick paper and quickly reverse onto a suitable flameproof serving dish. Spread the remaining sauce over the top and down the sides of the meatloaf using a round-bladed knife. Cook uncovered for 1 minute on HIGH or brown under the grill/broiler. Garnish with parsley sprigs, chives and carrot flowers.

This page: Turkey Fillet en Papillote. Facing page: Chinese Meatballs (top) and Saucy Meatloaf (bottom).

Lamb Chops with Currant Sauce

PREPARATION TIME: 5 minutes

MICROWAVE COOKING TIME: 6 minutes

SERVES: 4 people

TOTAL CALORIES: 760

4 120g/4oz loin lamb chops, well
    trimmed
45g/1½ oz/¼ cup currants
90ml/6 tbsps water
30g/1oz/½ cup fresh brown breadcrumbs
Pinch ground cloves
40ml/2½ tbsp red wine
1.25ml/¼ tsp butter
Cooked French/green beans to garnish

Arrange the chops in a shallow dish or preheated, oiled browning dish, the bones towards the centre. Cover with wax/greaseproof paper and cook for 2½ minutes on HIGH. Place the currants in a bowl with the water, cover and cook for 2 minutes on HIGH. Add all the remaining ingredients, cover and cook for 1½ minutes on HIGH. Transfer the chops to a micro-proof serving dish and top each with the sauce. Cook uncovered for 5 minutes on LOW. Garnish with the French/green beans.

Liver and Tomato Slaw

PREPARATION TIME: 15 minutes

MICROWAVE COOKING TIME: 14 minutes plus heating browning dish

SERVES: 4 people

TOTAL CALORIES: 1230

285g/10oz white cabbage, finely
    shredded
1 small onion, peeled and finely chopped
1 carrot, peeled and grated
60ml/4 tbsps/¼ cup natural low fat
    yogurt
15ml/1 tbsp horseradish sauce
15ml/1 tbsp low calorie mayonnaise/
    salad dressing
15ml/1 tbsp finely chopped parsley
15ml/1 tbsp vegetable oil

450g/1lb lambs liver, trimmed and sliced
Salt
Freshly ground black pepper
8 tomatoes, sliced
5ml/1 tsp gravy powder

Mix the cabbage, onion and carrot in a large bowl. Combine the yogurt, sauces and parsley in a smaller bowl. Season the liver with salt and pepper. Preheat a large browning dish to maximum, add the oil and quickly brown half of the liver slices on both sides. Remove them from the browning dish and set aside. Reheat the browning dish for 2 minutes on HIGH, then brown the remaining liver slices. Layer the liver slices and tomatoes in the browning dish or a suitable casserole, finishing with a layer of tomato. Sprinkle with the gravy powder. Cover and cook for 8-10 minutes on HIGH until the liver is just cooked. Cover and leave to stand for 5 minutes. Meanwhile cook the vegetables uncovered for 4 minutes on HIGH, stirring once. Stir the sauce into the warm vegetables and serve with the liver.

Chicken Escalopes in Paprika Sauce

PREPARATION TIME: 20 minutes

MICROWAVE COOKING TIME: 16-18 minutes plus standing time

SERVES: 4 people

TOTAL CALORIES: 876

15g/½ oz/1 tbsp butter
1 small green pepper, cored, seeded and
    diced
1 small onion, peeled and finely chopped/
    minced
1 garlic clove, peeled and crushed
7.5ml/1½ tsp mild paprika
15g/1 tbsp all-purpose/plain flour
140ml/¼ pint/⅔ cup dry white wine
140ml/¼ pint/⅔ cup hot chicken stock
2 tomatoes, skinned and chopped
Salt
Freshly ground black pepper
4 120g/4oz boneless chicken breasts,
    skinned

Put the butter in a medium bowl and

add the pepper, onion and garlic. Cover and cook for 4-5 minutes on HIGH, stirring occasionally, until the vegetables are tender. Stir in the paprika and flour, and cook uncovered for 1 minute on HIGH. Stir in the wine, stock and tomatoes and season to taste with salt and pepper. Cook uncovered for 4 minutes on HIGH until the mixture thickens, stirring occasionally during cooking. Cover tightly and set aside. Arrange the chicken in a shallow dish, cover and cook for 3 minutes on HIGH. Reposition and turn the pieces over, then cover and cook for 2-3 minutes on HIGH until the chicken is cooked. Leave for 1 minute, then uncover and transfer the chicken to a hot serving dish. Pour the sauce over, cover and cook for 2 minutes on HIGH until the sauce is hot.

Tropical Lamb Kebabs

PREPARATION TIME: 20 minutes plus standing time

MICROWAVE COOKING TIME: 18-20 minutes

SERVES: 4 people

TOTAL CALORIES: 920

450g/1lb lean leg of lamb, cut into
    2½ cm/1 inch cubes
2.5ml/½ tsp meat tenderising powder
3 thick slices fresh pineapple, each cut
    into 3 wedges
Salt
1.25ml/¼ tsp ground cumin
1.25ml/¼ tsp turmeric
15ml/1 tbsp black treacle/molasses
1 small onion, peeled and sliced into thick
    rings
¼ head Chinese leaves, shredded
Alfalfa to garnish

Sprinkle the lamb with meat tenderising powder and set aside in a cool place for 1 hour. Thread the

Facing page: Lamb Chops with Currant Sauce (top left) and Liver and Tomato Slaw (top right and bottom).

meat cubes and pineapple wedges alternately onto twelve cocktail sticks. Season with salt and sprinkle with cumin and turmeric. Put the treacle/molasses into a shallow dish and heat uncovered for 20 seconds on HIGH. Carefully place kebabs in the dish, turning them in the molasses mixture until they are well coated. Cook uncovered for 15-20 minutes on LOW until the lamb is just cooked. Serve on a bed of onion and Chinese leaves. Garnish with alfalfa.

Kidneys in Creamy Wine Sauce

PREPARATION TIME: 15 minutes

MICROWAVE COOKING TIME: 12 minutes

SERVES 4 people

TOTAL CALORIES: 540

450g/1lb/8 lambs kidneys, skinned
1 medium onion, peeled and very finely
*   chopped*
1 small garlic clove, peeled and crushed
*   with 2 5ml/½ tsp salt*
30ml/2 tbsp medium red wine
10ml/2 tsp French/Dijon mustard
Shake Tabasco (optional)
Freshly ground black pepper
60ml/4 tbsp/¼ cup low fat skimmed
*   milk soft cheese (Quark)*

Quarter the kidneys, removing the core with scissors. Set aside. Mix the onion, garlic and wine together in a casserole dish, cover and cook for 3 minutes on HIGH. Stir in the mustard, Tabasco and pepper to taste, then stir in the kidneys. Cover and cook for 3 minutes on HIGH. Stir and cook for a further 2 minutes on HIGH until the kidneys are just pink inside. Stir in the cheese (Quark) and cook uncovered for 4 minutes on LOW, stirring once during cooking.

This page: Chicken Escalopes in Paprika Sauce. Facing page: Tropical Lamb Kebabs (top) and Kidneys in Creamy Wine Sauce (bottom).

Fillet Steak au Poivre

PREPARATION TIME: 5 minutes

MICROWAVE COOKING TIME:
4-6 minutes plus heating browning dish

SERVES: 4 people

TOTAL CALORIES: 1150

4 120g/4oz fillet steaks
15ml/1 tbsp brandy
15ml/1 tbsp vegetable oil
30ml/2 tbsp green peppercorns
60ml/4 tbsp/¼ cup soured cream

Salt
4 small tomatoes, halved and cooked

First brush the steaks with brandy and then with the oil. Crush the peppercorns with a rolling pin and press onto one side only of each steak. Preheat a large browning dish to maximum, then immediately press in the steaks, peppercorn side uppermost. Cook uncovered for 1 minute on HIGH. Turn steaks over and for medium rare, cook uncovered for a further 3 minutes on HIGH. (Shorten or lengthen the

This page: **Fillet Steak au Poivre.**
Facing page: **Aubergine/Eggplant Loaf (top) and Okra Alabama (bottom).**

cooking time according to preference.) Remove the steaks to a hot serving platter. Stir the cream into the juices remaining in the dish and add salt to taste. Spoon the cream over the steaks and serve immediately, accompanied by a green salad and tomato halves.

*Microwave*

LOW CALORIE

VEGETABLE DISHES

Okra Alabama

PREPARATION TIME: 10 minutes

MICROWAVE COOKING TIME: 16 minutes

SERVES: 4 people

TOTAL CALORIES: 120

450g/1lb okra
225g/8oz can chopped tomatoes
4 spring onions/scallions, peeled, trimmed
and finely sliced
Dash Worcestershire sauce
Dash Tabasco
Salt
Freshly ground black pepper
5ml/1 tsp cornstarch/cornflour
15ml/1 tbsp cold water

Wash, top and tail the okra, place in a casserole and add the tomatoes and their juice, the onions, sauces and seasoning to taste. Mix well, then cover and cook for 10 minutes on HIGH, stirring occasionally. Remove the lid and cook uncovered for a further 5 minutes on HIGH, stirring twice during cooking. Transfer the okra with a slotted spoon to a warm serving dish. Blend the cornstarch/cornflour and cold water together and stir into the cooking liquor. Cook uncovered for 1 minute on HIGH, stirring once during cooking until thickened. Pour the sauce over the okra and serve immediately.

Aubergine/Eggplant Loaf

PREPARATION TIME: 15 minutes

MICROWAVE COOKING TIME: 14-18 minutes

SERVES: 4 people

TOTAL CALORIES: 442

450g/1lb aubergine/eggplant
1 small onion, finely chopped/minced
Pinch salt
5ml/1 tsp oregano

1 egg
30ml/2 tbsp skimmed milk powder
75ml/5 tbsp/⅓ cup fresh breadcrumbs
2.5ml/½ tsp ground coriander
Freshly ground black pepper
15ml/1 tbsp grated Parmesan cheese

Rinse, dry, then peel and thinly slice the aubergine/eggplant. Place in a bowl with the onion, salt and oregano. Cover and cook for 6-8 minutes on HIGH until the aubergine/egg plant is soft. Stir the mixture occasionally during cooking. Transfer the mixture to the blender and add the egg, milk powder, 60ml/4 tbsp/¼ cup of the breadcrumbs, the coriander and pepper to taste. Process to mix coarsely, then put the mixture into a suitable loaf-shaped microwave dish. Cook uncovered for 8-10 minutes on LOW, then turn out on to a flameproof serving dish. Mix the Parmesan cheese with the remaining breadcrumbs, sprinkle over the top of the loaf, then brown under the grill/broiler.

Pancakes Provençale

PREPARATION TIME: 15 minutes plus cooking the pancakes

MICROWAVE COOKING TIME: 12-14 minutes

SERVES: 4 people

TOTAL CALORIES: 585

PANCAKE BATTER
2.5ml/½ tsp vegetable oil
50g/2oz/½ cup all-purpose/plain flour
Pinch salt
1 small egg
140ml/¼ pint/⅔ cup skimmed milk

2 medium green peppers, cored, seeded and diced
1 large red pepper, cored, seeded and diced

1 large onion, peeled and finely chopped/ minced
1 garlic clove, peeled and crushed
1 small courgette/zucchini, topped, tailed and diced
3 tomatoes, skinned and chopped
5ml/1 tsp chopped basil leaves
30ml/2 tbsp tomato purée/paste
30g/1oz/¼ cup grated Edam cheese
Salt
Freshly ground black pepper
Parsley sprigs to garnish

Use the oil to grease a 7 inch non-stick pan, then make up the batter and cook four pancakes in the usual way. Put the peppers, onion and garlic in a bowl, cover and cook for 5-6 minutes on HIGH. Add the courgette/zucchini, cover and cook for 5-6 minutes on HIGH until all the vegetables are soft. Stir in the tomatoes, basil, tomato purée/paste and cheese, cover and cook for 2 minutes on HIGH. Season to taste with salt and pepper. Divide the mixture between the pancakes, roll up, place on a suitable serving dish and reheat, uncovered, on HIGH for 1 minute Serve at once.

Cauliflower Parma

PREPARATION TIME: 10 minutes

MICROWAVE COOKING TIME: 12-13 minutes

SERVES: 4 people

TOTAL CALORIES: 344

15ml/1 tbsp flour
Salt
Freshly ground black pepper
1 small onion, peeled and cut into rings
15g/½ oz low calorie margarine
450g/1lb cauliflower florets
2 thin slices Parma ham, diced
2.5ml/½ tsp dried marjoram, soaked in 5ml/1 tsp cold water for 15 minutes before draining

Season the flour with salt and pepper, toss in the onion rings, then

**This page: Cauliflower Parma.
Facing page: Pancakes Provençale.**

shake off the surplus flour. Put the margarine in a casserole and cook for 20 seconds on HIGH until melted, then add the onion rings and cook uncovered for 4-5 minutes on HIGH, turning them over once until golden. Fill a 570-850ml/1-1½ pint/2½-3 cup basin with cauliflower florets, arranging them so that the cauliflower shape is reconstructed in the base. Cover and cook for 6 minutes on HIGH or until only just tender. Leave to stand covered. Stir the ham and drained marjoram into the onions, cover and cook for 1 minute on HIGH. Turn the cauliflower out on to a hot serving dish, reshaping the vegetables if necessary, and garnish with the ham and onion mixture.

Tomato Supper Ring

PREPARATION TIME: 10 minutes plus setting time

MICROWAVE COOKING TIME: 1 minute

SERVES: 6 people

TOTAL CALORIES: 340

430ml/¾ pint/2 cups tomato juice
15g/½ oz powdered gelatine
5ml/1 tsp fresh lemon juice
15ml/1 tbsp tomato purée/paste
Salt
Freshly ground black pepper
120g/4oz cooked mixed diced vegetables
120g/4oz cooked chicken, diced
Lettuce leaves and onion rings to garnish

Rinse a 570ml/1 pint/2½ cup ring mould with cold water and shake out the surplus. Put 75ml/5 tbsp/⅓ cup of tomato juice into a bowl and cook uncovered for 40 seconds on HIGH until hot but not boiling. Sprinkle gelatine over the surface and stir thoroughly. Cook uncovered for a further 20-30 seconds on HIGH, then stir briskly until dissolved. Whisk in the remaining tomato juice, the lemon juice and tomato purée. Season to taste with salt and pepper. Set aside in a cool place until just on the point of setting. Mix in the vegetables and chicken, then pour into the mould and leave in a cool

place until set. When ready to serve, arrange a salad of lettuce and onion rings on a suitable dish, dip the base of the mould in hot water, then turn out onto the salad.

Poached Fennel

PREPARATION TIME: 5 minutes

MICROWAVE COOKING TIME: 12 minutes plus standing time

SERVES: 4 people

TOTAL CALORIES: 124

2 large fennel bulbs
15ml/1 tbsp fresh lemon juice
60ml/4 tbsp water
5ml/1 tsp fennel seeds
5ml/1 tsp vegetable oil
Salt
Freshly ground black pepper

Wash the fennel, remove a slice from the bottom and discard the outside leaves if necessary. Cut each bulb into six or eight wedges. Combine the lemon juice, water, fennel seeds and oil in a casserole and season to taste with salt and pepper. Put in the fennel, cover with a lid and cook for 12 minutes on HIGH, repositioning the wedges once during cooking. Leave to stand for 3-4 minutes, then serve hot.

Hot Cucumber in Ginger Mint Sauce

PREPARATION TIME: 10 minutes

MICROWAVE COOKING TIME: 13-15 minutes

SERVES: 4 people

TOTAL CALORIES: 239

1 large cucumber
½ small onion, peeled and finely chopped/minced
15ml/1 tbsp vegetable oil
15g/½ oz/1 tbsp all-purpose/plain flour
140ml/¼ pint/⅔ cup home-made chicken or vegetable stock
Salt
Freshly ground black pepper
Few sprigs fresh ginger mint

Peel the cucumber, roughly chop and reserve the peel. Cut the cucumber into half lengthwise, then into 1cm/½ inch chunks and set aside. Combine the onion and oil in a bowl, cover and cook for 2 minutes on HIGH. Stir in the flour and stock, then cook for 2 minutes on HIGH, whisking once during and once after cooking. Season to taste with salt and pepper, stir in most of the mint, reserving some for garnish if desired and add the chopped cucumber peel. Cover and cook for 6-8 minutes on LOW, stirring once during cooking. Liquidise in the blender and adjust the seasoning if necessary. Put the cucumber chunks into a dish, cover and cook for 2 minutes on HIGH until only just tender. Mix in the sauce and cook uncovered for 1 minute on HIGH. Garnish with the reserved mint leaves if desired.

Artichokes Sauce Maigre

PREPARATION TIME: 10 minutes

MICROWAVE COOKING TIME: 30-31 minutes

SERVES: 4 people

TOTAL CALORIES: 95

4 well-rounded globe artichokes
140ml/¼ pint/⅔ cup hot water
5ml/1 tsp lemon juice

SAUCE
200g/7oz can tomatoes
2 spring onions/scallions, trimmed and finely sliced
1.25ml/¼ tsp bay leaf powder
Salt
Freshly ground black pepper
5ml/1 tsp cornstarch/cornflour

Remove tips from leaves and long stem from base of artichokes. Wash artichokes thoroughly. Combine water and lemon juice in a large, deep casserole and arrange the artichokes bottom ends towards the outside. Cover tightly and cook for

Facing page: Hot Cucumber in Ginger Mint Sauce (top) and Tomato Supper Ring (bottom).

Remove the tough ends from the asparagus, then pare or scrape the stalks. Arrange the asparagus in two layers in a rectangular casserole so that half the stalks point in one direction and the other half in another. Smaller spears should be placed in the centre. Pour in the stock, cover and cook for 9-14 minutes on HIGH until the tips are just tender (cooking time depends upon the size of the asparagus). While the asparagus is cooking mix the cream and lemon juice together, and season to taste with salt and pepper. Serve the asparagus well drained with a light dressing of the cream.

Yogurty Sweetcorn

PREPARATION TIME: 5 minutes	
MICROWAVE COOKING TIME: 8 minutes	
SERVES: 4 people	
TOTAL CALORIES: 380	

1 small onion, peeled and finely chopped/ minced
15ml/1 tbsp vegetable oil
225g/8oz/1½ cups frozen corn/ sweetcorn kernels
Salt
Freshly ground black pepper
60ml/2 fl oz/¼ cup natural low fat yogurt
5ml/1 tsp cornstarch/cornflour
Chopped chives to garnish

Mix the onion and oil together in a medium casserole, cover and cook for 3 minutes on HIGH. Stir in the sweetcorn and season to taste with salt and pepper. Cover and cook for 4 minutes on HIGH, stirring once during cooking. Blend together the yogurt and cornstarch/cornflour and stir into the sweetcorn. Cover and cook for 1 minute on HIGH. Stir and serve garnished with the chopped chives.

10 minutes on HIGH. Reposition artichokes, replace cover and cook for 10 minutes on HIGH or until a leaf pulls away easily. Leave to stand covered while preparing the sauce. Drain tomatoes, reserving the juice. Put the tomatoes and onions in a bowl, and cook uncovered for 8 minutes on HIGH, stirring occasionally. Add the bay leaf powder and salt and pepper to taste. Blend cornstarch/cornflour with the reserved juice, stir into the mixture and cook uncovered for 2-3 minutes on HIGH, stirring occasionally until the sauce thickens. Drain the artichokes and serve the sauce as a hot dip.

Fresh Asparagus with Soured Cream

PREPARATION TIME: 5-10 minutes	
MICROWAVE COOKING TIME: 9-14 minutes	
SERVES: 4 people	
TOTAL CALORIES: 220	

450g/1lb asparagus
140ml/¼ pint/⅔ cup well-flavoured chicken stock
60ml/4 tbsps/¼ cup soured cream
1.25ml/¼ tsp fresh lemon juice
Salt
Freshly ground black pepper

This page: Poached Fennel (top) and Persian Courgettes/Zucchini (bottom). Facing page: Fresh Asparagus with Soured Cream.

Persian Courgettes/ Zucchini

PREPARATION TIME: 5 minutes

MICROWAVE COOKING TIME:
4 minutes plus standing time

SERVES: 4 people

TOTAL CALORIES: 295

450g/1lb firm courgettes/zucchini
1.25ml/¼ tsp coriander
1.25ml/¼ tsp ground cardamom
1.25ml/¼ tsp salt
1.25ml/¼ tsp freshly ground black pepper
30g/1oz/⅙ cup seedless raisins
30g/1oz/¼ cup chopped cashew nuts

Rinse, top and tail the courgettes/ zucchini and cut them into 5cm/ 2 inch sticks. Mix the spices and seasoning together. Arrange layers of courgettes/zucchini in a small dish, sprinkling each layer with the spice mixture, the raisins and the nuts. Cover and cook for 4 minutes on HIGH, then leave to stand for 2 minutes. Stir just before serving.

Spinach and Pepper Casserole

PREPARATION TIME: 15 minutes

MICROWAVE COOKING TIME:
24-25 minutes

SERVES: 4 people

TOTAL CALORIES: 491

450g/1lb spinach, tough stalks removed
1 medium red pepper, cored, seeded and cut into thin strips
1 medium green pepper, cored, seeded and cut into thin strips
4 celery stalks, thinly sliced
2 medium onions, peeled and finely chopped/minced
30g/1oz/⅙ cup sultanas/golden raisins, chopped
1.25ml/¼ tsp sweet paprika
Generous pinch sugar
Pinch ground cinnamon
5ml/1 tsp salt
30ml/2 tbsp tomato purée/paste
10ml/2 tsp cornstarch/cornflour
30g/1oz/¼ cup grated Cheddar cheese
30ml/2 tbsp fresh breadcrumbs

Wash the spinach in plenty of cold water and shake off the excess water. Put the spinach in a roasting bag and seal loosely with an elastic band, leaving a gap for steam to escape. Put the bag upright in the microwave and cook for 5-6 minutes on HIGH. Drain, reserving the liquid. Put the peppers, celery and onion into a shallow casserole, cover tightly and cook for 15 minutes on HIGH, stirring several times during cooking. Stir in the spinach, cover and set aside. Mix together the sultanas/ raisins, paprika, sugar, cinnamon, salt, tomato purée, cornstarch/cornflour and reserved spinach liquor (approximately 10 tbsps) and cook for 2-3 minutes on HIGH, stirring occasionally until thickened. Stir into the vegetables, then cover and cook for 2 minutes on HIGH. Spoon into individual flame-proof dishes. Mix the cheese and breadcrumbs together, sprinkle over the vegetables and brown under the grill/broiler.

Austrian Red Cabbage

PREPARATION TIME: 10 minutes

MICROWAVE COOKING TIME:
15 minutes

SERVES: 4-6 people

TOTAL CALORIES: 276

450g/1lb red cabbage, thick stem removed
2 red dessert apples, cored
30g/1oz/⅙ cup raisins
140ml/¼ pint/⅔ cup salted water
15ml/1 tbsp fresh lemon juice
Freshly ground black pepper
Sweetener
15ml/1 tbsp soured cream

Finely shred the cabbage and put into a large casserole. Grate in the apple and add the raisins, salted water, lemon juice and a dash of pepper. Cover and cook for 15 minutes on HIGH or until the cabbage is just tender, stirring three times during cooking. Leave to stand covered for 5 minutes, then sweeten to taste. Swirl the soured cream on top just before serving.

Brussels Sprouts in Orange Juice

PREPARATION TIME: 5 minutes

MICROWAVE COOKING TIME:
8 minutes plus standing time

SERVES: 4 people

TOTAL CALORIES: 147

1 large orange
2.5ml/½ tsp salt
450g/1lb Brussels sprouts, fresh or frozen

Grate the orange zest and set aside. Squeeze the juice into a casserole and stir in the salt. Trim and rinse the fresh sprouts, then stir the vegetables into the orange juice. Cover and cook for 8 minutes on HIGH, until the sprouts are tender, stirring once during cooking. Leave covered for 5 minutes, then drain and serve sprinkled with the grated zest.

Carrot Ramekins

PREPARATION TIME: 10 minutes

MICROWAVE COOKING TIME:
17-20 minutes

SERVES: 4 people

TOTAL CALORIES: 459

120ml/8 tbsp water
Salt
285g/10oz carrots, peeled and finely sliced
280ml/½ pint/1¼ cups skimmed milk
3 eggs, at room temperature, beaten
1.25ml/¼ tsp mustard powder
Freshly ground black pepper

Put the water into a dish and add salt to taste. Stir in the carrots, then cover and cook for about 6 minutes on HIGH until soft. Drain and set aside. Meanwhile grease four individual ramekin dishes. Put the milk in a bowl and heat uncovered for 1-2 minutes on HIGH until warm. Beat in the eggs, mustard powder and

Facing page: Austrian Red Cabbage (top), Spinach and Pepper Casserole (centre) and Yogurty Sweetcorn (bottom).

season to taste with salt and pepper. Divide the carrots between the dishes, then pour in the milk mixture. Cover each ramekin with cling film/plastic wrap and arrange in a circle in the microwave. Cook for 10-12 minutes on LOW or until just set. Turn out if desired. Serve warm or cold.

Mushrooms in Tarragon Sauce

PREPARATION TIME: 5 minutes

MICROWAVE COOKING TIME: 7-8 minutes

SERVES: 4 people

TOTAL CALORIES: 324

450g/1lb button mushrooms, quartered
15ml/1 tbsp vegetable oil
15g/½ oz skimmed milk powder
30ml/2 tbsp all-purpose/plain flour
Salt
Freshly ground black pepper
1.25ml/¼ tsp dried tarragon
60ml/4 tbsp/¼ cup medium white wine
Fresh tarragon leaves to garnish

Put the mushrooms into a large bowl, add the oil and stir to coat them. Cover and cook for 5 minutes on HIGH, stirring occasionally. Remove the mushrooms with a slotted spoon and set aside. Whisk the milk powder and flour into the juices remaining in the bowl and season to taste with salt and pepper. Add the dried tarragon. Cook uncovered for 30 seconds on HIGH, then whisk in the wine and cook for a further 1-1½ minutes on HIGH, whisking frequently until thickened. Stir in the mushrooms and cook uncovered for 1 minute on HIGH, stirring once during cooking. Stir again before serving. Garnish with fresh tarragon leaves.

Chicken Stuffed Peppers

PREPARATION TIME: 20 minutes

MICROWAVE COOKING TIME: 19 minutes

SERVES: 4 people

TOTAL CALORIES: 532

4 180g/6oz green peppers
2 225g/8oz cans tomatoes
3 stalks celery, finely chopped/minced
1 small onion, peeled and finely chopped/minced
5ml/1 tsp chopped basil
Small clove garlic, peeled and crushed
225g/8oz cooked chicken, chopped
15ml/1 tbsp cornstarch/cornflour

Remove a slice from the top of each pepper. Discard the core and seeds. Chop and reserve the flesh from the pepper lids. Drain the tomatoes, reserving the juice. Mix the chopped peppers, celery, onion, basil,

This page: **Carrot Ramekins (top) and Chicken Stuffed Peppers (bottom). Facing page: Stuffed Crispy Potatoes (top) and Mushrooms in Tarragon Sauce (bottom).**

tomatoes and garlic together in a bowl, cover and cook for 7 minutes on HIGH, stirring occasionally until the vegetables are tender. Season to taste with salt and pepper, then mix in the chicken. Stuff the mixture into the peppers, then stand them in a shallow dish, cover and cook for 10 minutes on HIGH. Give each pepper a half turn halfway through

cooking. Transfer the peppers to a
serving plate and keep warm. Blend
the cornstarch/cornflour with the
reserved tomato juice and stir into
the juices remaining in the dish.
Cook uncovered for 2 minutes on
HIGH, stirring occasionally until
thickened. Serve the sauce with the
peppers.

Savoury Celery

| **PREPARATION TIME:** 15 minutes |
| **MICROWAVE COOKING TIME:** 14-15 minutes |
| **SERVES:** 4 people |
| **TOTAL CALORIES:** 250 plus approximately 100 for corn chips |

1 head/bunch celery, rinsed, trimmed and
*   cut into 2.5cm/1 inch lengths*
60ml/4 tbsps chicken stock
120g/4oz chicken livers, rinsed and
*   trimmed*
Salt
Freshly ground black pepper
15ml/1 tbsp all-purpose/plain flour
15g/½ oz corn chips, lightly crushed

Put the celery into a casserole with
the chicken stock. Cover and cook
for 12 minutes on HIGH or until the
celery is tender, stirring twice during
cooking. Meanwhile coarsely chop
the livers and season to taste with
salt and pepper. Mix in the flour, then
add the livers to the celery, stirring
thoroughly. Cover and cook for
2-3 minutes on HIGH or until the
liver is cooked. Garnish with crushed
corn chips.

Stuffed Crispy Potatoes

| **PREPARATION TIME:** 10 minutes |
| **MICROWAVE COOKING TIME:** 20-25 minutes |
| **SERVES:** 4 people |
| **TOTAL CALORIES:** 635 |

2 285g/10oz baking potatoes
15ml/1 tbsp vegetable oil
1 small green pepper, cored, seeded and
*   diced*
1 small onion, peeled and chopped

1 clove garlic, peeled and crushed
Pinch ground ginger
Pinch saffron powder
Salt
Freshly ground black pepper

Wash and dry the potatoes and prick
deeply with a fork. Place on paper
towels and cook uncovered for
5 minutes on HIGH. Reposition and
turn the potatoes over and continue
cooking for 5-6 minutes until soft.

**This page: Leeks Mimosa. Facing
page: Brussels Sprouts in Orange
Juice (top) and Savoury Celery
(bottom).**

Cut in half lengthwise and scoop out
the pulp. Mash lightly with a fork.
Arrange the potato skins in a shallow
dish and pour a little of the oil
around the insides. Brush the
remaining oil over the outside of the

skins. Cook uncovered for 4-6 minutes on HIGH until the skins are crispy, removing each skin as it is ready. Put the green pepper, onion, garlic, ginger and saffron in a small bowl and season to taste with salt and pepper. Cover tightly and cook for 3-4 minutes on HIGH until soft. Mix into the mashed potatoes, then pile the mixture into the potato skins. Reheat uncovered for 2-3 minutes until hot.

Leeks Mimosa

PREPARATION TIME: 10 minutes	
MICROWAVE COOKING TIME: 13-14 minutes	
SERVES: 4-6 people	
TOTAL CALORIES: 325	

280ml/½ pint/1¼ cups hot water
Salt
6 medium leeks (each weighing approximately 120g/4oz), washed and trimmed
10ml/2 tsp cornstarch/cornflour
15ml/1 tbsp cold water
60ml/4 tbsp skimmed milk soft cheese (Quark)
Freshly ground black pepper
1 hard boiled/hard cooked egg
5ml/1 tsp freshly chopped parsley

Pour the hot water into a shallow dish and add salt to taste. Cut the leeks so that there is an equal amount of white and green and put in the dish. Cover and cook for 12 minutes on HIGH until tender, repositioning the leeks once during cooking. Meanwhile blend the cornstarch/cornflour and cold water together in a jug, then separate the yolk and the egg white. Sieve the yolk and chop the white separately. When the leeks are tender, transfer them to a warm serving dish using a slotted spoon. Stir 140ml/¼ pint/⅔ cup of the liquid into the blended cornflour. Cook uncovered for 1-2 minutes on HIGH, stirring occasionally until thickened. Season the cheese with pepper and stir into the thickened juices. Spoon over the leeks and garnish with the egg white, yolk and parsley.

DESSERTS

Apple Snow

PREPARATION TIME:	15 minutes
MICROWAVE COOKING TIME:	5½-7 minutes
SERVES:	4 people
TOTAL CALORIES:	385

450g/1lb dessert apples, peeled, cored and
   sliced
5ml/1 tsp finely grated lemon zest
2 egg whites
30g/1oz/2 tbsp sugar
2 drops almond essence/extract
15g/½ oz flaked/slivered almonds

Put the apple and lemon zest in a
medium bowl, cover tightly and cook
for 4-5 minutes on HIGH until
pulpy. Purée in the blender. Beat the
egg whites until stiff and fold half the
mixture into the apple purée. Beat
the sugar and almond essence/extract
into the remaining beaten whites.
Half-fill four sundae dishes with the
purée and pile the mallow on top.
Arrange the dishes in a circle in the
microwave and cook uncovered for
1½-2 minutes on HIGH until the
mallow puffs up. Sprinkle with flaked
almonds and quickly brown at a
15cm/6 inch distance from a hot
grill/broiler.

Rhubarb, Orange and Strawberry Comfort

PREPARATION TIME:	5 minutes
MICROWAVE COOKING TIME:	10-12 minutes
SERVES:	4-6 people
TOTAL CALORIES:	202

450g/1lb canned rhubarb, cut into
   2.5cm/1 inch lengths
1.25ml/¼ tsp ground ginger
1 298g/10½ oz can mandarin orange
   segments in natural juice
Liquid sweetener
30ml/2 tbsp low fat natural yogurt
180g/6oz strawberries, halved and rinsed
30ml/2 tbsp crunchy muesli

**This page: Rhubarb, Orange and
Strawberry Comfort (top) and
Apple Snow (bottom). Facing page:
Hot Fruit Salad Cups.**

Put the rhubarb in a large bowl, add
the ground ginger and strain in the
juice from the mandarin oranges.
Cover and cook for 10-12 minutes on
HIGH, stirring twice during cooking

until the rhubarb is mushy. Mix in sweetener to taste. Stir in the yogurt and fold in the orange segments, cover and leave to cool. Reserve four strawberries for decoration and thinly slice the remainder. Mix the sliced strawberries into the rhubarb, then spoon the mixture into individual goblets. Just before serving, sprinkle with the muesli and top with a half or whole strawberry.

Tipsy Berries

PREPARATION TIME: 5 minutes

MICROWAVE COOKING TIME:
7 minutes plus chilling

SERVES: 4-6 people

TOTAL CALORIES: 408

30ml/2 tbsps sugar
225ml/8 fl oz/1 cup sweet red wine
30ml/2 tbsps tequila
Low calorie sweetener
450g/1lb raspberries
120g/4oz blackcurrants } *or use all*
120g/4oz redcurrants } *blackcurrants*

Mix the sugar and the wine in a medium bowl and cook uncovered for 2 minutes on HIGH. Stir until the sugar is dissolved. Cook uncovered for 5 minutes, then stir in the tequila and add liquid sweetener to taste. Trim and rinse the fruit and place in a serving bowl, then pour the syrup over. Chill thoroughly in the refrigerator, stirring occasionally.

Hot Fruit Salad Cups

PREPARATION TIME: 10 minutes

MICROWAVE COOKING TIME:
6½ minutes

SERVES: 4 people

TOTAL CALORIES: 457

2 large oranges
30g/1oz/2 tbsps sugar
5ml/1 tsp rum
1 small dessert apple
1 slice fresh or canned pineapple
1 banana
8g/¼ oz shelled pistachios, skinned and chopped

Halve the oranges and put in a shallow dish, cut side down. Cook uncovered for 2 minutes on HIGH until the juice can be easily squeezed. Gently squeeze the juice and scrape out most of the flesh. Set the shells aside. Stir the sugar into the juice and cook uncovered for 1-1½ minutes on HIGH until boiling. Stir, then cook uncovered for 2 minutes on HIGH. Add the rum. Core and cube the apple, cut the pineapple into wedges and peel and slice the banana, and mix all the fruit into the juice. Cook uncovered for 30 seconds on HIGH, then stir and cook for a further 30 seconds on HIGH. Spoon the fruit into the orange shells and pour the syrup over. Decorate with pistachio nuts.

Blackberry and Raspberry Jellies

PREPARATION TIME: 5 minutes

MICROWAVE COOKING TIME:
7 minutes plus setting time

SERVES: 4 people

TOTAL CALORIES: 290

225g/8oz fresh or frozen blackberries
225g/8oz fresh or frozen raspberries
Approximately 225ml/8 fl oz/1 cup fresh orange juice
30ml/2 tbsps cold water
10ml/2 tsp gelatine
Liquid sweetener
4 rosettes whipping cream

Put the blackberries in one bowl and the raspberries in another and cook each separately, uncovered, for 3 minutes on HIGH or until the juice runs freely. Strain the juices into a wide-necked jug and make up to 280ml/½ pint/1¼ cups with the orange juice. Put the water into a small dish or glass and cook for 30 seconds on HIGH until hot but not boiling. Sprinkle the gelatine over the surface and stir thoroughly. Cook for 20 seconds on HIGH, then stir until the gelatine is completely dissolved. Leave to cool for a few moments before pouring into the fruit juices. Stir in liquid sweetener to taste. Chill until just beginning to set. Divide the blackberries between four tall glasses and cover with the jelly. Refrigerate until set, then top up with the raspberries. Decorate each with a rosette of cream.

Home Made Yogurt

PREPARATION TIME: 5 minutes

MICROWAVE COOKING TIME:
12-13 minutes plus setting time

MAKES:
approximately 570ml/1 pint/2½ cups

TOTAL CALORIES: 262

430ml/¾ pint/2 cups skimmed milk
60ml/4 tbsps skimmed milk powder
60ml/4 tbsps low fat yogurt

Put the milk in a large bowl and cook uncovered for 2 minutes on HIGH. Stir and cook for a further 2-3 minutes on HIGH until the milk boils. Reduce the setting and cook uncovered for 8 minutes on DEFROST (35%), stirring occasionally until the milk is slightly reduced. Whisk in the milk powder and leave to cool until comfortable to the touch. Whisk in the yogurt, then pour into a wide-necked flask or divide between the glasses in a yogurt maker. Cover and leave for 8 hours until the yogurt is just set, then refrigerate covered for a further 3-4 hours.

Chocolate Creams

PREPARATION TIME: 5 minutes

MICROWAVE COOKING TIME:
5 minutes plus chilling time

SERVES: 4 people

TOTAL CALORIES: 568

30g/1oz/¼ cup cocoa powder, sifted
45g/1½ oz/⅓ cup custard powder
570ml/1 pint/2½ cups skimmed milk

Facing page: Home Made Yogurt (top) and Tipsy Berries (bottom).

Low calorie sweetener
1 milk coated chocolate digestive/
  Graham cracker, grated

Mix the cocoa and custard with a little of the cold milk in a medium bowl. Whisk in the remaining milk and cook uncovered for 5 minutes on HIGH, whisking frequently until thickened. Add sweetener to taste. Divide the cream between four individual moulds and leave to cool for 30 minutes, then cover with cling film/plastic wrap and refrigerate until cold. Remove the cling film/plastic wrap and decorate the tops of the creams with grated biscuit/cracker.

Coffee Soufflés

PREPARATION TIME: 20 minutes

MICROWAVE COOKING TIME: 40 seconds

SERVES: 4 people

TOTAL CALORIES: 795

140ml/¼ pint/½ cup double strength hot
  black coffee
15ml/1 tbsp powdered gelatine
2 eggs, separated
30ml/2 tbsp sugar
170ml/6 fl oz/¾ cup canned evaporated
  milk, well chilled
2.5ml/½ tsp vanilla essence/extract
1 small bar dairy flake chocolate, finely
  crushed
4 rosettes whipping cream

Cut four strips wax/greaseproof paper and attach to four individual ramekins with an elastic band, making sure that the collars protrude 2.5cm/1 inch above the rims. Put half the coffee in a medium jug and heat uncovered for 30 seconds on HIGH. Sprinkle on the gelatine and stir to dissolve. If necessary return to the microwave for a further 10 seconds. Beat the egg yolks and sugar until thick and mousse-like. Beat in the remaining coffee, then mix in the dissolved gelatine. In another bowl whisk the milk and vanilla essence/extract until very thick, then fold into the coffee mixture. Leave in a cool place until on the point of setting, then beat the egg whites until

stiff and fold into the mixture. Pour evenly into the prepared dishes and chill until set. With the aid of a round-bladed knife dipped into hot water, remove the paper collars. Decorate the soufflés with crushed flake and a cream rosette.

This page: Blackberry and Raspberry Jellies. Facing page: Chocolate Creams (top) and Apple and Cherry Sponge Cakes (bottom).

Beat the eggs, cream of tartar, sugar and vanilla essence/extract together until thick. Fold in the flour and the chopped apple. Divide the mixture between approximately fifteen double thickness paper cases and sprinkle the cherries over each. Arrange five at a time in a circle in the microwave and cook for 45 seconds to 1 minute on HIGH until the cakes are just dry on top. Do not overcook.

Baked Bananas Sauce au Poire

PREPARATION TIME: 15 minutes	
MICROWAVE COOKING TIME: 6 minutes	
SERVES: 4 people	
TOTAL CALORIES: 375	

1 large orange
2 ripe pears
Low calorie sweetener
4 small bananas

Pare thin strips of orange and shred finely. Put into a jug, cover with cold water and cook on FULL POWER for 2 minutes or until tender. Drain and set aside. Halve the orange and squeeze the juice of one half into a blender. Remove and chop the segments from the remaining half of orange and set aside. Peel, core and cut up the pears, and blend with the orange juice to a smooth purée, adding sweetener to taste. Peel the bananas and put into a small dish. Cook uncovered for 2 minutes on HIGH, then reposition the fruit, placing the two outside bananas into the middle. Pour the pear purée over the bananas and cook uncovered for 2 minutes on HIGH. Top with the chopped orange and decorate with the reserved shreds. Serve immediately.

Apple and Cherry Sponge Cakes

PREPARATION TIME: 15 minutes	
MICROWAVE COOKING TIME: 2-3 minutes	
MAKES: approximately 15	
TOTAL CALORIES: 590	

2 large eggs
Pinch cream of tartar
25g/1oz/2 tbsps sugar
2.5ml/½ tsp vanilla essence/extract
60g/2oz/½ cup all-purpose/plain flour, sifted
1 dessert apple, peeled, cored and finely chopped
30g/1oz/⅛ cup glacé/candied cherries, finely chopped

This page: Coffee Soufflés. Facing page: Baked Bananas Sauce au Poire.

Microwave
JAMS AND PRESERVES

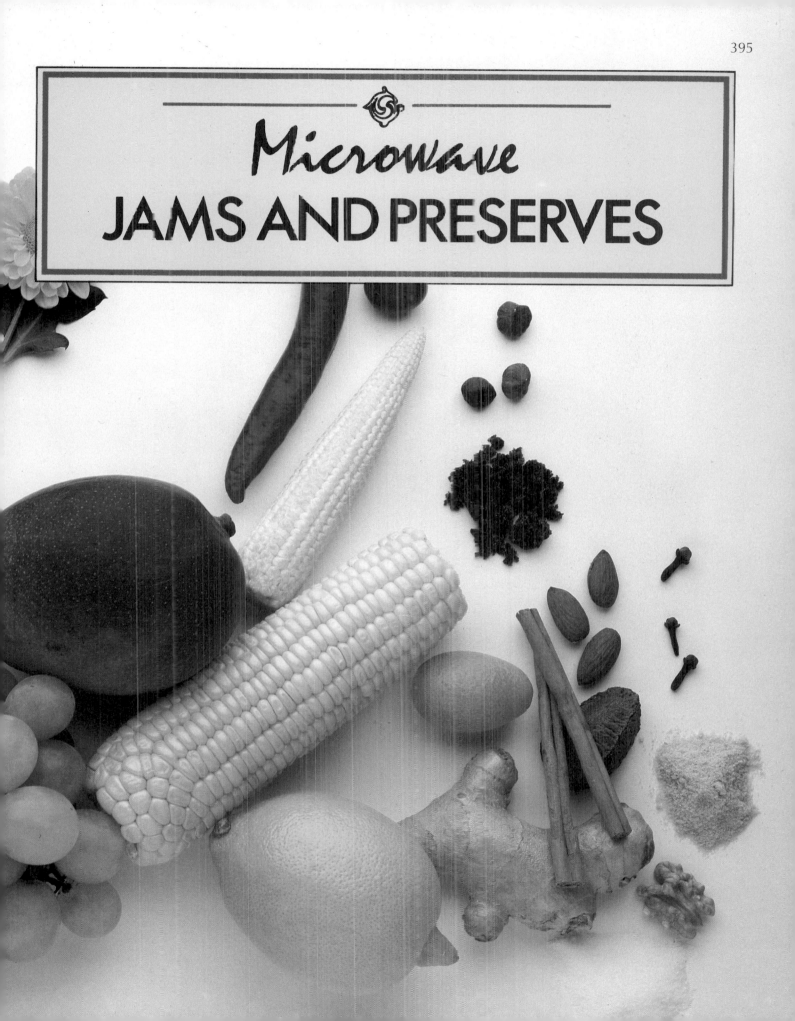

Microwave
JAMS AND PRESERVES

Preserving in a microwave oven brings an old-fashioned art up to date, enabling you to make smaller batches of jams, jellies and relishes than would be possible by conventional cooking. Preserves of all kinds are ready in a fraction of the time they take with ordinary methods and without all the stirring and constant attention.

The even distribution of energy in a microwave oven means that the food is heated from all sides, thus avoiding the problem of burned sugar on the bottom of the pan, which can spoil the taste of your preserves and make cleaning difficult.

Perfect jams and preserves can be made in the microwave using equipment as basic as the largest glass bowl that will fit in your oven, and a roll of plastic wrap. The usual type of preserving jar can be used and in the case of jams and jellies any attractive microwave-proof jar will do, with the top sealed with paraffin.

To sterilize jars, simply pour in 1 inch of water and heat for 2-3 minutes on the highest setting. Let the water boil for 1 minute and drain upside down on paper towels. Sterilize non-metallic lids and seals in a bowl of boiling water for 2-3 minutes on high. For long-term storage, jars can be sterilized in the conventional way.

To seal your preserves, follow the instructions for the particular kind of jar you choose. If using paraffin, melt it in the normal way as it is resistant to microwave energy. Pour jam or jelly into sterilized jars and allow it to set slightly. Carefully pour over a layer of melted paraffin and leave to solidify.

Like all good homemade things, microwave preserves have no additives to prolong their shelf life, and it is wise to store jars in the refrigerator after opening. Pickles, relishes and whole preserved fruit are best stored in the refrigerator as soon as they are bottled. Canning of fresh vegetables should never be attempted in a microwave oven since cooking times and sterilization procedures aren't adequate to prevent food poisoning.

Pectin plays an important role in successful jams and jellies. It is the clear, jelly-like substance found naturally in fruit that makes jams and jellies set. Apples, currants, plums and citrus fruits are high in pectin, while cherries, berries, rhubarb and tropical fruits like papayas are low. Our grandmothers and great grandmothers had to add chopped apple or lemon juice to fruit low in pectin in order to make jams set. Today, however, we can use the bottled or powdered pectin to set jams and jellies – even those made from fruit juice, wine or tea.

All recipes in this book were tested using an oven with a 700 watt maximum setting, although the suggested times should be taken as basic guidelines – experiment with your oven and make your own changes accordingly. Hopefully, these recipes will encourage you to become adventurous: to produce your own creations or adapt old favourites. Even grandma would approve of that!

Quantities of ingredients in each recipe are given in metric, imperial and U.S. measures, and it should be noted that these are not interchangeable.

PRESERVES, JAMS AND SPREADS

Ginger Pear Jam

PREPARATION TIME: 15 minutes

MICROWAVE COOKING TIME:
35-38 minutes

MAKES:
Approximately 900g/2lbs/4 cups

900g/2lbs/firm pears
450g/1lb/2 cups sugar
45g/1½ oz/¼ cup grated fresh ginger root
1 lemon

Peel and core the pears, and cut them into thick slices. Keep the peels and cores. Peel the lemon and scrape off any white pith remaining on the peel. Squeeze the lemons and mix the juice with the pears in a large bowl. Add the ginger root. Cut the lemon peel into short, thin strips and add to the pears. Tie up the peels and cores of the pears, and the pith and seeds of the lemons in cheesecloth. Put the cheesecloth bag into the bowl with the pears, and cover with pierced plastic wrap. Cook for 15 minutes on HIGH, stirring frequently. Add the sugar and cook uncovered for a further 20 minutes on HIGH or until thickened. Stir frequently. Test by stirring with a wooden spoon. If the spoon leaves a channel, setting point has been reached. If not, cook for a further 2-3 minutes on HIGH. Pour into hot, sterilized jars. Seal and cover.

This page: Ginger Pear Jam (top) and Strawberry and Banana Jam (bottom).
Facing page: Three-Fruit Marmalade (top) and Orange and Grapefruit Marmalade with Whiskey (bottom).

Apple and Calvados Jam

PREPARATION TIME: 15 minutes

MICROWAVE COOKING TIME:
30-33 minutes

MAKES:
Approximately 900g/2lbs/4 cups

900g/2lbs apples
Juice and grated rind of 1 lemon
140ml/¼ pint/½ cup water
140ml/¼ pint/½ cup Calvados
900g/2lbs/4 cups sugar

Peel and core the apples and cut lengthwise into thick slices. Put into a large bowl with the water, lemon juice and rind, and cover with pierced plastic wrap. Cook for 15 minutes on HIGH, stirring occasionally. Stir in the sugar. Cook, uncovered, for a further 15 minutes on HIGH. Put a spoonful of the syrup onto a cold plate. If it forms a skin and the syrup wrinkles when the plate is tilted, setting point has been reached. If not, cook for another 2-3 minutes on HIGH. Add the Calvados. Pour into hot, sterilized jars. Seal and cover.

Orange and Grapefruit Marmalade with Whiskey

PREPARATION TIME: 15 minutes

MICROWAVE COOKING TIME:
40-43 minutes, and 30 minutes standing time

MAKES:
Approximately 450g/1lb/2 cups

2 oranges
2 small grapefruit
450g/1lb/2 cups brown sugar
425ml/14 fl oz/1¾ cups water
60ml/4 tbsps/¼ cup Bourbon or Scotch
30g/1oz/1 tbsp butter (if necessary)

Peel the fruit and scrape some of the white pith off the peel. Cut the peel into shreds and squeeze the juice. Put the remaining pith and seeds into cheesecloth, and tie. Put the juice, peel and cheesecloth bag into a large bowl. Boil the water for 3-4 minutes on HIGH and add 120ml/¼ pint/

½ cup water to the bowl. Stir the ingredients and leave for 30 minutes. Add remaining water, cover with pierced plastic wrap, and cook for 20 minutes on HIGH. Uncover, and squeeze the juice from the cheesecloth bag. Stir in the sugar and cook uncovered for another 20 minutes on HIGH, stirring every 5 minutes. The marmalade should boil rapidly. Test by putting a spoonful onto a cold plate. Leave for 2-3 minutes and if a skin forms and the marmalade wrinkles when the plate is tilted, setting point has been reached. If the marmalade is still too liquid, cook for a further 2-3 minutes on HIGH. Stir in the whiskey. If the marmalade is bubbly and cloudy, 30g/1oz/1 tbsp butter stirred through the hot mixture will help to clear it. Pour into hot, sterilized jars, seal and cover.

Plum Nuts Jam

PREPARATION TIME: 15-20 minutes

MICROWAVE COOKING TIME:
30-33 minutes

MAKES:
Approximately 900g/2lbs/4 cups

900g/2lbs plums
900g/2lbs/2 cups sugar
30ml/2 tbsps lemon juice
180g/6oz/1 cup roasted hazelnuts, chopped

Put the plums into a large bowl with the lemon juice. Cover with pierced platic wrap and cook for 10 minutes on HIGH, stirring occasionally. Leave to cool slightly and remove the stones from the plums. Stir in the sugar and nuts. Cook uncovered for 20 minutes, stirring every 5 minutes. Test the jam by stirring with a wooden spoon. If it leaves a channel, the setting point has been reached. If not, cook for a further 2-3 minutes on HIGH. Pour into hot, sterilized jars. Seal and cover.

Plum Nuts Jam (above right) and Apple and Calvados Jam (far right).

Black Raspberry and Apple Preserves

PREPARATION TIME: 15 minutes

MICROWAVE COOKING TIME:
22-25 minutes plus 30 minutes standing time

MAKES:
Approximately 450g/1lb/2 cups

275g/9oz/1½ cups black raspberries, washed
225g/½lb apples, peeled, cored and chopped
90ml/5 tbsps/⅓ cup water
500g/1lb/2 cups sugar

Put the fruit into a large bowl with the water. Cover the bowl with pierced plastic wrap and cook for 7 minutes on HIGH. Give the jam ½ hour's standing time. Stir in the sugar and cook uncovered for 15 minutes on HIGH. Test the jam by stirring with a wooden spoon. If the spoon leaves a channel, the setting point has been reached. If not, cook for a further 2-3 minutes on HIGH. Pour into hot, sterilized jars. Seal and cover.

Blueberry Jam with Cassis

PREPARATION TIME: 10 minutes

MICROWAVE COOKING TIME:
18-20 minutes

MAKES:
Approximately 900g/2lbs/4 cups

900g/2lbs/4 cups blueberries
60ml/4 tbsps water
180g/6oz/¾ cup sugar to every 240g/½ pint/1 cup fruit juice
30ml/2 tbsps lemon juice
90ml/5 tbsps/⅓ cup pectin
60ml/4 tbsps/¼ cup crème de cassis (blackcurrant liqueur)

Put the blueberries, lemon juice and water into a large bowl and cook, covered with pierced plastic wrap, for 3 minutes on HIGH. Stir occasionally. Measure the fruit juice and add the sugar. Cook, uncovered, for 10 minutes on HIGH. Stir once after 5 minutes, and add the pectin

during the last 2 minutes of cooking time. Test by stirring with a wooden spoon. If the spoon leaves a channel in the jam, then setting point has been reached. If the jam is still liquid, cook for a further 2 minutes on HIGH. Stir in the cassis and pour into hot, sterilized jars. Seal and cover.

Strawberry and Banana Jam

PREPARATION TIME: 10 minutes

MICROWAVE COOKING TIME:
15-18 minutes

MAKES:
Approximately 900g/2lbs/4 cups

This page: Black Raspberry and Apple Preserves.
Facing page: Blueberry Jam with Cassis.

500g/1lb 2oz/3 cups strawberries, washed and sliced
3 bananas, peeled and cut into chunks
15ml/1 tbsp lemon juice
675g/1½lbs/3 cups sugar
90ml/5 tbsps/⅓ cup pectin

Put the strawberries and bananas into a large bowl and stir in the lemon juice. Cover the bowl with pierced plastic wrap and cook for 15 minutes on HIGH. Add the sugar and cook uncovered for a further 15 minutes

on HIGH, stirring every 3 minutes. Add the pectin during the final 3 minutes. Stir with a wooden spoon, and if the spoon leaves a channel, then setting point has been reached. If the jam is still liquid, cook for a further 2-3 minutes on HIGH. Pour into hot, sterilized jars. Seal and cover.

Lemon Lime Curd

PREPARATION TIME: 10 minutes

MICROWAVE COOKING TIME: 17-19 minutes

MAKES: Approximately 675g/1½lbs/3 cups

Grated rind and juice of 2 lemons
Grated rind and juice of 1 lime
225g/8oz/1 cup sugar
40g/1½ oz/⅓ cup sweet butter
3 eggs, beaten

Put the rind and juice into a large bowl with the butter and cook uncovered for 3 minutes on HIGH until the butter melts. Add the sugar and stir in well. Cook for 2 minutes on HIGH. Stir again to help dissolve the sugar and strain on the eggs, Stir well to blend thoroughly. Cook uncovered for 12-14 minutes on LOW, stirring every 2 minutes. Do not allow the mixture to boil. Keep a bowl of iced water on hand in case the mixture curdles. If it does, put it immediately in the iced water to stop the cooking. The curd is cooked when it coats the back of a spoon. Put into dry jars, and cover. Best stored in the refrigerator.

Chocolate, Orange and Hazelnut Spread

PREPARATION TIME: 10 minutes

MICROWAVE COOKING TIME: 8-10 minutes

MAKES: Approximately 225g/½lb/1 cup

60g/2oz/½ cup unsweetened cocoa
30g/1oz/¼ cup butter
60g/2oz/¼ cup sugar

Juice and rind of half an orange
1 egg, beaten
15ml/1 tbsp evaporated milk
125g/4oz/½ cup ground hazelnuts

Put the butter and sugar into a deep bowl and cook for 2 minutes on HIGH. Add the orange rind and juice, cocoa and evaporated milk, and stir well. Strain on the egg and heat well to blend thoroughly. Cook uncovered for 4 minutes on LOW, stirring once. Stir in the hazelnuts and cook for 2 minutes on HIGH. Do not allow to boil rapidly. Have a bowl of iced water ready. If the mixture curdles, put it into the iced water to stop the cooking. Leave to cool, then pour into a dry jar. Store in the refrigerator.

Three-Fruit Marmalade

PREPARATION TIME: 15 minutes

MICROWAVE COOKING TIME: 40-43 minutes, and 30 minutes standing time

MAKES: Approximately 450g/1lb/2 cups

2 limes
2 tangerines
2 lemons
500ml/1 pint/2 cups water
450g/1lb/2 cups sugar
30g/1oz/1 tbsp butter (if necessary)

Peel the fruit and scrape some of the white pith off the peel. Cut the peel into shreds and squeeze the juice. Put the remaining pith and seeds into cheesecloth, and tie. Put the juice, peel and cheesecloth bag into a large bowl. Boil in the water for 3-4 minutes on HIGH. Add 120ml/ ¼ pint/½ cup water to the bowl, stir the ingredients, and leave for half an hour. Add remaining water, cover with pierced plastic wrap and cook for 20 minutes on HIGH. Uncover and squeeze the juice out of the cheesecloth bag. Stir in the sugar and cook uncovered for another 20 minutes on HIGH, stirring every 5 minutes. The marmalade should come to a rapid boil. Test by putting a spoonful onto a cold plate. Leave

for 2-3 minutes, and if the marmalade forms a skin and wrinkles when the plate is tilted, setting point has been reached. If it is still too liquid, cook for a further 2-3 minutes. If it looks bubbly and cloudy, 30g/1oz/1 tbsp of butter stirred through the hot mixture will help to clear it. Pour into hot, sterilized jars. Seal and cover.

Rhubarb and Raspberry Jam

PREPARATION TIME: 10 minutes

MICROWAVE COOKING TIME: 13-15 minutes

MAKES: Approximately 900g/2lbs/4 cups

340g/12oz/2 cups rhubarb, cut in small pieces
340g/12oz/2 cups red raspberries
900g/2lbs/4 cups sugar
45ml/3 tbsps lemon juice
60ml/4 tbsps/¼ cup pectin for every 500ml/1 pint/2 cups cooked fruit

Put the rhubarb into a large bowl and cover with pierced plastic wrap. Cook for 2 minutes on HIGH and add the raspberries. Re-cover the bowl and cook for 1 minute on HIGH. Add the sugar and lemon juice, and stir well. Cook uncovered for 10 minutes on HIGH, stirring frequently. Measure the fruit and juice and add the necessary pectin, stirring well to mix. Cook for a further 1 minute on HIGH. Test the jam by stirring with a wooden spoon. If it leaves a channel, the setting point has been reached. If not, cook for a further 2-3 minutes on HIGH. Pour into hot, sterilized jars. Seal and cover.

Facing page: Lemon Lime Curd (top) and Chocolate, Orange and Hazelnut Spread (bottom).

with a wooden spoon. If the spoon leaves a channel, the setting point has been reached. If not, cook for a further 2-3 minutes on HIGH. Pour into hot, sterilized jars. Seal and cover.

Apricot Jam

PREPARATION TIME: 10 minutes

MICROWAVE COOKING TIME: 25-28 minutes

MAKES: Approximately 900g/2lbs/4 cups

675g/1½lbs/4 cups sliced apricots
800g/1¾lbs/3½ cups sugar
30ml/2 tbsps water
15ml/1 tbsp lemon juice
2 whole cloves

Put the apricots, water, lemon juice and cloves into a large bowl. Cook, covered with pierced plastic wrap, for 10 minutes on HIGH, stirring frequently. Remove the cloves and add the sugar, stirring well. Cook for 15 minutes on HIGH, stirring every 5 minutes. Put a spoonful of the jam onto a cold plate. If a skin forms and the jam wrinkles when the plate is tilted, setting point has been reached. If the jam is still liquid, cook for a further 2-3 minutes on HIGH. Pour into hot, sterilized jars. Seal and cover.

Pineapple and Coconut Jam

PREPARATION TIME: 10-15 minutes

MICROWAVE COOKING TIME: 15-18 minutes

MAKES: Approximately 900g/2lbs/4 cups

675g/1½lbs/4 cups crushed canned pineapple, drained
15ml/1 tbsp lemon juice
60ml/4 tbsps/¼ cup bottled pectin
180g/6oz/1 cup shredded coconut, fresh or packaged
450g/1lb/2 cups sugar

Put the pineapple into a large bowl. Add the lemon juice and, if using

Quince and Cardamom Preserves

PREPARATION TIME: 15 minutes

MICROWAVE COOKING TIME: 30-33 minutes

MAKES: Approximately 900g/2lbs/4 cups

900g/2lbs quinces
225g/8oz/1 cup sugar for every 240ml/ ½ pint/1 cup liquid and fruit
240ml/½ pint/1 cup water
1 orange, sliced thinly
30ml/2 tbsps cardamom pods

This page: Pineapple and Coconut Jam (top) and Rhubarb and Raspberry Jam (bottom). Facing page: Apricot Jam (top) and Quince and Cardamom Preserves (bottom).

Peel and slice the quinces. Put the peels, half the sliced orange and water into a large bowl and cook for 10 minutes on HIGH. Measure the jam, and stir in the sugar. Crush the cardamom pods and add only the seeds to the juice and sugar. Stir in the sliced quinces and the remaining orange slices, and cook uncovered on HIGH for 20 minutes, stirring every 5 minutes. Test the jam by stirring

fresh pineapple, 120ml/¼ pint/½ cup water. Cover the bowl with pierced plastic wrap and cook for 5 minutes on HIGH. Add the sugar, pectin and coconut. Cook uncovered for 10 minutes on HIGH. Stir with a wooden spoon, and if the spoon leaves a channel in the jam, then setting point has been reached. If the jam is still liquid, cook for a further 2-3 minutes on HIGH. Pour into hot, sterilized jars. Seal and cover.

Paradise Jam

PREPARATION TIME: 20 minutes

MICROWAVE COOKING TIME:
21-23 minutes

MAKES:
Approximately 900g/2lbs/4 cups

1 large papaya
2 passion fruit
1 guava
180g/6oz/1 cup crushed pineapple
800g/1¾lbs/2 cups sugar
140ml/¼ pint/½ cup water
60ml/4 tbsps/¼ cup liquid pectin
15ml/1 tbsp lime juice

Peel and chop the papaya finely. Cut the passion fruit in half and scoop out the pulp and seeds. Add to the papaya. Peel and chop the guava. Put the fruit, lime juice and water into a large bowl. Cover with pierced plastic wrap and cook for 10 minutes on HIGH, stirring frequently. Stir in the sugar and cook uncovered for another 10 minutes on HIGH. Add the pectin and cook for 1 minute on HIGH. To test the jam, stir with a wooden spoon. If the spoon leaves a channel, the setting point has been reached. If not, cook for 2-3 minutes on HIGH. Pour into hot, sterilized jars. Seal and cover.

Kiwi Fruit and Apple Honey

PREPARATION TIME: 10 minutes

MICROWAVE COOKING TIME:
15-18 minutes

MAKES:
Approximately 450g/1lb/2 cups

4 kiwi fruit
2 apples, peeled, cored and chopped
5ml/1 tsp lemon juice
120ml/¼ pint/½ cup water
450g/1lb/2 cups sugar
450g/1lb/2 cups honey
Green food coloring (optional)

This page: Paradise Jam.
Facing page: Kiwi Fruit and Apple Honey.

Peel and chop the kiwi fruit. Heat the sugar, honey and water in a large bowl for 5 minutes on HIGH, to melt the sugar. Add the kiwi fruit, apple and lemon juice, and cook uncovered for

minutes on HIGH, stirring frequently until thick and creamy. Cook for an additional 2-3 minutes on HIGH if necessary. Work in a food processor to make a smooth purée. Add food coloring if desired. Put in hot, sterilized jars. Seal and cover.

Brandy Peach Jam

PREPARATION TIME: 15 minutes

MICROWAVE COOKING TIME: 30-33 minutes

MAKES:
Approximately 900g/2lbs/4 cups

675g/1½lbs/4 cups peaches, peeled and sliced
800g/1¾lbs/3 cups sugar
15ml/1 tbsp water
15ml/1 tbsp lemon juice
Half a cinnamon stick
60ml/4 tbsps/¼ cup brandy

Put the sugar, water, lemon juice and cinnamon into a large bowl. Cook for 10 minutes on HIGH, stirring frequently. Put the peaches into

This page: Whole Strawberry Preserves with Grand Marnier. Facing page: Brandy Peach Jam (top) and Autumn Jam (bottom).

boiling water for 1-2 minutes to loosen the skin. Cut in half, remove the stones and cut into thick slices. Add the peaches to the hot syrup and cook uncovered for 20 minutes on HIGH stirring every 5 minutes. Put a spoonful of the syrup onto a cold plate. If a skin forms and the syrup wrinkles when the plate is

tilted, setting point has been reached. If the syrup is still liquid, cook for a further 2-3 minutes on HIGH. Add the brandy and pour into hot, sterilized jars. Seal and cover.

Rose Petal and Cherry Preserves

PREPARATION TIME: 15 minutes

MICROWAVE COOKING TIME: 25-27 minutes

MAKES: Approximately 900g/2lbs/4 cups

675g/1½lbs/4 cups cherries
800g/1¾lbs/3½ cups sugar
Handful/1 cup rose petals, washed and dried
60ml/4 tbsps/¼ cup pectin
60ml/4 tbsps/¼ cup water
1.25ml/¼ tsp rose water

Wash, halve and stone the cherries. Put into a large bowl with the water. Cover with pierced plastic wrap and cook for 5 minutes on HIGH. Add the pectin during the last 5 minutes of cooking time. Stir in the sugar and rose water and cook, uncovered, for a further 20 minutes on HIGH. Test by stirring with a wooden spoon. If the spoon leaves a channel, then setting point has been reached. If not, cook a further 2-3 minutes on HIGH. Stir in the rose petals and pour into hot, sterilized jars. Seal and cover.

Whole Strawberry Preserves with Grand Marnier

PREPARATION TIME: 10 minutes

MICROWAVE COOKING TIME: 15 minutes

MAKES: Approximately 900g/2lbs/4 cups

900g/2lbs/4 cups strawberries
900g/2lbs/4 cups sugar
15ml/1 tbsp lemon juice
30ml/2 tbsps Grand Marnier

Hull the strawberries, using only firm, unblemished berries. Wash them and leave to dry. Toss the berries and sugar gently in a large bowl and leave until the juice begins to run. Cook uncovered for 5 minutes on HIGH or until the jam comes to a rapid boil. Stir occasionally, add the lemon juice, and continue cooking for 10 more minutes on HIGH, or until the syrup thickens. Put a spoonful of the syrup on a cold plate. Leave for 2-3 minutes. If the syrup forms a skin and the surface wrinkles when the plate is tilted, setting point has been reached. If the syrup is still liquid, cook for a further 2-3 minutes on HIGH. Stir in the Grand Marnier, but do not overstir or the berries will break. Pour into hot, sterilized jars. Seal and cover.

Autumn Jam

PREPARATION TIME: 15 minutes

MICROWAVE COOKING TIME: 35-38 minutes

MAKES: Approximately 900g/2lbs/4 cups

180g/6oz/1 cup apples, peeled, cored and chopped
180g/6oz/1 cup pears, peeled, cored and chopped
180g/6oz/1 cup plums, stoned and chopped
140ml/¼ pint/½ cup water
30ml/2 tbsps lemon juice
180g/6oz/¾ cup sugar for every 240ml/ ½ pint/1 cup of cooked fruit

Put the fruit into a large bowl with the water and lemon juice. Cover and cook for 10 minutes on HIGH, stirring occasionally. Measure the fruit, and add an equal amount of sugar. Cook uncovered for 25 minutes on HIGH. Test by stirring with a wooden spoon. If the spoon leaves a channel, setting point has been reached. If not, cook for a further 2-3 minutes on HIGH. Pour into hot, sterilized jars. Seal and cover.

Right: Rose Petal and Cherry Preserves.

Pineapple Grapefruit Marmalade

PREPARATION TIME: 15 minutes

MICROWAVE COOKING TIME:
44-46 minutes and 30 minutes standing time

MAKES:
Approximately 900g/2lbs/4 cups

1 fresh pineapple
1 grapefruit
500ml/1 pint/2 cups water
225g/8oz/1 cup sugar
15g/½ oz/1 tbsp butter (if necessary)

Peel and cut the pineapple into small pieces. Peel the grapefruit and scrape some of the white pith off the peel. Cut the peel into shreds. Squeeze the juice, and put the remaining pith and

This page: **Peach Butter with Bourbon (top) and Apple Butter (bottom).**
Facing page: **Pineapple Grapefruit Marmalade (top) and Plum Butter (bottom).**

seeds into cheesecloth, and tie. Put the juice, peel, cheesecloth bag and pineapple into a large bowl. Boil the water for 3-4 minutes on HIGH. Add 125ml/¼ pint/½ cup water to the

bowl, stir the ingredients, and leave for 30 minutes. Add the remaining water, cover with pierced plastic wrap, and cook for 20 minutes on HIGH. Uncover, and squeeze the juice out of the cheesecloth bag. Stir in the sugar. Cook uncovered for another 20 minutes, stirring every 5 minutes. Test by putting a spoonful of the marmalade onto a cold plate. If it forms a skin and wrinkles when the plate is tilted, setting point has been reached. If not, cook for a further 2-3 minutes on HIGH. If the mixture is bubbly and cloudy, 1 tbsp butter stirred through the hot marmalade will help to clear it. Pour into hot, sterilized jars. Seal and cover.

Plum Butter

PREPARATION TIME: 10 minutes

MICROWAVE COOKING TIME: 15-18 minutes

MAKES: Approximately 900g/2lbs/4 cups

900g/2lbs plums
225g/8oz/1 cup sugar
5ml/1 tsp ground ginger
60ml/4 tbsps/¼ cup water

Wash the plums, cut them in half and remove the stones. Put them, with the ginger and water, into a large bowl and cover with pierced plastic wrap. Cook for 10 minutes on HIGH, stirring frequently. Stir in the sugar, and cook uncovered for a further 5-8 minutes on HIGH. Put the contents of the bowl into a food processor and purée until smooth. Strain if necessary. The mixture should be thick and creamy. If it is not thick enough, put back into the bowl and cook for a further 2-3 minutes on HIGH. Pour into hot, sterilized jars. Seal and cover.

Cherry and Almond Preserves

PREPARATION TIME: 20 minutes

MICROWAVE COOKING TIME: 20-28 minutes

MAKES: Approximately 900g/2lbs/4 cups

675g/1½lbs/4 cups cherries
900g/2lbs/4 cups sugar
60ml/4 tbsps/¼ cup bottled pectin
60g/2oz/½ cup slivered almonds
140ml/¼ pint/½ cup water
1.25ml/¼ tsp almond extract

Wash, stem and stone the cherries. Put them in a large bowl with the water and almonds. Cover with pierced plastic wrap and cook for 5 minutes on HIGH. Stir in the sugar and almond extract, and cook for a further 15-20 minutes, uncovered, on HIGH. Add the pectin during the last 5 minutes of cooking. Test the preserves by stirring with a wooden spoon. If the spoon leaves a channel, then the setting point has been reached. If not, cook for a further 2-3 minutes on HIGH. Pour into hot, sterilized jars. Seal and cover.

Peach Butter with Bourbon

PREPARATION TIME: 15 minutes

MICROWAVE COOKING TIME: 17 minutes

MAKES: Approximately 900g/2lbs/4 cups

900g/2lbs peaches
225g/½ lb/1 cup honey
1.25ml/¼ tsp ground cloves
2.5ml/½ tsp ground nutmeg
30ml/2 tbsps water
30ml/2 tbsps Bourbon

Put the peaches into boiling water for 1-2 minutes to loosen the peel. Cut in half, remove the stones and chop the fruit into small pieces. Combine with all the other ingredients, except the Bourbon, in a large bowl. Cover with pierced plastic wrap and cook for 17 minutes on HIGH, stirring frequently. Add the Bourbon and pour the contents of the bowl into a food processor. Purée until smooth.

Cherry and Almond Preserves (right).

The mixture should be thick and creamy. If it is not thick enough, return to the bowl and cook for another 2-3 minutes on HIGH. Pour into hot, sterilized jars. Seal and cover.

Elderberry Jam

PREPARATION TIME: 10 minutes

MICROWAVE COOKING TIME:
20-28 minutes, and 10 minutes standing time.

MAKES:
Approximately 900g/2lbs/4 cups

*675g/1½lbs/4 cups elderberries
   (substitute raspberries, blackberries,
   gooseberries or loganberries, if desired)
675g/1½lbs/3 cups sugar
1 apple, peeled, cored and grated
15ml/1 tbsp lemon juice*

Wash the berries and put into a large bowl. Add the grated apple and lemon juice, and cover with pierced plastic wrap. Cook for 7-8 minutes on HIGH and leave to stand for 10 minutes, covered. Stir in the sugar and cook uncovered for 15-20 minutes on HIGH. Test by stirring with a wooden spoon. If it leaves a channel, the setting point has been reached. If not, cook for a further 2-3 minutes on HIGH. Pour into hot, sterilized jars. Seal and cover.

Grape Jam

PREPARATION TIME: 15 minutes

MICROWAVE COOKING TIME:
21 minutes

MAKES:
Approximately 900g/2lbs/4 cups

*675g/1½lbs/4 cups Concord grapes
900g/2lbs/4 cups sugar
30ml/2 tbsps water
30ml/2 tbsps lemon juice
60ml/4 tbsps/¼ cup pectin*

Cut the grapes in half and remove the seeds. Put them, the lemon juice and the water into a large bowl. Cover with pierced plastic wrap and cook for 10 minutes on HIGH, stirring frequently. Stir in the sugar

and cook uncovered on HIGH for another 10 minutes. Stir twice while cooking. Add the pectin and cook for 1 minute on HIGH. Pour into hot, sterilized jars. Seal and cover.

Apple Butter

PREPARATION TIME: 10 minutes

MICROWAVE COOKING TIME:
17-18 minutes

MAKES:
Approximately 900g/2lbs/4 cups

*900g/2lbs apples
225g/8oz/1 cup brown sugar*

*5ml/1 tsp ground cinnamon
60ml/4 tbsps water or apple juice*

Cut the apples in quarters, but do not peel or remove the stems and cores. Put into a large bowl with the cinnamon and apple juice. Cover with pierced plastic wrap and cook for 10 minutes on HIGH. Push the apple mixture through a strainer to extract all of the pulp. Discard the seeds and cores. Turn the apple mixture into a large bowl and stir in the sugar. Cook for a further 7-8 minutes on HIGH. The mixture should be thick and creamy. Pour into hot, sterilized jars. Seal and cover.

Microwave
JAMS AND PRESERVES

PRESERVED WHOLE FRUIT

Preserved Kumquats

PREPARATION TIME: 15 minutes

MICROWAVE COOKING TIME:
22 minutes

MAKES:
Approximately 675g/1½ lbs/3 cups

340g/12oz/2 cups whole kumquats
450g/1lb/2 cups sugar
350ml/¾ pint/1½ cups water
30ml/2 tbsps Cointreau

Cut a cross in the top of each kumquat. Put the sugar and water into 2 450g/1lb/2 cup jars and cook uncovered for 4 minutes on HIGH. Put the kumquats into the jars, cover with plastic wrap, and cook for 18 minutes on HIGH or until the kumquats look clear. Remove the plastic wrap and stir in the Cointreau. Seal and cover the jars.

Apples in Ginger Wine

PREPARATION TIME: 15 minutes

MICROWAVE COOKING TIME:
8 minutes

MAKES:
Approximately 900g/2lbs/4 cups

675g/1½lbs apples, peeled, cored and
  sliced (use a variety that holds its shape
  when cooked)
180ml/6 fl oz/¾ cup green ginger wine
180ml/6 fl oz/¾ cup water
675g/1½ lbs/3 cups sugar

Put the sugar, wine and water into 2 450g/1lb/2 cup preserving jars. Cook uncovered for 4 minutes on HIGH. Put the apples into the jars, cover the

jars with plastic wrap, and cook for 2 minutes on HIGH. Reduce the power to MEDIUM and cook for a further 2 minutes. Remove the plastic wrap, seal the jars, and then cover them.

Facing page: Grape Jam (top) and
Elderberry Jam (bottom).
This page: Preserved Kumquats
(top) and Apples in Ginger Wine
(bottom).

Cherries and Peaches in Kirsch

PREPARATION TIME: 20 minutes

MICROWAVE COOKING TIME:
14 minutes

MAKES:
Approximately 900g/2lbs/4 cups

450g/1lb peaches
225g/8oz/1¼ cups cherries
60g/2oz/½ cup whole blanched almonds
350ml/¾ pint/1½ cups water
675g/1½lbs/3 cups sugar
¼ cup kirsch

Put the peaches into boiling water for 1-2 minutes to loosen the skin. Peel, cut the peaches into quarters, and discard the stones. Take the stems off the cherries. Put the water and sugar into 2 450g/1lb/2 cup jars, and cook uncovered for 4 minutes on HIGH. Add the cherries, peaches and almonds, and cover each jar with plastic wrap. Cook for 5 minutes on HIGH, then reduce the power to MEDIUM and cook for a further 5 minutes. Remove the wrap and stir in the kirsch. Seal and cover the jars.

Brandied Apricots

PREPARATION TIME: 10 minutes

MICROWAVE COOKING TIME:
11 minutes

MAKES:
Approximately 900g/2lbs/4 cups

900g/2lbs apricots
675g/1½lbs/3 cups sugar
1 stick cinnamon
180ml/6 fl oz/¾ cup brandy
180ml/6 fl oz/¾ cup water

Put the sugar, brandy and water into 2 450g/1lb/2 cup jars. Put half the stick of cinnamon into each jar and cook uncovered for 4 minutes on HIGH. Wash the apricots. Put them into the jars and cover with plastic wrap. Cook for 2 minutes on HIGH. Reduce power to MEDIUM and cook for a further 5 minutes. Remove the wrap, and seal and cover the jars.

Spiced Orange Slices

PREPARATION TIME: 10 minutes

MICROWAVE COOKING TIME:
16 minutes

MAKES:
Approximately 675g/1½lbs/3 cups

3-4 oranges
340g/12oz/1½ cups sugar
240ml/½ pint/1 cup water
240ml/½ pint/1 cup white wine vinegar
1 cinnamon stick
2 whole all-spice berries
4 whole cloves

Slice the oranges into 5mm (¼") rounds, discard the ends and remove any seeds. Put the sugar, water, vinegar and whole spices into a bowl or 2 450g/1lb/2 cup jars. Cook uncovered for 6 minutes on HIGH. Put in the orange slices and cover with plastic wrap. Cook for 10 minutes on MEDIUM or until the orange rind looks clearer. Remove the plastic wrap, seal and cover.

Rum Fruit Compote

PREPARATION TIME: 20 minutes

MICROWAVE COOKING TIME:
20-23 minutes

MAKES:
Approximately 900g/2lbs/4 cups

500g/1lb 2oz/3 cups mixed fruits
(peaches, pears cherries, plums,
pineapple or apples)
450g/1lb/2 cups brown sugar
500ml/1 pint/2 cups water
240ml/½ pint/1 cup dark rum

Peel the apples and pears, cut into quarters and remove the cores. Put the peaches into boiling water for 2-3 seconds to loosen the skin, then cut into quarters and remove the stones. Cut the plums in half and

Right: Cherries and Peaches in Kirsch.

remove the stones. Peel the pineapple, cut it into quarters, remove the core and cut into 1.5cm (½") thick chunks. Wash the cherries and leave on the stems if desired. Put the sugar and water into a large bowl. Cook uncovered for 5 minutes on HIGH, stirring frequently. If using

apples or under-ripe pears, cook them first for 3 minutes on HIGH. Add all the other prepared fruit and stir well. Cover with pierced plastic wrap and cook for 15 minutes on MEDIUM, stirring carefully so that the fruit does not break up. If the fruit does not look translucent and is

This page: Rum Fruit Compote. Facing page: Brandied Apricots (top) and Spiced Orange Slices (bottom).

still very firm, cook for another 3 minutes on HIGH. Stir in the rum. Pour into hot, sterilized jars. Seal and cover. Keep in a cool place.

Plums in Port

PREPARATION TIME: 15 minutes

MICROWAVE COOKING TIME:
14 minutes

MAKES:
Approximately 900g/2lbs/4 cups

675g/1½lbs plums, halved and stoned

675g/1½lbs/3 cups sugar
350ml/¾ pint/1½ cups ruby port
2 whole cloves

Put the sugar and port into 2 450g/
1lb/2 cup jars, and put a clove into
each jar. Cook uncovered for 4
minutes on HIGH. Put in the plums,
cover with plastic wrap, and cook for
5 minutes on HIGH. Reduce the

This page: Plums in Port.
Facing page: Grapes in Alsace
Wine.

power to MEDIUM and cook for a
further 5 minutes. Remove the wrap.
Seal and cover the jars.

Microwave
JAMS AND PRESERVES

SWEET AND SAVOURY JELLIES

large bowl. Stir in the sugar and cover with pierced plastic wrap. Cook for 10 minutes on HIGH, stirring occasionally. Stir in the pectin and cook uncovered for 1 minute on HIGH, then add the grapes. Pour into hot, sterilized jars, seal and cover.

Apple and Thyme Jelly

PREPARATION TIME: 10 minutes

MICROWAVE COOKING TIME:
20-23 minutes

MAKES:
Approximately 450g/1lb/2 cups

350ml/¾ pint/1½ cups unsweetened clear apple juice
140ml/¼ pint ½ cup cider vinegar
550g/1lb 4oz/2½ cups sugar
90ml/5 tbsps/⅓ cup pectin
Small handful/¼ cup fresh thyme leaves
Green food coloring (optional)

Pour the apple juice and vinegar into a large bowl and stir in the sugar. Add the thyme, cover with pierced plastic wrap and cook for 10 minutes on HIGH. Stir in the pectin and cook for a further 10 minutes uncovered on HIGH. The jelly must boil rapidly. Test by putting a spoonful onto a cold plate. Leave for 2-3 minutes, and if a skin forms and the surface of the jelly wrinkles when the plate is tilted, setting point has been reached. If the jelly is still liquid, cook for a further 2-3 minutes on HIGH. Stir in the food coloring. Pour into hot, sterilized jars. Seal and cover.
Note: Other herbs, such as basil, rosemary, marjoram, sage, or a mixture of several different herbs, may be used.

Grapes in Alsace Wine

PREPARATION TIME: 10 minutes

MICROWAVE COOKING TIME:
25 minutes

MAKES:
Approximately 450g/1lb/2 cups

500ml/1 pint/2 cups white wine, such as

Gewürztraminer or Rhine
550g/1lb 4oz/2½ cups sugar
15ml/1 tbsp white wine vinegar
90ml/5 tbsps/⅓ cup bottled pectin
90g/3oz/½ cup seedless green grapes
90g/3oz/½ cup purple grapes, halved and seeded
Small bunch tarragon leaves

Pour the wine and vinegar into a

uncovered for 10 minutes on HIGH. The jelly should boil rapidly. Test by putting a spoonful onto a cold plate. Leave for 2-3 minutes. If a skin forms and the surface of the jelly wrinkles when the plate is tilted, setting point has been reached. If the jelly is still liquid, cook for a further 2-3 minutes on HIGH. Allow to cool slightly, and carefully stir in the flower petals. Pour into hot, sterilized jars. Seal and cover.

Paw-Paw (Papaya) Jelly

PREPARATION TIME: 10 minutes

MICROWAVE COOKING TIME:
25-28 minutes

MAKES:
Approximately 450g/1lb/2 cups

900g/2lbs/3 or 4 papayas
225g/8oz/1 cup sugar for every
*   250ml/½ pint/1 cup juice*
15ml/1 tbsp lemon juice
1 orange
250ml/½ pint/1 cup water
90ml/5 tbsps/⅓ cup pectin (if necessary)

Wash and cut the papayas into small pieces, discarding the seeds, and put into a large bowl. Squeeze the orange and add the juice and lemon juice to the bowl with the papayas. Put in the orange skins and seeds and water, cover with pierced plastic wrap, and cook for 10 minutes on HIGH. Strain and measure the juice. Stir in the sugar and cook for a further 15 minutes on HIGH, stirring frequently. Test the jelly by putting a spoonful onto a cold plate. Leave for 2-3 minutes, and if the jelly forms a skin and wrinkles when the plate is tilted, setting point has been reached. If the jelly is still liquid, cook for a further 2-3 minutes on HIGH, adding the pectin if necessary for setting. Strain the pour into hot, sterilized jars. Seal and cover.

Chrysanthemum and Green Peppercorn Jelly

PREPARATION TIME: 10 minutes

MICROWAVE COOKING TIME:
20-23 minutes

MAKES:
Approximately 675g/1½lbs/3 cups

500ml/1 pint/2 cups unsweetened clear
*   apple juice*
340g/12oz/1½ cups sugar
90ml/5 tbsps/⅓ cup pectin
15ml/1 tbsp lemon juice
1 tbsp green peppercorns, packed in brine,
*   well drained*
Handful/1 cup chrysanthemum petals,
*   rinsed and dried (nasturtium or*
*   carnation petals may be substituted)*

Pour the apple juice into a large bowl and stir in the sugar and lemon juice. Cover with pierced plastic wrap and cook for 10 minutes on HIGH. Stir in the pectin and peppercorns and cook

**This page: Chrysanthemum and Green Peppercorn Jelly.
Facing page: Apple and Thyme Jelly (top) and Paw-Paw (Papaya) Jelly (bottom).**

Port and Cranberry Jelly

PREPARATION TIME: 10 minutes

MICROWAVE COOKING TIME:
15-18 minutes

MAKES:
Approximately 675g/1½lbs/3 cups

500ml/1 pint/2 cups ruby port

*180g/6oz/1 cup whole cranberries,
　washed*
550g/1lb 4oz/2½ cups sugar
90ml/5 tbsps/⅓ cup pectin
1 bay leaf
15ml/1 tbsp lemon juice

Pour the port into a large bowl with
the lemon juice. Stir in the sugar,
cover with pierced plastic wrap and

**This page: Port and Cranberry
Jelly.
Facing page: Mint and Apple Jelly
(top) and Apple Cider Jelly
(bottom).**

cook for 5 minutes on HIGH, stirring
once. Uncover, and add the cranberries, bay leaf and pectin. Cook
uncovered for a further 10 minutes or

until the cranberries are tender. Test the jelly by putting a spoonful onto a cold plate. If the jelly forms a skin and wrinkles when the plate is tilted, the setting point has been reached. If the jelly is still liquid, cook for a further 2-3 minutes on HIGH. Pour into hot, sterilized jars. Seal and cover. Store in the refrigerator.

Spiced Tea Jelly

PREPARATION TIME: 10 minutes

MICROWAVE COOKING TIME: 18-19 minutes

MAKES: Approximately 450g/1lb/2 cups

500ml/1 pint/2 cups boiling water
4 tbsps loose tea
Rind of 1 orange
1 cinnamon stick
4 whole cloves
1 all-spice berry
175ml/6 fl oz/⅔ cup pectin
150g/5oz/⅔ cup sugar

Boil the water for about 3-4 minutes in a large glass measuring cup. Pare the rind of an orange. Put the tea into a large bowl with the orange rind, spices, sugar and pectin. Cook uncovered for 15 minutes on HIGH. Strain into hot, sterilized jars. Seal and cover.

Apple Cider Jelly

PREPARATION TIME: 10 minutes

MICROWAVE COOKING TIME: 20-23 minutes

MAKES: Approximately 450g/1lb/2 cups

500ml/1 pint/2 cups clear apple juice or cider
450g/1lb/2 cups sugar
5ml/1 tsp lemon juice
90ml/5 tbsps/⅓ cup bottled pectin
1 cinnamon stick (optional)

Pour the apple juice into a large bowl and stir in the sugar and lemon juice. Add the cinnamon stick (if desired), cover and cook for 10 minutes on

HIGH. Remove the cinnamon, stir in the pectin and cook uncovered for 10 minutes on HIGH. The jelly should boil rapidly. Test by putting a spoonful onto a cold plate. Leave for 2-3 minutes and if a skin forms and the surface of the jelly wrinkles when the plate is tilted, setting point has been reached. If the jelly is still liquid, cook for a further 2-3 minutes on HIGH. Pour into hot, sterilized jars. Seal and cover.

Mint and Apple Jelly

PREPARATION TIME: 10 minutes

MICROWAVE COOKING TIME: 20-25 minutes

MAKES: Approximately 450g/1lb/2 cups

500ml/1pt/2 cups unsweetened clear apple juice
450g/1lb/2 cups sugar
20ml/1½ tbsps cider vinegar
90ml/5 tbsps/⅓ cup pectin
Handful/1 cup chopped mint leaves
500ml/1 pint/2 cups water

Put the apple juice into a large bowl with the vinegar and water. Cover with pierced plastic wrap and cook for 10 minutes on HIGH. Add the sugar, half the mint leaves, and the pectin, and stir well. Cook uncovered for a further 10 minutes on HIGH. The jelly should boil rapidly. Test by putting a spoonful onto a cold plate. Leave for 2-3 minutes and if a skin forms and the surface of the jelly wrinkles when the plate is tilted, setting point has been reached. If the jelly is still liquid, cook for a further 2-3 minutes on HIGH. Strain and leave to cool slightly. Add the remaining mint and pour into hot, sterilized jars, seal and cover.

Peppered Grapefruit Jelly

PREPARATION TIME: 15 minutes

MICROWAVE COOKING TIME: 45 minutes, and 30 minutes standing time

MAKES: Approximately 450g/1lb/2 cups

3 grapefruit
Juice of 1 lemon
1 tbsp crushed black peppercorns
90ml/5 tbsps/⅓ cup bottled pectin
60ml/4 tbsps/¼ cup white rum
225g/8oz/1 cup sugar for every 240ml/½ pint/1 cup of juice

Peel the grapefruit and scrape off any white pith. Shred the peel finely and squeeze the juice from the grapefruit and lemon. Put the pith and seeds into cheesecloth and tie it into a bag. Measure the juice and boil an equal amount of water for 3-4 minutes on HIGH. Put the juice, cheesecloth bag, peel and half the water into a large bowl, and leave for 30 minutes to stand. Cover the bowl with pierced plastic wrap and cook for 20 minutes on HIGH. Uncover, remove the cheesecloth bag and press out the juice. Discard the bag. Add the sugar and cook uncovered for 25 minutes on HIGH, stirring frequently. Add the rum and pectin during the last 10 minutes of cooking time. The jelly should boil rapidly. Test by putting a spoonful onto a cold plate. Leave for 2-3 minutes, and if a skin forms and the surface of the jelly wrinkles when the plate is tilted, setting point has been reached. If the jelly is still liquid, cook for a further 2-3 minutes on HIGH. Stir in the peppercorns and pour into hot, sterilized jars. Seal and cover.

Beet and Chive Jelly

PREPARATION TIME: 15 minutes

MICROWAVE COOKING TIME: 17-20 minutes

MAKES: Approximately 450g/1lb/2 cups

Facing page: Spiced Tea Jelly (top) and Peppered Grapefruit Jelly (bottom).

3 large uncooked beets
140ml/¼ pint/½ cup pectin
140ml/¼ pint/½ cup distilled white
  vinegar
225g/8oz/1 cup sugar
Small handful/½ cup chopped chives

Peel and slice the raw beets. Put into a large bowl and cover with water. Cover with pierced plastic wrap and cook for 7 minutes on HIGH. Drain and mix with the pectin, sugar and vinegar, and re-cover the bowl. Cook for 10 minutes on HIGH or until boiling. To test, put a spoonful of the jelly onto a cold plate. If it forms a skin and wrinkles when the plate is tilted, setting point has been reached. If not, cook for a further 2-3 minutes on HIGH. Stir in the chives and pour into hot, sterilized jars. Seal and cover.

Guava and Lime Jelly

PREPARATION TIME: 10 minutes

MICROWAVE COOKING TIME:
20-23 minutes

MAKES:
Approximately 450g/1lb/2 cups

900g/2lbs guavas
Sugar
3 limes
500ml/1 pint/2 cups water
140ml/¼ pint/½ cup pectin

Wash and cut the guavas into large pieces. Peel the limes and scrape any white pith off the peel. Cut the peel into strips. Squeeze and limes and put the juice with the guavas into a large bowl. Wrap the remains of the limes in a cheesecloth and tie it into a bag. Put the bag into a bowl with the fruit. Add the water and stir the ingredients to mix. Cover the bowl with pierced plastic wrap and cook for 10 minutes on HIGH. Strain, measure the juice, and add 1 cup sugar for every cup of liquid. Add the peel and pectin, and cook uncovered

Guava and Lime Jelly (right) and Hot Pepper Jelly (far right).

for a further 10 minutes. The jelly should boil rapidly. Test by putting a spoonful onto a cold plate. Leave for 2-3 minutes and if the jelly forms a skin and wrinkles when the plate is tilted, setting point has been reached. If the jelly is still liquid, cook for a further 2-3 minutes on HIGH. Pour into hot, sterilized jars. Seal and cover.

Strawberry and Pink Champagne Jelly

PREPARATION TIME: 10 minutes

MICROWAVE COOKING TIME: 15 minutes

MAKES: Approximately 675g/1½lbs/3 cups

500ml/1 pint/2 cups pink Champagne, or sparkling wine
180g/6oz/1 cup strawberries, halved
550g/1lb 4oz/2½ cups sugar
90ml/5 tbsps/⅓ cup pectin

Pour the Champagne into a large bowl. Stir in the sugar and cover and cook on HIGH for 10 minutes. Stir in the pectin and cook uncovered for 5 minutes on HIGH. Carefully stir in the strawberries and pour into hot, sterilized jars. Seal and cover. Jelly is best stored in the refrigerator.

Hot Pepper Jelly

PREPARATION TIME: 10 minutes

MICROWAVE COOKING TIME: 12 minutes

MAKES: Approximately 900g/2lbs/4 cups

3 sweet red peppers
1 green pepper
2 hot chili peppers
675/1½lbs/3 cups sugar
240ml/½ pint/1 cup white wine vinegar
200ml/6oz/¾ cup pectin

Remove the cores and seeds from the peppers. Chop them all finely in a food processor or by hand. Put into a large bowl with the vinegar and cover with pierced plastic wrap. Cook for

2 minutes on HIGH. Stir in the sugar and cook for another 10 minutes, uncovered, on HIGH. Add the pectin during the last 3 minutes of cooking. Pour into hot, sterilized jars, seal and cover.

This page: Beet and Chive Jelly. Facing page: Strawberry and Pink Champagne Jelly.

Microwave

JAMS AND PRESERVES

CHUTNEY, PICKLES AND RELISHES

Pickled Orange Beets

PREPARATION TIME: 15 minutes

MICROWAVE COOKING TIME:
24 minutes

MAKES:
Approximately 450g/1lb/2 cups

340g/12oz/2 cups sliced beets
Grated rind and juice of 1 orange
120g/4oz/½ cup sugar
240ml/½ pint/1 cup distilled white
  vinegar
240ml/½ pint/1 cup cooking liquid from
  the beets
1.25ml/¼ tsp ground nutmeg
Salt

Peel and slice the beets and put into a
large bowl with enough water to
cover and add a pinch of salt. Cover
with pierced plastic wrap and cook
for 4 minutes on HIGH. Mix the
orange rind and juice, sugar, vinegar,
nutmeg and 240ml/½ pint/1 cup of
the beet cooking liquid together in a
large bowl. Cook uncovered for 15
minutes on HIGH. Add the beets
and cook for a further 5 minutes
uncovered on MEDIUM. Pour into
hot, sterilized jars. Seal and cover.

Fennel Preserves with Aquavit

PREPARATION TIME: 15 minutes

MICROWAVE COOKING TIME:
20-25 minutes

MAKES:
Approximately 900g/2lbs/4 cups

2-3 bulbs Florentine fennel
225g/8oz/1 cup sugar

240ml/½ pint/1 cup distilled white
  vinegar
240ml/½ pint/1 cup water
15ml/1 tbsp caraway seeds
120ml/¼ pint/½ cup aquavit
Salt

**This page: Pickled Orange Beets.
Facing page: Fennel Preserves
with Aquavit (top) and Pickled
Carrots and Walnuts (bottom).**

Cut the root ends off the bulbs and cut the fennel into 1.5cm (½″) slices. Include the green tops. Put the sugar, vinegar, water, caraway seeds and a small pinch of salt into a large bowl or 2 450g/1lb/2 cup jars. Cook uncovered for 10 minutes on HIGH, stirring frequently. Add the fennel, cover with pierced plastic wrap and cook for 10 minutes on MEDIUM or until the fennel looks translucent. Stir frequently. Stir in the aquavit and pour into sterilized jars. Seal and cover.

Pickled Carrots and Walnuts

PREPARATION TIME: 15 minutes

MICROWAVE COOKING TIME: 32 minutes

MAKES: Approximately 900g/2lbs/4 cups

900g/2lbs carrots
240ml/½ pint/1 cup cider vinegar
500ml/1 pint/2 cups reserved cooking liquid from the carrots
450g/1lb/2 cups sugar
1.25ml/¼ tsp ground nutmeg
1.25ml/¼ tsp ground ginger
2 whole cloves
120g/4oz/1 cup walnut halves
Salt

Peel the carrots and chop roughly. Put into a large bowl with water to cover and a good pinch of salt. Cover with pierced plastic wrap and cook for 7 minutes on HIGH. Mix the vinegar, spices, sugar and 500ml/1 pint/ 2 cups of liquid from the carrots. Cook uncovered for 15 minutes on HIGH. Add carrots and walnuts and cook uncovered for 10 minutes on MEDIUM, or until the carrots look translucent. Pour into hot, sterilized jars. Seal and cover.

Sweet and Sour Onions

PREPARATION TIME: 20 minutes

MICROWAVE COOKING TIME: 15 minutes

MAKES: Approximately 900g/2lbs/4 cups

675g/1½lbs/4 cups button or pickling onions
340g/12oz/1½ cups light brown sugar
500ml/1 pint/2 cups cider vinegar
140ml/¼ pint/½ cup water
15ml/1 tbsp mustard seed
½ cinnamon stick
Salt

Put all the ingredients except the onions into a large bowl. Cook uncovered for 5 minutes on HIGH, stirring frequently. Remove the cinnamon. Pour boiling water onto the onions to loosen the skins and make them easier to peel. When peeled, put the onions into the bowl with the other ingredients and cook for 10 minutes on HIGH. Pour into hot, sterilized jars. Seal and cover.

Pepper Relish

PREPARATION TIME: 15 minutes

MICROWAVE COOKING TIME: 15-18 minutes

MAKES: Approximately 900g/2lbs/4 cups

275g/9oz/1½ cups sweet red pepper, diced
275g/9oz/1½ cups green pepper, diced
275g/9oz/1½ cups sweet banana pepper, diced
180g/6oz/1 cup onion, diced
Tarragon
Ground cloves
5ml/1 tsp celery seed
500ml/1 pint/2 cups distilled white vinegar
340g/12oz/1½ cups sugar
Salt
Pepper

Put a pinch of tarragon and ground cloves into a large bowl with all the other ingredients except the peppers, salt and pepper. Cook for 5 minutes

Right: Sweet and Sour Onions.

2 red chili peppers, seeds removed and cut
    into thin strips
1 piece ginger root, peeled and cut into
    strips
5ml/1 tsp soy sauce
240ml/½ pint/1 cup rice vinegar
60ml/4 tbsps sherry
60ml/4 tbsps sugar
2 pieces star anise
Salt

Mix the soy sauce, vinegar, sherry,
sugar, salt and star anise together in a
large bowl. Cook uncovered for
5 minutes on HIGH. If the ears of
corn are small, use whole; if large, cut
in half lengthwise. Add them to the
bowl along with the ginger and chili
peppers. Stir well, cover with pierced
plastic wrap, and cook for 3 minutes
on HIGH. Pour into hot, sterilized
jars, cover and seal. Best stored in the
refrigerator.

Green Tomato Relish

PREPARATION TIME: 15 minutes

MICROWAVE COOKING TIME:
30 minutes

MAKES:
Approximately 900g/2lbs/4 cups

1.2kg/2½lbs green tomatoes
3 onions, chopped
150g/5oz/⅔ cup brown sugar
90g/3oz/½ cup dried currants
1.25ml/¼ tsp ground ginger
1.25ml/¼ tsp mustard seed
240ml/½ pint/1 cup cider vinegar
Salt
Pepper

Put the tomatoes into boiling water
for 1-2 minutes to loosen the peel,
then cut into dice. Put all the
ingredients except the sugar, salt and
pepper into a large bowl. Cover with
pierced plastic wrap and cook for 15
minutes on HIGH. Stir in the sugar,
salt and pepper, and cook uncovered
for 15 minutes on HIGH, stirring

on HIGH, stirring frequently. Add
the peppers and cook, covered with
pierced plastic wrap, for a further 10
minutes on HIGH. Test by putting a
spoonful of the syrup onto a cold
plate. It should thicken immediately.
If not, cook for a further 2-3 minutes
on HIGH. Season with salt and
pepper, and pour into hot, sterilized
jars. Seal and cover.

Chinese Corn Pickles

PREPARATION TIME: 8 minutes

MICROWAVE COOKING TIME:
8 minutes

MAKES:
Approximately 450g/1lb/2 cups

225g/8oz/1½ cups baby corn ears

**This page: Chinese Corn Pickles.
Facing page: Green Tomato Relish
(top) and Pepper Relish (bottom).**

frequently until thickened. Pour into hot, sterilized jars. Seal and cover. Best stored in the refrigerator.

Curried Fruit

PREPARATION TIME: 15 minutes

MICROWAVE COOKING TIME: 15-18 minutes

MAKES:
Approximately 900g/2lbs/4 cups

3 apples, peeled, cored and sliced thickly
6 apricots, stoned and sliced thickly
180g/6oz/1 cup pineapple chunks
90g/3oz/½ cup raisins
225g/8oz/1 cup light brown sugar
140ml/¼ pint/½ cup distilled white
   vinegar

This page: Curried Fruits. Facing page: Apple and Fig Chutney (top) and Pineapple, Mango and Mint Chutney (bottom).

140ml/¼ pint/½ cup water
4 whole cloves
30ml/2 tbsps mild curry powder
5ml/1 tsp coriander seeds

Put all the fruit except the apricots into a large bowl and toss to mix. Put the remaining ingredients into a large glass measuring cup and cook uncovered for 5 minutes on HIGH. Pour onto the fruit and mix well. Cook uncovered for 10 minutes on HIGH, stirring frequently. Add the apricots during the last 3 minutes. If the apples do not look clear, cook for an additional 2-3 minutes on HIGH. Pour into hot, sterilized jars. Seal and cover. After opening, store in the refrigerator.

Chow-Chow (Mustard Pickles)

PREPARATION TIME: 20 minutes

MICROWAVE COOKING TIME:
22-23 minutes

MAKES:
Approximately 900g/2lbs/4 cups

340g/12oz/2 cups pickling cucumbers, diced
340g/12oz/2 cups onions, chopped
340g/12oz/2 cups cauliflower, in small florets
340g/12oz/2 cups green peppers, diced
15ml/1 tbsp yellow mustard
1.25ml/¼ tsp turmeric
2.5ml/½ tsp mustard seed
30g/1oz/2 tbsps flour
60g/2oz/¼ cup sugar
240ml/½ pint/1 cup white distilled vinegar
1.25ml/¼ tsp thyme
1 bay leaf
1.25ml/¼ tsp salt

Put the first 4 ingredients into a bowl with salt. Cover with water and leave to stand for 30 minutes. Cover with pierced plastic wrap and cook on MEDIUM for 15 minutes. Leave to stand, covered. In a deep bowl, combine the remaining ingredients and beat until smooth. Cover with pierced plastic wrap, and cook for 7-8 minutes on MEDIUM, stirring frequently until thick. Do not allow to boil. Drain the vegetables and mix with the mustard sauce. Heat through for 1 minute on HIGH and remove the bay leaf. Pour into hot, sterilized jars. Seal and cover.

Red and White Radish Preserves

PREPARATION TIME: 15 minutes

MICROWAVE COOKING TIME:
15 minutes

MAKES:
Approximately 450g/1lb/2 cups

180g/6oz/1 cup sliced red radishes
180g/6oz/1 cup sliced white (daikon) radishes
15ml/1 tbsp grated fresh ginger root
15ml/1 tbsp lemon juice
500ml/1 pint/2 cups honey
90g/3oz/½ cup Brazil nuts, roughly chopped
500ml/1 pint/2 cups water

Cut the radishes into 5mm (¼") thick slices. Put the water into a large bowl and cook for 3-4 minutes on HIGH, or until the water boils. Add the radishes and cook for 1 minute, uncovered. Drain them and mix with the honey, lemon juice, ginger and nuts. Cook uncovered for 10 minutes on HIGH. Pour into hot, sterilized jars. Seal and cover. Best stored in the refrigerator.

Apple and Fig Chutney

PREPARATION TIME: 15 minutes

MICROWAVE COOKING TIME:
30-33 minutes

MAKES:
Approximately 450g/1lb/2 cups

340g/¾lb apples
180g/6oz/1 cup chopped dried or fresh figs
225g/8oz/1 cup brown sugar
90g/3oz/½ cup chopped onion
45g/¼ cup raisins
240ml/½ pint/1 cup cider vinegar
½ tbsp coriander seeds, crushed lightly
½ tsp ground ginger
¼ tsp Cayenne pepper
Salt

Peel, core and chop the apples roughly. Put all the ingredients except the sugar, salt and Cayenne pepper, into a large bowl. Cover with pierced plastic wrap and cook for 15 minutes

on HIGH, stirring frequently. Stir in the sugar, Cayenne pepper, and a pinch of salt. Cook uncovered for a further 15 minutes on HIGH, stirring every 5 minutes, or until thickened. Test by stirring with a wooden spoon. If the spoon leaves a channel, setting point has been reached. If not, cook for a further 2-3 minutes on HIGH. Pour into hot, sterilized jars, seal and cover.

Pineapple, Mango and Mint Chutney

PREPARATION TIME: 20 minutes

MICROWAVE COOKING TIME:
30-35 minutes

MAKES:
Approximately 900g/2lbs/4 cups

500g/1lb 2oz/3 cups fresh pineapple, chopped
1 large mango, peeled and chopped
225g/8oz/1 cup sugar
500ml/1 pint/2 cups distilled white vinegar
180g/6oz/1 cup white raisins
2 tbsps chopped fresh mint
¼ tsp ground nutmeg
1 small piece ginger root
Salt

Sprinkle the pineapple with a good pinch of salt and leave for half an hour. Peel the ginger root and cut into thin slivers. Drain the pineapple and rinse in cold water. Put all the ingredients except the sugar into a large bowl. Cover with pierced plastic wrap and cook for 15 minutes on HIGH, stirring frequently. Add the sugar and cook uncovered for a further 15 minutes on HIGH or until thickened. Stir frequently. Test by stirring with a wooden spoon. If the spoon leaves a channel, then setting point has been reached. If not, cook for a further 5 minutes on HIGH. Add another pinch of salt if necessary and pour into hot, sterilized jars. Seal and cover.

Facing Page: Red and White Radish Preserves (top) and Chow-Chow (Mustard Pickles) (bottom).

further 2-3 minutes on HIGH. Pour into hot, sterilized jars, seal and cover.

Bread and Butter Pickles

PREPARATION TIME: 10 minutes

MICROWAVE COOKING TIME:
11 minutes

MAKES:
Approximately 900g/2lbs/4 cups

*675g/1½lbs 4 cups pickling cucumbers,
  sliced to 5mm (¼") thick
500ml/1 pint/2 cups distilled white
  vinegar
450g/1lb/2 cups sugar
1.25ml/¼ tsp turmeric
30ml/2 tbsps mustard seed
Cayenne pepper
1.25ml/¼ tsp alum
15ml/1 tbsp water
Salt*

Mix the cucumbers with the salt, alum and water, and leave for 1 hour. Rinse well under cold water and dry. Sterilize 2 450g/1lb/2 cup jars and divide all the ingredients except the cucumbers between them, adding a good pinch of Cayenne pepper. Stir well and cook uncovered for 8 minutes on HIGH. Add the cucumbers, cover with plastic wrap and cook for a further 3 minutes on MEDIUM. Do not let the cucumbers boil in the liquid. Seal and cover the jars.

Tarragon Vinegar Pickles

PREPARATION TIME: 15 minutes

MICROWAVE COOKING TIME:
13 minutes

MAKES:
Approximately 900g/2lbs/4 cups

*675g/1½lbs/4 cups whole small pickling
  cucumbers
225g/8oz/1 cup sugar
360ml/¾ pint/1½ cups white wine
  vinegar
120ml/¼ pint/½ cup water
1 large bunch tarragon
Black peppercorns
1.25ml/¼ tsp alum*

Pumpkin Chutney

PREPARATION TIME: 20 minutes

MICROWAVE COOKING TIME:
45-48 minutes

MAKES:
Approximately 900g/2lbs/4 cups

*675g/1½lbs/4 cups pumpkin, peeled and
  cubed
450g/1lb/2 cups light brown sugar
1 lemon, thinly sliced
1 tbsp grated ginger root
300ml/12 fl oz/1¼ cups water
240ml/½ pint/1 cup cider vinegar
180g/6oz/1 cup raisins*

This page: Pumpkin Chutney.
Facing page: Bread and Butter
Pickles (top) and Tarragon
Vinegar Pickles (bottom).

Put the pumpkin, lemon slices, ginger root, raisins, water and vinegar into a large bowl. Cover with pierced plastic wrap and cook for 15 minutes on HIGH, stirring frequently. Stir in the sugar thoroughly and cook uncovered for a further 20 minutes on HIGH, or until thickened. Test by stirring with a wooden spoon. If the spoon leaves a channel, setting point has been reached. If not, cook a

15ml/1 tbsp water
Salt

If the cucumbers are small, leave
them whole; if not, cut them into
quarters lengthways. Salt them, mix
with the alum and water, and leave
for 1 hour. Rinse under cold water
and dry. Put the sugar, vinegar, water,
tarragon and peppercorns into a
bowl, or 2 450g/1lb/2 cup jars. Cook
uncovered for 10 minutes on HIGH.
Put in the cucumbers, cover with
plastic wrap and cook on MEDIUM
for 3 minutes or until the cucumbers
lose their bright green color. Seal and
cover the jars.

Watermelon and Lime Pickles

PREPARATION TIME: 20 minutes
plus overnight standing

MICROWAVE COOKING TIME:
25 minutes

MAKES:
Approximately 900g/2lbs/4 cups

675g/1½lbs/4 cups watermelon rind, cut
    into cubes
3 limes
240ml/½ pint/1 cup distilled white
    vinegar
140ml/¼ pint/½ cup lime juice
340g/12oz/1½ cups sugar
1 stick cinnamon
2 whole cloves
2.5ml/½ tsp powdered alum
Salt

Save the rinds from a watermelon
and peel off the dark green skin.
Scrape off any remaining flesh and
cut the rind into 2.5cm (1") cubes.
Mix the alum together with a pinch
of salt and the cold water. Pour over
the rind and add more water to cover.
Leave to stand overnight. Rinse
under cold water and drain. Slice
2 limes into thin rounds and squeeze
the juice from the third lime.
Combine the juice, vinegar, spices
and sugar in a large bowl and cook
uncovered for 10 minutes on HIGH.
Remove the spices and add the
prepared watermelon rind. Cook un-

covered for 15 minutes on MEDIUM,
or until the rind looks translucent.
Stir occasionally. Add the lime slices
during the last 3 minutes. Pour into
hot, sterilized jars. Seal and cover.

Spicy Cantaloupe Pickles

PREPARATION TIME: 15 minutes

MICROWAVE COOKING TIME:
15 minutes, plus 2 hours soaking time

MAKES:
Approximately 900g/2lbs/4 cups

2 cantaloupe melons, slightly under-ripe
340g/12oz/1½ cups sugar
350ml/¾ pint/1½ cups distilled white
    vinegar
140ml/¼ pint/½ cup water
4 whole cloves
1 stick cinnamon

This page: Corn Relish.
Facing page: Watermelon and
Lime Pickles (top) and Spicy
Cantaloupe Pickles (bottom).

Cut the melons in half and remove
the seeds. Cut the melons into
quarters and remove the rind. Cut
the flesh into 2.5cm (1") chunks.
Mix the sugar, spices, water and
vinegar together in a large bowl and
cook uncovered on HIGH for
10 minutes. Put in the cantaloupe
and leave to soak in the syrup for
2 hours. After the melon has soaked
up some of the syrup, cook for a
further 5 minutes on HIGH or just
until the syrup comes to the boil.
Pour into sterilized jars, seal and
cover. Once the jars have been
opened, store the pickles in the
refrigerator.

Corn Relish

PREPARATION TIME: 15 minutes

MICROWAVE COOKING TIME:
20-23 minutes

MAKES:
Approximately 900g/2lbs/4 cups

340g/12oz/2 cups frozen or fresh corn
2 red peppers, diced
180g/6oz/1 cup chopped celery
1 onion, chopped
120g/4oz/½ cup sugar
300ml/12 fl oz/1¼ cups distilled white
   vinegar
1 tbsp cornflour/cornstarch
180ml/7 fl oz/¾ cup water
8ml/½ tbsp celery seed
5ml/1 tsp mustard seed
1.25ml/¼ tsp turmeric
Salt
Pepper

Put all the ingredients except the
corn, sugar, salt and pepper into a
large bowl and stir well to mix in the
cornstarch. Cover with pierced
plastic wrap and cook on HIGH for
5 minutes, stirring occasionally. Add
the corn, sugar, salt and pepper,
mixing thoroughly. Cover and cook
for a further 15-18 minutes on HIGH,
stirring frequently until thickened.

Chili Sauce

PREPARATION TIME: 15 minutes

MICROWAVE COOKING TIME:
30 minutes

MAKES:
Approximately 900g/2lbs/4 cups

675g/1½lbs tomatoes, peeled and diced
3 large onions, chopped
2 green peppers, diced
180g/6oz/⅔ cup brown sugar
240ml/½ pint/1 cup cider vinegar
1.25ml/¼ tsp ground cloves
1.25ml/¼ tsp ground cinnamon
5ml/1 tsp mustard seed
5ml/1 tsp celery seed
2.5ml/½ tsp chili powder
Pinch ground all-spice
1 bay leaf
Salt
Pepper

Put all the ingredients except the
sugar, salt and pepper into a large
bowl. Cover with pierced plastic
wrap, and cook for 15 minutes on
HIGH. Stir in the sugar, salt and
pepper, and cook uncovered for a
further 15 minutes on HIGH or until
the mixture thickens. Remove the
bay leaf, and pour into hot, sterilized
jars. Seal and cover. Best stored in
the refrigerator.

Cranberry Orange Relish

PREPARATION TIME: 15 minutes

MICROWAVE COOKING TIME:
11 minutes

This page: Cranberry Orange
Relish.
Facing page: Chili Sauce (top) and
Mock Mincemeat (bottom).

MAKES:
Approximately 900g/2lbs/4 cups

800g/1¾lbs/5 cups whole cranberries
3 small oranges
180g/6oz/¾ cup sugar
180ml/7 fl oz/¾ cup red wine
2.5ml/½ tsp ground all-spice
15ml/1 tbsp red wine vinegar (optional)

Squeeze the juice from the oranges.
Scrape the white pith from the peel

600ml/1¼ pints/2½ cups water
140ml/¼ pint/½ cup white wine vinegar
22ml/1½ tbsps ground mustard
10ml/2 tsps mustard seed
Salt

Put the sugar, mustard powder and
seed, water, vinegar and a pinch of
salt into a large bowl and mix the
ingredients together thoroughly.
Cook on HIGH, uncovered, for
4 minutes. Add all the fruit and stir
well. Leave to stand covered for
30 minutes. Cook uncovered for
10 minutes on HIGH. Pour into hot,
sterilized jars. Seal and cover. After
opening, store in the refrigerator.

Mock Mincemeat

PREPARATION TIME: 15 minutes

MICROWAVE COOKING TIME:
22 minutes

MAKES:
Approximately 900g/2lbs/4 cups

900g/2lbs apples, peeled, cored and
    chopped
300g/10oz/1¾ cups seedless raisins
120g/4oz/½ cup candied peel, chopped
120g/4oz/½ cup dark brown sugar
2.5ml/½ tsp nutmeg
10ml/2 tsps cinnamon
2.5ml/½ tsp ground cloves
1.25ml/¼ tsp ground ginger
180ml/7 fl oz/¾ cup water
Grated rind and juice of 1 orange
60ml/4tbsps/¼ cup rum

Put all the ingredients except the rum
and sugar into a large bowl. Cover
with pierced plastic wrap and cook
for 15 minutes on HIGH. Add the
sugar and cook a further 2 minutes,
uncovered, on HIGH. Put into hot,
sterilized jars and fill to within 2.5cm
(1") of the top. Cover each jar with
plastic wrap and cook for a further
5 minutes on HIGH. Remove the
wrap and stir in the rum. Seal and
cover the jars.

and chop the peel in a food
processor. Wash the cranberries, add
them to the food processor and chop
roughly. Put the sugar, orange juice
and all-spice into a large bowl and
cook uncovered for 4 minutes on
HIGH. Add the cranberries, orange
rind and wine, and cook for
5 minutes on HIGH, stirring
frequently. Cook until the rind and
cranberries are just tender. Taste, add
the red wine vinegar if the mixture is
too sweet, and continue to cook for
2-3 minutes on HIGH. Pour into hot,
sterilized jars. Seal and cover
Best kept in the refrigerator.

Mustard Fruit

PREPARATION TIME: 15 minutes

MICROWAVE COOKING TIME:
14 minutes, plus 30 minutes standing
time

MAKES:
Approximately 900g/2lbs/4 cups

225g/8oz/1½ cups dried fruit (prunes,
    apricots, peaches, pears, apples, figs),
    left whole
225g/8oz/1½ cups candied fruit
    (cherries, citron peel, pineapple slices or
    pieces), left whole
340g/12oz/1½ cups sugar

**This page: Mustard Fruit.
Facing page: Lemon Vinegar (top)
and Garlic Vinegar (bottom).**

FLAVOURED SYRUPS AND VINEGARS

Garlic Vinegar

PREPARATION TIME: 5 minutes

MICROWAVE COOKING TIME:
1½ minutes

MAKES:
Approximately 500ml/1 pint/2 cups

500ml/1 pint/2 cups cider vinegar
3 cloves garlic, peeled
1 bay leaf

Thread the cloves of garlic onto a
wooden skewer. Put this into a
500ml/1 pint/2 cup bottle of cider
vinegar, along with the bay leaf. Cook
for 1½ minutes on HIGH or until the
bottle is warm. Check after 30
seconds to make sure that the bottle
is not overheating. Cover while still
warm and store in a cool, dark place
for 2 weeks before using.
Keeps 2 months.

Raspberry Syrup

PREPARATION TIME: 5 minutes

MICROWAVE COOKING TIME:
10 minutes

MAKES: 900g/2lbs/4 cups

900g/2lbs/5 cups red raspberries, fresh or
*   frozen*
340g/12oz/1½ cups sugar
180ml/7 fl oz/¾ cup water
60ml/4 tbsps/¼ cup raspberry liqueur
*   (optional)*
Half a cinnamon stick
15ml/1 tbsp lemon juice

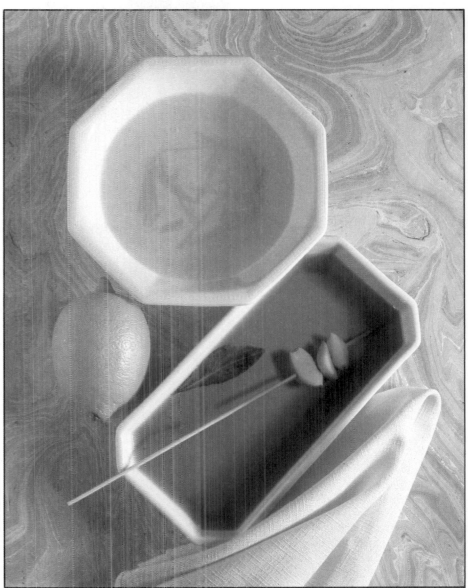

Wash the raspberries and put into a
large bowl with the water and the
cinnamon. Cover with pierced plastic
wrap and cook for 3 minutes on
HIGH or until the berries break up.
Strain and mix with the sugar.
Remove the cinnamon and return
the liquid to the bowl. Cook
uncovered for 7 minutes on HIGH.
Add the raspberry liqueur (if
desired), and lemon juice to taste.
Pour into bottles or jars, and cover.
Keep in a refrigerator. Drink mixed
with 2 parts soda water or dry white
wine to 1 part syrup, or use with
desserts.

Blueberry Syrup

PREPARATION TIME: 5 minutes

MICROWAVE COOKING TIME:
10 minutes

MAKES:
Approximately 900g/2lbs/4 cups

675g/1½lbs/4 cups blueberries, fresh or
*   frozen*
225g/8oz/1 cup sugar
140ml/¼ pint/½ cup water
60ml/4 tbsps/¼ cup crème de cassis
*   (optional)*
15ml/1 tbsp lemon juice

Wash the blueberries, and put into a
large bowl with the water. Cover
with pierced plastic wrap and cook
for 3 minutes on HIGH, or until the
berries break up. Strain and mix with
the sugar. Return to the bowl and
cook uncovered for 7 minutes on
HIGH. Stir in the cassis (if desired),
and lemon juice to taste. Pour into
bottles or jars, and cover. Keep in a
refrigerator. Drink mixed with 2 parts
soda or dry white wine to 1 part
syrup, or use with desserts.

Rosemary Vinegar

PREPARATION TIME: 5 minutes

MICROWAVE COOKING TIME:
1 minute

MAKES:
Approximately 240ml/½ pint/1 cup

240ml/½ pint/1 cup red wine vinegar
6 sprigs fresh rosemary
3 black peppercorns

Put the rosemary into a bottle with
the red wine vinegar. Add the
peppercorns and cook for 30 seconds
to 1 minute on HIGH until the bottle
is warm to the touch. After 15
seconds, check the temperature of
the bottle to make sure it is not overheating. Cover while still warm and
keep in a cool, dark place for 2 weeks
before using. Keeps about 2 months.

Cherry Vinegar

PREPARATION TIME: 5 minutes

MICROWAVE COOKING TIME:
1½ minutes

MAKES:
Approximately 500ml/1 pint/2 cups

90g/3oz/½ cup red or black cherries,
*   stems left on*
240ml/½ pint/1 cup distilled white
*   vinegar*
Pinch sugar

Put all the ingredients into a bowl
and cook, covered, for 1½ minutes on
HIGH. Check after 30 seconds to
ensure the mixture is not overheating. If the cherries do not color
the vinegar, crush them slightly and
heat for 30 seconds more on HIGH.
Pour into bottles and seal while still
warm. Store in a cool place for
2 weeks before using.
Keeps 2 months.

Lemon Vinegar

PREPARATION TIME: 5 minutes

MICROWAVE COOKING TIME:
1½ minutes

MAKES:
Approximately 240ml/½ pint/1 cup

240ml/½ pint/1 cup distilled white
*   vinegar*
Juice and rind of 1 lemon
2.5ml/½ tsp sugar

Pour the lemon juice and vinegar
together into a bottle. Add the sugar
and cook for 1½ minutes on HIGH
or until the bottle is just warm to the
touch. Check the bottle after 30
seconds to make sure it is not overheating. Shred the lemon rind finely
and push into the bottle. Cover the
bottle while still warm, and store in a
cool, dark place for 2 weeks before
using. Keeps 2 months.

**This page: Blueberry Syrup (top)
and Raspberry Syrup (bottom).
Facing page: Cherry Vinegar (top)
and Rosemary Vinegar (bottom).**

Microwave BAKING

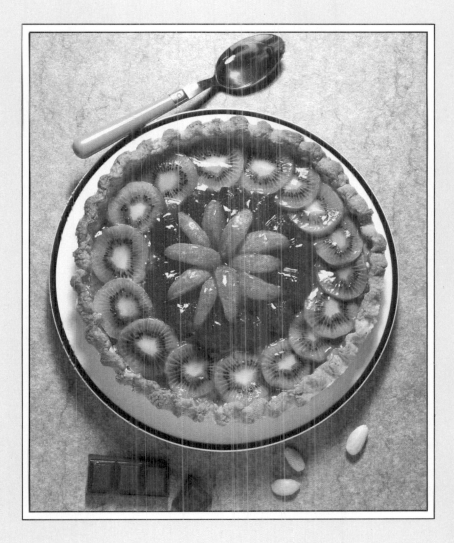

Microwave
BAKING

Microwave baking will be a pleasant surprise if you love fresh-baked goods but not the long baking time. A single layer of cake will bake in 5-10 minutes, and a loaf of bread in 9-12 minutes.

At the start, the following points are worth remembering:

When baking in square or loaf dishes the mixture in the corners will cook more quickly than in the centre. Wrapping the corners of the dish so that 5cm/2 inches of the mixture are protected will help prevent drying out.

Placing dishes on a rack or inverted saucer will allow heat to circulate underneath and help cook the bottom of cakes, bread or pastry evenly. Allowing the dish to stand on a flat surface for 5-10 minutes after baking will help the base to set.

Liquids do not evaporate as quickly in a microwave oven, so only add enough to bring the mixture to the proper consistency. When experimenting with conventional recipes, remember to cut down on the liquid.

Microwave ovens will cut the rising time for yeast dough almost in half. Place the prepared dough in a lightly-greased bowl large enough to allow the dough to double in bulk. Set the bowl in a shallow dish of hot water and cover tightly with plastic wrap/cling film. Microwave for one minute on MEDIUM setting and leave to stand for 15 minutes. Repeat

the process until the dough has doubled in size. Loosen the covering as the dough grows.

Bread dough and other baked mixtures will not brown in a conventional microwave oven. Combination ovens, which use convection heat *and* microwave energy, will produce lightly-browned baked goods in about the same length of time as regular microwave ovens and they also give a crisper crust. But with such a variety of toppings, even conventionally microwaved cakes, breads and cookies/biscuits can have an appealing finish.

Pastry baking has always been viewed as a microwave problem area. However, the edges of a pastry shell bake to a surprisingly crisp and flaky texture. Pre-baking a pastry shell unfilled, is not recommended in a combination oven, but in a regular microwave oven it can produce a crisper base, as can the use of a rack or inverted saucer under the dish while baking. Leave the unfilled shell to cool on a flat surface for 5-10 minutes and the residual heat will help the bottom of the pastry to bake more evenly.

Microwave baking puts delicious desserts, cakes and pastries within easy reach. A microwave oven gives new meaning to that old cliché – the best thing since sliced bread!

Note: All recipes were tested in an oven with a maximum power of 700 watts and a combination oven with a maximum power of 600 watts.

Microwave
BAKING

YEAST BREADS

Honey Savarin with Strawberries

PREPARATION TIME: 1 hour

MICROWAVE COOKING TIME:
7 minutes plus 1 minute
standing time

MAKES: 1 ring

180ml/6 fl oz/⅔ cup milk
15ml/1 tbsp/1 package active dry yeast
10ml/2 tsps sugar
150g/5oz/⅔ cup butter
4 eggs
Pinch salt

SYRUP
140ml/¼ pint/½ cup honey
90ml/3 fl oz/⅓ cup water
45ml/1½ fl oz/3 tbsps brandy

ACCOMPANIMENT
Whipped cream
Fruit

Heat the milk for 30 seconds on HIGH. Mix in the sugar and yeast. Sift the flour and salt into a large mixing bowl and warm for 15 seconds on HIGH. Make a well in the centre of the flour and pour in the yeast mixture. Cover the yeast with a sprinkling of flour and leave until frothy, about 30 minutes. Stir together to form a batter. Soften the butter for 10 seconds on HIGH and add to the batter with the beaten eggs. Beat well for about 10 minutes by hand or machine. Butter a tube dish/ring mould thoroughly and pour in the savarin batter. Cover the ring dish with greased plastic wrap/cling film and leave in a warm place 30-40 minutes. When the mixture has risen halfway up the sides of the

dish, cook on HIGH for 7 minutes. The savarin is done when the top looks dry. Leave to stand on a flat surface for 1 minute before turning out onto a rack. Place the honey and the water in a deep bowl and cook on HIGH for 7 minutes. Stir in the

**This page: Cinnamon Fruit Braid/
Plait. Facing page: Honey Savarin
with Strawberries.**

brandy and spoon the syrup over the cake to soak through. Serve with fresh fruit and cream.

Cinnamon Fruit Braid/ Plait

PREPARATION TIME: 1-2 hours

MICROWAVE COOKING TIME:
8 minutes plus 5 minutes
standing time

MAKES: 1 loaf

BREAD DOUGH
285g-340g/10-12oz/2½-3 cups all-
   purpose/plain flour
30g/1oz/2 tbsps sugar
5ml/1 tsp salt
60g/2oz/¼ cup butter or margarine
60ml/2 fl oz/¼ cup water
140ml/¼ pint/½ cup milk
15ml/1 tbsp/1 package active dry yeast
1 egg

FILLING
3 apples, peeled and roughly chopped
180g/6oz/1 cup raisins
90g/3oz/½ cup chopped candied/glacé
   citrus fruit
90g/3oz/½ cup chopped dried apricots
120g/4oz/½ cup brown sugar
60g/2oz/¼ cup melted butter
30g/1oz/¼ cup all-purpose/plain flour
15ml/1 tbsp allspice

TOPPING
30g/2 tbsps melted butter
15ml/1 tbsp sugar
5ml/1 tsp ground cinnamon

Sift the dry ingredients for the dough together into a large bowl and make a well in the centre. Heat the water for 30 seconds on HIGH until warm to the touch. Stir in the yeast. Heat the milk and butter together for 30 seconds on HIGH and beat in the egg. Add to the yeast and pour into the well in the flour and gradually beat the liquid into the dry ingredients until well incorporated. Turn the dough out onto a lightly floured surface and knead about 10 minutes or until the dough is smooth and springs back when lightly touched. Form into a ball and put into a lightly greased bowl. Turn dough over to coat all sides. Cover the bowl with plastic wrap/cling film or a clean towel. Leave in a warm place for 1-1½ hours or until doubled in bulk. Alternatively, cover the bowl very loosely and set in a dish of hot

water in the microwave oven at MEDIUM for 1 minute or on LOW for 4 minutes. Leave the dough to stand for 15 minutes. Repeat the process until the dough has doubled in bulk. This should cut the rising time almost in half. To shape the dough, punch it down and knead again, lightly, about 2 minutes. Roll out to a rectangle 20cm x 25cm/ 8 inches x 10 inches. Cut the long edges at 2.5cm/1 inch intervals into 7.5cm/3 inch strips on the diagonal. Mix the filling ingredients together and mound down the centre of the dough. Fold over the strips from alternating sides, down the length of the bread. Cover loosely with greased plastic wrap/cling film and leave to rise in a warm place for 30 minutes, or use the microwave rising method. Brush with the remaining melted butter, mix the sugar and cinnamon together and sprinkle over the top. Bake 6 minutes on MEDIUM, giving the baking sheet a quarter turn every minute. Increase the setting to HIGH and cook 1-2 minutes further, turning as before. The top should spring back when lightly touched if the bread is done. Leave on the baking sheet for 5 minutes before removing to a wire rack to cool.

Cinnamon Raisin Swirl

PREPARATION TIME: 1-2 hours

MICROWAVE COOKING TIME:
7-8 minutes plus 5 minutes
standing time

MAKES: 1 loaf

285g-340g/10-12oz/2½-3 cups all-
   purpose/plain flour
30g/1oz/2 tbsps sugar
5ml/1 tsp salt
60g/2oz/¼ cup butter or margarine
60ml/2 fl oz/¼ cup water
140ml/¼ pint/½ cup milk
15ml/1 tbsp/1 package active dry yeast

FILLING
90g/3oz/¾ cup flour
120g/4oz/½ cup brown sugar
30ml/2 tbsps ground cinnamon
60g/2oz/¼ cup butter or margarine
120g/4oz/¾ cup raisins

TOPPING
30g/1oz/2 tbsps butter or margarine,
   melted
15ml/1 tbsp cinnamon
60g/2oz/¼ cup brown sugar

Prepare the dough as in the cheese and chive spiral loaf. Once the dough has been prepared and has risen to double in bulk, punch it down and knead it again lightly, about 2 minutes. Roll out to a 20cm/8 inch rectangle. Cut the butter for the filling into the flour and stir in the sugar and cinnamon. Add the raisins and scatter the filling evenly over the dough. Roll up from the long edge to the long edge. Seal the ends and tuck them under. Put into a lightly greased loaf dish, about 22.5cm x 12.5cm/ 9 inch x 5 inch. Cover the dish loosely and leave in a warm place until doubled in bulk, about 30 minutes. Alternatively, follow the microwave rising method. Brush the top with melted butter. Mix together the topping ingredients and sprinkle over the bread. Cook on MEDIUM for 6 minutes. Increase the temperature to HIGH and cook 1-2 minutes. The top should spring back when lightly touched if the bread is done. Leave in the dish on a flat surface for 5 minutes before removing to a wire rack to cool.

Holiday Fruit Brioche

PREPARATION TIME: 1-2 hours

MICROWAVE COOKING TIME:
8-10 minutes

MAKES: 1 loaf

285g-340g/10-12oz/2½-3 cups all-
   purpose/plain flour
30g/1oz/2 tbsps sugar
5ml/1 tsp salt
60g/2oz/¼ cup butter or margarine
60ml/2 fl oz/¼ cup water
140ml/¼ pint/½ cup milk
15ml/1 tbsp/1 package active dry yeast
180g/6oz/1 cup candied/glacé fruit
90g/3oz/⅓ cup chopped almonds
1 egg, beaten with a pinch of salt
Powdered/icing sugar

Sift the dry ingredients together into

Cinnamon Raisin Swirl (top) and Holiday Fruit Brioche (bottom).

should cut the rising time almost in half. To shape the dough, punch it down and knead again lightly, about 2 minutes. Grease a brioche mould very well. Form ⅔ of the dough into a smooth ball and put into the oiled mould. Form the remaining ⅓ of the dough into a smaller ball and put in the centre of the dough in the brioche mould. Lightly flour the handle of a wooden spoon and stick the handle of the spoon through both balls of dough to stick them together. Cover the brioche mould with plastic wrap/cling film and set in a warm place for 30 minutes or until nearly doubled in bulk. The microwave rising method may be used as well. Brush the top of the brioche with the beaten egg and microwave on MEDIUM for 6 minutes. Increase the temperature to HIGH and cook for 1-2 minutes. If the dough still appears wet, cook an additional 2 minutes on HIGH. The top should spring back when lightly touched if the brioche is done. Leave in the dish for 5 minutes before removing to a wire rack to cool. Sprinkle with powdered/icing sugar before serving.

Cheese and Chive Spiral Loaf

PREPARATION TIME: 1-2 hours
MICROWAVE COOKING TIME: 10 minutes
MAKES: 1 large loaf

400g-450g/14-16oz/3½-4 cups all-purpose/plain flour
30g/1oz/2 tbsps sugar
5ml/1 tsp salt
30ml/2 fl oz/¼ cup water
140ml/¼ pint/½ cup milk
60g/2oz/¼ cup butter or margarine
15ml/1 tbsp/1 package active dry yeast

FILLING
120g/4oz/½ cup grated Cheddar cheese
60g/2oz/1 cup fresh breadcrumbs
45g/1½ oz/3 tbsps chopped chives
30g/1oz/¼ cup crushed cheese biscuits/ crackers
30g/2 tbsps melted butter or margarine

a large bowl and make a well in the centre. Heat the water for 1 minute on HIGH until warm to the touch. Stir in the yeast. Heat the milk and butter together for 30 seconds on HIGH and beat in the egg. Add the yeast and pour into the well in the centre of the flour. Gradually beat the liquid into the dry ingredients until well incorporated. Add the almonds and the candied/glacé fruit and turn out onto a floured surface. Knead the dough for about 10 minutes, until the fruit and nuts are well mixed in and the dough is smooth and springs back when lightly touched. Form into a ball and put into a lightly greased bowl. Turn the dough over to coat all sides. Cover the bowl with plastic wrap/ cling film or clean towel. Leave in a warm place for 1-1½ hours or until doubled in bulk. Alternatively, cover the bowl loosely and set it in a dish of hot water in the microwave oven on MEDIUM for 1 minute or LOW for 4 minutes. Leave the dough to stand for 15 minutes. Repeat until the dough is doubled in bulk. This

Sift the dry ingredients into a large bowl and make a well in the centre. Heat the water for 1 minute on HIGH until warm to the touch. Stir in the yeast. Heat the milk and butter together for 30 seconds on HIGH and beat in the egg. Add to the yeast and pour into the well in the flour and gradually beat the liquid into the dry ingredients until well incorporated. Turn the dough out onto a lightly floured surface and knead about 10 minutes or until the dough is smooth and springs back when lightly touched. Form into a ball and put into a lightly greased bowl. Turn the dough over to coat all sides. Cover the bowl with plastic wrap/cling film or a clean towel. Leave in a warm place for 1-1½ hours or until doubled in bulk. Alternatively, cover the bowl very loosely and set it in a dish of hot water in the microwave on MEDIUM for 1 minute or LOW for 4 minutes. Leave the dough to stand for 15 minutes. Repeat the process until the dough has doubled in bulk. This should cut the rising time in half. To shape the dough, punch it down and knead again, lightly, about 2 minutes. Roll out to a 20cm/8 inch rectangle. Mix together the filling ingredients and sprinkle over the surface. Roll up from the long edge to the long edge. Sprinkle a greased loaf dish with additional crushed biscuits/crackers. Seal the ends and put, seam side down, into a prepared loaf dish, approximately 22.5cm x 12.5cm/9 inches x 5 inches. Cover and leave to rise until doubled in bulk, about 30 minutes, or follow the microwave rising method. Brush with butter and sprinkle on the biscuits/crackers. Place dish on an inverted saucer or a rack. Cook on MEDIUM 6 minutes. Increase the setting to HIGH and cook 1-2 minutes. The top should spring back when lightly touched if the bread is done. Leave in the dish for 5 minutes before turning out onto a wire rack to cool.

Pâté en Brioche

PREPARATION TIME: 1-2 hours

MICROWAVE COOKING TIME: 8 minutes plus 5 minutes standing time

MAKES: 1 loaf

285g-340g/10-12oz/2½-3 cups all-purpose/plain flour
30g/1oz/2 tbsps sugar
5ml/1 tsp salt
60g/2oz/¼ cup butter or margarine
30ml/2 fl oz/¼ cup water
140ml/¼ pint/½ cup milk
15ml/1 tbsp/1 package active dry yeast
1 egg

FILLING
1 can pâté

COATING
1 egg, beaten with a pinch of salt
Poppy seeds
Dry breadcrumbs

Sift the dry ingredients together into a large bowl and make a well in the centre. Heat the water for 30 seconds

This page: Caraway Rye Sticks (top) and Pumpernickel Rolls (bottom). Facing page: Pâté en Brioche (top) and Cheese and Chive Spiral Loaf (bottom).

on HIGH, until warm to the touch. Stir in the yeast. Heat the milk and butter together for 30 seconds on HIGH and beat in the egg. Add the yeast and pour into the well in the flour and gradually beat the liquid into the dry ingredients until well incorporated. Turn the dough out onto a lightly floured surface and knead about 10 minutes or until the dough is smooth and springs back when lightly touched. Form into a ball and put into a lightly greased bowl. Turn the dough over to coat all sides. Cover the bowl with plastic wrap/cling film or a clean towel. Leave in a warm place for 1-1½ hours or until doubled in bulk. Alternatively, cover the bowl very loosely and set it in a dish of hot water in a microwave oven on MEDIUM for 1 minute, or 4 minutes on LOW. Leave the dough to stand for 15 minutes. Repeat until the dough has doubled in bulk. This should cut the rising time almost in half. To shape the dough punch it down and knead again, lightly, about 2 minutes. Roll out to a rectangle about 20cm/8 inches long. Place the pâté in the middle of the bread and roll the bread carefully around it. Tuck in the end and put the loaf seam side down into a lightly greased loaf tin, about 22.5cm x 12.5cm/ 9 inch x 5 inch. Cover the dish with plastic wrap/cling film and set in a warm place for 30 minutes or until nearly doubled in bulk. The microwave rising method may also be used. Cook on MEDIUM for 6 minutes. Increase the temperature to HIGH and cook 1-2 minutes. The top should spring back when lightly touched if the bread is done. Leave in the dish 5 minutes before removing to a wire rack to cool. Slice and serve cold as an appetizer or for picnics.

Caraway Rye Sticks

PREPARATION TIME: 1-2 hours

MICROWAVE COOKING TIME: 6-8 minutes

MAKES: 16 rolls

350g/12oz/3 cups rye flour
120g/4oz/1 cup all-purpose/plain flour
5ml/1 tsp salt
5ml/1 tsp brown sugar
280ml/½ pint/1¼ cups milk
15ml/1 tbsp/1 package active dry yeast
30g/2 tbsps butter or margarine
30ml/2 tbsps caraway seeds

TOPPING
1 egg, beaten with a pinch of salt
Caraway seeds
Coarse salt

Sift the flours into a large bowl with the salt and make a well in the centre. Add the caraway seeds. Heat the milk for 15 seconds on HIGH and stir in the yeast. Add the butter and the sugar and stir to dissolve. Pour into the dry ingredients and stir to incorporate. Turn out onto a floured surface and knead for 10 minutes. Shape the dough into a ball and put into a lightly greased bowl. Turn to coat all sides. Cover with plastic wrap/cling film or a clean towel and leave in a warm place 1-1½ hours, or until doubled in bulk. Alternatively, put the bowl into a dish of hot water and heat in the microwave oven for 1 minute on HIGH or 4 minutes on LOW. Leave the bowl to stand for 15 minutes. Repeat the process until the dough has doubled in bulk. To shape, turn the dough out onto a floured surface and knead again lightly, about 2 minutes. Divide the dough into 16 pieces. Shape into sticks, slightly thicker in the centre. Place on lightly greased microwave baking sheets and cover loosely with greased plastic wrap/cling film. Leave in a warm place 30 minutes or until doubled in size. The microwave rising method may also be used. Brush each roll with the beaten egg and sprinkle with caraway seeds and salt. Microwave 3-4 minutes on HIGH per batch. Transfer the rolls to a wire rack and serve warm.

Whole-Wheat Loaf

PREPARATION TIME: 1-2 hours

MICROWAVE COOKING TIME: 10 minutes

MAKES: 1 loaf

350g/12oz/3 cups whole-wheat flour
120g/4oz/1 cup all-purpose/plain flour
5ml/1 tsp salt
280ml/½ pint/1¼ cups milk
15ml/1 package active dry yeast
30g/2 tbsts butter or margarine
5ml/1 tsp brown sugar

TOPPING
1 egg, beaten with a pinch of salt
Bran

Sift the flours and the salt into a large bowl. Reserve half the bran from the whole-wheat flour and return the rest to the bowl and make a well in the centre of the ingredients. Heat the milk for 15 seconds on HIGH. Melt the butter and dissolve the yeast. Stir in the sugar and pour into the well in the bowl and stir to gradually incorporate the ingredients. Turn out onto a floured surface and knead for 10 minutes. Put the dough into a lightly greased bowl and turn over to coat all sides. Cover with plastic wrap/cling film or clean towel. Leave to rise 1-1½ hours in a warm place. Alternatively, place in a dish of hot water and put into the microwave oven for 1 minute on HIGH, or 4 minutes on LOW. Leave the dough to stand for 15 minutes. Repeat until the dough has doubled in bulk. This should cut the rising time in half. To shape the dough, punch it down and knead again lightly, about 2 minutes. Roll out to a rectangle and then roll up tightly. Seal the ends and tuck under slightly. Put into a lightly greased loaf dish, about 22.5cm x 12.5cm/9 inch x 5 inch. Cover the loaf dish lightly and leave to rise in a warm place for about 30 minutes, or use the microwave rising method. Brush the top of the loaf with lightly beaten egg and sprinkle on the remaining bran. Cook on MEDIUM for 6 minutes and give the dish a quarter turn every minute. Increase the temperature to HIGH and cook for 1-2 minutes, rotating as before.

Facing page: Whole-Wheat Loaf (top) and Poppy Seed Braid/Plait (bottom).

The top should spring back when lightly touched if the bread is done. Leave it in the dish for 5 minutes before removing to a wire rack to cool.

Pumpernickel Rolls

PREPARATION TIME: 1-2 hours

MICROWAVE COOKING TIME: 6-8 minutes

MAKES: 16 rolls

350g/12oz/3 cups dark rye or whole-wheat flour
120g/4oz/1 cup all-purpose/plain flour
15ml/1 tbsp/1 package active dry yeast
5ml/1 tsp dill seed
5ml/1 tsp salt
60g/2oz/¼ cup vegetable shortening
150ml/¼ pint/½ cup dark molasses/ black treacle
140ml/¼ pint/½ cup water
1 egg

TOPPING
60g/2 tbsps/¼ cup butter, melted
Sesame seeds

Sift the flours and salt into a large bowl. Heat the water for 30 seconds on HIGH and add the yeast. Stir in the shortening, molasses/treacle and egg. Pour into the dry ingredients and add the dill seeds. Stir well to incorporate all the ingredients. Turn out onto a floured surface and knead 10 minutes, until the dough is smooth and springs back when lightly touched. Form the dough into a ball and put into a lightly greased bowl. Turn to coat all sides. Cover with plastic wrap/cling film or a clean towel. Leave in a warm place to rise for 1-1½ hours or put the bowl into a dish of hot water in the microwave oven and heat on HIGH for 1 minute or on LOW for 4 minutes. Leave to stand for 15 minutes. Repeat the process until the dough has doubled in bulk. To shape the dough punch it down, turn it out of the bowl and knead, lightly, for 2 minutes. Divide into 16 pieces and shape into round rolls and knots. Place the rolls in a circle on microwave baking sheets. Cover loosely with greased plastic wrap/cling film and leave in a warm place for 30 minutes, or until the rolls have doubled in size. The microwave rising method may also be used. Melt the butter for 30 seconds on HIGH and brush over the surface of the rolls. Sprinkle on the sesame seeds and cook on HIGH for 3-4 minutes, turning the rolls over once during cooking. Cook in 2 batches. When the rolls are cooked, transfer to a cooling rack and serve warm.

Poppy Seed Braid/Plait

PREPARATION TIME: 1-2 hours

MICROWAVE COOKING TIME: 10 minutes

MAKES: 1 loaf

450g/1lb/4 cups all-purpose/plain flour
5ml/1 tsp salt
280ml/½ pint/1¼ cups milk
5ml/1 tsp sugar
15ml/1 tbsp/1 package active dry yeast
45g/3 tbsps butter or margarine
1 egg, beaten with a pinch of salt
Poppy seeds

Sift the salt and the flour together into a large bowl and make a well in the centre. Heat the milk for 1 minute on HIGH until warm to the touch. Stir in the sugar and the yeast. Add the butter and stir to melt. Pour into the well in the centre of the flour and gradually beat the liquid into the dry ingredients until well incorporated. Turn the dough out onto a lightly floured surface and knead about 10 minutes or until the dough is smooth and springs back when lightly touched. Form it into a ball and put into lightly greased bowl. Turn the dough over to coat all sides. Cover the bowl with plastic wrap/cling film or clean towel. Leave in a warm place for 1-1½ hours or until doubled in bulk. Alternatively, cover the bowl very loosely and set in a dish of hot water in a microwave oven on MEDIUM for 1 minute or on LOW for 4 minutes. Leave the dough to stand for 15 minutes. Repeat until the dough has doubled in bulk. This should cut the rising time in half. To shape the dough, punch it down and knead again lightly, about 2 minutes.

Divide the dough into thirds and roll each third into a sausage shape. Plait/braid the thirds beginning in the middle and working out to the ends. Turn the ends under and place the dough on a microwave baking sheet. Cover very loosely and leave to rise about 30 minutes or use the microwave rising method. Brush with the egg and sprinkle over the poppy seeds. Cook 1 minute on HIGH. Lower the setting to LOW and cook for 9 minutes. The top of the bread should spring back when lightly touched if it is done. Leave the bread on a sheet for 5 minutes before removing to a wire rack to cool.

Coffee Almond Ring

PREPARATION TIME: 1-2 hours

MICROWAVE COOKING TIME: 8 minutes plus 5 minutes standing time

MAKES: 1 ring

225g-340g/10-12oz/2½-3 cups all-purpose/plain flour
30g/1oz/2 tbsps sugar
5ml/1 tsp salt
60g/2oz/¼ cup butter or margarine
60ml/2 fl oz/¼ cup water
140ml/¼ pint/½ cup milk
15ml/1 tbsp/1 package active dry yeast
1 egg

FILLING
1 can almond paste/2 packages ground almonds mixed with 1 egg white

ICING DECORATION
225g/8oz/2 cups powdered/icing sugar, sifted
Milk
Candied/glacé cherries
Angelica
Toasted almonds

Sift the dry ingredients together into a large bowl and make a well in the centre. Heat the water for 30 seconds on HIGH until warm to the touch. Stir in the yeast. Heat the milk and butter together for 30 seconds on HIGH and beat in the egg. Add to the yeast and pour into the well in

Above: Coffee Almond Ring.

the flour and gradually beat the liquid into the dry ingredients until well incorporated. Turn the dough out onto a lightly floured surface and knead about 10 minutes or until the dough is smooth and springs back when lightly touched. Form into a ball and put into a lightly greased bowl. Turn the dough over to coat all sides. Cover the bowl with plastic wrap/cling film or a clean towel. Leave in a warm place for 1-1½ hours or until doubled in bulk. Alternatively, cover the bowl very loosely and set it in a dish of hot water in the microwave oven on MEDIUM for 1 minute, or on LOW for 4 minutes. Leave the dough to stand for 15 minutes. Repeat the process until the dough has doubled in bulk. This should cut the rising time almost in half. To shape the dough, punch it down and knead again, lightly, about 2 minutes. Roll out to a 30cm/12 inch rectangle. Spread with the almond paste. Roll up from the long edge to the long edge. Place the roll on a microwave baking sheet and form into a ring, sealing the ends together well. Cut at 5cm/2 inch intervals and turn each section on its side. Cover with lightly greased cling film/plastic wrap and leave in a warm place 30 minutes, until doubled in bulk. The microwave rising method may also be used. Brush with milk and cook for 6 minutes on MEDIUM. Increase the temperature to HIGH and cook 1-2 minutes, turning as before. The top of the ring should spring back when lightly touched if it is done. Leave on the baking sheet 5 minutes before removing to a wire rack to cool. Mix the icing/powdered sugar with enough milk to make a thick but pourable icing. Drizzle the icing over the top of the ring and decorate with the cherries and angelica.

Microwave
BAKING

QUICK BREADS

Strawberry Shortcakes

PREPARATION TIME: 25 minutes

MICROWAVE COOKING TIME:
2-3½ minutes

SERVES: 6 people

120g/4oz/1 cup all-purpose/plain flour
Scant 10ml/1½ tsps baking powder
30g/1oz/2 tbsps butter or margarine
90ml/3 fl oz/⅓ cup milk
Salt
30g/1oz/2 tbsps sugar

TOPPING
Ground browned almonds
30g/1oz/2 tbsps butter

Sift the flour with a pinch of salt and baking powder. Cut in the butter or margarine until the mixture resembles fine breadcrumbs and stir in the sugar. This may be done in a food processor. Add the milk and stir or process just until the dough comes together. Knead lightly and roll out 1.25cm/½ inch thick. Cut out rounds with a 7.5cm/3 inch cutter. Melt the remaining butter 30 seconds on HIGH. Brush the tops of each biscuit and sprinkle on the ground browned almonds. Microwave on HIGH for 2-5 minutes until well risen. Turn the biscuits every 1 minute to cook evenly. Remove to a wire rack to cool. Split and serve filled with strawberries and whipped cream.

Baking Powder Biscuits

PREPARATION TIME: 15 minutes

MICROWAVE COOKING TIME:
2½-5½ minutes

MAKES: 8 or 9 biscuits

120g/4oz/1 cup all-purpose/plain flour
Scant/10ml/1½ tsps baking powder
30g/1oz/2 tbsps butter or margarine
90ml/3 fl oz/⅓ cup milk
Salt

TOPPING
30g/1oz/2 tbsps butter
Dry breadcrumbs
Paprika

Sift the flour with a pinch of salt and baking powder. Cut in the butter or margarine until the mixture

This page: Strawberry Shortcakes. Facing page: Fruit Scones (top) and Baking Powder Biscuits (bottom).

resembles fine breadcrumbs. This may be done in a food processor. Add the milk and stir or process just until the dough comes together. Knead lightly and roll out 1.25cm/½ inch thick. Cut out rounds with a 5cm/2 inch cutter. Melt butter 30 seconds on HIGH. Place biscuits

mixture thoroughly. Fill into paper cups/cases in a microwave muffin/patty pan. Fill the cups half-full with the batter and sprinkle the ground browned almonds on top of each muffin. Microwave 3-5 minutes on HIGH. If the muffins still look moist in spots, they will dry out during standing.

Cornmeal and Bacon Muffins

PREPARATION TIME: 15 minutes

MICROWAVE COOKING TIME: 5-7 minutes

MAKES: 8-10 muffins

60g/2oz/½ cup all-purpose/plain flour
60g/2oz/½ cup yellow cornmeal
6 strips bacon/smoked streaky bacon
1 small sweet red pepper, diced
15ml/1 tbsp sugar
10ml/2 tsps baking powder
60ml/2 fl oz/¼ cup oil
1 egg, beaten
Salt
Paprika

Heat a browning dish for 5 minutes on HIGH. Add the oil and cook the bacon until crisp, about 2 minutes. Crumble the bacon and combine with the rest of the ingredients except the paprika. Mix well to blend thoroughly. Fill into paper cups/cases in microwave muffin/patty pans. Fill each cup half-full with the batter. Microwave for 3-5 minutes on HIGH. If the muffins still look moist in spots, they will dry during standing. Serve warm or allow to cool.

on a baking sheet. Brush the top of each biscuit with the butter and sprinkle on the crumbs and paprika. Microwave on HIGH for 2-5 minutes, until well risen. Turn the biscuits every 1 minute to cook evenly. Serve with butter or honey or thinly sliced country ham.

Honey Whole-Wheat Muffins

PREPARATION TIME: 15 minutes

MICROWAVE COOKING TIME: 7-9 minutes

MAKES: 8-10 muffins

120g/4oz/1 cup whole-wheat flour
Scant 10ml/1½ tsps baking powder
Pinch ground ginger
Salt

This page: **Apple Pecan Streusel Cake.** Facing page: **Honey Whole-Wheat Muffins** (top) and **Cornmeal and Bacon Muffins** (bottom).

30g/2 tbsps dark brown sugar
60ml/2 fl oz/¼ cup honey
90ml/3 fl oz/⅓ cup milk
60ml/2 fl oz/¼ cup oil
1 egg, beaten
30g/1oz/¼ cup chopped almonds

TOPPING
Ground browned almonds

Sift the flour with the baking powder, salt and ginger into a large bowl. Return the bran from the whole-wheat flour to the ingredients in the bowl. Stir in the brown sugar and add the honey, milk, oil and egg. Stir in the almonds and blend the

Apple Pecan Streusel Cake

PREPARATION TIME: 25 minutes

MICROWAVE COOKING TIME: 13 minutes plus 10 minutes standing time

MAKES: 1 cake

180g/6oz/1½ cups all-purpose/plain flour, sifted

180g/6oz/¾ cup brown sugar
5ml/1 tsp baking powder
5ml/1 tsp nutmeg
5ml/1 tsp cinnamon
2.5ml/½ tsp baking soda
180ml/6 fl oz/¾ cup milk with 15ml/
    1 tbsp lemon juice or vinegar
120g/4oz/½ cup butter or margarine
1 egg, beaten

TOPPING
1 apple, peeled and thinly sliced
90g/3oz/⅓ cup brown sugar
30g/1oz/¼ cup all-purpose/plain flour
60g/2oz/½ cup coarsely chopped pecans
30g/1oz/2 tbsps butter or margarine

Combine all the cake ingredients and mix for about 30 seconds, or until fairly smooth. Do not overbeat. Pour in a 16cm/8 inch round dish. Scatter over the apples. Do not put too many apples in the centre. Melt the butter for the topping for 30 seconds on HIGH. Mix in the remaining topping ingredients and sprinkle over the apples and batter. Microwave 6 minutes on MEDIUM. Increase to HIGH and cook 6 minutes more. Leave to stand on a flat surface for 10 minutes before serving. Serve warm or allow to cool.

Fruit Scones

PREPARATION TIME: 15 minutes
MICROWAVE COOKING TIME:
3-4 minutes
MAKES: 6-8 scones

225g/8oz/2 cups all-purpose/plain flour
15ml/1 tbsp baking powder
60g/2oz/¼ cup butter or margarine
30g/1oz/2 tbsps sugar
30g/1oz/¼ cup golden raisins
1 egg, beaten
60ml/2 fl oz/¼ cup milk

GLAZE
1 egg white, lightly beaten
30g/1oz/2 tbsps sugar
15ml/1 tbsp ground cinnamon

Sift the flour, salt and baking powder into a large bowl and cut in the butter or margarine until the mixture resembles fine breadcrumbs. This

may be done in a food processor. Add the sugar and the raisins and stir in by hand. Stir in the beaten egg and enough milk to form a soft dough. The dough should not be too sticky. Knead the dough lightly into a ball, then flatten by hand or with a rolling pin to about 1.25cm/½ inch thick. Cut into a 5cm/2 inch rounds or squares. Place the scones in a circle on a microwave baking-sheet and brush the tops with lightly beaten egg white. Combine the sugar and the cinnamon and sprinkle over the tops of each scone. Microwave on HIGH for 3-4 minutes, changing the position of the scones from time to time. Serve warm with cream or butter and jam.

Cheese and Dill Bread

PREPARATION TIME: 20 minutes
MICROWAVE COOKING TIME:
15 minutes plus 5-10 minutes
standing time
MAKES: 1 loaf

225g/8oz/2 cups all-purpose/plain flour
Scant 10ml/1½ tsps baking powder
2.5ml/½ tsp baking soda
30ml/2 tbsps chopped dill
10ml/2 tsps brown sugar
60g/2oz/½ cup shredded Colby/Red
    Leicester cheese
90g/3oz/⅓ cup butter or margarine
180ml/6 fl oz/⅔ cup milk with 15ml/
    1 tbsp lemon juice or vinegar
1 egg, beaten

TOPPING
30g/2 tbsps dry breadcrumbs
30g/2 tbsps grated Parmesan cheese
15ml/1 tbsp chopped dill

Combine the flour, baking powder, soda, salt and sugar in a food processor. Work in the butter and add the dill and grated cheese. Add the egg and milk. This can also be done with an electric mixer. Spread into a 22.5cm x 12.5cm/9 inch x 5 inch loaf dish lined with wax/greaseproof paper. May also be baked in a round dish. Sprinkle over the topping and cover the edges of the dish with foil to cover the mixture

2.5cm/1 inch. This will prevent the edges of the bread drying out before it is completely cooked. Microwave for 10 minutes on MEDIUM. Increase the setting to HIGH and cook a further 5 minutes. Remove the foil during the last 5 minutes of cooking. In a microwave-convection combination oven, cook on the highest temperature setting for 14 minutes. Leave the bread to stand on a flat surface for 5-10 minutes before removing from the dish to serve.

Whole-Wheat Soda Bread

PREPARATION TIME: 15 minutes
MICROWAVE COOKING TIME:
8 minutes plus 10 minutes
standing time
MAKES: 1 round loaf

225g/8oz/2 cups whole-wheat flour
225g/8oz/2 cups all-purpose/plain flour
10ml/2 tsps baking soda
10ml/2 tsps cream of tartar
30g/1oz butter or margarine
10ml/2 tsps brown sugar
280ml/½ pint/1 cup milk with 15ml/
    1 tbsp vinegar or lemon juice

TOPPING
15g/½ oz/4 tbsps oatmeal/porridge oats

Sift the flours into a large bowl and return the bran to the bowl. Add the soda, cream of tartar and sugar. Rub in the butter until the mixture resembles fine breadcrumbs. This may be done in a food processor. Stir in the milk until the mixture forms a soft dough. Knead lightly until smooth. Shape into a round on a microwave baking sheet. Mark into 4 sections and sprinkle over the oats. Cook on MEDIUM 5 minutes. Cook on HIGH for 3 minutes. Leave to stand for 10 minutes on a flat surface and then cool on a wire rack before serving.

Facing page: Cheese and Dill Bread (top) and Whole-Wheat Soda Bread (bottom).

Hazelnut Date Bread

PREPARATION TIME: 20 minutes

MICROWAVE COOKING TIME:
15 minutes plus 5-10 minutes
standing time

MAKES: 1 loaf

180g/6oz/1½ cups whole-wheat/
  wholemeal flour
180g/6oz/¾ cup brown sugar
5ml/1 tsp baking soda
1 egg, beaten
200ml/6 fl oz/¾ cup water
180g/6oz/1 cup dates, stoned and
  chopped
60g/2oz/½ cup toasted, chopped
  hazelnuts

Combine the dates and water and
heat for 5 minutes on HIGH. Leave
to stand 5 minutes. Cream the butter
and sugar together. Sift in the baking
soda, flour and the pinch of salt. Add
the dates and liquid along with the
egg, beating until smooth. Stir in the
nuts and spread into a 22.5cm x
12.5cm/9 inch x 5 inch loaf dish
lined with wax/greaseproof paper.
Cover the ends of the dish with foil
to cover the mixture 2.5cm/1 inch.
This will prevent the mixture from
drying out on the sides before the
bread is completely cooked. Cook on
MEDIUM for 10 minutes. Increase
the setting to HIGH and cook for
further 5 minutes. Remove the foil
halfway through the last 5 minutes of
cooking. In a microwave-convection
combination oven, cook on the
highest temperature setting for
14 minutes. Leave to stand on a flat
surface for 5-10 minutes before
removing from the dish to serve.

Pumpkin Raisin Bread

PREPARATION TIME: 20 minutes

MICROWAVE COOKING TIME:
15 minutes plus 5-10 minutes
standing time

MAKES: 1 loaf

120g/4oz/1 cup all-purpose/plain flour
180g/6oz/¾ cup sugar
5ml/1 tsp baking powder

5ml/1 tsp baking soda
5ml/1 tsp allspice
5ml/1 tsp ground cinnamon
5ml/1 tsp ground ginger
140ml/¼ pint/½ cup oil
2 eggs, beaten
120g/4oz/¾ cup raisins
225g/8oz/1 cup canned or cooked
  pumpkin

Sift the flour, salt, baking powder,
soda and spices into a large bowl.
Beat in the remaining ingredients,
except the raisins, with an electric
mixer for about 2 minutes. Stir in the
raisins by hand and spread the
mixture into a 22.5cm x 12.5cm/
9 inch x 5 inch loaf dish lined with a
strip of wax/greaseproof paper.
Cover the ends of the dish with foil

**This page: Pumpkin Raisin Bread
(top) and Hazelnut Date Bread
(bottom). Facing page: Cranberry
Orange Bread.**

to cover 2.5cm/1 inch of the mixture.
This will prevent the mixture from
drying out on the sides before the
bread is completely cooked. Remove
the foil after 5 minutes of cooking
time. Cook for 10 minutes on
MEDIUM. Increase the temperature
to HIGH and cook for a further
5 minutes. In a microwave-convection
combination oven, cook on the
highest temperature setting for
14 minutes. Leave to stand for
5-10 minutes on a flat surface before
removing from the dish to serve.

Banana Coconut Bread

PREPARATION TIME: 20 minutes

MICROWAVE COOKING TIME:
17 minutes plus 5-10 minutes
standing time

MAKES: 1 loaf

2 bananas
180g/6oz/1½ cups all-purpose/plain
   flour
180g/6oz/¾ cup sugar
150g/5oz/½ cup plus 2 tbsps butter or
   margarine, well softened
2 eggs
90ml/3 fl oz/⅓ cup milk
15ml/1 tbsp lemon juice
5ml/1 tsp baking soda
90g/3oz/½ cup shredded coconut
60g/2oz/½ cup chopped macadamia
   nuts (optional)

TOPPING
60g/2oz/½ cup all-purpose/plain flour
60g/2oz/¼ cup dark brown sugar
30g/2 tbsps butter or margarine

**This page: Banana Coconut Bread.
Facing page: Black Bottom Pie
(top) and Orange Hazelnut Pie
(bottom).**

Mash the bananas with an electric
mixer or in a food processor. Soften
the butter 5 seconds on HIGH and
add to the bananas. Sift in the flour
and the remaining bread ingredients
in the order given. Beat until well
blended, about 2 minutes. Line a
22.5cm x 12.5cm/9 inch x 5 inch loaf
dish with wax/greaseproof paper and
spread in the bread mixture. Sprinkle
over the topping evenly and cover
the ends of the dish with foil to cover
the mixture 2.5cm/1 inch. This
prevents the sides from drying out
before the bread is completely
cooked. Cook on MEDIUM for
about 10 minutes. Increase to HIGH
and cook for 5 minutes. Remove the
foil halfway through the last

5 minutes of cooking. In a microwave-
convection combination oven, cook
on the highest temperature setting
for 14 minutes. Leave to stand for
5-10 minutes on a flat surface before
removing from the dish to serve.

Cranberry Orange Bread

PREPARATION TIME: 20 minutes

MICROWAVE COOKING TIME:
15 minutes plus 5 minutes
standing time

MAKES: 1 loaf

180g/6oz/1 cup cranberries, roughly
   chopped
Juice and rind of 1 orange
Water
120g/4oz/½ cup sugar
150g/5oz/⅓ cup butter or margarine
2 eggs, beaten
10ml/2 tsps baking powder
2.5ml/½ tsp baking soda
60g/2oz/½ cup chopped Brazil nuts
1.25ml/¼ tsp ginger
150g/5oz/1¼ cups all-purpose/plain
   flour

Grate the rind from the orange and
set it aside. Squeeze the juice and
measure the amount. Add enough
water to make 280ml/½ pint/1 cup
liquid. Sift the flour with the baking
powder, soda, salt and ginger. Cut in
the butter or margarine until the
mixture resembles fine breadcrumbs.
Stir in the sugar and add the beaten
eggs, orange juice and water, orange
rind and the cranberries. Mix until
well blended and pour into a
22.5cm x 12.5cm/9 inch x 5 inch loaf
dish lined with a strip of wax/
greaseproof paper. Wrap foil on the
sides of the dish to cover the batter
2.5cm/1 inch. This will prevent the
mixture drying out before the bread
is cooked. Cook for 10 minutes on
MEDIUM. Remove the foil. Increase
the setting to HIGH and cook a
further 5 minutes. In a microwave-
convection combination oven, cook
on the highest temperature setting
for 14 minutes. Leave to stand on a
flat surface for 5-10 minutes before
removing from the dish to serve.

Microwave
BAKING

PIES & QUICHES

Orange Hazelnut Pie

PREPARATION TIME: 20 minutes

MICROWAVE COOKING TIME:
13-17 minutes

SERVES: 6-8 people

PASTRY
120g/4oz/1 cup all-purpose/plain flour
90g/3oz/⅓ cup butter or margarine
30g/1oz/2 tbsps shortening
15g/1oz/¼ cup ground hazelnuts
60ml/2-4 tbsps cold water

FILLING
3 eggs
120g/4oz/½ cup brown sugar
Grated rind of 1 orange
60ml/4 tbsps/¼ cup orange juice
15g/½ oz/1 tbsp flour
Pinch of salt
120g/4oz/1 cup roasted hazelnuts,
   roughly chopped

DECORATION
140ml/¼ pint/½ cup whipped cream
6-8 orange slices
Small sprigs of mint

Cut the butter or margarine and
shortening into the flour with a
pinch of salt until mixture resembles
fine breadcrumbs. Add the nuts and
enough liquid to bring the dry
ingredients together into a ball. It
may not be necessary to add all the
water. This may be done by hand or
in a food processor. Roll out to a
circle at least 5cm/2 inches larger
than the dish. Fit into a pie dish and
crimp the edges if desired. Prick the
base and sides well with a fork. Cook
on HIGH for 5-7 minutes on an
inverted saucer or a rack. If the
pastry begins to develop brown

spots, cover them with a piece of foil. If the pastry bubbles up, press it gently back into place. Allow to cool slightly before filling. Mix all the filling ingredients together, except the nuts, with an electric mixer. Stir in the nuts by hand and cook about 3 minutes, stirring frequently. Pour into the pastry shell and cook on MEDIUM 8-10 minutes or until nearly set. The filling will set further as the pie cools. Serve with whipped cream and garnish with orange slices and sprigs of mint.

Note: If using a combination setting in a microwave-convection oven, use the highest temperature and bake the filling and pastry together for about 20 minutes. Do not pre-cook the filling or pre-bake the pastry.

Black Bottom Pie

PREPARATION TIME: 25 minutes plus chilling time

MICROWAVE COOKING TIME: 7½-13½ minutes

SERVES: 6-8 people

PASTRY
120g/4oz/1 cup all-purpose/plain flour
90g/3oz/⅓ cup butter or margarine
30g/1oz/2 tbsps shortening
Pinch of salt
60g/2oz/½ cup toasted desiccated coconut
30-60ml/2-4 tbsps cold water

FILLING
15ml/1 tbsp gelatine
60ml/2 fl oz/¼ cup water
570ml/1 pint/2 cups milk
80g/6oz/¾ cup sugar
25ml/1½ tbsps cornstarch/cornflour
3 eggs, separated
45g/1½ oz/1½ squares unsweetened cooking chocolate
5ml/½ tsp vanilla extract/essence
15ml/1 tbsp rum
60g/2oz/¼ cup sugar

DECORATION
Toasted coconut
Grated chocolate
140ml/¼ pint/½ cup whipped cream

Sift the flour with a pinch of salt. Cut the butter or margarine and shortening into the flour until the mixture resembles fine breadcrumbs.

Add the coconut and enough liquid to bring the dry ingredients together into a ball. It may not be necessary to add all the water. This may be done in a food processor or by hand. Roll out to a circle at least 5cm/2 inches larger than the dish. Fit into a pie dish or a removable base dish and crimp the edges if desired. Prick the base and the sides of the pastry well with a fork. Cook on HIGH 5-7 minutes. If the pastry begins to brown in spots, cover with a bit of foil. If the pastry bubbles up, press gently back into shape. Sprinkle the gelatine on top of the water in a small ramekin/custard cup and leave to soak. Put the egg yolks, sugar and cornstarch/cornflour together in a deep bowl and pour on the milk. Heat on medium for 2-4 minutes, stirring frequently until thickened. Melt the chocolate for 2 minutes on MEDIUM. Take 280ml/½ pint/1 cup of the custard and mix it with the melted chocolate and vanilla. Pour into the pastry shell and smooth out. Leave to cool. Melt the gelatine for 30 seconds on HIGH and stir into the remaining custard along with the rum. Put into a bowl of ice water and stir constantly until beginning to thicken. Beat the egg whites until stiff but not dry and fold into the custard. Pour carefully on top of the chocolate layer and refrigerate until firm. Decorate with cream, coconut and chocolate.

Fresh Fruit Pizza

PREPARATION TIME: 25 minutes

MICROWAVE COOKING TIME: 6-9 minutes

SERVES: 8 people

PASTRY
120g/4oz/1 cup all-purpose/plain flour
90g/3oz/⅓ cup butter or margarine
30g/1oz/2 tbsps shortening
Pinch of salt
30g/1oz/2 tbsps ground almonds
30-60ml/2-4 tbsps cold water

FILLING
225g/8oz/2 cups ricotta cheese
120g/4oz/1 cup plain/semi-sweet chocolate, finely chopped
60g/2oz/½ cup toasted almonds, finely chopped
30ml/2 tbsps honey
Milk or cream
2 kiwi fruits, peeled and sliced
120g/4oz/1 cup strawberries, hulled and halved
2 peaches or tangerines/satsumas

GLAZE
140ml/¼ pint/½ cup apricot jam, strained
Squeeze of lemon juice

Cut the butter or margarine and shortening into the flour with the pinch of salt until mixture resembles fine breadcrumbs. Add the almonds and enough of the liquid to bring the dry ingredients together into a ball. It may not be necessary to use all the water. This may be done by hand or in a food processor. Roll out to a circle at least 5cm/2 inches larger than the baking dish. Fit into a pie dish or a removable base dish and crimp the edges of the pastry if desired. Prick the base and the sides of the pastry well with a fork. Cook on HIGH for 5-7 minutes. If the pastry begins to develop brown spots, cover with a piece of foil. If the pastry bubbles up, press gently back into place. A removable base dish may be set on a rack to allow air to circulate underneath the pastry, or a pie dish may be placed on an inverted saucer. For the filling, mix the cheese, chocolate, almonds and honey together. Thin with milk or cream, if necessary, to bring to a spreading consistency. Spread evenly over the base of the cooled pastry. Put the jam and lemon juice into a deep bowl and heat on HIGH for 1-2 minutes. Thin with more juice or water if necessary. Peel and remove the pith from all of the tangerine segments or, if using peaches, peel and slice thinly. Arrange the fruit in circles on top of filling. Spoon or brush the glaze over the fruit, covering it evenly and filling in any spaces completely with more glaze. Cool to set before cutting to serve.

Facing page: Fresh Fruit Pizza.

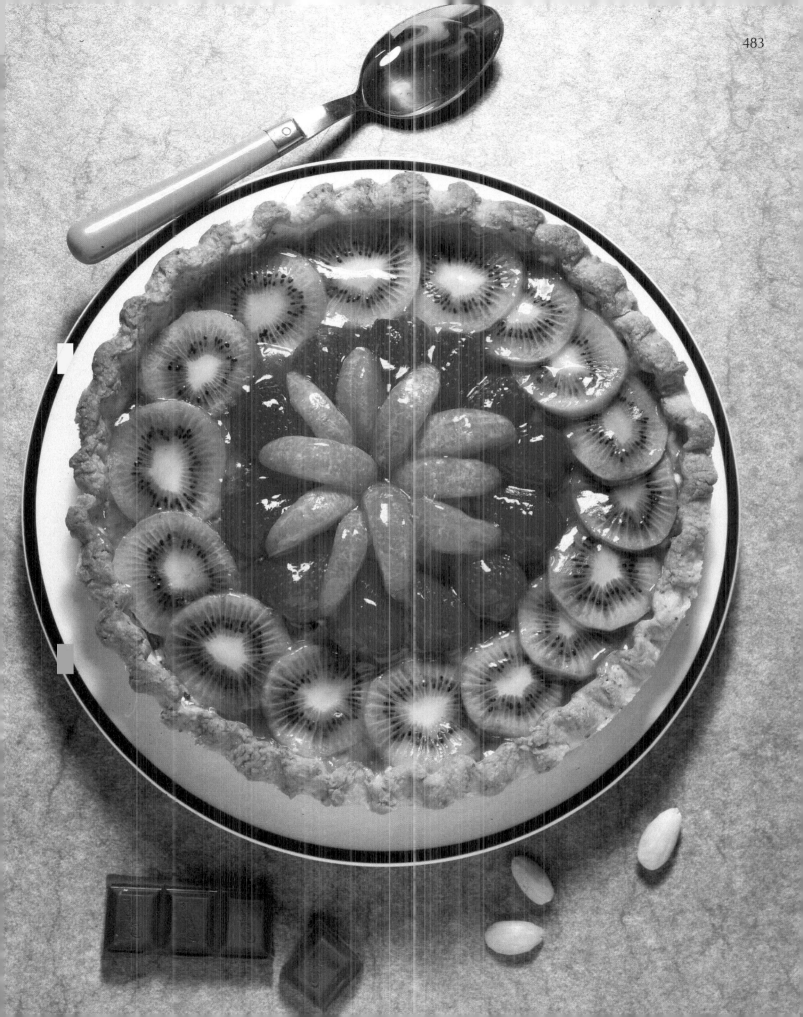

Deep Dish Pizza

PREPARATION TIME: 25 minutes

MICROWAVE COOKING TIME:
19½-22½ minutes plus 5 minutes
standing time

SERVES: 6-8 people

PASTRY
120g/4oz/1 cup all-purpose/plain flour
90g/3oz/⅓ cup butter or margarine
30g/1oz/2 tbsps shortening
Pinch of salt
40g/2 tbsps chopped mixed herbs
30-60ml/2-4 tbsps cold water

FILLING
30ml/2 tbsps oil
1 onion, chopped
1 clove garlic, chopped
1 green pepper, chopped
225g/8oz mushrooms, sliced
225g/8oz canned plum tomatoes
60ml/2 fl oz/¼ cup tomato purée/paste
*5ml/1 tsp each chopped basil, oregano
   and parsley*
Salt and pepper
1 small can anchovies, drained
*120g/4oz/1 cup shredded Mozzarella
   cheese*
60g/2oz/¼ cup grated Parmesan cheese

Sift the flour with a pinch of salt.
Cut the butter or margarine and
shortening into the flour until the
mixture resembles fine breadcrumbs.
Add the chopped herbs. Add enough
liquid to bring the dry ingredients
together into a ball. It may not be
necessary to add all the water. This
may be done by hand or in a food
processor. Roll out a circle at least
5cm/2 inches larger than the baking
dish. Prick the base and sides well
with a fork. Cook on HIGH 5-7
minutes on an inverted saucer or a
rack. If the pastry begins to brown in
spots, cover with bits of foil. If the
pastry begins to bubble up, press it
gently back into shape. Cook the
onions, green pepper, mushrooms
and garlic in oil for 30 seconds on
HIGH in a large bowl, loosely
covered. Add the tomatoes, purée/
paste, herbs, salt and pepper and
cook a further 4 minutes on HIGH,
uncovered, until reduced. Pour into
the pastry shell and top with the

**This page: Raspberry Soufflé Pie.
Facing page: Spinach and Bacon
Quiche (top) and Deep Dish Pizza
(bottom).**

anchovies and sprinkle with cheeses.
Cook 10 minutes on MEDIUM on a
rack or inverted saucer. Leave to
stand 5 minutes before serving.

Spinach and Bacon Quiche

PREPARATION TIME: 25 minutes

MICROWAVE COOKING TIME:
17-19 minutes plus 5 minutes
standing time

SERVES: 6-8 people

PASTRY
120g/4oz/1 cup all-purpose/plain flour
90g/3oz/⅓ cup butter or margarine
30g/1oz/2 tbsps shortening
Pinch of salt
30g/1oz/¼ cup ground walnuts
30-60ml/2-4 tbsps cold water

FILLING
6 strips bacon/smoked, streaky bacon
1 shallot, finely chopped
225g/8oz fresh spinach, well washed
4 eggs
*140ml/¼ pint/½ cup single/light cream
   or milk*
120g/4oz/1 cup shredded cheese
Nutmeg
Salt and pepper

Sift the flour with a pinch of salt. Cut in the butter or margarine and shortening until the mixture resembles fine breadcrumbs. Add the walnuts and enough liquid to bring the dry ingredients together into a ball. It may not be necessary to add all the water. This may be done in a food processor or by hand. Roll out to a circle at least 5cm/2 inches larger than the dish. Fit into a pie dish or removable base dish and crimp the edges of the pastry if desired. Prick the base and sides well with a fork. Cook on HIGH for 5-7 minutes on an inverted saucer or rack. If the pastry begins to develop brown spots, cover with pieces of foil. If the pastry bubbles up, press gently back into place. Heat a browning dish for 5 minutes on HIGH. Cook the bacon 2 minutes per side. Drain and leave in strips. Cook the shallot in the bacon fat for 1 minute on HIGH and drain. Cook the spinach in 2 tbsps of water in a large bowl covered loosely with plastic wrap/cling film. Reserve 30ml/2 tbsps of the cheese for the top of the quiche. Mix the eggs, cream or milk, salt, pepper, nutmeg and remaining cheese. Drain the spinach well and chop finely. Add the spinach to the egg mixture and pour into the pastry. Arrange the strips of bacon on top like the spokes of a wheel. Sprinkle on the reserved cheese and cook on a rack or inverted saucer for 7-8 minutes until the filling is softly set in the middle. Leave to stand for 5 minutes before serving.

Note: If using a microwave-convection combination oven, choose the highest temperature setting. Fill the unbaked pastry with the filling and bake for about 21 minutes.

Sour Cream, Apple and Raisin Pie

PREPARATION TIME: 25 minutes

MICROWAVE COOKING TIME: 17-20 minutes

SERVES: 6-8 people

PASTRY
120g/4oz/1 cup all-purpose/plain flour
15ml/1 tbsp sugar/caster sugar
10ml/2 tsps ground cinnamon
90g/3oz/⅓ cup butter or margarine
30g/1oz/2 tbsps shortening
Pinch of salt
30-60ml/2-4 tbsps cold water

FILLING
3 eggs, separated
280ml/8oz/1 cup sour cream
30g/1oz/2 tbsps flour
180g/6oz/¼ cup sugar
Pinch cinnamon, clove, and nutmeg
120g/4oz/1 cup raisins
2 small apples, peeled, cored and sliced thinly
140ml/¼ pint/½ cup milk

MERINGUE
3 egg whites
180g/6oz/¾ cup brown sugar
1.25ml/¼ tsp cream of tartar

Sift the flour, sugar and the cinnamon with a pinch of salt. Cut in the butter or margarine and shortening until it resembles fine breadcrumbs. Add enough liquid to bring the dry ingredients together into a ball. It may not be necessary to add all the water. This may be done by hand or in a food processor. Roll out to a circle at least 5cm/2 inches larger than the dish. Fit into a pie dish and crimp the edges of the pastry if desired. Prick the base and the sides of the pastry well with a fork. Cook on HIGH for 5-7 minutes on an inverted saucer or a rack. If the pastry begins to brown in spots, cover them with a piece of foil. If the pastry bubbles up, press it gently back into place. Beat the sugar, egg yolks and flour together in a deep bowl. Add the spices, milk and sour cream. Cook on HIGH for 2 minutes and then stir. Add the raisins and continue cooking until thickened – about 6 minutes. Cover and set aside. Cook the apples 1-2 minutes on HIGH and add to the sour cream mixture. Stir well and spoon into the pastry. Spread to smooth out completely. Beat the whites and the cream of tartar until stiff but not dry. Gradually beat in the brown sugar until stiff peaks form. Spread over

the filling to cover completely to the pastry edge. Cook on MEDIUM about 5 minutes or until the meringue is set. May be served slightly warm or cold.

Key-Lime Pie

PREPARATION TIME: 20 minutes

MICROWAVE COOKING TIME: 10-12 minutes

SERVES: 5-8 people

PASTRY
120g/4oz/1 cup all-purpose/plain flour
30g/2 tbsps cocoa
15ml/1 tbsp sugar
90g/3oz/⅓ cup butter or margarine
30g/1oz/2 tbsps shortening
Pinch of salt
30-60ml/2-4 tbsps cold water

FILLING
400g/14oz/1 can sweetened condensed milk
3 eggs, separated
180g/6oz/¾ cup sugar/caster sugar
Grated rind and juice of 3 limes
1 drop yellow food colouring (optional)
1 drop green food colouring (optional)

DECORATION
Grated chocolate
Lime slices

Sift the flour with the pinch of salt, sugar and cocoa. Cut in the butter or margarine and the shortening until the mixture resembles fine breadcrumbs. Add enough liquid to bring the dry ingredients together into a ball. It may not be necessary to use all the water. This may be done by hand or in a food processor. Roll out to a circle at least 5cm/2 inches larger than the dish. Fit into a pie dish and crimp the edges of the pastry if desired. Prick the base and sides well with a fork. Cook on HIGH 5-7 minutes on an inverted saucer. If the pastry bubbles up, press gently back into place. For the filling, combine the egg yolks, milk, rind and juice of the limes and colouring. Beat until smooth. Pour into the baked pastry shell. Beat the egg whites until stiff but not dry. Beat in the sugar gradually until stiff peaks form. Beat

Above: Sour Cream, Apple and Raisin Pie (top) and Key-Lime Pie (bottom).

in the cream of tartar. Spread the meringue evenly over the lime filling out to the pastry edge. Cook on MEDIUM for 5 minutes or until the meringue sets. Allow to cool completely and then chill. Decorate with grated chocolate and lime slices before serving.

Raspberry Soufflé Pie

PREPARATION TIME: 25 minutes plus chilling time

MICROWAVE COOKING TIME: 5½-7½ minutes

SERVES: 6-8 people

PASTRY
120g/4oz/1 cup all-purpose/plain flour
90g/3oz/⅓ cup butter or margarine
30g/1oz/2 tbsps shortening
Pinch of salt
30-60ml/2-4 tbsps cold water
10ml/2 tsps instant coffee

FILLING
120g/4oz/1 cup raspberries, fresh or
    frozen
60ml/2 fl oz/¼ cup lemon juice and
    water, mixed
15g/½ oz/1 tbsp unflavoured gelatine
130g/6oz/¾ cup sugar/caster sugar
3 eggs, separated
280g/½ pint/1 cup whipped cream

DECORATION
6-8 whole raspberries
140ml/¼ pint/½ cup whipped cream

Sift the flour and the pinch of salt into a bowl and cut in the shortening and butter or margarine until the mixture resembles fine breadcrumbs. Mix the coffee and the water and add to the dry ingredients to bring them together into a ball. It may not be necessary to add all the water and coffee. This may be done in a food processor or by hand. Roll out to a circle at least 5cm/2 inches larger than the baking dish. Fit into a pie dish or a removable base dish. Crimp the edges if desired. Prick the base and the sides of the pastry well with a fork. Cook on HIGH 5-7 minutes. If the pastry begins to brown in spots, cover with a bit of foil. If the pastry bubbles up push gently back into place. To prepare the filling, purée the raspberries in a blender or food processor and sift to remove the seeds. Sprinkle the gelatine on top of the juice and water in a small ramekin/custard cup. Leave to stand 5 minutes. Beat the egg yolks and sugar until thick and mousse-like. Fold in the raspberry purée. Melt the gelatine for 30 seconds on HIGH. Pour into the egg yolk mixture, stirring constantly. Put into a bowl of ice water and stir until starting to thicken. Beat the egg whites until stiff, but not dry. Allow the raspberry mixture to thicken until it begins to hold its shape. Then fold the egg whites into the raspberry mixture along with the cream and pour into the pie shell, mounding in the center. Refrigerate until firm. Decorate with rosettes of cream and whole raspberries.

Apple and Rose Petal Pie

PREPARATION TIME: 25 minutes

MICROWAVE COOKING TIME: 22-26 minutes

SERVES: 6-8 people

PASTRY
120g/4oz/1 cup all-purpose/plain flour
90g/3oz/⅓ cup butter or margarine
30g/1oz/2 tbsps shortening
Pinch of salt
30-60ml/2-4 tbsps cold water

FILLING
8-10 apples/4-5 cups peeled, sliced apples
150g/5oz/⅔ cup sugar
1 cup rose petals, washed and dried
30g/1oz/2 tbsps flour
Pinch ginger

TOPPING
Pastry trimmings
5ml/1 tsp cinnamon
10ml/2 tsps sugar

Sift the flour and the pinch of salt into a bowl. Cut in the butter or margarine and shortening until the mixture resembles fine breadcrumbs. Add enough liquid to bring the dry ingredients together into a ball. It may not be necessary to add all the water. This may be done in a food processor or by hand. Roll out to a circle at least 5cm/2 inches larger than the baking dish. Fit into a pie dish or a removable base dish and crimp the edges of the pastry if desired. Prick the base and sides well with a fork. Cook on HIGH 5-7 minutes on a rack or an inverted saucer. If the pastry begins to brown in spots, cover with pieces of foil. If the pastry bubbles up, press gently back into place. Cut the pastry trimmings into circles or flower shapes. Prick lightly with a fork and sprinkle with cinnamon sugar. Cook 2-4 minutes on HIGH arranged in a circle on a microwave baking sheet covered with wax/greaseproof paper. Combine all the filling ingredients and put into the pastry shell. Cook 15 minutes on HIGH or until the apples are done. Top with the pastry cut-outs before serving.

This page: Apple and Rose Petal Pie (top) and Cherry Streusel Pie (bottom). Facing page: Sweetcorn and Tomato Quiche.

Cherry Streusel Pie

PREPARATION TIME: 20 minutes

MICROWAVE COOKING TIME: 22 minutes

SERVES: 6-8 people

CINNAMON PASTRY
120g/4oz/1 cup all-purpose/plain flour
90g/3oz/⅓ cup butter or margarine
Pinch of cinnamon
90ml/3 fl oz/⅓ cup cold water
Pinch salt

CHERRY FILLING
2 450g/1lb cans pitted red cherries
1.25ml/¼ tsp almond essence/extract
150g/5oz/⅔ cup sugar
30g/1oz/2 tbsps flour

STREUSEL TOPPING
60g/2oz/½ cup all-purpose/plain flour
45g/1½ oz/3 tbsps butter or margarine

30g/1oz/¼ cup chopped almonds
30ml/1 fl oz/2 tbsps water

ICING
120g/4oz/1 cup icing/powdered sugar
30ml/1 fl oz/2 tbsps water
Few drops almond essence/extract

Sift the flour for the pastry with the cinnamon and a pinch of salt. Cut in the butter or margarine until the mixture resembles fine breadcrumbs. This may be done in a food processor. Add enough water to bring the ingredients together into a ball. Chill for 10 minutes and roll out to a circle at least 5cm/2 inches larger than the baking dish. Fit the pastry into a 20cm/8 inch pie dish and crimp the edges if desired. Place on a rack or inverted saucer. Prick the base well with a fork and cook for 5-7 minutes on HIGH. If the pastry bubbles up, press gently back into place. If brown spots appear, cover them with foil and continue baking. Mix the filling ingredients and pour into the pastry shell. Sift the flour for the topping and cut in the butter or margarine until the mixture resembles fine breadcrumbs. This may be done in a food processor. Stir in the almonds and add just enough water to make a crumbly mixture. Sprinkle the topping over the filling and cook a further 12 minutes on MEDIUM, or until the filling just begins to bubble. Sift the icing/powdered sugar and beat in the water and almond extract/essence. Add more water if necessary, but the icing should not be too thin. Allow the pie to cool completely before drizzling over the icing.

Sweetcorn and Tomato Quiche

PREPARATION TIME: 25 minutes

MICROWAVE COOKING TIME: 17-19 minutes plus 5 minutes standing time

SERVES: 6-8 people

PASTRY
120g/4oz/1 cup whole-wheat flour
90g/3oz/⅓ cup butter or margarine
30g/1oz/2 tbsps shortening

Pinch of salt
30-60ml/2-4 tbsps cold water

FILLING
1 green pepper, diced
1 small onion, chopped
10ml/2 tsps oil
1 cup frozen corn, defrosted
4 eggs
140ml/¼ pint/½ cup single/light cream or milk
120g/4oz/1 cup shredded cheese
15ml/1 tbsp chopped parsley
15ml/1 tbsp chopped dill
Salt and pepper
2 tomatoes, sliced in rounds

Sift the flour with a pinch of salt and return the bran to the bowl. Cut the butter or margarine and shortening into the flour until the mixture resembles fine breadcrumbs. Add enough liquid to bring the dry ingredients together into a ball. It may not be necessary to use all the water. This may be done in a food processor or by hand. Roll out to a circle at least 5cm/2 inches larger than the dish. Fit into a pie dish or a removable base dish and crimp the edges if desired. Prick the base and sides well with a fork and cook on HIGH 5-7 minutes on an inverted saucer or a rack. If the pastry begins to brown in spots, cover with pieces of foil. If the pastry bubbles up, press it gently back into place. Put the oil, pepper and onion into a small bowl. Cover loosely and cook 30 seconds on HIGH. Add the corn and cook a further 30 seconds. Combine with all the remaining ingredients except the tomatoes. Pour into the pastry shell and return the dish to a rack or inverted saucer. Cook 7 minutes on MEDIUM. Arrange the tomato slices on top and cook a further 5 minutes, until softly set in the middle. Leave to stand 5 minutes before serving. *Note:* If using a microwave-convection combination oven, choose the highest temperature setting. Fill the unbaked pastry with the filling and bake about 21 minutes.

Microwave
BAKING

COOKIES/BISCUITS

60g/2oz/½ cup roasted cashew nuts
Milk (as needed)

Beat together the butter and the sugar until light and fluffy. Add the egg, water and vanilla. Sift in the baking powder, salt and flour. Beat until just blended and stir in the nuts and the chocolate chips/drops by hand. Add enough milk to bring to dropping consistency. Drop by rounded 5ml/1 tsp amounts on wax paper/greaseproof paper in a circle of 6 cookies. Cook on MEDIUM 2-3 minutes per batch. Cookies may also be cooked in a microwave-convection combination oven for 3 minutes. When the tops look set the cookies are done. Remove on a paper and cool on a flat surface before serving.

Lemon-Iced Molasses/ Treacle Cookies

PREPARATION TIME: 20 minutes

MICROWAVE COOKING TIME: 12-18 minutes

MAKES: 48 cookies

120g/4oz/½ cup butter or margarine
120g/4oz/½ cup dark brown sugar
1 egg
30ml/2 tbsps molasses/treacle
10ml/2 tsps baking powder
225g/8oz/2 cups whole-wheat flour
Pinch salt
5ml/1 tsp allspice
2.5ml/½ tsp ginger

This page: Chocolate Cherry Slices. Facing page: Lemon-Iced Molasses/Treacle Cookies (top) and Chocolate Chip Cashew Cookies (bottom).

Chocolate Chip Cashew Cookies

PREPARATION TIME: 20 minutes

MICROWAVE COOKING TIME: 12-18 minutes

MAKES: 48 cookies

120g/4oz/½ cup butter or margarine
120g/4oz/½ cup light brown sugar
1 egg
15ml/1 tbsp water
10ml/2 tsps vanilla extract/essence
Pinch salt
10ml/2 tbsps baking powder
225g/8oz/2 cups all-purpose/plain flour
120g/4oz/1 cup chocolate chips/drops

ICING

450g/1lb icing/powdered sugar
140ml/¼ pint/½ cup hot water
Yellow food colouring (optional)
Juice of 1 lemon
Rind of 1 lemon cut in thin strips

Beat the sugar and the butter together until light and fluffy. Beat in the egg gradually. Stir in the molasses/treacle and sift in the baking powder, flour, salt and spices. Stir together well and drop in 2.5cm/1 inch balls on wax/greaseproof paper on a microwave baking sheet. Arrange in a circle of 8 balls. Cook on MEDIUM for 2-3 minutes per batch, until the tops look set. Remove on a paper and cool on a flat surface. Prepare the icing by mixing the icing sugar and the hot water together. Add the lemon juice, strips of lemon rind and yellow food colouring, if using. Once the cookies are cool coat with the icing and leave to set completely before serving.

Chocolate Peppernuts

PREPARATION TIME: 15 minutes

MICROWAVE COOKING TIME:
24-32 minutes

MAKES: 48 cookies

60g/2oz/¼ cup butter or margarine
225g/8oz/1 cup sugar/caster sugar
60g/2oz/2 squares unsweetened
  chocolate
10ml/2 tsps baking powder
2 eggs
225g/8oz/2 cups all-purpose/plain flour
5ml/1 tsp black pepper
Pinch salt
Icing/powdered sugar

Heat the butter and chocolate in a deep bowl on MEDIUM for 2-3 minutes. Beat in the sugar and eggs. Sift in the baking powder, salt, pepper and flour. Blend until well incorporated and chill until firm. Shape into 2.5cm/1 inch balls. Cook 6 at a time in a circle on waxed/greaseproof paper on a microwave baking sheet for 3 minutes on MEDIUM per batch. The cookies may also be cooked for 4 minutes on

a combination setting of a microwave-convection oven. Cool on a paper on a flat surface until firm. Sprinkle with icing sugar before serving.

Rum-Raisin Cookies

PREPARATION TIME: 20 minutes

MICROWAVE COOKING TIME:
12-18 minutes

MAKES: 48 cookies

45ml/3 tbsps dark rum
120g/4oz/1 cup raisins
120g/4oz/½ cup butter or margarine
120g/4oz/½ cup sugar/caster sugar
1 egg
10ml/2 tsps baking powder
225g/8oz/2 cups all-purpose/plain flour
Milk (as needed)
Pinch salt

Combine the rum and raisins in a small bowl. Cover loosely and heat 10 seconds on HIGH. Leave to soak. Beat the butter and sugar together until light. Beat in the egg gradually. Sift in the baking powder, flour and salt. Stir into the egg mixture until well mixed. Add the raisins and any remaining rum. If the mixture is very stiff, add some milk to bring to dropping consistency. Drop in a circle in rounded teaspoonfuls onto wax/greaseproof paper on a baking sheet. Cook on MEDIUM for 2-3 minutes or until the surface looks set. Cookies may also be cooked on a combination setting in a microwave-convection oven for 3 minutes. Remove the cookies on a paper to cool on a flat surface. Leave to cool completely before serving.

Chocolate Cherry Slices

PREPARATION TIME: 25 minutes

MICROWAVE COOKING TIME:
12 minutes

MAKES: 32 cookies

120g/4oz/½ cup butter or margarine
180g/6oz/1½ cups all-purpose/plain
  flour
1 egg

120g/4oz/½ cup icing sugar/powdered
  sugar
2.5ml/½ tsp cream of tartar
2.5ml/½ tsp baking soda
60g/2oz unsweetened chocolate, melted
Pinch salt
48 glacé/candied cherries, halved
60g/2oz/½ cup chopped, unblanched
  almonds
120g/4oz semi-sweet/plain chocolate

Melt the unsweetened chocolate 2 minutes on MEDIUM. Cool slightly. Beat all the ingredients together until a dough forms. Form into 4 sausage shapes about 2.5cm/1 inch thick. Press on 8 rows of 3 cherries and sprinkle over the almonds. Bake on sheets of wax/greaseproof paper on microwave baking sheets for 3 minutes on MEDIUM or until the top is set. Slice into 8 2.5cm/1 inch fingers while still slightly warm. Cool on paper or on a flat surface. Melt the plain/semi-sweet chocolate for 2 minutes on MEDIUM. Drizzle over the cookies while the chocolate is still warm. Allow the chocolate to set completely before serving.

Walnut Fingers

PREPARATION TIME: 20 minutes

MICROWAVE COOKING TIME:
12 minutes

MAKES: 32 cookies

120g/4oz/½ cup butter or margarine
1 egg
180g/6oz/1½ cups all-purpose/plain
  flour
120g/4oz/½ cup icing/powdered sugar
2.5ml/½ tsp cream of tartar
2.5ml/½ tsp baking soda
Pinch salt
60g/2oz/½ cup ground walnuts
2.5ml/½ tsp vanilla essence
32 walnut halves
Icing/powdered sugar

Beat the butter or margarine until soft, add the remaining ingredients

Facing page: Rum-Raisin Cookies (top) and Chocolate Peppernuts (bottom).

except the ground walnuts and beat until a stiff dough forms. Stir in the nuts. Form into 4 long sausage shapes about 2.5cm/1 inch thick. Place on sheets of wax paper/ greaseproof paper on microwave baking sheets and flatten slightly. Push walnut halves down the centre of each strip. Cook 2 strips at a time for 3 minutes on MEDIUM or until set on top. Slice into 2.5cm/1 inch fingers while still slightly warm. Cool on the paper or on a flat surface. Sprinkle with icing sugar/powdered sugar when cold.

Butter Pecan Bars

PREPARATION TIME: 25 minutes

MICROWAVE COOKING TIME:
12-13 minutes

MAKES: 12-16 bars

90g/3oz/¾ cup whole-wheat flour
60g/2oz/¼ cup butter or margarine
60g/2oz/¼ cup brown sugar
2 eggs
90ml/3oz/⅓ cup plain yogurt
2.5ml/½ tsp baking powder
1.25ml/¼ tsp baking soda
Pinch salt
30g/1oz/¼ cup chopped pecans

TOPPING
120g/4oz/½ cup butter or margarine
225g/8oz/1 cup dark brown sugar
60g/2oz/½ cup chopped pecans
30ml/2 tbsps plain yogurt

Mix the butter and sugar together with an electric mixer until light and fluffy and add the eggs and remaining ingredients and beat about 1 minute. Stir in the nuts by hand. Spread into a 20cm/8 inch square dish. Cover the corners with foil and place on a rack or inverted saucer before baking. Cook for 6 minutes on HIGH. Remove the foil halfway through. Melt the butter for the topping for 1 minute on HIGH. Stir in the sugar and the nuts and cook for 3 minutes on HIGH. Add the yogurt. Spread the topping onto the bar mixture and cook on HIGH for 2-3 minutes until beginning to bubble. Cool and cut into bars.

Cranberry Bars

PREPARATION TIME: 15 minutes

MICROWAVE COOKING TIME:
10 minutes

MAKES: 12-16 bars

120g/4oz/½ cup butter or margarine
150g/5oz/⅔ cup brown sugar
90g/3oz/1 cup instant oatmeal/oat flakes
120g/4oz/1 cup all-purpose flour/plain flour
Pinch salt
120g/4oz/1 cup whole cranberry sauce
60g/2oz/½ cup chopped walnuts

This page: Butter Pecan Bars (top) and Chocolate Chip Brownies (bottom). Facing page: Butterscotch Brownies (top) and Cranberry Bars (bottom).

Beat together the butter or margarine and sugar until light and fluffy. Sift in the flour and salt. Add the oatmeal and blend until the mixture resembles coarse breadcrumbs. Press ⅔ of the mixture in the bottom of a 20cm/8 inch square baking dish. Put the dish onto a rack or inverted saucer. Cook on MEDIUM for 5 minutes or until just firm. Mix the cranberry sauce and walnuts together,

and spread over the base. Crumble remaining oatmeal mixture over the top and cook on HIGH for 5 minutes. Cut into squares while slightly warm. Allow to cool in the dish on a flat surface. Remove from the dish when cool.

Peanut Butter Thumb Print Cookies

PREPARATION TIME: 25 minutes

MICROWAVE COOKING TIME: 24 minutes

MAKES: 48 cookies

120g/4oz/½ cup butter or margarine
120g/4oz/1 cup smooth or crunchy peanut butter
225g/8oz/1 cup light brown sugar
2 eggs
2.5ml/½ tsp baking soda
340g/12oz/3 cups all-purpose/plain flour
2 egg whites
120g/4oz/1 cup coarsely chopped roasted peanuts
Grape or blackcurrant jelly
Redcurrant jelly or raspberry jam

Mix together the butter and the sugar until light and fluffy. Add the peanut butter and the eggs. Sift in the flour and the soda. Add a pinch of salt if using unsalted peanuts. Shape into 2.5cm/1 inch balls. Roll in lightly beaten egg white and then in the chopped roasted peanuts. Chill for 10 minutes. Press a well in the centre of each cookie. Fill with 5ml/1 tsp jelly or jam. Arrange in a circle on wax paper/greaseproof paper. Cook for 4 minutes on MEDIUM. Cool on a flat surface before serving.

Chocolate Chip Brownies

PREPARATION TIME: 20 minutes

MICROWAVE COOKING TIME: 5-6 minutes

MAKES: 12-16 bars

60g/2oz unsweetened/plain chocolate
120g/4oz/½ cup butter or margarine
225g/8oz/1 cup sugar/caster sugar

5ml/1 tsp instant coffee dissolved in 10ml/2 tsps hot water
90g/3oz/¾ cup all-purpose/plain flour
2.5ml/½ tsp baking powder
2 eggs
Pinch salt
120g/4oz/1 cup whole pecans
60g/2oz/½ cup chocolate chips/drops

Combine unsweetened chocolate, butter, sugar and dissolved coffee in a mixing bowl. Microwave on MEDIUM for 3-4 minutes or until the chocolate melts and the sugar

dissolves. Beat in the eggs and sift in the flour, baking powder and salt. Stir well to blend the mixture. Spread into a 20cm/8 inch square dish. Cover the corners of the dish with foil and put the dish on a rack or an inverted saucer. Cook on HIGH for 5 minutes. Sprinkle on the chips and nuts and remove the foil. Cook further 2 minutes. Cool on a flat surface and cut into even squares while slightly warm. Leave to cool completely before removing from the dish.

Sugar Plums

PREPARATION TIME: 25 minutes

MICROWAVE COOKING TIME:
24 minutes plus 1 minute
standing time

MAKES: approximately 48 cookies

90g/3oz/⅓ cup butter or margarine
180g/6oz/¾ cup dark brown sugar
1 egg
30ml/2 tbsps brandy
150g/5oz/1¼ cups all-purpose/plain
*   flour*
225g/8oz/2 cups mixed glacé/candied
*   fruit, chopped*
120g/4oz/½ cup raisins
120g/4oz/½ cup dates, chopped
120g/4oz/1 cup chopped toasted
*   almonds*
2.5ml/½ tsp baking soda
Pinch of salt

ICING
450g/1lb/4 cups icing/powdered sugar
140ml/¼ pint/½ cup hot water
Almond, vanilla and peppermint
*   essence/extract*
Lemon juice
Food colouring
Coloured sugar
Granulated sugar

Beat the brown sugar and the butter
together until light and fluffy. Beat in
the egg gradually. Stir in the brandy,
fruit and almonds. Sift in the flour,
baking soda and salt and stir together
well. Form into a ball and wrap well.
Refrigerate until firm. Shape into
1.25cm/½ inch balls. Place 8 balls in a
circle on a sheet of waxed/
greaseproof paper on a microwave
baking sheet and cook on MEDIUM
for 4 minutes per batch. Leave to
stand 1 minute and remove to a rack
to cool completely. Mix the icing/
powdered sugar and water together
and divide the mixture into 4
separate bowls. Tint 1 batch pink and
flavour with almond, 1 white,
flavoured with vanilla, 1 yellow,
flavoured with lemon juice and
1 green, flavoured with mint. Coat an
equal number of cookies with each of
the icings and sprinkle coloured
sugar on the top while the icing is
still slightly damp.

Butterscotch Brownies

PREPARATION TIME: 15 minutes

MICROWAVE COOKING TIME:
7 minutes

MAKES: 12-15 bars

120g/4oz/½ cup butter or margarine
180g/6oz/¾ cup brown sugar
2 eggs
2.5ml/½ tsp vanilla
90g/3oz/¾ cup all-purpose/plain flour
2.5ml/½ tsp baking powder
Pinch salt
60g/2oz/½ cup raisins
120g/4oz/1 cup roughly chopped walnuts
Icing/powdered sugar

Melt the butter for 1 minute on
HIGH. Stir in the sugar until well

**Facing page: Walnut Fingers (top)
and Peanut Butter Thumb Print
Cookies (bottom). This page: Sugar
Plums.**

blended. Beat in the egg. Sift in the
flour, baking powder and salt. Stir
well and add the raisins. Pour into a
20cm/8 inch square dish. Cover the
corners of the dish with foil. Place
the dish on a rack or on an inverted
saucer. Cook for 5 minutes on
HIGH. Remove the foil, sprinkle on
the nuts and press down lightly.
Cook a further 2 minutes on
MEDIUM. Cut into bars while still
slightly warm. Cool in a dish on a flat
surface. Remove from the dish when
cool.

Microwave
BAKING

CAKES

Jam and Cream Sandwich/Layer Cake

PREPARATION TIME: 25 minutes

MICROWAVE COOKING TIME:
13-21 minutes plus 5 minutes
standing time

SERVES: 6-8 people

CAKE
225g/8oz/1 cup butter or margarine
225g/8oz/1 cup sugar/caster sugar
2.5ml/½ tsp vanilla extract/essence
225g/8oz/4 cups all-purpose/plain flour
10ml/2 tsps baking powder

ICING
225g/8oz/2 cups powdered/icing sugar
140ml/¼ pint/½ cup hot water
Redcurrant jelly or seedless raspberry jam

FILLING
140ml/¼ pint/½ cup whipped cream
60ml/4 tbsps strawberry or raspberry jam

Line 2 20cm/8 inch cake dishes with
2 layers of wax/greaseproof paper.
Beat the butter or margarine to
soften. Beat in the sugar until light
and fluffy. Beat in the eggs, one at a
time, mixing until the mixture is
light. Beat in the vanilla and fold in
sifted flour and baking powder.
Divide the mixture between the
2 dishes and smooth the tops. Bake
on highest setting of a combination
microwave-convection oven for
12 minutes, or on MEDIUM in a
conventional microwave oven for
6 minutes per layer, increasing to
HIGH for 2-8 minutes per layer, until
done. The cake will look set on the
top and the mixture will pull away
from the sides of the dish when done.
Cool 5-10 minutes on a flat surface

before transferring to a cooling rack
to cool completely. Remove the
paper from the cakes and choose the
layer with the flattest top and spread
the other with jam. Spread over the
cream and then press on the top
layer. Mix the powdered/icing sugar
and the water together until of thick

**This page: Jam and Cream
Sandwich/Layer Cake. Facing
page: Black Forest Torte.**

coating consistency. Pour the icing on
the top layer and allow to set briefly
but not completely. Fill a piping bag
fitted with a small nozzle with the

redcurrant jelly or raspberry jam. Pipe thin lines of jelly or jam onto the icing. Draw a knife blade or a skewer back and forth through the icing and the jelly to feather the lines. This must be done quickly before the icing sets completely. Allow to set thoroughly before slicing to serve. *Note:* It may be necessary to heat the redcurrant jelly for the feathered lines for 1 minute on HIGH to soften before piping. If the jelly appears full of lumps rub through a fine strainer before using.

Lemon-Glazed Gingerbread

PREPARATION TIME: 20 minutes

MICROWAVE COOKING TIME: 10-13 minutes plus 5-10 minutes standing time

SERVES: 6-8 people

90g/3oz/⅓ cup vegetable shortening
90g/3oz/⅓ cup light brown sugar
180g/6oz/1¼ cups all-purpose/plain flour
Pinch salt
2.5ml/½ tsp baking soda
1.25ml/¼ tsp ground cloves
2.5ml/½ tsp ground cinnamon
2.5ml/½ tsp ground ginger
90ml/3 fl oz/⅓ cup molasses/treacle
60ml/2 fl oz/¼ cup hot water

GLAZE
90g/3oz/¾ cup sugar/caster sugar
25g/1½ tbsps butter or margarine (optional)
Juice and rind of 1 small lemon
200ml/6 fl oz/¾ cup water

TOPPING
280ml/½ pint/1 cup whipped cream
140ml/¼ pint/½ cup sour cream or yogurt
Sugar to taste

Beat the shortening to soften. Beat in the sugar until mixture is light and fluffy. Add the flour, sifted if necessary, salt, soda and spices. Mix the molasses/treacle, water and eggs together. Pour into the mixture and beat by hand or machine until just mixed. Spread into a 20cm/8 inch round baking dish. Cook on MEDIUM for 6 minutes and then increase the setting to HIGH and cook 1-4 minutes until set. Cool on a flat surface for 5-10 minutes before transferring to a serving dish. To prepare the glaze, pare the rind from the lemon and scrape off any white pith. Cut the rind into thin slivers and set aside. Combine the remaining ingredients and cook for 2 minutes on HIGH, stirring every 1 minute until the sauce begins to thicken. Add the strips of lemon rind and cook an additional 1 minute on HIGH, stirring once. Do not overcook. The sauce will thicken as it cools. Mix the topping ingredients together. Spoon some of the glaze over the cake, top with the sour cream mixture and pour over the remaining glaze as a sauce.

Pineapple-Apricot Upside-Down Cake

PREPARATION TIME: 25 minutes

MICROWAVE COOKING TIME: 9-15 minutes plus 5-10 minutes standing time

SERVES: 6-8 people

CAKE
90g/3oz/⅓ cup butter or margarine
150g/5oz/⅔ cup sugar/caster sugar
2.5ml/½ tsp vanilla extract/essence
2 eggs
120g/4oz/1 cup all-purpose/plain flour
Scant 10ml/2 tsps baking powder
60-90ml/2-3 fl oz/¼-⅓ cup milk

TOPPING
1 small fresh pineapple, peeled, cored and sliced or 9 canned pineapple rings
3-4 fresh apricots or 6-8 canned apricot halves
6-8 walnut halves
60g/2oz/¼ cup butter or margarine
120g/4oz/½ cup light brown sugar

Beat the margarine or butter until soft. Beat in the sugar gradually until the mixture is light and fluffy. Beat in the eggs gradually and add vanilla essence/extract. Stir in the flour and baking powder, sifting if necessary. Add enough of the milk to make the mixture of dropping consistency. Melt the butter or margarine in a 20cm/8 inch round dish for 1 minute on HIGH. Sprinkle the sugar evenly over the butter and top with the pineapple rings cut in half and placed in the middle. Around the outside edge place the walnut halves, rounded sides down. Cover each walnut half with an apricot, cut side down. Top with the cake mixture and carefully spread it over the topping. Put the dish on a rack or an inverted saucer and cook 6 minutes on MEDIUM. Increase the setting to HIGH and cook a further 3-8 minutes or until the top appears set. Cool on a flat surface for 5-10 minutes before turning out onto a serving dish. Serve warm with whipped cream.

Passion Cake

PREPARATION TIME: 20 minutes

MICROWAVE COOKING TIME: 14-22 minutes

SERVES: 8-10 people

CAKE
285g/10oz/2½ cups all-purpose/plain flour
225g/10oz/1¼ cups sugar/caster sugar
225g/8oz carrots, finely grated
225g/8oz canned pineapple, drained and finely chopped
15ml/1 tbsp ground cinnamon
10ml/2 tsps ground allspice
10ml/2 tsps baking powder
4 eggs
180g/6oz/⅔ cup butter or margarine
60g/2oz/½ cup chopped walnuts

FROSTING
2-225g/8oz packages cream cheese
60g/2oz/½ cup icing/powdered sugar
Juice of 1 lemon
Milk

DECORATION
Walnut halves tossed in powdered/icing sugar

Facing page: Lemon-Glazed Gingerbread (top) and Pineapple-Apricot Upside-Down Cake (bottom).

Line 2 21.5cm/9 inch sandwich layer cake dishes with 2 circles of wax/greaseproof paper. Beat the sugar and butter together until light and creamy. Beat in the eggs gradually. Add the carrots, pineapple and walnuts. Sift the flour, baking powder and spices into the mixture and fold in. Divide the mixture between the 2 dishes and bake 1 layer at a time for 6 minutes on MEDIUM per layer. Increase the setting to HIGH and continue to cook for 1-5 minutes more per layer. Cook both layers at a time on the highest setting of a combination microwave-convection oven for 12 minutes. Leave the cakes to stand for 5-10 minutes before turning out to cool on a wire rack. Beat the cheese, sugar and lemon juice together until smooth and spreadable. Add milk, if necessary, until the frosting is of the right consistency. Sandwich the layers together with half the frosting and spread the rest on the top. Decorate with the sugar-coated walnuts around the outside edge of the cake.

Boston Caramel Cream Pie

PREPARATION TIME: 25 minutes

MICROWAVE COOKING TIME: 17½-20 minutes plus 5-10 minutes standing time

SERVES: 6-8 people

CAKE
90g/3oz/⅓ cup margarine or butter
150g/5oz/⅔ cup sugar/caster sugar
2 eggs
2.5ml/½ tsp vanilla extract/essence
150g/5oz/1¼ cups all-purpose/plain flour
Scant 10ml/2 tsps baking powder
60-90ml/2-3oz/¼-⅓ cup milk

FILLING
60g/2oz/¼ cup dark brown sugar
30g/1oz/2 tbsps cornstarch/cornflour
280ml/½ pint/1 cup milk
2 egg yolks
15ml/1 tbsp butter or margarine

ICING
15g/½ oz unsweetened cooking chocolate

120g/4oz/1 cup icing/powdered sugar
60ml/2 fl oz/¼ cup or more hot water
10ml/2 tsps vegetable oil
Note: If using plain/semi-sweet chocolate use 30g/1oz/2 tbsps less icing/powdered sugar

Mix the margarine or butter until soft. Beat in the sugar gradually until the mixture is light and fluffy. Beat in the eggs gradually and add the vanilla essence/extract. Sift in the flour and baking powder and fold in the dry ingredients. Add enough of the milk to make the mixture of dropping consistency. Line the bottom of a 20cm/8 inch round dish with 2 layers of wax/greaseproof paper. Cook on MEDIUM for 6 minutes. Increase the setting to HIGH and cook for 2-5 minutes more until the centre has risen and the surface appears set. Leave to cool on a flat surface for 5-10 minutes before removing from the baking dish. If using a combination microwave-convection oven use the highest temperature setting and cook for 11 minutes.
Put the sugar for the filling into a deep mixing bowl or glass measure. Heat for 30 seconds on HIGH until melted. Mix the milk into the cornstarch/cornflour and beat the mixture into the sugar. Cook on HIGH for about 6 minutes, stirring every 2 minutes until very thick. Beat the yolks together and add a spoonful of the hot mixture. Return the eggs to the remaining caramel mixture and blend well. Heat 1 minute on MEDIUM to cook the eggs. Beat in the butter. Put a damp greaseproof paper or wax paper onto the surface of the filling, and allow to cool slightly. Cut the cake layer in half horizontally and sandwich with the filling.
Melt the chocolate for the icing for 2 minutes on MEDIUM. Sift in the sugar and stir in enough water to make a thick but pourable icing. Beat in the oil to keep the icing shiny. Pour the icing all at once on top of the cake. Ease the icing out over the top of the cake with a palette knife/spatula and allow it to drip down the sides of the cake. Let the icing set completely before cutting to serve.

Black Forest Torte

PREPARATION TIME: 30 minutes

MICROWAVE COOKING TIME: 26-33 minutes

SERVES: 6-8 people

CAKE
60g/2oz/2 squares unsweetened chocolate
285g/11oz/1⅓ cups sugar/caster sugar
150g/5oz/⅔ cup butter or margarine
4 eggs
255g/9oz/1¼ cups all-purpose/plain flour
60g/2oz/½ cup cocoa
5ml/1 tsp baking soda
200ml/6 fl oz/¾ cup milk

PASTRY
150g/5oz/⅔ cup butter or margarine
60g/2oz/¼ cup sugar/caster sugar
2.5ml/½ tsp vanilla extract/essence
150g/5oz/1 cup all-purpose/plain flour
1 egg yolk
30ml/2 tbsps raspberry jam or redcurrant jelly, melted

FILLING
1-225g/8oz can dark, sweet cherries, pitted
15g/1 tbsp cornstarch/cornflour
30ml/2 tbsps kirsch
140ml/¼ pint/½ cup whipped cream, with sugar and kirsch to taste

ICING
570ml/1 pint/2 cups whipped cream
Grated chocolate
Maraschino/cocktail cherries

Mix the butter and sugar together for the pastry until well blended, stir in the egg yolk and vanilla. Stir in the flour until the mixture comes together. Rub well and chill 10 minutes. Roll the pastry out to 1.25cm/½ inch thick. Prick lightly and cut out into a 21.5cm/9 inch circle. Bake on a microwave baking sheet lined with waxed/greaseproof paper for 5-8 minutes on HIGH. Transfer to a wire rack to cool.

Facing page: Passion Cake (top) and Boston Caramel Cream Pie (bottom)

Line 2 20cm/8 inch round dishes with 2 layers of wax/greaseproof paper. Melt the chocolate for the cake 4 minutes on MEDIUM, stirring once or twice. Allow to cool slightly. Beat the butter or margarine and the sugar together until light. Add the eggs one at a time, beating well between each addition. Fold in the flour, cocoa and baking soda, sifting if necessary. Add the milk and melted chocolate, stirring well to mix, but not overbeating. Spread the butter into the prepared dishes and cook both layers for 12 minutes on the highest temperature in a combination microwave-convection oven or 6 minutes per layer on MEDIUM, increasing to HIGH for 2-5 minutes in a coventional microwave oven. Cool on a flat surface for 5-10 minutes before transferring to a wire rack.

Combine the cherries, juice and cornstarch/cornflour. Cook on HIGH for 3 minutes, or until thick. Stir in the kirsch and allow to cool. Melt the jam or jelly 1 minute on HIGH, and brush a thin layer over the surface of the pastry. Cut the

cake layers in half horizontally. Stick one layer onto the pastry base. Spread on the cherry filling. Sandwich with another cake layer. Top with the kirsch-flavoured cream. Top with the cake and cherry filling. End with a cake layer. Cover the top and sides with half of the remaining whipped cream. Sprinkle the grated chocolate on the sides and the top. Pipe a decoration of cream on top of the cake and decorate with the cherries.

Cherry Almond Cakes

PREPARATION TIME: 20 minutes

MICROWAVE COOKING TIME:
6 minutes

MAKES: 6-8 cakes

CAKES
4 eggs
120g/4oz/½ cup sugar/caster sugar
120g/4oz/1 cup all-purpose/plain flour
60g/2oz/¼ cup butter or margarine

ICING
60g/2oz/¼ cup butter or margarine
225g/8oz/2 cups icing/powdered sugar

15ml/1 tbsp single/light cream
1 jar maraschino/cocktail cherries, juice reserved

DECORATION
Maraschino cherries cut in half
Whole, unblanched almonds

Grease 6-8 custard cups or muffin/patty tins and place a circle of greaseproof paper in the bottom of each cup. Beat the eggs and sugar together until light and fluffy. Heat the butter 2 minutes on LOW to soften. Sift the flour, if necessary, and sprinkle over the surface of the beaten eggs. Pour on the butter and fold into the eggs with the flour. Spoon into the prepared dishes or pans and place on a rack or an inverted saucer. Cook on the highest setting of a combination microwave-convection oven for 5 minutes or on HIGH for 5 minutes in a conventional microwave oven. Leave to stand for 5-10 minutes on a flat surface before turning out onto a wire rack to cool. Reserve 4 cherries and chop the rest. Stir into the icing with the almonds and kirsch or flavouring. Add more cream if necessary to bring to a smooth spreading consistency. Turn the cakes over so that the base is larger in diameter than the top. Spread over the cherry icing and top each cake with half a maraschino/cocktail cherry and 1 blanched almond.

Bombe au Chocolat

PREPARATION TIME: 30 minutes

MICROWAVE COOKING TIME:
5-6 minutes

SERVES: 6-8 people

CAKE
4 eggs
120g/4oz/½ cup sugar/caster sugar
120g/4oz/1 cup all-purpose/plain flour
60g/2oz/¼ cup butter

ICING
30g/1oz unsweetened cooking chocolate
60g/2oz/¼ cup butter or margarine
90ml/3 fl oz/⅓ cup milk
450g/1lb/4 cups icing/powdered sugar
30ml/2 tbsps brandy

5 minutes, or on HIGH for 5-6 minutes in a conventional microwave oven. Leave to stand for 5-10 minutes before turning out onto a wire rack to cool. To prepare the icing, heat the chocolate, butter and milk for 3-4 minutes on MEDIUM. Stir occasionally until of creamy consistency. Stir in the remaining ingredients. Allow the icing to cool completely and beat until creamy. Add more milk if necessary. When the cake has cooled split in 4, divide the icing in half and flavour half with the brandy. Sandwich the layers together starting with the largest flat layer and ending with the small round layer on top. Cover the whole cake with the remaining chocolate icing and reserve about ⅓ for piping if desired. Pipe on rosettes or ropes of icing using a fluted tube/nozzle. Sprinkle over the nuts. Lightly sprinkle with icing/powdered sugar and decorate with the cherries.

Coffee and Lemon Petit Gateaux

PREPARATION TIME: 30 minutes

MICROWAVE COOKING TIME: 9 minutes

MAKES: 16 cakes

4 eggs
120g/4oz/½ cup sugar/caster sugar
120g/4oz/1 cup all-purpose/plain flour
60g/2oz/¼ cup butter or margarine

GLAZE ICING
450g/1lb/2 cups icing sugar
140ml/¼ pint/½ cup water
Juice of ½ lemon
30ml/2 tbsps instant coffee
Few drops yellow food colouring

BUTTERCREAM ICING
15g/1 tbsp butter
15g/1 tbsp milk
120g/4oz/1 cup icing sugar/powdered sugar
Few drops vanilla extract/essence

APRICOT GLAZE
225g/8oz/1 cup apricot jam, sieved
Juice of ½ lemon

Facing page: Bombe au Chocolat. This page: Coffee and Lemon Petit Gateaux (top) and Cherry Almond Cakes (bottom).

DECORATION
Chopped, browned almonds
Maraschino/cocktail cherries

Grease a 470ml/1 pint/2 cup round-based mixing bowl with butter and dust lightly with flour. Beat the eggs and sugar until light and fluffy. Heat the butter 2 minutes on LOW to soften. Sift the flour if necessary and sprinkle over the surface of the beaten eggs. Pour on the butter and fold into the egg mixture with the flour. Spread into the prepared bowl and place on a rack or an inverted saucer. Cook on a combination setting in a microwave-convection oven on the highest temperature for

Line a 20cm/8 inch square dish with 2 layers of wax/greaseproof paper. Beat the eggs and sugar until thick and mousse like. Heat the butter for 2 minutes on LOW to soften. Sift the flour, if necessary, and sprinkle over the surface of the beaten eggs. Pour on the butter and fold into the eggs with the flour. Spread into the prepared dish and place on a rack or an inverted saucer. Cook on the highest setting of a combination microwave-convection oven for 5 minutes or on HIGH in a conventional microwave oven for 5 minutes. Leave to stand for 5-10 minutes on a flat surface before turning out onto a wire rack to cool completely. Cut in desired shapes, rectangles or squares. The cake may also be cut with cookie/pastry cutters in rounds or heartshapes, but this will make less than 16 cakes. Cook the jam and lemon juice for 1 minute on HIGH. Brush the cakes on the tops and sides while the glaze is still warm and allow the glaze to set. Divide the icing sugar in half. Add lemon juice, half the water and yellow food colouring to one half. Beat until smooth. Heat the remaining water until boiling and dissolve the coffee. Add to the remaining sugar and beat until smooth. Pour the lemon icing over half of the cakes and the coffee icing over the other half and allow to set completely. Decorate with the buttercream icing using a small fluted pastry/piping nozzle and allow to set before serving.

Queen of Sheba

PREPARATION TIME: 25 minutes	
MICROWAVE COOKING TIME: 13-20 minutes	
SERVES: 6-8 people	

90g/3oz/⅓ cup butter or margarine
60g/2oz/2 squares unsweetened chocolate
180g/6oz/¾ cup sugar/caster sugar
3 eggs
120g/4oz/1 cup ground almonds
60g/2oz/¼ cup plain/all-purpose flour
2.5ml/½ tsp almond extract/essence

GLACÉ ICING
225g/8oz/2 cups icing/powdered sugar
30g/1oz/1 square unsweetened chocolate
60ml/2 fl oz/¼ cup water
15ml/1 tbsp vegetable oil

DECORATION
Blanched, halved almonds
Candied violet or rose petals

Line an 18cm/7 inch cake dish with 2 layers of wax/greaseproof paper. Melt the chocolate for 2 minutes on MEDIUM and set aside. Beat the butter or margarine and sugar together until light and creamy. Add the almond essence. Beat in the eggs 1 at a time. Cook on highest setting of a combination microwave-convection oven for 11 minutes, or cook for 12 minutes on MEDIUM increasing to HIGH for 1-6 minutes in a conventional microwave oven. Melt the chocolate for the icing in the water 2 minutes on MEDIUM. Pour into the icing/powdered sugar and beat until smooth. Add the oil to keep the icing shiny and more water if necessary to bring to thick coating consistency. Pour over the cake all at once and ease down the sides with a palette knife/spatula to cover completely. Allow to set slightly before arranging the decoration. Allow to set completely before slicing to serve.
Note: If using semi-sweet/plain chocolate in the cake and icing recipe omit 30g/1oz/2 tbsps of the required sugar for each.

Devil's Food Cake with Seafoam Icing

PREPARATION TIME: 25 minutes	
MICROWAVE COOKING TIME: 25-29 minutes	
SERVES: 6-8 people	

60g/2oz/2 squares unsweetened chocolate
150g/5oz/⅔ cup butter or margarine
285g/11oz/1⅓ cups sugar/caster sugar
4 eggs
255g/9oz/1¼ cups all-purpose/plain flour
120g/4oz/½ cup cocoa

5ml/1 tsp baking soda
200ml/6 fl oz/¾ cup milk

ICING
450g/1lb/2 cups sugar
180ml/6 fl oz water
Small pinch cream of tartar
4 egg whites
5ml/1 tsp vanilla essence/extract
90g/3oz plain/semi-sweet chocolate

Line 2 20cm/8 inch round dishes with 2 layers of wax/greaseproof paper. Melt the chocolate for the cake for 1 minute on MEDIUM, stirring once or twice. Allow to cool slightly. Meanwhile, beat the butter or margarine and sugar together until light. Add the eggs one at a time, beating well between each addition. Fold in the flour, baking soda and cocoa, sifting if necessary. Add milk and chocolate, stirring to mix well but not overbeating. Spread the batter into the prepared dishes. Cook both layers for 12 minutes on the highest temperature in a combination microwave-convection oven, or 6 minutes per layer on MEDIUM increasing to HIGH for 2-5 minutes in a conventional microwave oven. Cool on a flat surface for 5-10 minutes before turning out onto a wire rack to cool completely. To prepare the icing combine the water and sugar in a deep bowl. Cook to a syrup, stirring frequently. The syrup should register 130°C/240°F on a sugar thermometer. Beat the egg whites with the cream of tartar until stiff peaks form. Gradually beat in the sugar syrup until the icing is stiff and glossy. If the icing will not stiffen beat in up to 225g/8oz/2 cups icing/powdered sugar. Add vanilla essence. Sandwich the layers with the icing, reserving enough for the top and sides. Swirl the icing on the top and sides and melt the chocolate on MEDIUM for 2 minutes. Drizzle the chocolate on top of the cake and allow it to drip down the sides. Allow the icing and the chocolate to set before slicing to serve.

Facing page: Devil's Food Cake with Seafoam Icing (top) and Queen of Sheba (bottom).

Microwave
BAKING

DESSERTS & CONFECTIONERY

Danish Fruit Shortcake

PREPARATION TIME: 25 minutes

MICROWAVE COOKING TIME:
9 minutes plus 1 hour minimum
standing time

SERVES: 6-8 people

60g/2oz/½ cup icing/powdered sugar
225g/8oz/2 cups plain/all-purpose flour
150g/4½ oz/⅔ cup butter or margarine
2.5ml/½ tsp vanilla extract/essence
1 egg
450g/1lb strawberries
225g/8oz/1 cup redcurrant jelly or
seedless raspberry jam
280ml/½ pint/1 cup whipped cream
Mint leaves

Work the flour and sugar briefly in a
food processor to sift. Add the
butter, cut into small pieces and add
vanilla essence/extract. Work until
the mixture resembles fine
breadcrumbs. Add the egg and work
until the mixture comes together. If
the mixture is too soft at this point
chill for 15-20 minutes. Line a large
glass pie dish or flan dish or a large
baking sheet with wax/greaseproof
paper. Press out the dough into a
20cm-22cm/8-9 inch round. Crimp
the edges and chill for 15 minutes.
Cook 8 minutes on LOW. Leave to
cool on a baking sheet or in the dish
for 1 hour or more before removing.
Pastry may also be cooked in a
combination microwave-convection
oven for 8 minutes on a moderate
temperature setting. Lift the pastry
carefully onto a serving dish. If the
strawberries are small leave them
whole, otherwise cut in half
lengthwise. Heat the jelly or jam in a
jar or deep bowl for 1 minute on
HIGH, stirring once, to help soften.

**This page: Chocolate Orange
Cheesecake. Facing page: Danish
Fruit Shortcake.**

Brush the pastry with the hot glaze
and leave to set for a minute.
Arrange the strawberries, cut side
down if sliced. Brush with the hot
glaze and leave to cool and set. Whip
the cream and pipe rosettes around
the edge of the strawberries and
decorate each rosette with a mint leaf
before serving.

Chocolate Orange
Cheesecake

PREPARATION TIME: 25 minutes

MICROWAVE COOKING TIME:
15 minutes

SERVES: 8-10 people

CRUST
60g/2oz/¼ cup butter
360g/12oz/1½ cups crushed chocolate
cookies/biscuits
FILLING
60g/2oz semi-sweet/plain chocolate
30ml/2 tbsps water

the cake. Mix the remaining chocolate and water for 30 seconds to 1 minute on MEDIUM, stirring until smooth. Drizzle over the oranges. Allow the chocolate to set before serving.

Hazelnut Meringues with Black Cherry Sauce

PREPARATION TIME: 20 minutes

MICROWAVE COOKING TIME: 6 minutes

SERVES: 8-10 people

MERINGUES
1 egg white
300g/10oz/2½ cups icing/powdered sugar
45g/1½ oz/¼ cup finely chopped, browned hazelnuts
470ml/1 pint/2 cups whipped cream

SAUCE
225g/8oz can dark sweet cherries, pitted
30g/2 tbsps cornstarch/cornflour
15ml/1 tbsp kirsch or cherry brandy

DECORATION
Cocoa powder

Beat the egg white lightly and add the icing/powdered sugar and hazelnuts. Stir to form a pliable dough. Roll the dough into a thin sausage about 1.25cm/½ inch thick. Cut into small pieces and place well apart on greaseproof/wax paper on a microwave baking sheet. Flatten the pieces slightly. Cook for 1 minute on HIGH until dry. The meringues will triple in size. Leave to cool on a wire rack. Combine the cornstarch/cornflour and cherries. Cook 5 minutes on HIGH stirring once after 2 minutes. When thickened, add the kirsch or cherry brandy and set aside. Cut a long strip of wax/greaseproof paper about 2.5cm/1 inch wide, line up half the meringues and lay the strip across them. Sprinkle cocoa powder on the exposed ends of both sides of the meringues. Spread the undecorated meringue with whipped cream and place the decorated meringues on top. Serve with the cherry sauce.

2 225g/8oz packages cream cheese
150g/5oz/⅔ cup sugar/caster sugar
90ml/3 fl oz/⅓ cup plain yogurt
Grated rind and juice of 1 orange
4 eggs

TOPPING
2 oranges, peeled and segmented
30g/1oz semi-sweet/plain chocolate
15ml/1 tbsp water

Melt the butter for the crust 1 minute on HIGH. Crush the biscuits/cookies in a food processor and add the butter. Place the crust onto a base of a 20cm/8 inch dish with a removable base, if possible. Cook the crust for 1 minute on HIGH. Melt the chocolate for the filling with the water for 30 seconds on MEDIUM,

This page: Hazelnut Meringues with Black Cherry Sauce. Facing page: Chocolate Brandy Cake.

stirring occasionally. Mix the remaining ingredients for the filling until smooth. Cook for 4 minutes on HIGH, stirring well every 2 minutes. Pour ⅓ of the filling onto the crust base. Drizzle ⅓ of the chocolate onto the filling and carefully marble it through using a skewer or a knife. Do not disturb the base. Repeat until all the filling and chocolate are used. Cook an additional 10 minutes on MEDIUM or until softly set in the centre. Chill until firm. Remove the cake to a serving dish and arrange the orange segments around the edge of

Chocolate Brandy Cake

PREPARATION TIME: 20 minutes plus chilling overnight

MICROWAVE COOKING TIME: 7 minutes

SERVES: 8 people

340g/12oz plain/semi-sweet chocolate
120g/4oz/½ cup butter
60ml/2 fl oz/¼ cup brandy
2 eggs
250g/8oz/2 cups digestive, sweetmeal biscuits or graham crackers, coarsely crushed
60g/2oz/½ cup chopped almonds
280ml/½ pint/1 cup whipped cream
Candied violet or rose petals
Toasted almonds
Slivers of angelica

Melt the chocolate and butter together on MEDIUM for 5 minutes. Beat in the eggs and heat a further 2 minutes on MEDIUM stirring twice to thicken the eggs. Stir in the brandy, biscuits and chopped almonds. Spread into a 17cm/7 inch springform or removable base pan. Chill overnight until firm. Transfer to a serving dish and decorate with rosettes of cream, almonds, angelica and candied violet or rose petals.

Lemon Ginger Pudding Cake

PREPARATION TIME: 20 minutes

MICROWAVE COOKING TIME: 12 minutes

SERVES: 6 people

180g/6oz/¾ cup white sugar/caster sugar
120g/4oz/1 cup all-purpose/plain flour
10ml/2 tsps baking powder
30g/2 tbsps butter
Grated rind and juice of 1 lemon
2 pieces preserved or crystallised ginger, chopped
140ml/¼ pint/½ cup milk
225g/8oz/1 cup brown sugar
420ml/¾ pint/1½ cups cold water

Sift the flour if necessary and combine with 180g/6oz/¾ cup white sugar and baking powder. Melt the butter for 1 minute on HIGH and combine with the milk, lemon juice and rind and ginger. Beat the liquid ingredients into the dry ingredients and spoon into a 22cm/9 inch round baking dish. Scatter the brown sugar over the top and pour over the cold water. Cook on MEDIUM for 10 minutes and 2 minutes on HIGH, or 12 minutes on a combination setting in a microwave-convection oven. Pudding will separate into a cake layer on top and a sauce underneath. Do not allow the pudding to overcook. Serve warm or chilled with whipped cream.

Chocolate Flans

PREPARATION TIME: 20 minutes

MICROWAVE COOKING TIME: 24-25 minutes

SERVES: 6-8 people

CARAMEL
140ml/¼ pint/½ cup water
120g/4oz/½ cup granulated sugar

CUSTARD
3 eggs
60g/2oz semi-sweet/plain chocolate
420ml/12 fl oz/1½ cups milk
1 cinnamon stick

DECORATION
6-8 pecan halves
Chocolate curls

Put water and sugar for the caramel into a deep bowl or glass measure. Stir well. Cook on HIGH for 12 minutes until golden. Stir once or twice at the beginning of cooking to help dissolve the sugar. Do not overcook the caramel; it will continue to darken after it is removed from the oven. Pour the caramel quickly into 6-8 ramekin dishes/custard cups that have been warmed briefly in the oven. Leave the caramel to cool and harden. Melt the chocolate in the milk for 5 minutes on HIGH with the cinnamon. Beat the egg and strain on the milk, blending well. Discard the cinnamon stick. Pour onto the hardened caramel in each dish. Put the dishes into a shallow dish in a circle with enough hot water to come halfway up the sides. Cook on LOW for 7-8 minutes or until set. Chill completely and turn out onto serving plates. Decorate with chocolate curls and pecans.

Chocolate Almond Pudding Cake

PREPARATION TIME: 20 minutes

MICROWAVE COOKING TIME: 12 minutes

SERVES: 6 people

180g/6oz/¾ cup sugar/caster sugar
120g/4oz/1 cup all-purpose/plain flour
10ml/2 tsps baking powder
30g/2 tbsps butter
45g/3 tbsps cocoa
150ml/¼ pint/½ cup milk
2.5ml/½ tsp almond extract/essence
60g/2oz/½ cup chopped almonds
120g/4oz/½ cup brown sugar
120g/4oz/½ cup sugar
60g/2oz/4 tbsps cocoa
420ml/¾ pint/1½ cups cold water

Sift the flour if necessary and combine with 180g/6oz/¾ cup sugar. Melt butter 1 minute on HIGH and combine with 45g/3 tbsps cocoa, almond extract/essence and milk. Beat the liquid ingredients into the dry ingredients and fold in the nuts. Spoon into a 22cm/9 inch round baking dish. Scatter the brown sugar, remaining white sugar and cocoa over the top without mixing. Pour over the water and bake on MEDIUM for 10 minutes and 2 minutes on HIGH, or 12 minutes on a combination setting of a microwave-convection oven. The pudding will separate into a cake layer on top and a sauce underneath. Do not overbake. Serve with whipped cream if desired.

Facing page: Lemon Ginger Pudding Cake (top) and Chocolate Almond Pudding Cake (bottom).

Cherry Nut Balls

PREPARATION TIME: 20 minutes

MICROWAVE COOKING TIME:
10-13 minutes

MAKES: about 16 balls

225g/8oz/2 cups glacé/candied cherries
180g/6oz/¾ cup sugar/caster sugar
120g/4oz/½ cup butter or margarine
60g/2oz/2 cups crisp rice cereal, crushed
60g/2oz/½ cup chopped walnuts
1 egg
30ml/2 tbsps evaporated milk
Desiccated coconut

Combine butter and sugar in a medium bowl. Cook for 4 minutes on HIGH. Chop the cherries finely and add to the bowl. Stir well and cook 1 minute further on HIGH. Mix the egg and the milk. Add gradually to the hot cherry mixture, stirring well. Cook on MEDIUM for 5-8 minutes or until the mixture comes together in a ball when stirred. Mix in the cereal and nuts, and shape into 2.5cm/1 inch balls. Roll in desiccated coconut and allow to set before serving. Cherry nut balls keep 2 weeks in an airtight container.

White Coffee Creams

PREPARATION TIME: 20 minutes

MICROWAVE COOKING TIME:
10-11 minutes plus 30 minutes standing time

SERVES: 6-8 people

280ml/½ pint/1 cup milk
8 coffee beans
3 eggs
60g/2oz/½ cup sugar/caster sugar
140ml/¼ pint/½ cup single light cream

SAUCE
225g/8oz/2 cups blackberries,
  blackcurrants or raspberries
15ml/1 tbsp lemon juice
Icing/powdered sugar to taste
Water

**This page: Cherry Nut Balls (top)
and Chocolate Truffles (bottom).
Facing page: Chocolate Flans (top)
and White Coffee Creams (bottom).**

Chocolate Truffles

PREPARATION TIME: 20 minutes

MICROWAVE COOKING TIME:
4½ minutes

MAKES: 30 balls

180g/6oz chocolate chips/drops
10ml/2 tsps instant coffee or brandy
10ml/2 tsps light/single cream
2 egg yolks
15g/½ oz/1 tbsp butter

COATING
Cocoa
Ground blanched almonds

Melt the chocolate with the coffee, if using, for 4½ minutes on MEDIUM. Add the remaining ingredients and beat well until thick and cool. If using brandy, add with the rest of the ingredients. Chill until firm. Roll into 2.5cm/1 inch balls. Roll half in the cocoa and half in the ground, blanched almonds.

DECORATION
Whole berries
Mint leaves

Put the coffee beans and milk into a small, deep bowl. Heat 3 minutes on HIGH. Set aside 30 minutes to infuse. Beat the egg and the sugar together until thick. Strain on the milk and add the cream. Pour into 6-8 ramekin dishes/custard cups. Put into a shallow dish in a circle with enough hot water to come halfway up the sides of the dishes. Cook on LOW for 7-8 minutes or until set. Chill completely. Combine berries, juice and sugar in a blender or food processor, reserving 6-8 for decoration. Process until the berries break down. If the sauce is too thick add water to thin slightly. Strain to remove the seeds. Loosen the creams from the sides of the dishes and turn out onto individual plates. Pour round the sauce and decorate with the berries and mint leaves.

Rocky Road Fudge

PREPARATION TIME: 20 minutes

MICROWAVE COOKING TIME:
20 minutes

MAKES: 1lb

450g/1lb/2 cups sugar/caster sugar
200ml/6 fl oz/¾ cup milk
60g/2oz unsweetened chocolate
60g/2oz/¼ cup butter or margarine
10ml/2 tsps vanilla essence/extract
60g/2oz/1 cup miniature marshmallows
60g/2oz/½ cup coarsely chopped
*   walnuts*

Put the sugar and milk into a large bowl. Add the chocolate, finely chopped, and butter. Cover the bowl with pierced plastic wrap/cling film and cook on HIGH for 5 minutes or until boiling. Stir well and cook a further 15 minutes, uncovered, on MEDIUM. Stir frequently. The mixture should form a soft ball when a small amount is dropped into cold water. Leave to cool until barely warm. Beat in the vanilla essence and continue beating until the mixture thickens and starts to lose its shine.

Quickly add the nuts and marshmallows and spread into a 20cm/8 inch square dish lined with greaseproof/wax paper. Mark into squares and leave to set before removing from the dish.

Coffee Raspberry Roulades

PREPARATION TIME: 25 minutes

MICROWAVE COOKING TIME:
3 minutes per batch

SERVES: 6-8 people

15g/½ oz/1 tbsp butter
6 egg whites
340g/12oz/1½ cups sugar/caster sugar
10ml/2 tsps cornflour/cornstarch
5ml/1 tsp cream of tartar
5ml/1 tsp vinegar
10ml/2 tsps instant coffee dissolved in
*   5ml/1 tsp boiled water*
60g/2oz/½ cup toasted, sliced/flaked
*   almonds*

FILLING
280ml/½ pint/1 cup whipped cream
225g/8oz/2 cups raspberries, fresh or
*   frozen*

DECORATION
Icing/powdered sugar
Coffee bean dragées

Melt the butter for 30 seconds on HIGH. Line several baking sheets with wax/greaseproof paper and brush the paper with the melted butter. Beat egg whites until stiff but not dry. Beat in the sugar a spoonful at a time, beating well in between each addition. Mix the vinegar with the coffee and fold into egg whites with the cornflour/cornstarch and cream of tartar. Divide the mixture into 12 equal portions. Smooth each portion out into a rectangle about 1.25cm/½ inch thick on the baking sheets. Sprinkle on the almonds and cook for 3 minutes on HIGH per batch and leave to cool slightly. Sprinkle a sheet of wax/greaseproof paper or a clean towel with icing/powdered sugar and turn the roulades over almond side down. Whip the cream and spread half of it over the rolls and scatter on the

raspberries, reserving 12 for garnish. Roll up each roulade, from long end to long end as for a Swiss/jelly roll. Pipe the remaining cream on top using a rosette pastry tube/nozzle. Decorate with coffee bean dragées and remaining raspberries to serve.

Honeycomb

PREPARATION TIME: 20 minutes

MICROWAVE COOKING TIME:
10-16 minutes

MAKES: approximately 450g/1lb

225g/8oz/1 cup sugar/granulated sugar
280ml/8 fl oz/1 cup light corn syrup/
*   golden syrup*
15ml/1 tbsp white or wine vinegar
15ml/1 tbsp baking soda

COATING
225g/8oz semi-sweet/plain or milk
*   chocolate*

Line a 20cm/8 inch square dish with oiled foil. Combine sugar, syrup and vinegar in a large, deep bowl, cover with pierced plastic wrap/cling film and cook on HIGH for 3 minutes, stirring frequently to dissolve the sugar. Uncover and cook a further 4-10 minutes on HIGH, or until the mixture reaches 150°C/300°F on a sugar thermometer or until a small amount of the mixture forms brittle threads when dropped in cold water. Quickly add the soda to the mixture and stir it well. The mixture will foam when the soda is added. Pour into the prepared dish and leave until firm. Remove from the dish and break into pieces about 5cm/2 inch. The pieces will be irregular in shape. Melt the chocolate for 3 minutes on MEDIUM in a deep bowl. Coat half of the honeycomb with the chocolate and allow it to set before serving. The remaining honeycomb may be served plain.

Facing page: Honeycomb (top) and Rocky Road Fudge (bottom).

Steamed Chocolate-Fig Pudding

PREPARATION TIME: 20 minutes

MICROWAVE COOKING TIME:
7-9 minutes plus 5-10 minutes
standing time

SERVES: 6-8 people

90g/3oz/⅓ cup butter or margarine
225g/8oz/1 cup sugar/caster sugar
2 eggs
180g/6oz/1½ cups all-purpose/plain
  flour
30ml/2 tbsps cocoa powder
5ml/1 tsp baking soda
15ml/1 tbsp brandy
280ml/½ pint/1 cup water
120g/6oz/1 cup semi-sweet/plain
  chocolate chips/drops
225g/8oz/1½ cups dried figs, chopped
120g/4oz/1 cup toasted hazelnuts,
  chopped

Grease a 1150ml/2 pint/4 cup mixing
bowl or decorative mould very well
with butter or margarine. Beat the
remaining butter and sugar until light
and fluffy. Beat in the eggs one at a
time. Add the flour, unsifted, cocoa
and baking soda. Add the brandy,
water, figs, almonds and chocolate
chips/drops. Pour into the prepared
dish or mould. Cover with 2 layers of
pierced plastic wrap/cling film to
release the steam. Cook 7-9 minutes
on HIGH. Leave to stand 5-10
minutes before serving. Serve with
hard sauce/brandy butter or
whipped cream.

Steamed Raspberry Jam Pudding

PREPARATION TIME: 20 minutes

MICROWAVE COOKING TIME:
6-8 minutes plus 5-10 minutes
standing time

SERVES: 6 people

120g/4oz/½ cup raspberry jam
120g/4oz/½ cup butter or margarine
120g/4oz/½ cup sugar/caster sugar
2 eggs
5ml/1 tsp vanilla essence/extract

120g/4oz/1 cup all-purpose/plain flour
5ml/1 tsp baking powder
30ml/2 tbsps milk

Grease a 900ml/1½ pint/3 cup
mixing bowl or decorative mould
very well with butter or margarine.
Put the jam into the bottom. Cream
the remaining butter or margarine
and sugar until light and fluffy. Beat
in the eggs one at a time. Add the
vanilla, sift in the flour and baking
powder and fold in. If the mixture is
very stiff add up to 2 tbsps milk to

**This page: Coffee Raspberry
Roulades. Facing page: Steamed
Raspberry Jam Pudding (top) and
Steamed Chocolate-Fig Pudding
(bottom).**

bring to a soft dropping consistency.
Spoon the mixture on top of the jam.
Cover the top of the bowl or mould
with 2 layers of plastic wrap/cling
film pierced several times to release
steam. Cook 6-8 minutes on HIGH.
Leave to stand 5-10 minutes before
turning out to serve. Serve with
whipped cream or custard sauce.

My first experience with microwave cooking consisted of watching a demonstration by my Home Economics teacher during which she showed us the joys of popping corn, reheating hamburgers and scrambling eggs. Microwave ovens still do those things beautifully, but they have come a long way since then.

My second experience of microwave cooking was composed solely of reheating my lunch in the company canteen!

My third experience was more auspicious. I was able to have some instruction from a well-known expert in microwave cooking, and then, when I was teaching cookery myself, I was able to demonstrate some innovative and delicious recipes developed by my school. That was when my amazement at microwave cooking began.

Compiling and testing the recipes in this book has simply added to that amazement. As a professional cook trained in the classical methods, I was nothing if not suspicious of microwave ovens. But I was also curious, and anxious to learn more about this totally different way of cooking.

Certain things about the art of cooking in a microwave oven still impress me, even after all this time. The ease with which it can produce lump-free sauces is one of those things. It is even possible to cook sauces like a Hollandaise extraordinarily well in a microwave oven.

I was pleased to learn that the myth of the flabby, white chicken is just simply that. A whole bird will brown in a microwave oven, and so will large cuts of meat with a thin layer of fat on them. Besides, you will find yourself spoiled for choice with all the various marinades, bastes and coatings available to give colour and crispiness.

Speaking of browning, the browning dish has been a revelation, and I confess myself hopelessly addicted to it. I can't seem to stop thinking of ways to use it in microwave cooking. There are several different designs available, but they must all be preheated to work well. Butter browns in about half a second. I have used mine to toast nuts and seeds, make fried bread croutes and brown meat for stews as well as for cooking steaks and chops. It is even possible to brown flour to give colour to sauces and gravies. The list goes on and on, and I strongly recommend a browning dish as an essential piece of equipment.

New ovens are appearing all the time, with many new functions built into them. One of the ovens I used in compiling this book was a Brother Hi-Speed Cooker with the ability to cook with microwaves alone, convection heat alone, or a combination of the two. These combination ovens usually have a lower wattage than conventional microwave ovens, so they cook a little slower. Still, on the combination setting the results are impressive. In almost the same length of time as ordinary microwave cooking takes, you can have food that is browned as well as cooked, which is a plus for roasting meat. These ovens are especially good for pastry, that old microwave problem, and for baking in general.

In deciding what recipes to include, I first considered the sorts of cooking the microwave oven does best. It excels at cooking vegetables. Very little water is required, even for 450g/1lb of

vegetables, so all the textures, colours and nutrients remain in the food. Fish requires quick cooking, so it was an obvious choice. Including soups and starters/appetizers made a lot of sense because they can be reheated, and often cooked from the beginning, in their serving dishes, which is a great advantage for entertaining. Eggs, even when poached, cook very well in a microwave oven, and baked custards, which ordinarily take a while to cook, are fast and foolproof.

Other foods which need long cooking or preparation were next on the list. Large cuts of meat and less tender cuts benefit from being cooked in a microwave oven. Dried beans, peas and lentils cook in about half the time they would take if cooked conventionally, and a special microwave method eliminates the overnight soaking. When yeast doughs have help from a microwave they rise in about half the time.

Finally came the experiments with the recipes I was dubious about – soufflés, cakes, breads and meringues. I won't promise soufflés that never fall, but microwave soufflés are exceedingly light. Certain ingredients, such as cream of tartar, help stabilise the egg whites. Cakes and breads come out very soft and tender in a fraction of the conventional time. Meringues are the real magic trick, though. A microwave meringue mixture is a fondant-like paste which, when baked, triples in size and becomes crisp and light as a cloud.

My microwave oven comes to my rescue in a hundred different ways. It defrosts food, so I can be as forgetful as I like about taking food out of the freezer. It reheats whole meals quickly on the serving dish, a definite advantage when my husband comes home from the office, is absolutely starved and it is 10.00pm. I entertain quite a lot, and I think of my microwave oven as a modern equivalent of the kitchen maid. It is there at my disposal to cook and reheat vegetables, and to melt the butter to go with them. It reheats rice and pasta without extra water and without any loss of texture. It melts chocolate for special desserts and reduces wine or spirits for special sauces. It can even infuse after dinner coffee with the flavours of spice or orange.

My microwave oven helps me create 'convenience' foods of my own. I cook in quantity and freeze individual portions in micro-proof containers to keep on hand for quick meals. During a busy week I am constantly grateful for the defrosting and reheating abilities of my microwave oven, and no longer am I caught out by unexpected guests.

When I first saw that corn popping in a microwave oven so many years ago, I never thought I would one day compile such a large volume of recipes for microwave cooking. A good cookbook leads readers on to experiment and develop new ideas of their own. I hope this book does exactly that, and that you enjoy using it as much as I enjoyed writing it.

INDEX